Four Easy Steps to
Understanding Your Dreams

✷

1. Write down your dream
2. Look up the entry that best describes the opening scene
3. Look up the symbols and the situations that occurred in your dream
4. Discover what your dream actually means

Did You Know . . .

✷

. . . A dream can be a forewarning of things to come?

. . . Dreams can help you solve problems in your everyday life?

. . . Women dream more during PMS?

. . . Revelatory dreams are more common in men?

. . . Sleepwalking occurs most frequently in adolescence?

. . . You can control your dreams?

You can find the key to your inner
life in the . . .
Dream Dictionary

Dream Dictionary

*

An A to Z Guide to
Understanding Your
Unconscious Mind

TONY CRISP

A Dell Book

A Dell Book
Published by
Dell Publishing
Random House, Inc.

For information address Dell Publishing, New York, New York.

Dell® is a registered trademark of Random House, Inc., and the colophon is a trademark of Random House, Inc.

ISBN: 0-440-23707-6

Printed in the United States of America
Published simultaneously in Canada
February 2002

OPM   20 19 18 17 16 15 14

To my children
Mark, Helen, Neal, Leon, Quentin.
This is a fruit of my life.
It has grown out of the wonder and the pain,
the struggle, the goodness, and the vision,
that are the riches in my life.

Contents

✴

Introduction
*

A Dream is a mirror revealing your deepest self.

Most of us now have experience, directly or through films, of the monitors that sit next to a sick person in a hospital. We know that on the screen of the monitor a visible image can be displayed of the patient's heartbeat, their blood pressure, even their brain activity. Through ultrasound one can even see the body and movements of a baby within the mother's womb.

Your dreams are like those monitors. In the mirror of your dreams you can witness what is happening in your body, in your mind, and in your most guarded self and intuitions. The hospital monitor may show things happening in your body that you are usually unconscious of. Like the monitor, dreams show things that are deeply unconscious. In this way your dreams take you into the profoundly unknown of your personality and your felt but often unconscious links with the people and world around you. In the mirror of your dreams these things appear as external people and places depicting the subtle and otherwise unknown processes of your body, your mind, and your connection with others.

At first it may be difficult to believe or grasp that the persons or objects in your dreams, like the things seen on the hospital monitor, are depicting your internal feelings and mental structure. But the experience of thousands who have explored their dreams in depth point to this

1

Introduction

possibility. And it is around this approach that *Dream Dictionary* is written.

Dreams cannot be defined under any one heading. Like human beings, they are enormously varied in what they express. Just as you cannot say the human mind is simply a system of memory, you cannot say dreams are just the reflection of experienced events. Your mind can also solve problems, predict the outcome of what you do, play with possibilities through imagination. You can create new ideas out of old memories, or replay disturbing events in order to find ways of meeting them constructively. Being the mental phenomena they are, dreams deal with all of these issues and more.

How Do We Know Dreams Do All These Things?

Two of the major ways we know things in today's world are through validated scientific research, and through personal experience.

Through the scientific approach we know that each of us dream about five times every night, and while we dream our eyes move, following the action in the dream (Aserinsky and Kleitman, 1952; *The Dreaming Brain,* J. Allan Hobson,). This is known as rapid-eye-movements or REM sleep. It was later discovered that while dreaming, your voluntary muscles are paralyzed, making it impossible or difficult to move, thus sometimes giving rise to a feeling of being possessed by a force or power outside of your will.

Professor Jerome Siegel of the UCLA School of Medicine found that duck-billed platypuses have REM sleep, suggesting that this form of sleep and the process underlying dreaming developed in early mammals 250 million years ago.

More recently, studies of brain scans while subjects were dreaming have revealed that "dreams are formed by drawing on a well of emotional memories." (Dr. Chiara Portas of the Wellcome Department of Cognitive Neurology, Institute of Neurology, London.)

Because a dreaming person exhibits REM, researchers in sleep laboratories can wake people to discover what they are dreaming. According to sleep researcher Peretz Lavie, lawyers dream about courtrooms, doctors dream about operating rooms, students dream about classrooms. Dreams early in the night tend to deal with present situations, whereas dreams in the morning are more likely to go back to the dreamer's early childhood.

Several researchers have found evidence that a process of learning takes place during dreaming. Because of this, the theory that dreams are nothing more than a means of dumping mental garbage from memory has not been validated. Jerold M. Lowenstein, professor of medicine at the University of California at San Francisco, says, "Most researchers who study dreams reject" the idea of dreams as means of garbage dumping, "because dreams seem to have a narrative coherence and logic that goes beyond being just a random collection of impressions. They are convinced that REM sleep and dreams constitute a separate reality that plays a vital part in our lives and health, though the nature of that reality is not yet understood." (Quoted from the *Electronic Telegraph,* issue 952)

So why we need to sleep, or why we dream, still holds mysteries for the scientific community. This is because our brain and personality are such extraordinary and complex systems.

Human experience leaps beyond the laboratory. When we put together the massive information gathered from people's experience of dreaming over the centuries, the mystery of sleep and dreams speaks to us of many possibilities. Tens of thousands of hours have been spent by individuals exploring their dreams in therapeutic settings. From their experience we can see that dreams link with an internal process that attempts to move toward the healing of internal trauma and tension. For many people such

Introduction

work has been life transforming. From it they have learned that the dream process continually attempts personal growth.

There are numerous instances of highly creative dreams. From such widely diverse sources as Einstein and Robert Louis Stevenson, we can gather examples of dreams that have led to breakthroughs in science, in literature, in industry, and in medicine.

Doctors such as Bernard S. Seigal, clinical professor of surgery at Yale University School of Medicine, have promoted the use of dreams in the early diagnosis of illness. ("A Surgeon's Experience With Dreams," by Bernard Seigal, in *The Dream Network Bulletin,* February 1963.)

Dr. Charles Tart, while experimenting with a subject wired to an EEG machine, discovered that while the subject was in a state that was neither sleep nor wakefulness she was able to read a hidden number in an envelope out of sight of her sleeping body. This and thousands of other out-of-body and near-death experiences suggest sleep and dreams reveal to us the most profound aspects of existence. (From The Zz files, a report by Joseph Bullman on *The Secrets of Sleep,* a television documentary. The feature appeared in the *Electronic Telegraph* issue 1093.)

How Your Dreams May Help You

Understanding your dreams can definitely help you to creatively find your way through the difficulties you face in work, in relationships, in discovering your potential, and in your personal growth. They can do this because they profoundly reflect truths about your makeup, your strengths and weaknesses. Dreams have access to the enormous resources of your total memories, and to the sources of your creativity. A dream can leap beyond the responses and viewpoints you may be stuck in while awake, and show you a completely new approach to what you confront.

Observing your dreams can radically improve your

health and way of life. This is because dreams not only combine the needs of your waking self, but also show you what your deepest physical and transcendent needs are. If we use the analogy of a car, your conscious need might be to hurry to an appointment, but the car might be badly in need of a service, or out of oil and gas. Your dreams can show you when your way of life is stressing your body or emotions. They can depict in their imagery what situations allow you to express your potential more fully. They can even point directly to what foods will help and heal.

Because dreams give you the most convincing virtual reality known, they can provide you with riches of experience you could get in no other way. There is a huge difference between being told or reading something, and experiencing it. In your dreams you can experiment in a completely safe environment with relationships, sex, creativity, giving birth, and different approaches to situations. Nothing else but dreams can offer you such a treasure. Nothing else can so enlarge your experience of yourself and life.

So What's Stopping You?

If exploring dreams is so great, why aren't more people doing it?

Well, you could ask why more people do not speak French or German as a second language. After all, it would be a great benefit to speak several foreign languages. The answer is, of course, that we have to bring something to the process of learning that we are not bringing without help. The huge amount of information in this book has done a lot of the work for you. Nevertheless, you will gain even more from your dreams if you learn a few skills in understanding their perspective and language.

If you get to know enough people well, it soon becomes obvious they all have slightly different ways of seeing and responding to events. But it might come as a surprise to

Introduction

realize that within yourself exist very different ways of responding to and becoming aware of things. Previously, I used the analogy in which the needs of a driver and the needs of the car being driven were compared. There is a difference similar to this in the way your dreams depict you and the way you see yourself. Dreams have a more global view of your life and your place in the world. Your waking view may be much more involved in what confronts you this week, today, this minute. Dreams present a view that more fully scans all your past experience, and this more inclusive view of yourself has a lot to offer. It reminds you of the passionate drives that have motivated you over the years, and can bring renewal when difficulties sap resolve. It shows you where you are on the map of life, and what lies before you in your growth and possibilities. Dreams present you with a diagram of where you have come from, and where you are heading. Dreams are like the helicopter in the sky that can see if your direction is taking you down a dead-end road, or onto a highway leading to wider opportunities. They also present the needs of your body and its mysterious working, along with aspects of your mind you might not access in waking life.

Dreams do not express this wider perspective in words or the neat phrases of spoken language. This is partly because dreams arise from a part of your brain that developed long before speech arose in human beings. We know that skilled actors and actresses can lead us to feel and experience things simply through the way they hold their body, how they interact with other people, a sound they make, or their movements. This is exactly how dreams communicate with us. They use interaction with other people or animals to depict ideas and feelings. They use lighting and color to show mood and emotions. They use images and people with whom you have particular feelings or thoughts to portray something important to you.

All of us have such linked feelings about the everyday things around us. If you own a car, you will have particular feelings about it. What are they? Do you feel happy with it? Or perhaps it is not as good as you would like? If you do not own a car, you will still have feelings about cars. Do those feelings have to do with your ambition to gain a car, or to do with feelings about your social standing, or what a mess cars make of your living environment?

Perhaps you have none of the feelings mentioned, but the example is only given to illustrate a truth about dreams. Namely that you have feelings or ideas associated with each of the objects, places, and people around you. In your dreams the image of the place or person is used to depict those feelings or ideas. However, you may not have taken note of the feelings you have about things, and this is exactly why a dream arises—to show you just how you are reacting to something. Or the events and people in the dream depict something in their drama.

As an example of this, a young boy of five, after his pet mouse had given birth to several babies, dreamt the babies opened their eyes. We explored the dream and he said that a pet was something that couldn't do anything for itself and needed looking after. When asked if he had any feelings about this, he said that sometimes he felt like a pet because he couldn't do things for himself without his parents' consent. We looked at what it meant that the babies had opened their eyes, and he said that when baby mice open their eyes it means they are ready to be independent. This led him to realize that he wanted to be more independent. So from that time on, he started doing more things for himself instead of depending on his parents.

This lovely simple dream shows how it reflected the boy's feelings about wanting to be independent, and used his associations with and knowledge of his pets to bring this to his attention. If he had been fully aware of his urge to be independent he would most likely not have had the dream. The dream put his previously unconscious feelings into a drama that, when he gave it a little thought, helped him understand his needs.

Introduction

Therefore, to gain help and inspiration from your dreams, you need to be ready to look at life in a fresh way. Open your mind to your wonderful possibilities, everything from problem-solving to having a sense of your future.

You will also learn, with the help of the many entries in this book, to define your feelings and associations with the characters, places, and things in your dreams. In this way you will open a truly wonderful doorway of understanding and experience. Entries such as those listing the possible meaning of the different parts of the body will help you define your associations with your dream images. Other entries, such as those describing how to explore your dreams in greater depth, will show you how to increase this skill. Quickly your dreams will come alive in a way that can transform your life. You will see that you have a source of insight that is truly a major guide in your life.

What This Book Offers

The information about dreams presented in this book has been gathered during forty years of working with and studying dreams and the dream process. It integrates the experience gained from personally helping hundreds of individuals explore their dreams. The examples used have been taken from a collection of 3,000 dreams put into a computer filing system (dtSearch). The filing system was also used to define general associations with commonly used dream images. However, the major input for definition has arisen from the actual exploration of dreams undertaken by individuals. These are people who have deeply felt the emotions and issues within their dreams, not simply talked them over to arrive at an intellectual interpretation. Or they are people who have written of their findings arising from similar work. Added to this are the commonly held associations we have through language and the way we use imagery within speech. Of course, your personal dream imagery may not be using commonly held associations, or those used by other people. So you must read the definitions with care and consider if these fit what is implied or dramatized in your dream.

The entries in the *Dictionary* contain explanations of the many different types of dreams and dream images. Despite some people's attempt to explain dreams in one simple formula, dreams cover a huge range of phenomena and human experience. So the subjects covered in the book are wide. There are thousands of entries on the researched meaning of the things, people, creatures, and places you may dream about. There are also many entries on special subjects such as **processing your dreams; symbols and dreaming; interpretation of dreams; recurring dreams; night-mares; precognition; science sleep and dreams;** and many more.

Therefore, if you have dreamt of such things as your teeth falling out; being chased; or your marriage partner dying, you will find an explanation of your dream in the following pages.

The aim of the book is to help you make connections between your dreams and your everyday life; to discover more fully the powerful emotions and reactions that unconsciously direct your decisions and responses in waking. The book is not an attempt to give you ideas to play with, to agree or disagree with, like fortune-telling. It can lead to real insights that empower you to make more of yourself, and find your way through the many decisions life confronts you with.

Using the Book

The *Dictionary* contains explanations on almost any type of dream subject. The entries are placed in alphabetical order for easy reference, but some, like *dog* or *running*, are placed in certain categories such as **animals** and **posture, movement, body language.** So, if you dreamt of a flying saucer landing in a field and aliens getting out and taking sheep and a dog back into the saucer, you could look up each of these subjects in the text. Turn to the F entries for **flying saucer;** the **animals** entry for *dog* and *sheep,* and so on.

Each entry gives the general meaning of the dream subject, just as an encyclopedia or dictionary does for a word. Several possible meanings are given, as in the example below.

> **perfume, scent, smell**   A smell can remind us of a particular situation or person; odor attracts, repulses, relaxes, or offends, so it can depict feeling responses or intuition, and may summarize what you feel about a person or situation; frequently in dreams a smell expresses an intuition of something rotten in one's life if the smell is bad; the rotten smell might mean "bad" emotions felt in a relationship; a hunch or feelings about something, as in the example; memories. <u>Good smell</u>: good feelings; nonverbalized intimations or love.
>
> Example: "I went back in time in circles, almost as if going unconscious. I went back and back and then there came this awful smell such as I've never experienced. I always felt it was the smell of death. I would wake terrified. One night my husband, a practical and down-to-earth man, said he would read me to sleep to see if it helped me not have the dream. It made no difference, I still had the nightmare. Imagine my surprise though. He said, 'I knew you'd had the dream again, for there was an awful smell in the room for a minute.' " (Mrs R.S.)
>
> Also explainable by the large number of idioms regarding smell. *Idioms:* on the right scent; throw someone off the scent; in bad/good odor with; odor of sanctity; smell a rat; smell of greasepaint; smells fishy; something stinks to high heaven; like stink; raise a stink; what you did stinks. See: *nose* under **body.**

The above entry on **perfume** is typical of most entries. The example it contains illustrates the entry, or an aspect of it. In general, the description of what the dream image means is set out first. The insertion of the semicolon (;) means that a separate suggestion for the meaning of the dream image is being given. We could therefore read it as saying, "Perfume or smell might remind us of a particular situation. It might depict feelings of repulsion or attraction. It might show 'bad' emotions felt in a relationship. It might depict a hunch or feelings about something. It might mean memories of something—depending on the smell."

To pack as much information into the available space, the semicolons have been used to shorten statements. Therefore, in using the entries to find meanings of dream images, consider each suggestion given.

Many entries, as with the above, also give variations, as with <u>Good smell.</u> The headings for these are underlined to make them easier to find. Because many dream images depict unconscious thought processes, as used in language, the section <u>Idioms,</u> also underlined, is frequently given. Standing in a pink room might well be your dream's way of saying you feel "in the pink." Coming down from a tall building to street level might be quickly understood by the idiom "coming down to earth."

"See" suggests the reading of other entries that might be useful. In this section when it says *nose* under **body,** this means look for the entry called **body,** and then find the subentry *nose* that is just below it. Sometimes a suggestion is made to "see" an example. This is because the example has in it mention of the symbol dealt with. To enormously extend the information offered about dreams, in many places a website is also suggested under the "see" option. The webpages given offer a very extended range of information about the topic being dealt with.

Throughout the dictionary, an effort has been made to list entries under the word you are likely to search for. For instance, an entry on the use of computers to file dreams would not be under a heading such as **dreams and computers**—but **computers and dreams.** Similarly, an entry

Introduction

would not be **dream movements,** but **movements while asleep.** Therefore, when searching for information on a topic, go to the word central to your search.

A dream has in it many sources of information. Not only is it helpful to consider the basic dream images, but also what is happening, how people are dressed, their posture, and what the dream environment is. A dream is often like a film. The background gives a lot of information making the foreground action meaningful. There is a great difference between a scene taking place in a farmyard than in a bedroom. So even things such as what hand was used, left or right, should be referred to. Entries in the *Dictionary*—such as **settings** and **posture**—help to understand this aspect of dreams.

Where sex or sexuality is mentioned, it is not simply referring to the sex act. It refers to sexuality in all its aspects. This includes the urge toward parenthood, and the love and caring connected with it.

This book is complete in itself. However, every publication has certain restrictions regarding size. This book includes all of the most frequently used dream images, and the most interesting features, such as "archetypes." For those interested, more features can be found on the author's website: *http://dreamhawk.com/d-ency.htm*.

Getting to Work on Your Dreams

The foundation of understanding your dreams begins with starting a dream journal. Buy yourself a good thick blank book, one that is attractive and reflects the value of your dreams and the work you will do with them.

If you have a computer, open a file called "Dream Journal" and record your dreams there. Or you can purchase special dream software such as Alchera. Alchera not only allows you to record your dreams, but also lets you develop your personal dream dictionary, and records many other facets of your dreams. See *http://mythwell.com/index.html*.

In whatever way you record your dreams, take time to write them out at length. Do not record them in note form. The details are important. Likewise, when you write your understanding of the dream, describe it as fully as possible. In this way your dream journal becomes a treasure house of information that grows over the years.

Of course, you can only record your dreams in your journal if you remember them. All of us dream each night, but many of us forget most of our dreams. So it is important to stimulate dream memory if you are to capture them. One of the best ways to do this is to become interested in what is happening in your dreams, and by trying to gain insight into any fragments of dreams you may catch. It is also important to ask yourself what you have dreamt as soon as you wake. As you wake, do not move your body or open your eyes. This often blasts away the subtle memories of dreams. The memory of dreams have a habit of melting like snowflakes held in a warm hand. Therefore it is also important to record your dream in some way as soon as you remember it.

Because writing takes time and effort, one of the easiest ways to immediately record your dream is with a small handheld tape recorder. You can later transcribe this into your journal. If you have a computer with voice recognition software, this is very easy to do.

Discovering the Meaning of Your Dream

When you have written down your dream, you can begin to unravel the threads that lead into the wonder of information your dream holds. Start by writing down the key words and phrases. To illustrate this we can use the following dream:

> I was leaving some people, like at a junior school. Some of the children tried to detain me with the attitude that I was defying

Introduction

> *teacher's authority, and they restrained me with the rules they re-strained themselves with. I broke free and walked off. (Timothy)*

Some of the key words here are "leaving," "people," "school," "children," "detain," "attitude," "defying," "teacher," "authority," "restrained," "free," "walked." Once you have written down the key words, look them up in the dictionary section wherever necessary. For instance, if you look up the word "leaving" the entry refers you to **departing.** This defines the possible meanings as "a breaking away from old or habitual patterns of behavior; leaving a situation, such as a relationship, a financial setup, or work; the struggle to become independent, as in leaving home; change."

Remember that each of the statements within the semicolons (;) are a separate suggestion of meaning. Do not hold rigidly to these definitions. They are only suggestions. Nevertheless, Timothy's dream is certainly about breaking away, and what he is moving away from obviously has to do with authority, and it is a relationship with authority learned at school.

In this way the dream already begins to release its meaning. If you consider the important phrases as well, and the drama they depict, this deepens the insight. For instance, the important phrases are "I was leaving," "children tried to detain me," "with the attitude," "I was defying," "they restrained me with the rules," "I broke free."

The next step is to take the dream out of its symbols and write a connected version of the key words and phrases as they refer to your everyday waking life and feelings. Prior to doing this you need to ask yourself how the key words and phrases link with your life. In the case of this dream, you would need to ask in what way you have been breaking away from attitudes to do with behavior dictated by rules and regulations learned as a child. You would also need to question yourself about the struggle the dream portrays of two opposing urges—the urge to conform, and the urge to go your individual way. What has happened, or is happening in your life, that links with this struggle? If you do this and write down the results, you might produce something like this:

> *The people I am leaving represent the attitudes I developed at school. I grew up in a small town that was separated by only a few years from the servant/master way of life. I was severely caned at school if I didn't conform to the rules dictated by teachers. Looking back I suppose the adults themselves were controlled by their own fears of authority. I see that at the moment I am beginning to be aware of how this influences my own choices and behavior in life, and am trying to move away from this. But as the dream suggests, it is a struggle, and I do it with some feelings of defying or challenging people around me. I would like to be independent without this personal struggle. But as the dream points out, I am learning to walk free. What I learn from the dream is to be more aware of this process taking place in my life.*

When working with this key-words approach, some of the questions you need to ask yourself are:

1. Are there particular feelings experienced, expressed, or dramatized in my dream as part of the plot? If so, can I relate them to what I am meeting in my waking life? See **emotions and mood.**
2. Is there a theme in my dream? Such themes might be: running away, looking for something, feeling lost, finding something new, relationship, work, etc. If possible put a name to the theme and consider how it relates to you. Also make a note of it to see if it occurs in other dreams. In this way you can see what the important issues are that your dreams are dealing with. Your life is itself a theme, and certain parts of your life story are extremely important and are explored in your dreams.
3. What aspects of me do the people, places, and animals depict? Try to define what these are. See if you can discover what comment the rest of the dream is making on these different aspects of yourself.

Introduction

Other features in the following pages give yet more hints on exploring your dreams. These can be read and used as you gain expertise in the methods just described. They include **amplification method; associations of ideas; plot of dream; peer dream work; processing your dreams; settings; symbols and dreaming.**

The World of Dreams

When we sleep and dream we enter a completely different realm of experience than when we are awake. It would be foolish to try to breathe under water in the physical world, but in dreams this is not only possible but lots of dreamers do it. In dreams we can fly. We can make love to men or women as we please, without fear of social or physical consequences. While dreaming we can die over and over. The dead can be reborn, and the world around us can be changed simply by changing our attitude. A monster pursuing us one moment can in an instant become a warm friend because we changed our fear to love.

In the world of dreams our most intimate fears and longings are given an exterior life of their own, in the form of the people, objects, and places of our dream. Therefore sexual drive may be shown as a person and how we relate to them; or given shape and color as an object; or given mood as a scene. Your feeling of ambition might thus be portrayed as a businessperson in your dream, your changing emotions as the sea or a river, while the present relationship you have with your ambition or emotions is expressed in the events or plot of the dream.

A dream portrays a part of you, such as your ambition, as being exterior to you. By showing your urges or fears as people or places exterior to you, your dreams are able to portray the strange fact that while, for instance, the love you have for another person is intimately yours, you may find such a feeling difficult to bear, as when one is married and falls in love with someone else. To observe our dilemma as if we were watching it as a play has very real advantages. The different factors of our situation, such as feelings for our marriage partner, our love of the new person, and social pressures such as our family's reactions, might all be shown as different people in the dream. We can therefore not only experience these as separate from our central self, but we define in the dream's action how we relate to them. Most important, we can *explore safely* the possible ways of living within, or changing, the factors involved.

Put in another way, because some of our feelings may never have been consciously felt or recognized, they cannot be grasped by us as a thinking or perceiving person. We cannot see them with our eyes, touch them with fingers, or smell them, let alone think about them. After all, they are unknown and formless. But a dream can portray what has not yet been put into words or organized into conscious thought by portraying it in images and drama. The dream is thus another *sense organ*, looking into areas we might not have any other way of examining.

Life's Great Work

When you realize each aspect of the dream, each emotion, each landscape and environment are materializations of your feelings and insights, you begin to see how you live in the midst of a world—the world of thoughts, feelings, values, judgments, fears—largely of your making. Whatever you think or feel, even in the depths of your being, becomes a material fact of experience in your dream. It is this inner universe that religion speaks of as heaven or hell. What you desire or fear, what you imagine and admire, also often takes form in the physical world in some way. So finding some degree of direction, mastery, or harmony within this world of your making is the great work of human life.

A

abandoned   Feeling unwanted, particularly by parents. May have become habitual. It can lead to feelings of being unloved in the midst of what is really a happy and caring relationship; sometimes self-pity; can represent big changes in your life, such as leaving home, or traveling and living in another country, so feeling abandoned by one's friends and support. Such dreams may occur if you had to spend time in hospital as a child, or one of your parents died. If <u>by a friend or relative:</u> anxiety about losing friendship, or of illness creating a loss. Being abandoned <u>in the sense of allowing sexual and emotional liberty:</u> finding a new freedom; dropping usual social codes and unashamedly expressing yourself; it can be an example of one of the functions of dreams, to release held-back sexuality and emotion. See **alone; hero/ine.**

abbey   See *abbey* under **house, buildings.**

abdomen   See *abdomen* under **body.**

abduction   <u>Happening to someone else:</u> the desire to influence or have power over someone. <u>Happening to yourself:</u> feeling influenced by someone or something else, against your inclinations or desires. This can occur when events in life, such as leaving school or home, push you into changes you do not embrace with pleasure. Or you may feel people you are involved with are forming a clique and pressuring you. Sometimes the pressure arises from within, from a part of you that is trying to emerge.

aboriginal   The unsophisticated; inner contact with the natural life-processes within; feeling unified with nature. This often brings an intuitive wisdom. See **Africa, African; black person; natives.**

abortion   Suggests an idea, a direction, or an area of one's feelings such as surround a love affair that has died or been lost; an attempted relationship, direction, or project is not supported by your confidence or desire. If <u>dream connects with actual abortion:</u> the emotions surrounding an actual experience of abortion; sense of guilt; the fears of damage to future possibility of childbearing; the feelings about loss of the baby. All these need to be healed in some measure. See **baby.**
   Example: "I dreamt that my mum had a miscarriage. When I woke up I knew she had split with her current boyfriend. She rang up and I said, 'Mum, don't tell me, I know why you've rung, you've broken with your boyfriend.' She was amazed and asked how I knew." (Jane)

above   See **positions.**

abroad   Your feelings about that country, or the culturally held view of it; being in a new or changed life situation. If <u>abroad or going abroad:</u> making a change, doing something new; wanting to escape your present environment; getting away from it all. If <u>someone or something arrives from abroad:</u> a change; something new arising in your life. If <u>you have lived in that country:</u> overall experience of that place. Were you happy there, lonely, what characteristics of the people did you take in? <u>Someone of the opposite sex from abroad:</u> hopes for a new relationship; a relationship that has new features; difficulties with intimacy in present relationship. See **travel.**

absorb

absorb Dreams often represent learning as an organic process. Ideas are taken in, digested, then form part of an organic whole in an integrated system. Seeing something absorbed in a dream may represent absorbing ideas, or even poisonous feelings, depending upon what the dream images are.

abyss <u>If feared:</u> fear of losing control; fear of failure; lack of confidence; loss of identity; feelings about death; the unconscious. Having these fears in no way suggests the external or internal world warrants anxiety. But lack of confidence will obviously hamper performance in dealing with the difficulties represented by the abyss. <u>Without fear:</u> being able to take risks, not being afraid of illness and death in a paralyzing way. The void depicts the aspect of human consciousness existing beyond the opposites, such as good and bad, right and wrong. Access to this gives tremendous liberation to the dreamer, freeing them from restricting rigid concepts or habits of thinking, responding, and relating. See **fall, falling; pit; void.**

accelerator See *accelerator* under **car.**

accident Anxiety; self-punishment or introverted aggression. Occasionally a warning to watch one's step as attitudes may be predisposing one toward dangerous situations. Many people have strong feelings of anxiety about any dream that shows them having an accident or being injured. Research does not support the idea that such dreams predict impending disaster. Some people do have occasional warning dreams. See **ESP in dreams.** <u>Accident at sea:</u> feelings of threat about relationship; a sense there is a problem building up. <u>Accident in car:</u> tension about your efforts to "get somewhere" or achieve your goals. Take care in driving for a few days. See **car.** <u>Accident in the home:</u> tension may be building up in your home life; occasionally means you have unconsciously noticed something might cause an accident in the home. Therefore check whatever it is that produced the accident—i.e., is stair carpet loose if you dream of falling down stairs? An <u>accident to someone else:</u> could be hidden aggression. <u>Plane crash:</u> worries about a project such as business collapsing or not coping financially. <u>Idioms:</u> accidentally on purpose; chapter of accidents. See **airplane.**

acid Something burning away at your feelings or confidence, perhaps guilt or anxiety; your vitriolic attack on someone else; fear of getting "burnt" or hurt. <u>Throwing acid on someone:</u> purposely hurting someone; putting them to the test by being hurtful. <u>Idioms:</u> acid tongue; come the old acid (try to deceive); the acid test.

acting, actor/actress See **famous people;** *actor/actress, acting* under **roles.**

active imagination Carl Jung several times described a technique for using imagination that allowed the spontaneous expression of the unconscious. Jung described active imagination as a putting aside of conscious criticism while we allow our irrational to play or fantasize. In relationship to a dream, this technique can be extraordinarily helpful and revealing. A way to learn the technique is to take a dream in which a fairly defined person appears. It can be a child or adult. Then sit in a quiet situation alone or with a sympathetic listener and purposefully create an internal feeling or attitude that is noncritical and meditative. It may help to imagine that you have dropped any critical feelings and are listening with open heart to a friend. The aim is to allow the friend to express without your intervention or direction. This attitude is applied to yourself.

Having developed the right attitude, then hold the dream in mind, imagine yourself back in the feelings and environment of the dream and simply watch to see what develops in your imagination. By doing this you are listening to the unconscious and observing how it intervenes and communicates with consciousness by introducing changes, imagery, and feelings into your contemplation of the dream. See *carrying the dream forward*, under **peer dream work.**

active/passive   You are in a passive role when you are an inactive observer in your dream, are all the time on the receiving end of dream action, or make no effort to move from discomfort. If this occurs frequently in your dreams, you are probably passive in your waking life. This habitual passivity can gradually be changed by such techniques as active imagination and imagining the dream forward. See **processing your dreams.**

ad   See **advertisement.**

address   Yourself; the way you live; your present style of life or status. Another person's address: contact with that person. Past address: the person you were, the traits you developed, what you faced in life at that time. To forget or lose your address: to lose sight of your goals or standards in life, or who you are. This suggests a loss of connection with, or a breakdown of the feelings and motivations that usually give you purpose and drive. Thus you would experience a sort of confusion about "where you live," i.e., your place in life and connection with others.

Adler, Alfred (1870–1937)   Born in Vienna, Austria. Studied medicine, and later became a disciple of Freud. Diverged from Freud over Freud's idea that the sexual impulse was all important in human behavior. Adler saw people as goal oriented, with an urge toward personal growth and wholeness. He stated that in dreams we can clearly see our aggressive impulses and desire for fulfillment. Dreams can also help the dreamer define two often conflicting aspects of their experience—their image or sense of themselves, and their sense of what is socially acceptable. Because we strive from our earliest years to have some control over ourselves and our surroundings, we may develop a style of life around a sense of inferiority or lack of power. So a person who feels vulnerable may become aggressive to compensate. Adler therefore felt that in dreams we not only see what we think of ourselves, and what our environmental situation is, but also find a definition of our techniques for satisfying our drive to deal with and succeed in the world.

adolescent   May refer to yourself and what you faced at that age; issues to do with sexual and social maturing; feelings about the opposite sex; undeveloped parts of self; potential for growth and creativity. See **boy; girl; individuation; man; woman.**

adventure   If difficult: Facing things about yourself that are painful or you wish to avoid; anxiety, or difficulties with change. On an interesting/pleasant adventure: undertaking something new and/or difficult; a new opportunity presenting itself; making a change; undertaking the journey to meeting oneself.

advertisement   A desire to have others know something about yourself; a way of bringing something to your attention; recognition of a need or opportunity. Advertisement for a job: desire for change; hope of something new; desire to find more satisfaction; recognition of opportunity.

advice   Being given advice: what you need to know but perhaps wouldn't take from someone else; intuition—occasionally of utmost importance, especially if the figure in the dream is one you feel natural respect or veneration for; feeling pressured by other people's opinions. Giving advice: conscience; sense of "ought" or "should"; what you desire to say but haven't; what you know to be useful unconsciously, but perhaps haven't accepted. See **voice; talking.**

affair   May depict feelings about infidelity; betrayal; failure; longing for love; feeling alone in a relationship. In general, dreaming of a pleasant affair is a way of enjoying or

affair

exercising the wonderful feelings of falling in love and sharing emotional and sexual pleasure. Having an affair in a
dream may help keep alive and active the ability to love and
be loved if there is not sufficient stimulus in waking life.

afraid   See **anxiety dreams; emotions, mood.**

Africa, African   This may refer to feelings about colored people or racial prejudices; Africa was the birthplace
for the human race, so may refer to personal origins; if one
is aware of particular associations, such as having lived in
Africa or studied it, then it would probably refer to those
associations. In dreams, white people often use tribal
Africans or Australian Aborigines to represent their own
natural inner life, the feeling urges or intuitions that guide
or beset them. See **aboriginal; black person; natives.**

afternoon   See **time of day.**

age   Youth: that period of your life and its major lessons;
lack of maturity; freshness and energy. Middle age: maturity; experience; facing old age and the changes it brings.
Old age: wisdom; experience; lacking of pliability and
freshness; worn-out or out-of-date.

air   Your ability to survive well or badly in an environment; the invisible but felt social atmosphere within which
you unconsciously exist and strive; support or lack of it
given by your confidence or social acclaim or condemnation; when we talk about "clearing the atmosphere" or
there being "something in the air," this is precisely what
dreams of air often refer to; can also refer to a fear of not
surviving in connection with what one is facing at the
time. In other words, a strong sense of being overwhelmed
by anxiety or some invading influence. See **breath; wind.**

air conditioner   Perhaps one's lungs; a way that you
"cool down" or calm your feelings or "blood pressure," so

a way of dealing with stress; relief. If <u>felt as cold:</u> Something causing emotional withdrawal or coldness.

airplane   Represents quick or dramatic life changes; taking a risk; vulnerable ideals, hopes, and plans; anxiety or fear; power to change, to transform one's situation, or to change or influence others; the desire to change one's lifestyle; getting away from the present situation or style of life. To climb aboard a plane is to embark upon dramatic movement from one way of life, or one situation in life, to another. It is a leap into the unknown, into chance—so it is a powerful symbol of change. Perhaps that flight into chance, into life and its mysterious possibilities might be okay. Or it might fall from the sky. Meanwhile, on the plane you will not have your feet on the ground, you will not be secure. The plans, the love, the hopes and efforts might work out or crash and lead to tragedy with all its rippling effects moving into the web of relationships and events connected with the flight of the plane.

An <u>attacking aircraft:</u> feeling attacked either by doubts and self-criticism, or by others.

Being <u>grounded:</u> sense of not getting anywhere; frustration; plans and hopes that haven't connected with achievement. <u>Difficulty landing:</u> difficulty achieving goal or making it real in a down-to-earth way; anxiety about where life events are taking you; feeling out of control or not being in control; difficulties or fears about being in someone else's hands. <u>Plane falling rapidly:</u> "pit" feeling in stomach that one gets when feeling anxiety about the outcome of a situation; sense of failure or guilt; apprehension about the future of a project or direction. <u>Plane journey:</u> a move toward independence; leaving home or friends; success. The plane is also a means of leaving things behind, rising above, or finding a way of escaping difficulties or the past. It is a way we move beyond the limitations of any one locality, racial customs, family attitudes, or religious environments. It is the power of the mind to move among and learn from or experience these many states of being. <u>Private plane:</u>

airplane

One's personal activities and plans not deeply connected with other people. The <u>crashed or wrecked plane:</u> worry about failing. Can be anxiety bringing down ambition or adventurousness; a loss of self-confidence or mental equilibrium; warning about a business project; broken dreams and hopes. <u>Watching a plane land safely:</u> The arrival back to oneself of the actions, words and energies sent out into the world. See **airport.**

airport   Making new departures; changes, hoped for or real; desire or need for adventure. This could be mentally, emotionally, or sexually; achieving goals; being en route to something, or something new in life; a checking of one's own values, identity, a sort of self-assessment in regard to independence and moving to new opportunities. Self-doubts and uncertainties at this stage stop you from attempting the new; occasionally the departure point for "higher planes"; considering that a flight might take us to new places, opportunities, or relationships, the airport can represent a terminus or change in connection with any of these. See **airplane; foreign countries.**

air raid   Feeling under attack, the severity depending on the dream damage. The attack might be emotional from people, or feelings we have about events around us. Things may be going badly at work, and comments be felt like bombshells. Very often, though, the threats are purely mental. We may read of an illness such as AIDS and the anxiety we connect with the idea has a devastating effect. <u>Idioms:</u> I feel blitzed; come as a bombshell; go down like a bomb; go like a bomb; put a bomb under someone; earn a bomb. See **airplane; war.**

air-sea rescue   Feeling at the mercy of powerful natural forces—emotions—that you are not dealing well with, otherwise you would not need to be rescued; difficulty in dealing with the demands of life generally, and a dangerous attraction to sinking or giving up; if you are seeing or actively helping in an air-sea rescue, this suggests an action to deal with feelings that might otherwise engulf you. See **sea.**

aisle   The aisle as a part of a building or plane, represents the way between opposites; a way through; being in public view if there are people about; the experience of connection with other people, or being connected by a common purpose or link. See **corridor.**

alcohol   An influence that changes the way you feel, moving you toward negative or positive feelings; a power that changes your heart and mind; prelude to friendliness or intimacy; an allowing into your life of another influence you do not immediately feel is your conscious will; sociability; dependence; alcohol dependence and the loss of control over oneself; in a religious sense the wine or spirit represents a life-changing influence, an influx of deep self-acceptance allowing something life-changing.

alien   Urges or feelings you find difficult to identify with; feelings of being an outsider in a group or society; can also be something very new and previously not experienced in regard to your potential or mind. Frequently the alien in your dream represents a meeting with the fuller potential you have.

alone   Sense of isolation; feelings of loneliness; independence, depending on dream feelings. <u>Idioms:</u> go it alone; alone together; alone = all-one.

altered states of consciousness   Dreams themselves are an altered state of consciousness. The term "ASC" refers to a significant change in what is considered normal waking awareness. Therefore a dream is an excellent example of an ASC. For instance, in dreams or in a state where the sense of oneself is diminished, people can sometimes do or experience things they cannot in "normal" waking life. Problems can be solved in an intuitive way, perception is heightened, some people look ahead to future events, or experience a view of things far distant from their physical body. There is also the possibility of healing processes released in the body. Memories of early childhood or even life in the womb are more readily accessible in the dream state than in waking life. Of course, it has to be said that although such things are possible, the run-of-the-mill altered state in dreams or fantasies has little or nothing of these splendid possibilities. Therefore part of the study of ASCs is to discover how we can, as humans, learn to use our potential more adequately. Nevertheless, the full surround virtual reality of a dream is definitely an ASC. See **ESP in dreams;** the definitions of dreaming under **Freud, Sigmund; out-of-body experience.**

ambulance   Most dreams about an ambulance involve feelings of emergency, or panic. Often the dream involves some injury or life-threatening situation to someone, so therefore concerns the stress you feel about some issue you are confronting. See **accident.**

American Indian   Natural wisdom; self-acceptance and wisdom based on the awareness of one's links with the world; the intuition or wisdom of the irrational or unconscious.

American Indian dream beliefs   In considering the beliefs of the Amerindian peoples, there is not a single belief system. Each tribe developed their own relationship with their inner life as it connected with and contributed to their external environment and needs. In looking at the fairly pure statements of traditional Amerindians in such books as *Black Elk Speaks,* and *Ishi,* it is fairly obvious, however, that dreams were generally considered a form of reality or information to be highly regarded. Black Elk became a revered medicine man of his tribe through the initiatory process of his dreams and their revelation. His dreams revealed rituals to be performed by the tribe that aided in healing social tensions. But these deeply perceptive social or psychological insights into his own people that arose in his dreams are only one of many facets the American native peoples found in their dream life. And, of course, Black Elk is only one of the men and women of the Native American people who were visionaries. See **Iroquoian dream cult.**

amnesia A dream may often show forgetfulness through the experience of sudden recall after a long period of not remembering—usually the avoidance or repression of seeing something about yourself in your life.

Example: "I am sleeping rough in a garden with a woman I do not love. I think I should try to make the best of the situation, but my feelings against it are too strong. Then I decide I don't ever want to live like that again, and tear up the mattress we slept on. As I do this I realize, as if waking from amnesia, that Pat lives just across the road. She has specially moved there because of our love. I realize with horror I had forgotten and may have lost her." (David H.)

amplification method An approach suggested by Carl Jung. In essence, it is to honor what the dream states. In the dream example above in the entry **amnesia,** David is sleeping on a mattress, but it could have been a bed or a hammock, or even a sleeping bag. So why a mattress and why in the garden, and why not alone? Having noted the specifics of your dream, you then amplify what you know about them. You ask yourself such questions as "What connections do I have with a mattress? What does sleeping on a mattress on the floor mean? Have I ever done it? When? Why? Where? In what circumstances? Does it represent some condition?" Thus you clarify as much information as you can about each dream specific. This includes memories, associated ideas, recent events, anything relevant. See **gestalt dream work.**

amusement park, arcade   Childlike playing at life; escapism; testing oneself to define self-image; practice run at taking risks. <u>Fear arising:</u> a sense of the pervading dangers underlying the surface impression of events; fear of the unknown emerging even in what appears to be pleasurable. If <u>enjoying oneself:</u> enjoyment of the varied experiences being met at the moment. See **fairground.**

analysis of dreams   All analyses of dreams rest upon concepts of what a dream is, what the events or images in the dream represent, and what we feel about them. Analyzing dreams has a very long history, and this history shows the various concepts different cultures had about dreams and dreaming. See **Greece (ancient) dream beliefs; history of dream beliefs; religion and dreams.**

   Most societies, ancient and modern, have had professional dream interpreters. India had its Brahmin *oneirocritics;* in Japan, the *om myoshi;* the Hasidic rabbis in Europe fulfilled this role; in ancient Egypt, the *pa-hery-tep;* ancient Greece had the priesthood within the Asclepian temples given to dreams; among the Aztecs, dream interpretation and divination were the prerogative of the priestly class *teopexqui,* the Masters of Secret Things; in today's world the Freudian and Jungian psychoanalysts fulfill this role. Some of the most ancient written documents are about dream interpretation and are direct expressions of the attempt to understand or interpret dreams. The Chester Beatty papyrus, for instance, dates from 1250 B.C., from Egypt. This contains records of two hundred dreams and their interpretations according to the priests of Horus. See Introduction; **gestalt dream work;** key words in Introduction; **peer dream work; plot of the dream; processing your dreams; series of dreams, working with; symbols and dreaming.**

analyst   See *analyst* under **roles.**

ancient   See **old, ancient, antique.**

anesthetic   Avoidance of painful emotions; indication that you are deadening pain, or that there is great pain to deaden; entering the unconscious; feeling overpowered; feelings about dying.

angel   The positive side of relationship with your mother or grandmother; religious concepts; sometimes feelings about death; unexpressed needs, or a need for a parent figure to guide or instruct in decision-making; wisdom arising from your wider awareness. The Hebrew word for angel is *"malak,"* meaning messenger. As a symbol it might therefore represent intuition of a wider truth than that encompassed by personal experience.

anger   Whether you show or repress anger in dreams is important. This is because like any other basic or instinctive response, anger uses tremendous resources of emotional and physical energy. The repression of emotional energy can be a key factor in the breakdown of health, and in positive and creative self-expression. Blocked emotional energy tends to act upon your mind and body. Anger may be a way of hiding vulnerability or real pain. In this case, it is important to feel the anger and discover what is underneath it. Sometimes deep feelings from childhood emerge once the anger has been felt. Such a surfacing of encapsulated emotions usually brings about deep insight into why certain traits are so powerful in one's nature. Holding the idea that we do not need to restrain anger in dreams can produce enormous changes in your dreams and in everyday life. Tests with women who had dreams in which they failed to express anger and who, in everyday life, were passive in situations calling for assertiveness, showed that when they learned to express anger in their dreams, they became easily assertive in daily life.

animals   Depending upon how the animal in your dream is presented, and what it is doing, dream animals represent your unedited feelings and drives, such as the fear reaction, anger, need for food, urge to breathe, sex or procreative drive, parental urges, drive for recognition or dominance in groups; survival drive; love of offspring; spontaneous feelings and affection; home-building. They depict these drives perhaps stripped of their social controls. Domestic animals are slightly different and need to be looked at in the entries below. See **birds; creatures; pets; reptiles, lizards, snakes; unconscious.**

animal situations   Animal with its young: parental feelings; basic childhood needs; ones childhood experience of being parented. Animal skin: the traits, power, or wisdom of the animal concerned. Attacked by an animal: see Wild animal(s) attacking below. Baby animal: sometimes connected with pregnancy or feelings about babies; yourself when young; feelings or memories concerning your babyhood; desire for babies; vulnerability; fundamental survival behaviors such as dependence, crying, and bonding. Domestic animal: urges in yourself that you have learned to meet and direct with reasonable success. They still have to be cared for, though, or they may react against what you ask of yourself. A horse, for instance, is broken in, or socialized when it is young, as we are. But if we are keeping a horse, we must still make sure it has proper food, exercise, and rest, as well as an expression for its herd instinct and sexual drive. What are your needs? A domestic animal such as a cat can also represent affection and one's need to care for someone. Eating the animal: integrating your natural wisdom and energy; absorbing strength from sources other than conscious personality; sensual pleasure and nutrition. Fear of animal: fear of your urges and desires. Herd of domesticated animals: feeling part of a group; if scared, then fear of group pressures. Hiding from or trapped by an animal: feeling controlled or threatened by your urges or emotions, such as anger or desire. See the *wolf* entry below. <u>Neglect, mutilation, or killing an animal:</u> neglect of your basic needs, such as those relating to sex, nutrition, body, and happy environment. <u>Talking, shining, holy, or wise animals:</u> important intuitive information; a meeting with the gathered wisdom you have unconsciously. <u>Taming or loved by a wild animal:</u> learning to relate to urges and energies in yourself that were previously unavailable to your will or needs. <u>Wild animal:</u> urges and spontaneous feelings that may not respond in the way we, or our social training, may wish. Wild animals in dreams are not something ultimately different to our personality. They are an expression of energies and needs that we have not previously related to in a cooperative or mutually helpful way. <u>Wild animal(s) attacking:</u> the wild animal represents unrepressed instinctive reactions, such as flight-or-fight, sex, and anger. In the attacking mode, however, it is unleashed aggression. In some dreams, being attacked depicts what we feel in relationship with other people. The attack, the criticism and malign emotions directed at us by others, are frequently shown as an animal attacking or biting us. Sometimes we may be aware of this, but often remarks are made that we miss, yet are sensed as an attack by our unconscious. <u>Wounded animal:</u> a hurt that has caused instinctive reaction, such as unreasoning reactive anger, fawning submission, or withdrawal.

alligator Feelings or fears of being attacked or overwhelmed, possibly from within oneself, or by a powerful mother—i.e., one's internal dependence upon mother.

ape Impulsive unreasoned urges such as self-centered grabbing of food or sexual expression without concern for the other person; mischievousness; mimicry; instinctive or intuitive wisdom about relationships, social interactions, and life; folly or foolishness or feeling like an idiot.

ass, donkey The basic life processes in the body that uphold or carry us through the years; the plodding long-suffering body; foolishness, a sort of living on whims and fancies, or being used and abused by others; stubbornness arising perhaps out of long-entrenched habits and automatic behavior, but also out of the hungers and needs of the body. If the ass or donkey is <u>being ridden by or pulling someone else:</u> you may be feeling you are doing all the hard work in a relationship, or working like a beast of burden. <u>Riding a donkey or ass:</u> this may represent humility or feeling in a lowly position. But may simply relate to one's relationship with the body's needs and responses.

baboon   See **ape.**

badger   May refer to badgering people, or feeling badgered; the quiet, unobtrusive, or even secluded life—so may refer to urges to get away from other people's influence or company; define what you associate with the badger, as there are very mixed general associations with this animal, far more so than with the fox, for instance.

bat   Thoughts or influences emerging from the unconscious; fear of the unconscious; being able to see in the dark—i.e., intuition. The Australian aborigines see the bat as the spirit of death.

bear   Feelings about being a solitary creature, capable of living alone and surviving; danger of sudden unpredictable responses; feelings of threat.

beast   Many dreams have as their main feature a beast that is of no particular characteristic or type. Often this beast is horrific and we feel such terror we cannot sustain the dream, and awaken in dread. Such a creature is a combination of many associations and fears. Perhaps it even holds in it memories of past hurts so deep we find it difficult to experience and redeem them. Thus it is an expression of drives and parts of our nature that have been repressed or avoided for one reason or another. See **nightmares.**

beaver Industriousness and independence; the word "beaver" sometimes has sexual connotations—the sexual organs; if there is emphasis on the beaver dam, then it may suggest either conserving one's energy and emotions, or holding back feelings. In the North American Indian traditions, the beaver was often a holy animal, and occasionally offered great wisdom to the dreamer. If the beaver speaks to you in the dream, it may be expressing innate or unconscious information or insights you have.

bird See **birds.**

buffalo See *bull; ox;* below.

bull Instinctive responses in us that are powerful enough to drag us along, cause us anxiety if we are in conflict with them, or carry us further in endeavors if we can work with them. Such instinctive urges may be in connection with sexual attraction and desire, feelings about people invading our territory, and protectiveness for family; sex drive, or the aspect of it that has generally been under control, but may occasionally be wild if provoked; the basic drives toward parenthood, and caring and providing via sex; an aggressive, "bullish" trait in oneself or someone else; personal traits to do with being very basic or earthy, and perhaps sexual in one's relationships; strength; ferocity; obstinacy; maleness; power. The <u>aggressive bull:</u> often shows the frustration arising from these basic drives being taunted or thwarted. For instance, a person may wish for a family, yet be frustrated by a form of sexuality in their partner that does not care for children. The <u>killed bull:</u> a killing of the natural drives to sex and procreation. If <u>sacrificed:</u> may show self-giving. The <u>ridden bull:</u> shows a harmony between self-awareness and its decision-making, and the basic "animal" drives. <u>Idioms:</u> like a bull at a gate; bull in a china shop; red flag to a bull; score a bull's-eye; sacred bull; take the bull by the horns.

camel   The ability to face difficult experiences—the dry place of life. Such dryness is when there is little satisfaction, no feelings, nothing growing in your experience. It may also link with patience, long-suffering, perseverance. Or having inner stores of sustenance; occasionally pregnancy, due to its hump.

cat   Because a cat is often an easy source of physical contact and affection it can depict the need to be cared for and warm affection, even sexual love accompanied with intense warm feelings; for some women cats are a substitute baby, it is therefore used in many dreams to represent a woman's urge or need to care for someone, or directly her need to reproduce, especially if she has bred cats; therefore, desire for sex; refined female sexuality or ruttiness, unless the cat is markedly a tom. In a man's dream: may refer to a woman or to the female, intuitive side of his nature; can be intuition and feelings, perhaps warning one through its sensitivity to moods, of unseen dangers; cattiness—showing one's "claws," jealousy, anger, or vindictiveness in a relationship; one's mother; independence; stealth; fertility; in some dreams a black cat definitely represents the fear of bad news or general fears. Jungians see the cat as representing a deep psychological secret, a hidden side of one's nature.

caterpillar   See **caterpillar**.

cow   Similar to the bull, but representing the female side of one's nature, especially the easy self-giving of oneself and one's body to others, or a baby; one's mother, motherliness, or the mother role; a woman; the forces of nature or life in oneself, especially as they relate to receptiveness or nurturing and the feminine that can lead or direct the masculine positive energy in oneself; being taken advantage of.

coyote   In general, similar to dog or fox—see below. It is sometimes used to represent the "trickster" element of life, as is the fox. See *fool, clown, trickster* under **archetypes**.

crocodile   See *alligator* above.

crow   See *crow, rook, raven* under **birds.**

cuckoo   See *cuckoo* under **birds.**

deer   The soul, the gentle harmless self that is often hurt or wounded by aggressiveness and cynicism, or by other people's criticism; vulnerability; the unsocialized or wild, but gentle side of our instincts; lovesickness. <u>In a man's dream:</u> the deer may depict a young woman the man is in pursuit of. <u>Male deer:</u> a man or ones relationship with a man.

dinosaur   Very basic urges such as survival, fear, repro- duction, and flight-or-fight reactions to situations. This does not make these "brutal." They are fundamental and necessary in today's life.

dog   Easy expression of such feelings as aggression— maybe because dogs show their teeth easily—sexuality, es- pecially male sexuality, friendship; the parts of self we usually keep out of sight, but may express spontaneously; easy-flowing natural feelings; devotion, perhaps to a lover or child; for some people a dog was the only source of ex- pressive love in their childhood, so may well depict this; fi- delity and faithfulness; as the sheepdog it is also the guardian of our welfare; like the cat, the dog can be a sub- stitute baby for childless women, or represent affection or caring; occasionally we depict a person, or what we feel about a person, through the character of a dog. See **cat.** In mythology the dog has symbolized the guardian of the gates of death, or a messenger between the hidden and the visible world. The dog was also thought of as a guide to or guardian of the hidden side of life. <u>Black dog:</u> depression or fear of death; a living energy in us that has gone "bad" and causes the depression or fear; urges that are largely unconscious; messenger related to someone dying. <u>Dog</u>

<u>attacking</u>: either being attacked by someone and so represents their anger or snide criticism, or your anger or aggression. <u>Dog on lead:</u> restrained or controlled urges; urges we have trained or directed; holding back or restraining parts of yourself. <u>Puppy:</u> youth, heedlessness, spontaneous affection and enthusiasm. It often represents a child, or feelings about wanting a child, being pregnant with a child, even one's own child; vulnerability or dependent needs; it can depict your need to care for or love something, or be loved; if neglected or mistreated, most likely indicates memories of pain from your childhood, or neglect of vulnerable parts of yourself. <u>Idioms:</u> die like a dog; dirty dog; dog-eared; dog-eat-dog; dog in the manger; gay dog; go to the dogs; let sleeping dogs lie; etc.

dolphin   See *dolphin, porpoise* under **fish, sea creatures.**

donkey   See *ass, donkey* above.

dove   See **birds.**

dragon   See **dragon.**

elephant   Although the elephant is much like any other animal in dreams, it tends to represent the power and influence of the potent emotional forces active in your body and mind that if you relate to well bring about health and success, and if you relate to badly bring about illness and ruin. If we <u>run from the elephant:</u> Being afraid of strength or inner power. The question is, can we meet this enormous energy in ourselves enough to direct it? Sometimes represents the collective unconscious. See what is said about *snake* under **reptiles, lizards, snakes,** to understand this power. <u>Elephant's trunk:</u> Sometimes a sexual symbol; ability to reach out for one's needs.

elk, moose   Like horse but wilder, less tamed—so the force of drives or emotions that carry us along or trample us. The moose or elk sometimes appears as a magical animal that brings a feeling of loving connection with the wild in us.

ferret, ermine Inquisitiveness, sexual forcefulness that can injure another person's feelings; the ability to ferret out things from the unconscious, but usually through force or fear or by denying other feelings; survival. The ermine was traditionally linked with virgin saints and thus purity. See **pet.**

fish See **fish, sea creatures.**

fly See **insects.**

fox Shrewdness in dealing with what faces the dreamer; a tricky person or relationship; street-wise; mistaken attitudes to a situation; shrewdness or wisdom gained from life experience; unpredictable behavior; the ability not to conform. See: *trickster* under **archetypes.**

frog See **reptiles, lizards, snakes.**

gazelle See *deer* above.

goat Rutting masculine sexuality, or if a female goat, the fertility and procreative power; ability to climb, personally or socially; tough ability to survive difficulties; sometimes connected with repressed natural drives that become reversed or evil/live when symbolizing the devil—or the animal drives or instinctive collective consciousness prior to ego development if connected with Pan; somebody butting into your life, or conflict with someone if the goat is attacking; surefootedness or meeting difficulties with ease; if you have kept goats it may well represent responsibility or caring. If you have bred them you might use the goat to depict your reproductive urges; in the Bible the goat represents the bad guys in the phrase "separating the sheep from the goats."

animals

hare Intuition; creative ideas; the crazy irrational notions we sometimes call intuition. This probably arose because of the hare's habit of suddenly bounding up from its hiding place unexpectedly, as intuitions often do; the victim or hunted feeling; swiftness; timidity or shyness. The hare occasionally appears as a supernatural figure giving advice, or as a sacrificial animal. As such, it depicts ability to make great changes in life, or to draw on potential that has enormous unexpressed resources.

hedgehog This probably refers to the sort of response we sometimes have of being easily hurt by situations or people's remarks or actions; could also suggest being very prickly, easily offended or irritated; memories that create pain or irritation; a vulnerable part of oneself that easily withdraws, but can react by hurting others.

hippopotamus In present times may be associated with being ungainly or overweight. In ancient Egypt the goddess Taueret was in the form of a pregnant hippopotamus with large sagging breasts. She represented motherhood and the care of children.

horse Pleasurable energy and exuberance, the sort of enthusiasm or feelings of well-being that can "carry" one through the day easily; dynamic sexual drive; the physical energy and life processes that "carry" us around. As such, it is the life processes that carry—or pull—us through growth and aging. Therefore, in old age the unbidden processes that move toward death may be depicted as the horse in a threatening role. The horse depicts human instincts that have been harnessed or socialized for generations, but have perhaps been let slide into nonuse. It is also survival drive, love, all yearning toward service, toward metamorphosis, all that has powerful energy to move us. <u>Black or dark horse:</u> unaccepted passions; threat of death; the unknown or threatening changes. <u>Blindered horse:</u> not allowing oneself to see what is happening around you; anxiety about life. <u>Controlling the horse, or fear of it:</u> trying to control, or fear of, feelings of love and sexuality, of natural drives and emotions that are powerful enough either to motivate us or drag us along unwillingly. <u>Dead horse:</u> serious loss of energy or motivation that could lead to illness or depression; an old and dying set of habits and motivations or way of life. <u>Falling off horse:</u> relating badly to one's urges and needs. This could result in tension, breakdown, or illness. <u>Grooming a horse:</u> taking care of one's basic needs, such as food, shelter, sex. <u>Horse and carriage:</u> the natural processes of life that move us through youth to old age; forces that can move us, either from within or as natural events. <u>Horse race:</u> the apparently random events of everyday life, and your relationship with people; everyday competition and where you rate yourself in it; what happens in the race shows how you are relating to opportunity, or how you feel about your accomplishments. The <u>winged horse:</u> shows how you are not limited to sexuality or survival, but can lift into wider activities—i.e., a woman turning her love of her children into social caring. See **Cayce, Edgar.** <u>Idioms:</u> back the wrong horse; from the horse's mouth; don't look a gift horse in the mouth; horse sense; you can lead a horse to water; wild horses; workhorse; horsing about; getting on your high horse; eat like a horse; beating a dead horse.

hyena   An attitude of living on other people's vulnerability or weakness; taking advantage of someone or being taken advantage of; underhandedness; messenger or bringer of death; feeling parasitized.

jackal   Like "dog," but a wild version; a trickster figure like coyote and fox; a deceiver; being a scavenger, it has sometimes been associated with death, as with crows and vultures; due to being able to see in the dark and the light, the jackal was seen by the Egyptians as a pathfinder in the underworld—i.e., the unconscious—leading the dead to the other world.

jaguar   Anger; power of assertion and fierceness.

kitten   A baby; feelings about babyhood or having a baby; caring urges, playfulness; youth.

lamb   The childlike, dependent, vulnerable part of self; new life, and so perhaps one's own child or childhood; innocence; Christ, as innocence and purity; the weakness of the lamb has enormous power, and can defeat evil. In ancient societies who bred sheep, the spring lambs were a sign of survival of the often harsh and hungry winter. At last there was food. So the sacrifice of the lamb was linked with the feeling of being given life and redemption.

leopard   As with any of the big cats, anger, temper; spitefulness, cruelty; courage; passion—even passion of caring for your children; because of the leopard's spots, which can be seen as eyes, the leopard has represented the Great Watcher—i.e., wider awareness.

lion/lioness   The power of physical strength, of temper, of emotions or sexuality; love that has become anger through jealousy or pain; leadership; one's father or fatherhood, or mother if it is a lioness; an image of the father/mother God; watchfulness or guardianship; self-assertion or boasting, because of the power of the lion's roar. Many children experience recurring dreams of a lion chasing them through their house. This is most likely due to a developing struggle with their natural feelings of anger and aggression. Parents might attempt to quiet or control the child's temper, or criticize it as "bad," therefore the child avoids or runs from it. <u>Idioms:</u> brave the lion's den; lion's share; head in the lion's mouth.

llama   This is simply another animal, so will have the basic associations of less restrained or socialized impulses, emotions, and sexuality. But its special associations might be that in its native country it is a beast of burden. It lives at high altitudes, so might represent hardiness or rarefied life.

lynx   Keenness of perception—lynx-eyed; vigilance; otherwise, same as other large cats. See *leopard* above.

mole   Living a secluded life; attitude of a recluse; short-sightedness; an avoidance of human company; unconscious forces or influence; something going on beneath the surface—this may be something you can't actually perceive, but suffer the consequences of, as with molehills; an undermining influence.

monkey   Foolishness; thoughtlessness; being ruled by impulse; one's instincts; the frivolous surface workings of the mind, or expression of frivolous emotion—or impulsive difficult-to-control urges; greediness and self-centeredness; frivolous; irrational in the sense of being stupid; mimicking or aping other people or the group, thus being a follower; the struggle involved in becoming conscious. But sometimes same as *ape*. <u>Idioms:</u> make a monkey of; monkey business; monkey with; monkey tricks; monkey's uncle; monkey on your back.

mouse   Minor irritations; fears and worries; the mousy or timid part of self; shyness; the activities within us—our house—that go on unconsciously, which might be important though small, or gnaw away at one; the sexual organ that goes in and out of a hole.

otter   Ability to meet the ever-changing moods and feelings without "drowning"; skill in seeing what is under the surface of everyday life and mind; ancient cultures saw the otter as a clean, holy creature.

ox   Interchangeable with the bull, except oxen may be castrated; strength; patient endeavor; wealth for people who live in agricultural lands; self-sacrifice; in China the ox or buffalo represented the untamed instinctive desires and reactions that need to be trained to a new relationship with the conscious self. See **bull.**

panther   Fierceness; temper; anger; in Christian symbolism it represented power to protect against evil. See *leopard* above.

pet   See **pet.**

pig   Fertility; physical appetites; life directed only by physical needs; sensuality; ungoverned passion or appetites; uncleanness; untamed human nature. The sow represents giving of oneself and sustenance; procreative fertility; lack of directive arising from anything other than sensory pleasure. <u>Idioms:</u> pig in a poke; happy as a pig in shit; make a pig of oneself; pig in the middle; pigs might fly; pigheaded.

porcupine   See *hedgehog* above.

porpoise   See *dolphin, porpoise* under **fish, sea creatures.**

rabbit   Sexuality—due to human associations with its rapid breeding; softness and non-aggression, sometimes to the point of depicting us as a victim, or foolishly passive—may thus represent unworldly idealism. Perhaps because of its tendency to be the victim of predators, is often used as a sacrifice in dreams, suggesting the hurt one might experience to the soft, vulnerable parts of oneself; feeling hounded by someone; vulnerable child self. If the <u>dreamer hunts rabbits:</u> some element of self or others being criticized, attacked, "hunted down," or hounded; instinctive urge to dominate. <u>Pet rabbit:</u> wanting to be petted or cared for; gentle contact and caring; responsibility. <u>Rabbit hole:</u> regression; a going within self; into the unconscious; the womb; attempting to escape from problems by turning within. See **unconscious.** <u>Rabbit in your garden:</u> a quiet attack on your resources or personal growth; also may connect with the general definitions above.

racoon The "bandit" part of oneself; scavenging for a living; the urges that express when not being watched.

ram Masculinity; sexual drive; the aggressive defensive side of "sheep"—i.e., of conformity, being one of the group, the passive employee; power of renewal; leader of a flock or group of people, or the less dominant aspects of self; being dominant or pushy. Idioms: battering ram; ramming one's point home; like a ram among sheep.

rat What is sick or negative; fear or anxieties; frightening instincts or urges; physical sickness or anxieties about health; feelings of sexual repulsion, or using sex to gain material aims; intuitions about a person being a "rat"—doing things behind one's back or underhandedly—or deserting a relationship when difficulties arise; threatening things going on without one being clear about what they are; seeing the underhanded side of oneself or others; the evil side of human nature; dirt and squalor; time gnawing away at your life; the unacceptable parts of oneself. Pet rat: quite different to general rat associations; vulnerability, instinctive intelligence, the caring feelings or drive to care; responsibility for caring. Idioms: rat on someone; rat race; smell a rat; feeling ratty; cornered rat; rats leave a sinking ship.

sea lion See **fish, sea creatures.**

seal See *seal* under **fish, sea creatures.**

sheep Conformity; feeling or being "one of the herd"; blind following of a leader or others; the aspects of oneself that are the same as other human beings; sheep may depict the way we might be led into situations, sometimes awful, by conforming to prevailing attitudes and social pressures; a passive female; vulnerability; sexual feelings about females.

animals

<u>Caring for sheep:</u> helping people to express more of their potential. <u>Herd of sheep, or sheep in rural setting:</u> innocence; natural feelings and peace; quietness of mind; following customs or a leader. <u>Idioms:</u> make sheep's eye at someone; follow like a sheep; being sheepish. See *shepherd* under **roles.**

stallion   See *horse* above.

tiger   Although similar in many ways to the lion, the tiger has a more feminine quality. It can therefore represent an angry woman; one's mother; a woman as a protector or destroyer; anger; spitefulness; the power and authority of one's animal strength; anxiety or fear; like any other animal, the tiger can also represent aspects of sexuality, depending on how it is presented in the dream. As a symbol of sex it would most likely include elements of uncertainty—will I be attacked or overwhelmed—power and instinctive responses. <u>Idioms:</u> fight like a tiger; paper tiger. See *lion* above.

toad   See *toad* under **reptiles, lizards, snakes.**

tortoise   See *tortoise* under **reptiles, lizards, snakes.**

turtle   See *shellfish* under **fish, sea creatures.**

wolf   Although the wolf can depict a feeling that "things" are out to get us, the wolf is often just fear. Fear is one of our instinctive reactions to situations, so is depicted by an animal. We may find ourselves a prisoner of such feelings. The wolf, as is suggested by such fairy stories as Red Riding Hood, also represents the female fear of powerful male sexuality; repressed sexuality or anger; emotions and drives you are frightened of.

antique   See **old.**

ants   See **insects.**

anxiety dreams   One of the most frequent dream themes is that of anxiety in some form. This may not be because most dreams are about things we fear, but simply because we remember those more than bland dreams. Fear is a basic and natural response to many life situations, and is not to be thought of as an illness. But excessive fear is detrimental to your well-being. In your dreams, all that can possibly disturb you is your memories, disturbing images, and your emotions. Your dream may be about a snake, or car accident—frightening things that in the dream appear to be exterior to you. Even so, it is your emotions involved in the image of the snake or situation that disturbs you, and these can be changed. If you can recognize what an enormous power your imagination has on your emotions and body, this can start the process of lessening anxiety. If you cannot meet your feelings of fear or emotional pain, you are controlled or trapped by them. Sometimes we need the help of a professional counselor to meet what we fear, but many anxieties can be met by using the simple techniques explained in **processing your dreams.** See **autonomous complex;** *wolf* under **animals; premenstrual tension; processing your dreams.**

apartment   See *apartment* under **house, buildings.**

ape   See *ape* under **animals.**

apocalypse   See **end-of-world dreams and fantasies.**

apple   See *apple* under **food.**

archetypes   Although the word "archetype" has a long history, Carl Jung used it to express something he observed in human nature. He said the archetypes are a tendency or instinctive trend in the human unconscious to express certain motifs or themes. These themes, such as death and rebirth are found throughout past- and present-day cultures in dreams and myths. Jung saw them as universal, and as existing innately within what he called the collective unconscious. They are particularly apparent in religious beliefs, in literature, and in the arts.

An easy way to understand archetypes is to remember that a man and woman have an archetypical shape—that is, a shape arising out of a fundamental pattern or mold. The woman's more rounded hips and larger breasts are typical of womanhood. They are universal, just as the heart or liver is. Each individual has unique features, but the basic "motif" remains the same. An archetype is similar to this, except that it relates to the mind. Just as we have internal organs in our body that are in virtually everyone else, we also have mental and emotional tendencies or structures that are typical. These are not so much organs of the mind as typical responses to life situations. One of these is that many people who have a near-death experience feel they are moving along a tunnel toward a light. So this is an archetype, or typical response, relating to that experience.

The archetypes are embodiments of behavioral stances that humans have developed over centuries. Countless people have lived these various modes of behavior—everything from hermit to leader, saint to horrific and malefic destroyer. These depict a direction each of us can go in making choices in life. Perhaps we only embody an archetype such as that of the sadist for moments, or perhaps our whole life is given to it. Whichever it is, our personal life and what we do are still only a tiny portion of the immense range of behavior, even within that one stance.

Below are some common archetypal symbols and their associated images. Remember that most images in your dreams are expressions of personal feelings and associations. It is only occasionally they connect your conscious self with the great pool of the collective experience. When they do, drink the waters.

anima   The female within the male, shown as a woman in a man's dream. Physically a man is predominantly male, but also has nipples and produces some female hormones.

Psychologically, we may only express part of our potential in everyday life. In a man, the more feeling and caring side may be given less expression. Apart from this, some functions, such as intuition and unconscious creativity, may also be held in latency. The female in male dreams may depict these secondary or latent characteristics. The femaleness or maleness must not be confused with personality. The conscious personality is a very flexible and shape-shifting thing. It can be male or female in quality, no matter what the body gender. But in dreams, the female is the receptive, creative aspect of this shape-shifting personality. See **woman.**

animus   The male within the female, shown as a man in a woman's dreams. Physically, a woman is predominantly female, but also has a clitoris and produces some male hormones. Psychologically, we may only express part of our potential in everyday life. In a woman, the more physically dynamic, intellectual, and socially challenging side of herself, such as assertiveness and taking charge of situations, may be given less expression. Apart from this, some features, such as innovation and creative rational thought, may be held in latency. The male in female dreams may depict these secondary or latent characteristics. In general we can say the man in a woman's dreams represents the woman's mental and social power, her ability to act creatively in "the world." It also holds in it an expression of her complex feelings about men, gained as experience mostly from her relationship with—or lack of relationship with—her father. The animus is also a synthesis of all her male contacts. So the whole realm of her experience of the male can be represented by the man in her dream, and is accessible through the image. Femaleness or maleness must not be confused with personality. The conscious personality is a very flexible and shape-shifting thing. It can be male or female in quality, no matter what the body gender. But in female dreams, the male is the dynamic, active aspect of this shape-shifting personality. See **man.**

ascetic   As a form of human behavior, the ascetic has an immensely long history and is seen in all cultures. In many chimpanzee groups there is a "monk" who lives alone. In dreams and visions, the ascetic links us with experience that comes from beyond personal life and memories, and from experience gained outside of living the social norm. It arises out of a sense of connection with something that unites all the separate people, creatures, and objects in the universe. The monk can also depict turning away from everyday life; discipline of the mind and emotions; rejection of or anxiety about the sexual roles. At a personal level the ascetic may connect with feelings of pain or failure in our experience of the sexual relationship or society. Through such pains, we may have withdrawn enthusiasm or involvement in what life offers. Positively it represents an internal question we may be unconsciously asking—What or who am I? Am I anything other than this changing body and constantly shifting emotions and thoughts?

beloved   See *lover* below.

blood   It represents the process of universal life in us. Thus wine/blood depicts the collective experience of human life. In other words, experience we can all share. It may be shown as red wine, the drinking of which, in some dreams, is realized to be wine and blood at the same moment. See *blood* under **body**.

Christ   Although people generally think of Christ as a historical figure, as a dream symbol he depicts powerful influences acting upon your personality. For a start, Christianity is a huge social and political force in the world. Many of us as children are educated to accept its beliefs. Therefore, Christ in dreams could easily depict this enormous influence and how we relate to it. But as an archetype, Christ is the cosmic mystery you have been born as. He was the very best of yourself you may have crucified in your way of living. Christ can also depict the sense of connection you have, perhaps unconsciously, with the rest of the world. See **religion and dreams;** *the self* below.

clown   See *fool, clown, trickster* below.

death   The *symbols of death* or the *fear of death* can be: sunset; evening; a crossed river or falling in a river; a skeleton; snarling dogs; sleep; anesthetic; gravestones; cemetery; blackness or something black; an old man or woman, or father time with a scythe; ace of spades; a fallen mirror; stopped clock; a pulled tooth; an empty abyss; the chill wind; falling leaves; a withering plant; an empty house; a lightning-struck tree; coffin; struggling breaths; the dead animal in the gutter; the rotting carcass; underground; the depths of the sea; falling into a hole or the void. What lies beyond death is conjecture, but the archetype of death we are considering is not completely about physical death. It is about observation of it in others, conceptions of it gained from our culture, and our impressions arising from seeing dead animals, rotting corpses. The images depict the feelings that generate around experiences and thoughts of it; attempts to deal with our aging and approach to death; social violence, plus what the deeper strata of mind releases in symbols or emotions regarding it. It is about how our sense of conscious personal existence meets the prospect of its disintegration. See *rebirth, resurrection* below.

devil   In Western culture there is a long history of struggle with sexuality. Even to dream of sex was considered a sign of the devil's influence. This struggle with internal urges, such as sex, anger, self-centeredness, is still a large part of life for many of us. The image of the devil represents this struggle, and also a force of negation that pulls us down, away from the possibility of personal transformation. The devil also represents the frustrated, inhibited side of self. See **devil.**

archetypes

father   The dream images representing father are many: God, a god, giant, tyrant, executioner, devil, Pan, older man, male leader figure, older male rival, king or emperor, holy man or priest, dominating boss, wise old man, the sun, bull—and of course, father. A child is, figuratively, like a growing plant. It takes in lumps of external material and transforms them into its own being. A child unconsciously either takes father or mother as its main model for structuring its behavior and aims. But also, huge areas of our basic self revolve around mother and father. The absence of an available father in the life of a child leaves an enormous imprint in the developing psyche. Our father in dreams therefore is most often the overall effect, habits, traits, that arise from experience—or lack of it—of our father. But we also have inborn expectations of needs in relationship. So the archetype of "father" is made up of these expectations and actual experience.

Our father is the great figure of original authority and strength in life—or lack of it. He therefore depicts relationship with outside authority or power. But there is also a cultural representation of what a father is, and each nation has particular ways of representing this. During our growth, and continuing throughout adulthood, we are confronted with literary, artistic, film, and dramatic representations of the role of father. These also form a powerful part of our inner "father." These, along with the deeply inbuilt expectations at an almost biological level of what our father is or should be, form our internal male parent, and in synthesis form the "father" archetype. See *animus* above; *father* under **family, family relationships.**

fool, clown, trickster   In several cultures the fool appears under the guise of idiot, trickster, harlequin, clown, or jester. In the Japanese story *Monkey*, this character is portrayed as Pig. In Britain it is Reynard the Fox, and in the U.S. Brer Rabbit. Charlie Chaplin is an image in the modern world for this crazy, unpredictable, yet wise clown. Jung puts all these figures under the name of Trickster, who he says represents the earliest and least developed period of life—or the least developed side of our personality. Like Pig, Trickster is a figure whose physical appetites and senses dominate his actions and decisions. His thinking does not rise above his belly or his genitals. Not understanding finer feelings, his responses to other people appear crude, self-centered, cynical, and unfeeling. In some of the stories, however, the difficulties of his exploits gradually bring about a transformation and he becomes a man instead of an animal. But there can also be a wise fool.

fugitive To forever feel you must avoid intimate human contact; to forever be running from something that is hard to define; to never be able to feel that where one is in life is home, a place to relax in, a place where you can feel peace and look around and take in the world instead of looking around to see where danger is—these are signs of the fundamental feeling of alienation or aloneness. All of these have anxiety, the fear reaction, and perhaps feelings of desertion at their root. As fear is one of the major reactions to life, some archetypical patterns of behavior have developed around the fear response. See **anxiety dreams; nightmares;** *Am I meeting the things I fear in my dream?* under **processing your dreams.**

the Great Mother The symbols are Virgin Mary, sometimes one's own mother, a divine female, an old or ageless woman, Earth, a blue grotto, the sea, a whale, a cave, a tree. Whatever the image it often contains great religious feeling or spiritual uplift. After all, mother was the most powerful being in our early world. "Did she admire hunters; then we would kill dragons and cleanse the world. Did she feel the weight of the world; then we would be the peacemaker and bring her joy." (W. V. Caldwell)

The symbols of mother represent not simply our relationship with her, but also how it influences our growth toward independence and mature love. As a baby we do not feel separate from mother. The gradual separation is

53

difficult. In some people it is never managed, even though they separate physically. Their mother, or their sense of their mother within them, still directs their decisions. The old joke about "My mother wouldn't like this" is true. In many older cultures this break was worked out in ritual tribal custom. At a certain age the children were taken from their parents' home and lived together with the other young males or females. Today we have to manage these subtleties of our psyche alone. A woman must find a way of transforming the pleasure—or absence of it—of her mother's breast into a love for a male. If she cannot she may wish to return to the breast of another female, or be the man her father never was for her. A man must find a way of transforming his unconscious desire for his mother into love of a woman which is more than that of a dependent or demanding baby or youth. If he cannot he may seek his mother in a likely woman, ignoring who that woman is as a real person. And this acceptance of our mother as she really is—a human being—precedes the acceptance of ourselves as we really are.

In the past she was known as Ishtar; Cybele; Rhea; Astarte; the Egyptian, Isis; Demeter; Hecate; Diana; Venus; Qwan Yin; Rhada. See **aura; compensation theory;** *mandala* under **shapes, symbols; ring.**

hermit   See *ascetic* above.

hero/ine   The archetype of the hero/ine has fascinated, taught, even ennobled human beings for thousands of years. It appears as Christ; Athena; Krishna; Mohammed; Mary; Ulysses; Superman; Florence Nightingale; a great game hunter; Hercules; or any film or TV hero, such as Captain Kirk or Dr. Who. We are the hero/ine of our life. We brave great dangers, face monsters, pass through difficult initiations. Fundamental to the whole drama of the hero/ine is the evolution of our identity from the depths of unconsciousness in the physical process of conception, through to developing self-awareness as an adult. From the great ocean of collective culture, language, and society, there is the gradual emergence of ourself as a mature individual. To do this we face death and rebirth several times as we metamorphose from baby to child; from child to adolescent; from adolescent to adult; from adult with youthful body to adult with aging body. It is such an incredible journey, so heroic, so impossible of achievement, so fraught with dangers and triumphs. It is the greatest story in the world, and you are the hero/ine.

king   In some ways the archetypal symbol of the king is not unlike that of the hero/ine and father. The difference is that the king is an established and acknowledged authority figure, whereas the hero is trying to deal with difficulties and meet strange fates and changes, and the father usually has a more personal connection. The king therefore represents control, or aspects of control, such as taking control, relinquishing control, reestablishing control, recognizing loss of control, and so on. The king is one of the most powerful symbols of fatherhood, which in its widest sense means the source that gave rise to us—as with the concept of God. But there is also a power aspect to the father, that often gives rise to dreams about fighting with, being unloved by, or killing or disempowering the father in some manner. See *father* under **family, family relationships; king.**

lover   At a straightforward level, the dreamt-of lover is an expression of all the emotional longing and unexpressed sensual desires we have. In the enjoyment or pain we feel in the dream, the lover is an enactment in the virtual reality of our dreams, of the perhaps secret desires we have, the unmet needs, the fears and pains we have in intimacy. As an archetypal image, it holds in it all the massive racial and cultural forces that attract and bind two people together—all the degrees and levels of maturity in love—and also all the attraction and difficulties we face in meeting our growth as a person toward wholeness. Because the image connects with all our personal and transpersonal experience of love, it may well hold in it the trauma of childhood abuse, which may work out in a series of dreams or fantasies regarding the lover. The lover is also a connection with the life beyond the boundaries of personal self. See **affair;** *anima* or *animus* above; *lover* under **roles; sex and dreams.**

martyr   The archetype of the scapegoat has, like all the others, different aspects. One can be a martyr in giving oneself to a cause, or one can be a martyr in that one forever feels one is being abused or used by others. There may be a sense of being asked too much by those around you or by the events of life. In such martyrdom there may be a hidden belief that if one does what is asked, if one sacrifices one's life for another, then one will be appreciated and loved. If one gives enough, maybe one will be recognized and rewarded? See **processing your dreams.**

monk   See *ascetic* above.

night journey   See *search for self* below.

outcast   Like many other animals, humans are very territorial and suspicious of anyone who is in some way different. Thus, living as an immigrant or child of an immigrant, being abused or abandoned in some way by one's parents, being different in some way, can all lead to a sense of being an outcast, and thus a connection with the archetypal feelings of abandonment or alienation. Living out this particular stance in life leads to the development of various attitudes to survive. There may be an intense form of independence, or hidden feelings of anger toward the nation or society one lives in. One may rebel against being a part of normalcy, even to rebelling against one's gender. The alienation can also occur because for one reason or another you cannot live within the patterns of behavior accepted, or built into, your family or social group. This is particularly evident in religious or political groups, which, to function well, require a high degree of conformity.

queen   Often represents our mother, or public acknowledgment or love. See *mother* under **family, family relationship;** *the Great Mother* below; **queen;** *king* above.

rebirth, resurrection   The *symbols of rebirth* are: the cave; an egg; spring; the tree; the cross; dawn; emerging out of the sea; the snake; the bird; a seed; arising from the earth or feces; a green shoot from a dead branch or trunk; phoenix; drinking alcohol or bloodred wine; flame; a pearl; the womb. Rebirth is as difficult to face as death. It holds within it not just the memories of the struggles and difficulties of physical birth and growth, but also the challenge of becoming the unknown future, the dark possibility, the new. See *death* above.

resurrection   See *rebirth, resurrection* above.

savior   See *Christ* above.

search for self   Each of us are constantly gathering information about who we are, what we are capable of, and what the meaning of life is. This is often put into an archetypal form—in expressions or themes as old as humanity—in the great quest, or the great pilgrimage. The search for God, the often extraordinary efforts people make to grow beyond the pain of childhood or adult trauma, the quest for knowledge when one truly tries to understand rather than simply remember facts, artists' attempts to go beyond themselves in creative acts, the quest for something self-existent or beyond change are all aspects of this search for self. Throughout history we have examples of how such quests were lived out. Mohammed, for instance, described in *The Night Journey*. In a dream he experienced a massive breakthrough into what he felt was a cosmic revelation. Our dreams often insist that the journey is everlasting, not even ending with death, but moving through the great cycles of the universe. Only by making the journey can we find wholeness and our place in life with any awareness. See **individuation.**

the self   Our conscious self or ego is only a tiny part of our totality, as is obvious when we consider how much of our memory or experience we can hold in mind at any one time. The self, as defined by Jung, is both what we are consciously aware of, and the massive potential remaining unconscious. That potential is not simply personal memories, but also areas of possibility beyond what we usually think of as our personal self. The self has no known boundaries, for we do not yet know the end of what the mind is capable of, or what consciousness is, or touches out of sight of waking.

the Shadow   Depicted as: a shadowy figure, often the same sex as dreamer but inferior; a zombie or walking dead; a dark shape; an unseen "Thing"; someone or something we feel uneasy about or in some measure repelled by; drug addict; pervert; what is behind one in a dream; anything dark or threatening; sometimes a younger brother or sister; a junior colleague; a foreigner; a servant; a gypsy; a prostitute; a burglar; a sinister figure in the dark. Usually there is an air of disrepute about the person, or of danger. In literature we find the Shadow depicted in such stories as *Dr. Jekyll and Mr. Hyde;* Wilde's *The Picture of Dorian Gray;* Hesse's *Steppenwolf,* and in many stories about werewolves or hauntings. Ackroyd, in his *Dictionary of Dream Symbols,* points to Cinderella as a Shadow figure, as she is seen as inferior by her socially accepted sisters, and is kept shut in the house, thus repressed. In occult literature the Shadow is called the Guardian of the Threshold. It is described as a great (subjective) figure we meet at a certain stage of growth. The Guardian holds in it all the negative deeds and aspects of self committed or developed in the past, even in past lives, that must be met and transformed. See **black person;** *black* under **color; shadow, shade.**

trickster   See *fool, clown, trickster* above.

wise old woman, wise old man   Jung classifies the wise old man/woman as a *"mana* personality." The word *"mana"* is

Melanesian and means holy or full of power. They are, of course, father and mother images, and carry many of the same features. The difference is in the quality of wisdom and sense of deep insight we find when we meet them in our dreams. <u>Wise old man:</u> he may appear in dreams as a king, magician, prophet, guru, guide, god, sage, authority figure, counselor, philosopher, priest, professor, judge, headmaster, doctor, alchemist, medicine man, sorcerer, wizard, necromancer, shaman, warlock, and others of like kind. Or he can be any man older than ourselves and radiating insight or power, creating in us a feeling of veneration. In general, depicts and offers guidance and rational wisdom gathered not only from one's own experience, but also cultural or universal experience. <u>Wise old woman:</u> appears as a grandmother; one's mother in old age; a goddess; a female figure depicting fertility, naked female with large breasts, vagina, or buttocks; queen or princess; an Eastern female; an old woman who radiates wisdom, authority, and unconditional love. In general, offers guidance and feeling wisdom gleaned from personal and cultural experience. One may even note from the wise old woman the signs of deep wisdom, which is a synthesis of what has arisen out of the pain and strength of the women in one's family, stretching back through time. Both of these figures tend to appear in dreams at times of great transition—perhaps because we need greater access to resources of insight and information at those times. During such periods of one's life, the aid these figures give can lead to greater self-actualization. The negative side of this archetype appears as a vengeful and destructive figure. In the case of the woman as a witch, or devouring female-figure, such as is seen in the Indian goddesses, such as kali. See *the Great Mother* above.

arena, amphitheater   A focus of attention; a mental capability to bring an unimaginable number of associated bits of information and experience together in considering something; area of conflict, attention, or turmoil;

something being dramatized or considered by dreamer; something being witnessed; a testing of oneself, as in a sporting event, especially if the area is a stadium rather than an arena; participation with others in life or endeavors. See **theater.**

argue Something you are feeling in conflict about and have opposing feelings on. Or it might show you releasing feelings about someone that you do not tell them to their face. It might refer to feelings about parents arguing, so depict the anxiety or anger you felt at the time.

Aristides A Greek who is thought to have written the first dream diary during the period of time dated 530 to 468 B.C. This diary, titled *The Sacred Teachings,* was a huge work five volumes in length—although twenty-seven portions of it may have been lost. The reason for the title is that many of the dreams concerned Aesculapius, the god of healing. They give accounts of how Aesculapius appeared to Aristides in his dreams and taught him various methods of healing illnesses. Many of these methods were what would be considered extreme today, consisting of bathing in icy cold streams, taking mud baths in freezing weather, and so on. See **Greece (ancient) dream beliefs.**

Aristotle on dreams Aristotle (384–322 B.C.), a Greek born in the Ionian city of Stagira was one of the first writers to attempt a study of the mind and dreams in a systematic way. He was the son of Nicomachus, the court physician to Amyntas III, king of Macydon. In 367 B.C. he went to Athens and studied at Plato's Academy, until Plato's death in 347 B.C. Along with Socrates and Plato, he became one of the great philosophers who were instrumental in forming the foundations of Western rational thinking.

Aristotle deals with the subtleties of sleep and dreams in three great treatises—*De Somno et Vigilia; De Insomnis;* and *De Divinatione Per Somnum (On Sleep and Dreams, On Sleeping and Waking,* and *On Divination Through Sleep).* The views on dreaming are developed out of Aristotle's concepts of mind and imagination, and his observation of how people deal with sleeping and waking. For instance, he saw imagination as the result of sensory and subjective perception occurring after the disappearance of the sensed object, recognizing that the human mind can form powerful and realistic "afterimages" of things no longer present. Aristotle carried this insight into the realm of sleep and applied it to dreaming. He added to this the observation that while awake we have the easy ability to distinguish between what is an external object and what is our imagined object. In sleep, however, this faculty disappears or is almost completely absent. This produces the sense of enormous reality we have in dreams, and the feeling that we are facing actual events and people. It is what Freud called the hallucinatory property of dreams. See **Freud, Sigmund; hallucinations and hallucinogens; Greece (ancient) dream beliefs.**

arm   See *arms* under **body.**

armor   The emotional and intellectual rigidity we use to protect ourselves from hurt. Can depict muscular tension that blocks free-flowing sexuality and feelings; defense systems, such as frantically arguing for our beliefs, or killing out feelings in a relationship; fear of getting hurt—but also ability to protect oneself from hurt or attack; barrier to stop other people "getting through to you"; hardness of heart; defensive attitudes; self-doubt; inner conflict. If the armor is seen as defensive, it may point to deep anxieties in regard to what is suggested by the dream action—such as relationship, work, health.

army   Some form of conflict, internal or otherwise; the forces or qualities you muster to deal with difficulties—i.e., courage, information; aggression or anger; attitudes necessary to face anxieties. See *soldier* under **roles; war.**

arrested   Suggests a restraint of self-expression by moral judgments or questions of right and wrong; restraint of one's anger or sexuality, or other "unlawful" feelings; a circumstance holding one back; held-back development or growth; a fear arising from a fearful relationship with authority or politics—such as is often dreamt by people who have survived harsh political regimes and terror of being arrested. See **policeman/woman.**

Artemidorus   To Artemidorus of Daldis we owe one of the first and most famous books on dream interpretation—*Oneirocritica (The Interpretation of Dreams)*. Artemidorus lived in Greece about 140 A.D., and almost certainly drew on older works, such as Assurbanipal's dream book. Clay tablets found at Nineveh, part of the library of the Assyrian king Assurbanipal—669 and 626 B.C.—tell of the importance of dreams in the life of kings and commoners. The Assurbanipal dream book is itself only a link in a chain of tradition, as the library possibly held records starting about 5000 B.C. If this is correct, the *Oneirocritica* links the remote past with present-day theories of dream interpretation. MacKenzie, in his book *Dreams and Dreaming*, makes this clear. He points out that in the Assurbanipal tablets it says that if a man flies frequently in his dreams he will lose his possessions. In *Zolar's Encyclopedia and Dictionary of Dreams*, printed in 1963 in the U.S., it says "Flying at a low altitude: ruin is ahead for you." Other obvious similarities suggest that the most recent of popular dream books is largely a copy of the most ancient. See **Greece (ancient) dream beliefs.**

artist   See *artist* under **roles.**

ascending   The rising feelings of passion or sexual pleasure; the transition from expressing energy genitally to expressing it in feelings and thoughts is often shown as ascending; in many past cultural traditions, ascent was associated with purification or refinement—as in the ascent to heaven, or a holy mountain; becoming more detached, or finding a different perspective; because we often move to a wider view of things, becoming more aware as we get higher, ascending is often linked with change, and perhaps leaving things behind, the dropping away of what occupied you below; an attempt to remove oneself from the difficulties or experiences of the world—there may be a link with losing touch with reality; moving toward achievement; may be a symbol of waking, such as ascending into wakefulness and descending into sleep.

ascetic   See *ascetic* under **archetypes; religion and dreams.**

Aserinsky, Eugene   In 1953 Aserinsky, while working under Kleitman in a sleep-study laboratory, was the first to observe the rapid eye movements—REM—now known to occur during dreaming. As Aserinsky had observed this in the sleep of babies, it was first assumed only to occur with infants. Later investigation proved it to occur with all people observed. This finding started a period of intense research into the psycho-physical functioning of dreams. Visit the website *http://www.srssleep.org/aserinsky.htm*.

ash, ashes   What remains in experience, perhaps as memory or wisdom, after the event or person has gone; purification; something that once moved us, but the feelings have burnt themselves out; death or fear of it; ashes also fertilize after a period of decay, death, or destruction; empty of life; made nothing of. Ash-filled air: enormous changes going on; great emotion, or emotion-filled events, creating confusion and perhaps danger. Ashes of someone or something: something or someone that existed in your life and was a living part of it, but has now gone. Perhaps feelings have burnt out and left only a shadow, ashes of what existed before. Idioms: rake over the ashes; reduced to ash; ashes to ashes, dust to dust. See **trees** for ash tree.

ass   See *ass, donkey* under **animals.**

association of ideas with dreams   Early in his work, Freud found that if he allowed his patients to talk freely, one idea led to another and they would uncover the origin of their neurosis. Freud himself suffered bouts of deep anxiety, and it was partly this that led him to explore the connection between association of ideas and dreams. In 1897 he wrote to his friend Wilhelm Fliess: "No matter what I start with, I always find myself back again with the neuroses and the psychical apparatus. Inside me there is a seething ferment, and I am only waiting for the next surge forward. I have felt impelled to start writing about dreams, with which I feel on firm ground."

This move toward dreams may have come about because in allowing his patients freedom to talk and explore the associations that arose—free association—Freud noticed that patients would often find a connection between the direction of their associations and a dream they had experienced. The more he allowed his patients to go in their own direction, the more frequently they mentioned their dreams. Also, talking about the dream often enabled the patient to discover a new and productive chain of associations and memories.

Freud began to take note of his own dreams and explore the associations they aroused. In doing so he was perhaps the first person to consciously and consistently explore a dream into its depths through uncovering and following obvious and hidden associations, and emotions connected with the dream imagery and drama. He did this to deal with his own neurosis, and says of this period, "I have been through some kind of neurotic experience, with odd states of mind not intelligible to consciousness, cloudy thoughts and veiled doubts, with barely here and there a ray of light."

Freud was not, of course, the first to recognize the connection between dream imagery and associated ideas. Artemidorus in the first century A.D. had already written about this. But even prior to this, Aristotle (384–322) had written on how the mind uses association. He had listed ways this happened—through similarity, difference, and contiguity. Prior to the publication of Freud's book *The Interpretation of Dreams,* David Hartley had written his work on psychology, titled *Observations on Man* (1749), and James Mill had written *Analysis of the Mind* (1829), both of which examined association and set the foundations for modern psychology in the Associationist movement. See **amplification method.**

astral travel See **altered states of consciousness; out-of-body experiences.**

astronaut See **space.**

atom bomb Anxiety regarding external world, political forces, etc., that the dreamer feels at the mercy of—often coupled with dreamer's survival strategies; the end of a particular world or way of life for the dreamer—i.e., the end of school life; divorce; loss of spouse; tremendous potential energy, but related to in a way that threatens the dreamer, and is therefore not harnessed; fear of the irrational forces of life and the unconscious that may destroy all we have built in our conscious self. See **end-of-world dreams and fantasies; explosion.**

attack, attacker Feeling attacked or threatened by one's own impulses, such as anger or sexuality; feeling surreptitiously attacked by other people and their attitude to you or their remarks; a subtle sense of being attacked by age, or a serious attack by an illness—one speaks of an asthma or virus attack, for instance, but also one may be attacked by a poison or food if one is allergic to it; one might personally attack an issue or a project, and so a dream might depict one attacking something in this sense; confidence may be attacked; it is a common term in sport or business, and so may refer to attitude or energy. This aspect of attack may also refer to one's beliefs, or to other people's, that may be attacked and threatened; attack is also sometimes a form of defense, so may suggest defensiveness about some issue or aspect of one's life. A positive side to attack is that we often feel attacked by an emerging new insight or positive personal change. We feel it as an attack because it threatens our old way of life, habitual way of doing things and thinking about things. <u>Attacked by animal:</u> introverting one's own aggression or sexuality; fear of one's own natural urges; anxiety about aggression in oneself or other people; feeling attacked by an external person. <u>Attacked by shadowy or frightening figure:</u> our childhood traumas and fears may take this guise in a dream. So in this case the attack is depicting feelings of fear and pain surrounding those past issues. How we meet such an attack is important—as, if we run from it, the trauma may remain largely unconscious, and therefore capable of influencing behavior negatively. See **fight; war.**

attic   See *attic* under **house, buildings.**

audience   <u>Standing in front of:</u> you might be dealing with an important issue in your life that attracts the attention of many associated ideas and feelings—thus audience participation or attention; desire for attention; baring one's soul; self-acceptance if the audience is positive, self-uncertainty if the audience is negative. <u>In the audience:</u> witnessing some emotion or process in yourself, considering some aspect of your life. See **arena; theater.**

aunt   See *aunt* under **family, family relationships.**

aura   Sometimes we touch a concept or feeling that has massive connections, so vast they begin to build up beyond usual levels of realization. We might call it a megaconcept, which goes on building and generating realizations we have never had before—that is, we have never made those connections before. An aura around an object, person, or animal depicts this mental function, which in the dream we are aware of more than we usually are. See *the self* under **archetypes.** The aura in dreams is also often associated with death, or the spirit of the person whose aura is seen—"spirit" being here used in the same way as "she had a fighting spirit." Therefore it might suggest awareness of wondrous or awful qualities of soul of the person or yourself. Occasionally the aura indicates a health problem. In such cases the dream would include some feeling or realization that the colors or marks in the aura showed an illness or upset in the system.

Australian aborigine dream beliefs   The Australian native peoples are divided into more than five hundred tribal groups. These tribes are also of two major types—those who live inland, and those who live along the coastline. The separation of tribes and the division provided by the environment led to differences in views about the nature of human life and death, and the part dreams played. But some beliefs, such as reincarnation and the "Dreamtime," were universally held. "Dreamtime" refers to an experience and to beliefs that are largely peculiar to the Australian native people. There are at least four aspects to Dreamtime—the beginning of all things; the life and influence of the ancestors; the way of life and death; and the sources of power in life. Dreamtime includes all of these four facets at the same time, being a condition beyond time and space as known in everyday life. The aborigines call it the "all at once" time instead of the "one thing after another" time. This is because they experience Dreamtime as the past, present, and future coexisting. This condition is met when the tribal member lives according to tribal rules, and then is initiated through rituals and hearing the myths of the tribe. The aborigine people believe that each person has a part of their nature that is eternal. This eternal being preexists the life of the individual, and only becomes a living person through being born to a mother. The person then lives a life in time, and at death melts back into the eternal life. See **altered states of consciousness.**

authority

authority   See **authority,** *leader* under **roles.**

automobile   See **car.**

autonomous complex   Many of the characters or elements of our dreams act quite contrary to what we consciously wish. This is why we often find it so difficult to believe all aspects of a dream are part of our psyche. These independent aspects of oneself are named autonomous complexes. Recent research into brain activity shows that, in fact, the brain has different layers or strata of activity. These strata often act independently of each other or of conscious will. Sensing them, as one might in a dream, might feel like meeting an opposing will. Integration with these aspects of self can be gained.

autopsy   Searching within oneself or one's life experiences for what has caused something in you to die or to stop functioning; examining the past for clues—perhaps for what has brought about present loss of motivation or sense of loss.

autumn   "The autumn of one's life"; mellow feelings; gradual but often pleasant decline; maturity; middle age; past the prime; a period of change when the old order of things is fading away, and the new has not shown itself; might be a time of harvesting what has grown or been developed in previous years or months; autumn in one's dream may also suggest a time that is not good for active creativity, but more suited to "being" rather than "doing." The falling leaves of autumn may therefore remind the dreamer that many attitudes or outworn—no longer necessary—ways of living and working are falling away and should not be held on to. <u>Autumn leaves:</u> old memories, skills, attitudes, things you have developed in life that are no longer performing a useful function due to the changes happening. They can therefore be dropped. If the <u>dreamer is in middle age:</u> represents these years of your life. The details of the dream show what you intuitively feel about these years and what can arise from them. It is therefore helpful to see if you can understand this season of your life and what it brings. It may be a time to rest and let go of some of the outer activities of the past.

avalanche   The power of frozen emotions. We can freeze desire, anger, or jealousy, etc., and the buildup of tension might then release in a dangerous way; associations with an avalanche also suggest that there is something that is delicately poised that if triggered can cause a disaster; fear of being overwhelmed by the release of emotions that had previously been held at bay—frozen or denied—and have been or might be released; anxiety about surviving a major upheaval or change in one's circumstances.

awake   See **wake up.**

awake, difficulty in waking sleeper   A few people exhibit the unusual symptom of being incredibly difficult to wake when they are asleep. In the book *Ramana Maharshi and the Path of Self Knowledge,* Arthur Osborne reports that family and friends of Ramana often found it difficult to wake him. So much so that school friends would sometimes carry him out of the dormitory and pour water over him or take advantage of him in other ways, and he still did not wake. Many people report a lesser degree of such inability to be woken, in which speaking while asleep occurs. Partners or parents report that the person asleep will talk to them as if awake, answer questions earnestly, even hold a conversation, but do not wake. This may be akin to sleepwalking. See **paralysis—while asleep or trying to wake.**

ax   See **weapons.** <u>Idioms:</u> ax to grind; to be axed (lose one's job).

B

baby Principally the dream baby represents your feelings, such as possessiveness, joy, curiosity, responding to the world without words or formed concepts, innocent love, infant trauma; intense dependence; feelings of helplessness; vulnerability; lack of responsibility; being cared for. Even as adults many of these early feeling responses still dominate the way we meet relationships and events. It is quite common, for instance, for adults to feel intense and destructive jealousy about their sexual partner. This is exactly the sort of feeling we experienced naturally as a baby and child, but in adulthood we seldom see them as feelings that we have not grown beyond. Instead we often rationalize them, blaming our sexual partner for them— i.e., "You made me jealous by showing affection for that other man/woman."

Also a new phase of life; a new idea; new activity—as when we say someone has a new baby, meaning new project or business. Often this "baby" is a part of the personality or ability that did not have a chance to "be born" or expressed before. Or it may be things learned in a rich life. Aborted baby: something lost that had been developing, such as a new facet of self, a relationship, or a new opportunity. If in a pregnant woman's dream, usually it is an expression of fears regarding the ability to carry the child to full term—but it is wise to have a checkup. See **abortion; pregnancy.** Adult body with baby head: an approach to life in which your thinking is still immature, even though

70

you are physically mature. Adopted baby: adopting a new stance in life, perhaps conceived by or seen in someone else; taking on the responsibility of something or someone that needs care and help to grow; if you are trying to adopt a baby it would reflect feelings or intuitions about this activity. Baby body with adult head: an adult intellect and rational thinking, or an adult self, but with emotional and sexual immaturity. Beautiful, gifted, or holy baby: emergence of a wider awareness, greater personal insight. It can show the emergence of previously unconscious parts of yourself. Boy baby: birth or emergence of a new phase of self-expression in terms of activity or achievement. In a male's dream, may suggest a new self emerging, or new aspects of self. Crying baby: your fundamental needs are not being met, or were not met in the past. These include basic things like feeling happy and relaxed in one's environment, feeling wanted and loved, having a sense of connection with other people. There may be something distressing you at a feeling/needing level that you are not acknowledging; a new project or aspect of self needing more care. Dropping a baby: carelessness in dealing with your basic needs, especially in relationship; mishandling an opportunity; betraying trust; feeling you have been "dropped" by someone, perhaps in a relationship; abortion. Girl baby: birth or emergence of new aspects of feelings and feeling relationship with others. But in a female's dream, may mean an emergence of a new phase or a new start in her life. Happy baby: feeling at ease with oneself and surroundings. It may be that something has happened in a relationship or environment that brings a deeper level of relaxation and sense of security. See **pregnancy; birth dreams during pregnancy.**

Babylonian dream beliefs Babylonian civilization lasted from 1800 B.C. till 600 B.C. It was an urban society with twelve or so cities in the nation, resting upon the agricultural land surrounding the cities. The social structure was headed by the king as absolute monarch. Under him were a group of appointed governors and administrators. Beneath this were freemen and then slaves. The culture lasted for about 1,200 years.

The psychological world ancient people's lived in was one filled with spirits and demons, gods and goddesses, good and evil forces. This is understandable when we realize our forebears had no clear conception of how natural forces, illness, the mind, worked. The many intangibles they were surrounded by, the immense uncertainties they faced, were quite usefully called spirits—invisible, mysterious, yet potent powers that could act upon them for good or ill. Their beliefs and observations regarding dreams were therefore deeply colored by their worldview. Death was a certainty, illness—physical or mental—was a possibility, love and reproduction were drives to be satisfied, and so dreams or myths centered on the way these needs could be met.

Dreams were classified into several types. Those of rulers and leaders such as priests were seen as one type, and those of common people as another. There was also a division between good dreams and bad dreams. If you go into any large bookstore and look at dream dictionaries written before the advent of modern psychotherapy, it can easily be seen that most definitions are still written in the same style—that the dream will bring good or bad luck regarding money, romance, or health. In fact, they are derivations of the ancient Babylonian dream books. These speculations, observations, and collection of folk beliefs were put into book form by the Babylonians, and are thought to have contained texts on dreams dating back to 5000 B.C. These ancient Babylonian dream dictionaries were copied and taken to the library at Nineveh by King Ashurbanipal. The great dream encyclopedist Artemidorus later drew on these records for his own learning. The part of the Jewish Talmud that was written during the Babylonian captivity is also full of dream interpretations and ways of dealing with dreams, and undoubtedly drew on the Babylonian library. Babylonian culture also produced one of the great, and certainly the oldest, literary works that includes a series of dreams. This is the *Epic of Gilgamesh*, which dates from about 2000 B.C. and is the oldest hero account. It is the story of how the king, Gilgamesh, searches for immortality, having lost his friend Enkidu. See **history of dream beliefs.**

bachelor   Man's dream: oneself if unmarried; desire for freedom, or comparison with present, if married. Woman's dream: possible hope for sexual partner; husband prior to marriage; unmarried male friend; or if the man is married in real life, hopes that he were single.

back   Back of or behind house, barrier, etc.: more private; intimate; less formal; surreptitious; out of sight; second best. When it is behind a wall or fence, then it may refer to barriers that get in the way of how we relate to people or situations. This could connect with such things as the class barrier or fears we have. Back, trunk: see *back* under **body.** Behind: repressed urges; one's past and memories; what is "behind" one, or is in the past, but may be influencing one again; one's inner feelings; inferior; out of sight. Being pushed back: feeling restrained or restricted; feeling others are holding you back. Returning, going back: being influenced by something from one's past, or meeting similar life situation as met in the past. Idioms: at the back of; at the back of one's mind; backroom boys; by the back stairs/door; behind one's back; take a backseat; back to earth; fell back; back row; held back. See **behind; front.**

backbone   See *back* under **body.**

backpack   See **knapsack.**

bacteria, germs, virus   A hidden attack that may weaken or even destroy your sense of well-being; anxieties that undermine your health; feelings that keep you away from

73

another person or situation—in case of infection; fear of inadequacy; sense of uncleanness; the word "germ" is also used extensively to suggest the beginning of something, the point from which great growth can occur, so if the dream does not suggest anxiety, there may be a positive connection with growth. <u>Bacterial warfare:</u> the undermining of one's personal or social well-being by surreptitious means. <u>Computer virus:</u> being got at by another person; something surreptitious that you feel might attack or undermine your work; a destroyer of calm and pleasure; energy that may be disruptive, but is like an automatic or habitual destructive process in you, depending on dream.

badge   Your identification with a particular group if the badge is connected with a group or organization; memories, experiences, things learned with a group or organization; an attitude suggested by the badge, such as courage or social recognition, or a role; a sense of achievement; a reminder of values held or strengthening beliefs. This is meant in the way a person will wear a Christian cross or St. Christopher medal to remind them of their moral decisions or help bring confidence in the face of anxiety; strength and feelings of authority, as one might have with a police badge; acknowledgment of attainment; if it is a name badge it most likely suggests one's own sense of identity—who you feel yourself to be in the circumstance of the dream.

bag   This has to do with the things, ideas, beliefs we carry about with us, or the way we collect things in a psychological way. For instance, one might "carry" a grudge or a feeling of inferiority for years, and it is just as much of a burden as carrying a loaded shopping bag. We might also collect or carry information or ideas. We might "buy" a suggestion from someone and carry it in this way until used or passed on; the basket is often used to represent the vagina or the ability to bear children; the word is occasionally used in English to mean a person who is morally loose or irritating—"she is a bag"; the phrase "don't put all your eggs in one basket" also shows how it is common to associate basket with the idea of collecting or holding on to things that are valuable. <u>Handbag:</u> more often depicts your identity. Our sense of identity is often dependent largely on social contacts and recognition. The bag, especially handbag, with all one's personal belongings and money, represents this social ability to get places and cope. Sometimes represents vagina, female sexuality. <u>Luggage:</u> the things we feel we need in order to survive; things we put away or hide from ourselves and others, therefore secrets, perhaps danger; skills or tools one has; may represent holiday or getting away from work or home; freedom or the ability to move; protective attitudes, as when one might carry something precious in a bag—such as a baby, small animal, or objects. <u>Bag of garbage:</u> desire, emotions, ideas you have discarded, or need to discard; rubbish being dumped on you by someone else. <u>Sleeping bag:</u> powerful sexual symbol—i.e., sexual intercourse or a sexual partner—especially if linked with a partner; could also represent the feelings of being in the womb, or wanting to sleep alone; may occasionally have the same significance as a body bag; warmth. <u>Idioms:</u> bag and baggage; windbag; in the bag; pack one's bag; punch bag.

baldness   See *hair* under **body.**

ball   See *sphere, ball* under **shapes, symbols.**

ball game   See **games, gambling.**

balloon   Party mood; something to celebrate; breasts; connection with sex through similarity to condom; the womb; something that can appear large, colorful and growing, but is only full of air we blow into it; life we give to things with our imagination and emotions—and can burst and disappear suddenly like a bubble; feeling fat and blown up. <u>Releasing a balloon:</u> hope; testing an idea or ideal to see where it takes you; letting go of something or someone; letting events decide the situation. See *sphere, ball* under **shapes, symbols.**

banana   Male penis; disguised sexual desire; enjoyment of sweet food, pleasure. <u>Taking one, handing one to someone:</u> desire to receive or have sexual relation. *Man eating one:* may be homosexual tendency.

band   Teamwork; sense of different parts of self working harmoniously; work for a musician; teenage emotions and feelings, perhaps to do with sexuality; comradeship.

bandage   Hurt feelings; past emotional injury; healing process; death; protection; a sign to others that you are vulnerable or hurt; protection within which healing can take place; fear of illness or death.

bank   Thoughts, worries, decisions about, or events to do with money and the whole lifestyle that goes with it. Therefore it may indicate dreams or hopes about the future; resources—financial, mental, and transcendent; one's internal sense of security—if threatened, then feelings of insecurity and fear; emotional resources, such as confidence and sexual certainty; social power; feeling of pressure about debts or social money situation; something you depend upon. <u>Idioms:</u> bank on; burst/break the bank. See **money.**

bank of river, field, canal   A barrier or safety measure—i.e., to stop the river flooding, a place in the sun, or an exposed place; a difficulty to be overcome; minor difficulty or obstruction; a boundary, such as the border of what you might permit sexually.

banquet   Social relationships; being recognized or seen as being chosen; feelings about class, social position, or status; business/sexual opportunity; feelings concerning eating and drinking; drive to impress, or being impressed.

baptism New influence entering your life, cleansing away old attitudes; opening to inner possibilities; life pervading and healing; an influx of what had been latent or potential in oneself; birth, or experiences connected with your birth; a reconnection of the conscious self with the deeper biological or psychological life. This may be allied with an old way of life or attitudes dying or passing away. See **compensation theory; religion and dreams;** *Christ* under **archetypes.**

bar Strength; male sexuality; rigidness; energy; symbol of power; lever to shift obstacles; an extension, barrier, fastening, or support; play on word suggesting the banning or exclusion of something, or an impediment; a means of discouragement, whether used as a weapon or as a physical barrier. Exercise bar: comment on your fitness, or what your body needs to get fit. If barring way: obstacle; block against self-expression. Metal bar: weapon; defensiveness; strength; penis. Idioms: raise the bar; color bar; barring the way.

barbarian A more instinctive, less restrained part of oneself. The barbarian often has a lot of shrewdness about human behavior, as this feeling level doesn't have the social complications of a more refined self, and may therefore "see" things as they are in a fundamental way.

barbecue Relaxed feelings of sociability; social relationships. See **food.**

barber, hairdresser Ability to change attitudes, thoughts, or opinions. Because we can change our social appearance by a haircut or style, it depicts changes of mind, change of image; being in someone else's hands or influence; in some dreams there appears to be a lot of anxiety or fear surrounding the barber dream.

barroom Often indicates how you relate to groups; relaxation or conflict with friends and others, depending on

barroom

action in dream. There may therefore be signs of aggressiveness or defensiveness; feelings about society; exploring ideas or feelings, as one might in a communicative atmosphere in a bar; hopes, fears, or expectations about finding a sexual partner. Therefore the meeting or avoiding of the complexities of relationship; gathering information or realizing things unconsciously gathered; can be difficulties regarding alcohol; one's technique for avoiding confrontation with loneliness, anxiety, sense of failure, etc.

bartender   See *bartender* under **roles.**

baseball   See *baseball* under **games, gambling.**

basement   See *basement, cellar* under **house, buildings.**

basketball   See **games, gambling.**

bat   <u>Cricket or baseball bat:</u> male sexuality; positive aggression; defensiveness. <u>A flying bat:</u> see *bat* under **animals.**

bath, bathing   Relaxation; cleansing; wanting to "come clean" or be rid of guilt. Such cleansing could depict a change of heart or forgiveness where old feelings are washed away; some bathing dreams or fantasies depict the bath as a form of ritual that is getting you ready for something, perhaps a radical change, but often to do with sexuality; the meeting with feelings or fears of relationship—perhaps meeting one's own male/female self more fully; vulnerability, nakedness, one's secrets; marriage/relationship intimacy; being immersed in an influence of some sort; deep sharing, perhaps blending of qualities; powerful change or renewal; may sometimes relate to feelings about life in the womb; need to cleanse the body internally. See **baptism.** <u>Bathing in a river:</u> being open to or under the influence of flowing feelings and urges within oneself; allowing oneself to be influenced from within by urges toward change, growth, or expansion of awareness. <u>Bathing in the sea:</u> being open to a more universal—less self-centered—awareness of one's relationship with life.

battery Resources of energy or vitality. Problems with the battery might depict health difficulties or even worries about heart weakness. <u>Dead battery:</u> suggests lack of motivation; a run-down condition regarding health or emotional energy; lack of resources or motivation.

battle Either an internal conflict, such as caused by struggles with one's own emotions or sexuality, or an emotional battle going on with someone else; something you are fighting for; feeling under attack; the struggle may be between unconscious drives, such as an urge to have a baby, and one's conscious decisions. Sometimes an internal "civil war" takes place between one's head and heart or intuitions; the struggle and conflicting emotions involved in making a decision; the carnage going on through childhood trauma or painful birth experience; a struggle against one's fears and doubts; memories, if you have been in a battle scene in waking life. <u>Idioms:</u> battle of the bulge; battle of the sexes; battle stations; battle your way through; battle ready; battle scarred; battleship.

battlefield An area of conflict within oneself or one's life situation; the struggle or conflict going on within a relationship; may also represent one's working environment if it is a place of competition or fight; you are fighting a "battle"—such as a battle regarding giving up smoking, or dieting.

bay Similar to **beach,** but the crescent shape sometimes depicts a woman's sexuality and openness to mating; receptiveness. <u>Boat sailing into bay:</u> something coming into your life; a new event or relationship. <u>Sailing across the bay:</u> the passage of time or events; distance to travel, in the sense of covering ground in one's life. <u>Sailing into bay:</u>

arriving at a calmer situation in life, feeling easier because you are no longer "at sea" about something. <u>Whales or other creatures in bay:</u> something important and deeply felt being realized or confronted. Usually this is about emotions or drives being felt strongly. <u>Idioms:</u> at bay; keep at bay.

beach Family gatherings or relaxation and intimacy; pleasure; state of mind in which you are open to intuitions and emotions; the state of mind that is open to pre- or non-verbal experiences, such as life in the womb, but links with waking consciousness and everyday life; a boundary, or threshold, between our individual self and effort, and our potential in the universal processes of life and death; a barrier or threshold such as fear or lack of confidence creates. To deal with such a barrier—crossing the ocean—we have to exhibit new skills or courage. To go farther we would have to swim or take a boat—so a change may be needed, new qualities must be developed; what we do on the beach may also depict how we deal with changing from one environment—school, work—to another, such as parenthood or retirement; the beach might be the place where aspects of the unconscious meet us—out of the sea. It thus illustrates how we draw on or avoid our potential; a place we are both seen by and see other people. So may relate to socializing and meeting people; the awe we feel when confronted by natural forces, therefore our relationship with life; simplicity of life; standing between the forces or primal life and the social human world, both of which we exist in. If there are <u>anxious feelings in connection with the beach:</u> this may show a feeling of being exposed to other people's scrutiny, or to the powerful forces we face in experiencing emotions, sexual drive, and social pressures. See **sea.**

bear See *bear* under **animals.**

beard See *hair* under **body.**

beast See *beast* under **animals; emotions, mood.**

beaver See *beaver* under **animals.**

bed See *bed* under **furniture, furnishings.**

bed-wetting If one <u>dreams of it but does not wet the bed:</u> possibly to do with allowing yourself freedom of expression, but with worry about social condemnation or propriety; anxiety that reduces you to childhood feelings with lack of self-control over emotions. This dream almost certainly links with childhood feelings to do with control or lack of control of one's body and drives. This is a very powerful area of feelings, and can leave strong influences in the adult personality. See **control, controlling.** Bed-wetting is technically known as enuresis. It is not unusual in children up to about three. After the age of three it is diagnosed as a disorder, but is not to be thought of as a serious condition. Up to fifteen percent of children continue bed-wetting to about five.

bee See **insects.**

beeper A reminder; a sense of a communication with another person that hasn't got through to you yet; intuition of another person's need for you; something nagging for attention.

beer See **alcohol.**

beetle See **insects.**

beggar The emotions, drives, and thoughts you seldom allow into expression. Feelings of failure. Desire to "drop out"; avoidance of involvement in society; a cringing, passive attitude; passive anger; feeling poor in spirit—"low."

behind The past; things you are unaware of; like a seashell on a beach, something that was "alive" and influential in your life at some time, but is now left behind,

behind

therefore someone or something being left; a phase of one's life that has been passed through. <u>Someone behind you:</u> something or someone you may not be aware of; you are turning your back on; the past; something or someone who is supporting you, backing you up, or that you gain strength from. See **back.**

bell   Warning; signal; calling for attention; summons; rejoicing; signal that someone has died; suggestion of a wedding. Occasionally a reference to breasts that swing like bells. <u>Telephone bell:</u> someone or something trying to get your attention. <u>Doorbell:</u> something new coming into your life—negative or positive depending on dream; hoping for contact with someone.

belongings   The degree to which you identify with, feel connected with, and perhaps even defined by your belongings is clear to see when they are either stolen or abused by someone else. Belongings may therefore represent the way of life you have managed to attain; the pleasure you get; your interests and absorptions; your connection and affections for other people if the belonging was given to you by someone else, or has links with them; the various inner needs, attitudes, and hopes one has. Another aspect of belongings is reflected by the fact that if living in someone else's house or on holiday, we may feel somewhat lost without the things we have at home to work/entertain/learn with. So belongings may depict urges, enthusiasms, and needs. The <u>loss of belonging:</u> the meaning is usually shown in the dream by what we feel at its loss.

below   See *below* under **positions.**

belt   If it is a belt such as on a car or machine, it depicts how power or energy is being directed or used. So problems with the belt would suggest that one's powerful drives, such as ambition, sexuality, desire for acclaim, are meeting with conflicts or obstructions, etc. If a <u>clothing belt:</u> see *belt* under **clothes.**

bent Feeling oneself or something is damaged or changed from its rightful function or property. See **bend.**

berries Very much depends on what the dream portrays. If they are poisonous, for instance, then it suggests the realization of possible contact with something that might poison your mind or feelings with fears or disturbing thoughts. If healthy, then the contact with possibly useful or nourishing experiences. See **food.**

beside See *adjacent, adjoining* under **positions.**

betrayal Becoming an adult, and maintaining one's equilibrium as an adult, means that we will have met and even dealt in betrayal. Feelings during babyhood and childhood suggest each of us is born with a tremendous need to be wanted and cared for. When innate need to be cared for is met with betrayal, the pain is enormous. In dreams betrayal is often shown in the form of abandonment or being left. But it can also be played out in scenes where someone is unfaithful in one form or another. Such dreams do not suggest the person in the dream is going to abandon us, just that we have a deep fear of abandonment.

bewitched Failing to see how we are being influenced either by an external person or by enchanting ideas and feelings we hold within. Bewitching feelings also arise from fantasies that may beguile us. A young woman may be swept away by fantasies of her own desirability, and of a wonderful man claiming her. Such fantasies, if they dominate, may cause the young woman to unwisely enter relationships with men who are other than the fantasy images she projects upon them. This can also occur from a powerful suggestion or association occurring during such impressive times as an operation or car accident. Traumas,

bewitched

such as a bad experience during a surgical operation, can also leave powerful feelings that dreams might present as being under a spell, or bewitched.

Bible Traditional moral standards; religion or one's feelings about it; one's most inclusive realizations, in which case see **aura;** those things one holds to be most true; as it represents traditional religion, it may depict one's conflicts or difficulties with religious organizations. See **religion and dreams.**

biceps See *arms* under **body.**

bicycle Personal effort or motivation through which you reach your goals. For many people a bicycle was their first experience of mastering a skill to gain greater freedom. Might therefore be youthful freedom or enthusiasm without responsibilities; the perseverance and confidence to master a skill; mental balance—confidence—enabling one to achieve goals; facing dangers in learning a skill or confidence; adolescent sexuality. Bicycle race or riding with many other people: dreams often use this scenario to represent an overall view of one's situation in life. It shows how you feel about your place in the human race, whether life is a struggle or pleasure, etc. See **race.** Falling off bike: losing balance—confidence; awkwardness; vulnerability. Flying on bike: the magic of believing in yourself. Riding a bicycle downhill: taking or facing a risk; being daring; need for care. Stolen bicycle: if you are using the stolen bicycle, it suggests a lack of confidence in your skills or resources. If you have had your bicycle stolen, then it is a feeling of losing your ability to get on through your efforts; loss of enthusiasm or confidence.

big See **size.**

bikini See *swimsuit* under **clothes.**

bill   See **check.**

billiards   See **games, gambling.**

billion   See *million, billion* under **numbers.**

binoculars   Seeing something or someone more clearly; the ability to pry into someone else's life; taking in one's environment and possibilities; the future.

birds   Imagination; intuition; the mind; freedom from restraints; thoughts or hidden wishes or hopes; longings to move beyond limitations or boundaries; expanded awareness—in this form, perhaps a large bird that can fly high, because wider awareness is like a higher, overall view of things. This may be painful or frightening as we approach it; the expansion of our viewpoint; the upliftment of our emotions or mind; transcendence; a link between the world we experience with our physical senses and the deep world of our often unconscious passions, intuitions, and insights; a woman—i.e., a "bird."
   The life cycle of a bird has so many similarities with important human stages of maturing we frequently use birds to represent important parts of our experience. A <u>huge bird:</u> the power of the collective mind or unconscious. It may uplift or be felt as threatening; something that can protect or be felt as a threat but can be a healing force; a threat; a parent. <u>Bird attacking:</u> fear of ideas, ideals, or opinions; verbal or mental (suggestions or suggestive behavior) attack by others; fear of the going beyond one's narrow boundaries; feeling criticized by a parent. <u>Black or carrion birds:</u> because such birds often feed on dead animals, they have the association with feelings about death or news of death. <u>Dead bird:</u> threat to ideals or hopes of freedom; feeling life is only material; feeling defeated or crushed; loss of sense of beauty or meaning in life; an ideal or hope has died; a flight of imagination or creativity has

birds

fallen. <u>Fighting birds:</u> family disputes; arguments about viewpoints. <u>Flying bird:</u> rising above something; an escape from a feeling of being trapped, or some fear; independence; freedom; self-expression; one's love or thoughts winging its way to someone; the sexual act—possibly because we may feel released and uplifted during sex. <u>Hatching from the egg:</u> our birth and infancy; rebirth. <u>In cage:</u> feelings of being restricted or trapped; holding back love or inspiration; safety in restriction; if there are positive feelings around the caged bird, it might suggest the need to withhold love or freedom; feeling trapped in a relationship. <u>Leaving nest:</u> gaining independence; meeting change; leaving a dependent relationship. <u>Making nest:</u> home-building; parental urges; partnership if with another bird. <u>Nest:</u> home; family environment; security; even the womb. The <u>baby bird:</u> our childhood.

blackbird, black bird   Unconscious urges. At times we may relate to enormous waves of feeling in an anxious way, and this relationship of anxiety may be represented by a black bird. The bird may be shown attacking something or oneself, because that is how we relate to the emotions or energies; feelings about death; the negative aspect of mother; something unconscious.

chicken   Nourishment; the female in a male; being "chicken." The <u>cock:</u> a male or the male sexual characteristics; confidence. The <u>hen:</u> mother; motherhood; being immersed in motherhood concerns and not having thoughts beyond that. <u>Chicks:</u> your babyhood and feelings or events associated with it, or to external baby or babies. May point to vulnerable people or assets. <u>Idioms:</u> chicken feed; chicken-hearted; she's no chicken; cock of the walk.

crow, rook, raven   Linked with death or feelings about death; bad news; fear; unconscious feelings. The negative aspect of father.

cormorant   Intellectual ideas that have the power to dig deep and bring up unconscious wisdom. You may be practising some form of introspection or self-examination.

crane   Inner feelings about wholeness; good luck. The ability to deal harmoniously with the libido or energy within.

cuckoo   Wanting to have, or feeling your partner is having, sex outside your relationship; pregnant with child of, or feelings connected with, another man than one's partner.

dove   Peace; awareness of one's potential; religious experience; relatedness.

eagle, buzzard, hawk   Sometimes the hunting, providing parent; dominance; a male figure; an uplifting power of feelings or ideas; a protective influence; a threatening influence. Often the ability to develop an integrated vision or perception out of a wide range of experience. This is because the height of the bird and its steady gaze give it unusual perception and wide awareness. See **aura** as it relates to megaconcept. Idioms: watch like a hawk; eagle-eyed.

feather, feathers   See **feather.**

goose/geese   Freedom; your soul; wanderlust; foolishness or group conformity. In some cases you might use the goose as a symbol for lifelong relationship.

owl   Because the owl sees in the dark, it represents our intuitive sense that "sees" what is happening in the subtle areas of feeling and perceptions. This sense "feeds" by watching or acting as an integrating function with the many dark or hidden aspects of your experience and behavior. The unconscious seems to have a sense of synthesis of all life and the owl speaks with this sort of collective wisdom; a wise advisor. Because of its connection with the hidden side of life, we may sometimes feel fear or danger in regard to the owl. In some mythologies the owl was connected with death, and might act as a messenger regarding the death of a family member. For instance, in Jewish tradition it is unlucky to dream of an owl, but okay to dream of any other bird. <u>Idioms:</u> wise old owl; wisdom of the owl; night owl; owlish (looking wise or solemn).

parrot   Repeating without judgment what others have said; accepting or copying something without evaluating it.

peacock   Pride; self-display; vanity; the desire to be more attractive; sometimes the same as *phoenix;* in some cultures the peacock represents the soul or psyche—one's sense of self with all one's individual memories and characteristics. Because the peacock could shed all its beautiful feathers and then grow them again, early Christians saw it as a symbol of resurrection and immortality. As the peacock is a male bird displaying for the sake of a mate, it can also obviously represent male sexuality in its proud, ostentatious, or displaying mode.

penguin   The penguin hardly ever appears in dreams—or, in fact, in literature generally. So I have not been able to gather from people's dreams how they use this symbol. From common associations, however, it is likely to represent foolishness; a difficult life situation; coldness in relationships.

phoenix   The ability to find a new impulse, new strength, new growth, even in death; the power in oneself to transform the dying, depressed, dark, and desperate into new endeavor and growth.

stork   The soul; symbol of birth or babyhood, and perhaps parenthood; the beauty of the wider awareness of the unconscious.

swan   Grace; beauty; dignity; in mythology, often represents the psyche or soul and its connection with the side of human nature usually hidden because unconscious; may be linked with an ending of something, due to the association with the "swan song"—a final act; amorousness. Also the ideal in sexuality, and as such may represent virginity or a blend of male and female.

vulture   A relative waiting for you to die—or vice versa; people around you trying to live on you—or vice versa; difficult feelings about dependents; an environment of ill will or hopelessness.
   Idioms: charm the birds from the trees; a bird told me; bird has flown; bird in the hand; bird of ill omen; free as a bird; odd bird.

birth   When we were born, one world of experience ended for us and another began. When we witness the birth of a new child, we see a new beginning, the emergence of a new being and life. Birth in a dream has the same meanings. The beginning of a new way of life, new attitude, new ability, new project. But also the death of the old. Can be about physical birth, its difficulties and trauma. But most difficult birth dreams are about coming to terms with life. Your birth dreams may be an expression of huge changes in your life that are occurring over quite long periods of time. The birth might have come after much has "died" or been lost. See **baby; hole; tunnel.**

birth dreams during pregnancy   Pregnancy is one of the most powerful experiences any woman can face. Her own body certainly changed enormously during her childhood and adolescence, but to meet such enormous physical, personal, and social changes as an adult is a huge challenge. A woman's dreams at such a time not only show some of the detailed events that are occurring physically, but also comment on psychological and relationship events and subtleties too.

birth dreams during pregnancy

Themes common in the dreams of pregnant women are those of animals and water. At first such dreams of water or animals may be calm, even healing, but later on in pregnancy there may be dreams of turmoil or even nightmares. Several studies show this is normal, in the sense that it is experienced by many women, and probably reflects the anxieties unconsciously held by the woman about her unborn baby and about birth. It is also very common for women to dream about actually having the baby, and these dreams are often bizarre or even disturbing to the dreamer. C. Winget and F. Kapp found that a high percentage of dreams showed this theme of anxiety, and by following their research through, they were able to observe that the more anxiety dreams a mother-to-be had, the easier the birth was. They conjecture that the anxiety dreams release a lot of tension and fear, and the mother is therefore more relaxed at the time of the birth—usually less than ten hours. (From, "The Relationship of the Manifest Content of Dreams to Duration of Childbirth in Primiparae." *Psychosomatic Medicine 34* (1972) The anxiety dreams include such images as giving birth to a baby who is only a few ounces in weight, the baby is malformed, the baby is born dead, the baby is blind or deaf or injured.

birth control Thoughts and feelings connected with preventing pregnancy—the action in the dream should show what the concerns are; connected with the urge toward parenthood and how you are relating to it; hope for or fear about pregnancy. Birth control devices: suppression of the urge toward parenthood; concerns about the method used, or comments from your feelings or unconscious about methods used; suggestion about using; worries about sexual contacts. It might also represent feelings or attitudes regarding responsibility. Certainly it connects in some way with sexual decisions and feelings.

birthday Good feelings; recognition and warmth regarding friends, or desire for it; a change happening; a special time when good things or favors can come to you. Someone else's birthday: reminder of social obligation to another person; showing of affection or otherwise; relaxed feelings.

bite   Aggression; the desire to suckle the breast hidden behind aggression—this applies to women equally as to men; a hurt from someone or something; something has got into you that has "wounded" you; fear of being hurt. See *teeth* under **body.**

black   See *black* under **colors.** For blackbird, black hole, blackberries, black tie, see respective entries—**birds, hole, food, clothes, etc**

black person   Depends what skin color one has. If white: one's natural drives, urges, longings, and emotions, uncluttered by intricate social taboos; feelings about black people; or if person is known, what you feel about them; one's unexpressed or repressed self—a "shadow" figure—therefore often depicting a depressed or unaccepted area of oneself; feeling downtrodden; underhanded. If black: as with any other person dream. See **people.**

blaming, being blamed   Most likely a direct expression of feelings one has about being blamed or blaming someone else. Therefore the things to watch for in the dream are—Blaming: What are you blaming someone or something else for? If you can clarify what it is, ask yourself if you are doing that in waking life, and how deeply you feel about the issue. How valid is the blaming? Is the blaming a way of avoiding responsibility or efforts to change? Blamed: Do you accept the blame and feel guilty or a failure? If so, it may show that you are taking on feelings of failure that will create guilt and conflict in you. There may also be excessive self-criticism arising. Perhaps there are things you have failed to see or accept, but feeling guilty isn't the best way to learn and improve one's performance. Better to look at events as learning experiences.

blanket Comfort; warmth—physical or emotional; an attitude we can hide under/behind; an attitude or experience we are wrapped/rapt in. In this case the color of the blanket would give a clue to what the feeling or attitude is; illness or injury; sexual activity; caring, as when we wrap someone in a blanket; withdrawal or vulnerability. See *bed* under **furniture, furnishings.**

blemish Feeling dissatisfied about something. See *skin* under **body.**

blindness Unwillingness or inability to "see" something; losing sight of something; not seeing traits that we don't like about ourselves or others; feelings of not knowing or being clear about where you are going in life, moving into things you do not understand; feeling lost or vulnerable; concealing something from yourself or others. <u>Idioms:</u> blind impulse; none so blind; turn a blind eye; blind leading blind; blind alley. See *eyes* under **body.**

blizzard An internal conflict or great unrest; feelings of disturbance, perhaps to do with coldness in a relationship; feeling emotionally battered or threatened; isolating influence. See **weather.**

blockage Usually depicts restrained or held-back emotions, energy, or thoughts. Common areas of blockage are the throat, where words or feelings can be blocked by tension or restraints such as anger or helplessness; the chest, most often the store of emotions, perhaps from many years ago; the genitals, where we might block desire, hunger, and the basic movement of our body toward pleasure. The blockage might be shown in dreams as a river being dammed, a traffic jam, a piece of machinery clogged, or some part of our body not functioning smoothly.

blood, bleeding See *blood* under **body;** *blood* under **archetypes.**

blowout   See *tire* under **car.**

blue   See *blue* under **colors.**

boarder   This depends more than most symbols on the subjective associations you have—whether you have been a boarder in a school or lodging house, or other people's home. <u>Lodger in other people's home:</u> feeling of not having one's own security or home; sense of sharing or being welcome; feelings of being an outsider. <u>Boarder at school:</u> feeling abandoned by family; in a learning situation, and one calling for independence. <u>In lodging house:</u> temporary situation; lack of personal resources or relationships; for some people represents a work situation.

boat, ship   Your journey through life and skills in meeting the rough and smooth experiences; in many dreams boats and ships appear to depict a situation or environment the dreamer is in. Because of the fact that once in the water it is difficult to leave the boat, the situation is often one that has certain bonds or commitments that may not be easy to leave or break away from—such as occurs in a close relationship or a work situation. The condition the boat depicts may be a physical one, such as a work opportunity, a place we live, a relationship that like any relationship offers certain opportunities and restrictions; a place of safety amidst the storms of life. Thus attitudes or strengths enabling the dreamer to meet difficulties.

   The various environments boats may be in show the condition or feelings surrounding you. For instance, being "at sea"—depending upon calmness or rough seas—shows the dreamer being away from a familiar base or in difficult or uncertain times. <u>Disembarking:</u> leaving a phase of life, such as motherhood, marriage, or a job. <u>Dry dock:</u> necessary changes being made; circumstances not conducive to be actively involved in a project or relationship; delays. <u>Embarking alone:</u> independence or loneliness. <u>Ferry boat:</u> if across a river, end of a relationship; transition

boat, ship

from one phase of life to another; the emotional connections in a relationship; death. <u>Journey by night:</u> classic archetype of searching for one's roots in life; the journey into one's unconscious experience. <u>Missing a boat:</u> missing opportunity; not grasping significance of events; not "making it" in a relationship. <u>Idioms:</u> burn one's boats; in the same boat; miss the boat; rock the boat; ships that pass; ship comes in; a tight ship; in a boat without a paddle. See **anchor; submarine.**

body   Because the body so potently depicts the image we have of ourselves, any distortions or collapse of the body image in our dreams suggests similar effects in our personality or the way we feel about ourselves. Listed below are first a series of general body descriptions and situations. Then at the end of those are parts of the body and situations relating to them, such as *face* and *legs*.

Body Situations

<u>Anesthetized body:</u> deadening of feelings; repression of love or anger; the "sleep" of passion, creativity, or reason; feelings connected with dying. <u>Appearance:</u> how you or others appear in a dream gives a lot of information. Most of this can be taken literally. So *smiling* would be referring to confidence and happiness, *frowning* to the reverse. Take time to consider if you are confident, happy, purposive in your dream. All these are scene setting for the rest of the dream. If you are tired and untidy in the dream, or your body is looking ill, then these factors represent the state of mind and perhaps even of health you are in or feel yourself to be in at the time of the dream. <u>Baby head on old body:</u> see **baby.** <u>Bodiless:</u> we build our identity and our sense of self out of our many interactions with other people and the world. In a real sense we create each other by believing in each other. Bodilessness may therefore show us feeling unrecognized, unnoticed, isolated by circumstances or attitudes; feelings of loneliness; being cut off from sexuality

and body drives. It also represents feelings about going beyond boundaries, realizing that identity does not depend upon the body, and sometimes about death. <u>Body being cut open:</u> a vital change being made in oneself; an emergency of emotional or physical nature; the release of deeply buried feelings or tension; release from restraints; in some women's dreams it occasionally represents a sexual relationship or painful sex; in times past it was sometimes used as an operation to release "evil spirits," so has the association of release of tension; a painful experience. <u>Bottom half of body:</u> sexuality and instincts; the animal, less rational, more passionate or "driven" aspect of self; the supporting sustaining aspect of self; the nourishing and reproductive process; the physiological or automatic motor energies; perhaps identified with the dreamer's mother. The lower body is therefore the energies or processes of life in us that move us without our will or even consent, such as the aging process, desire, fears, needs, and hungers; also frequently connected with falling in some way. <u>Burnt body—where burn is painful:</u> emotional hurt, the sort that can leave a deep impression—scar—on one; the burning often shows how we are dealing with emotional or sexual energy. So the suggestion is that we are relating to it is a self-destructive way. <u>Where the burning body is beautiful:</u> feeling of potential and wonder; realization of the wonderful inner potential; expressive direction of emotional or sexual energy. <u>Coldness of body:</u> repressed or resisted emotions and drives. This sort of cold or shivering often occurs as people start to release unconscious material; emotional coldness; without feelings; lack of motivation or enjoyment; the loss of something that warmed or enthused the dreamer; distancing oneself from others; fear or tension; actually being cold while asleep. <u>Coldness in lower part of body:</u> impotence; sexual coldness; restraint of passion and wanting. <u>Coldness in chest:</u> lack of feelings or emotional response; feeling "cold" toward someone; held-back emotions. <u>Cold feet:</u> fear; not wanting to do something; indecision. <u>Dead body:</u> the dead body depicts a whole set of personality traits, attitudes, or potentials, that have been denied life by us. We have not allowed them expression. A person hurt in love might kill out any feelings toward the opposite sex, for instance. <u>Diseased body:</u> a sick attitude in you; the sickness may depict a feeling state, or show how depleted you are in spirit and heart. Secondly the sickness may show an actual state in the body rather than a psychological state. <u>Dismembered body:</u> emotional or mental stress and breakdown. May be followed by emergence of new self; tearing oneself apart in facing a difficult situation; one's present inner and outer life falling apart. <u>Half a body:</u> if top missing, lack of thinking and higher emotion. If bottom, trauma to, loss or denial of, sexuality and sensuality. The half-body dreams certainly suggest some lack of balance between the conscious personality and the natural drives. <u>Injuries:</u> hurts; or events that may have led to emotional scars; internalized anger or aggression; attitudes or memories that are felt as hurts; imagined but felt hurts; body situations that are developing, perhaps out of internal stresses or emotions such as grief, but are still subliminal. See body areas below. <u>Leaving body:</u> getting away from the cares and responsibilities of physical life; reaching a powerful confrontation with feelings about life and death; shock or illness can cause this; exploring the idea of survival of bodily death; a result of remaining aware while falling asleep, thus being aware of the loss of sensory input, translated into the imagery of leaving the body. <u>Left side of body—if you are right-handed, the left of the body represents:</u> inner feelings that support outer action—such as confidence; our less used or supportive functions. If we are an intellectual, the left might depict one's feelings, intuitions, the irrational, and the right might depict orthodoxy, the rational, and accepted. The left may represent our mother's influence in our life and body, the right the influence of our father; the present, spatial awareness, synthesis of experience. This may be opposite for the left-handed, but not necessarily so, as the left-handed dreamer might share similar associations with "right." <u>Limbs, loss of:</u> usually pertains to the sense of inadequacy or lack of psychological function connected with the limb. Loss of a leg, for instance, would be lack of ability to stand up for oneself, stand one's ground—the strength that enables someone to meet opposition. Loss of an arm would relate to inadequacy in the ability to reach out and influence other people and the world, giving and receiving, keeping others at bay or holding on, depending on dream. See *arms* and *legs* in *parts of body* below. <u>Marks on the body:</u> because the flesh is what your life has created, your fate, or karma, any marks suggest something that you carry with you as your fate, or destiny. Some experience has marked you. The story of Cain and Abel illustrates this. <u>Maggots in body:</u> possible need to cleanse body of toxins or infection; sense of disease emotionally in that area of self; a feeling such as resentment eating away at one; decay; lacking life. <u>Murdered body:</u> often a period of one's life or aspects of oneself that have been angrily pushed out of consciousness because of their difficulties; an image of one's anger toward someone, or a member of one's family. Such anger is sometimes a defense against becoming aware of the root pain behind it. In such cases the murder in the dream may be a way of avoiding the pain; the murdered body may also show how you feel about being murdered by lack of love or a difficult birth; anger toward brother or sister. <u>Old head on baby body:</u> See **baby.** <u>Primitive body—such as prehistoric form:</u> strong basic responses such as anger, sexual drive, fear; like and dislike; territorial defense. Very often the dream shows the meeting with these basic responses. Perhaps something has released them more fully, or uncovered them. <u>Pulling things out of one's body:</u> becoming aware of feelings or parts of one's personality that were previously internal or unconscious; thoughts or attitudes that were previously taken to be important parts of oneself, now being seen as separate. <u>Right side of body—if you are right-handed, the right of the body represents:</u> outer activity and dominant functions; expressed abilities;

body

father's influence in life and body. If father is an anxious man there might be a lot more signs of stress on this side of the body. This is probably opposite for the left-handed. See **left, right.** <u>Sickness in body:</u> can refer to an awareness of illness in part of body shown. Most often depicts psychological problem symbolized by part of body—see body parts below. See *diseased body* above; **dead people dreams; hiding; illness.** <u>Top half of body:</u> thinking; feeling; rational conscious activity.

Parts of Body

In some cultures the areas of the body are sometimes thought of as sense organs. This may seem strange but it is very simple. If we had been castrated or had a hysterectomy prior to adolescence, we would have never properly developed sexually. Without that development we would not understand two people kissing, or what a mother was feeling when she held her baby. Out of sex drive develops a whole world of feelings and tenderness that enables us to understand many things we see in the world. It is therefore important when reading the particular descriptions below to remember that each area of your body, through its psychological counterpart, gives you some insight into yourself and life around you. That insight is missing if the area is injured or traumatized.

abdomen Almost half the dreams on file that mention abdomen, belly, or stomach show the dreamer being shot. This is about being hurt in our feeling connection with others, and our personal needs; the potential of fully active natural drives; hunger; longing to be held; desire to give of oneself. In the English language we use such phrases as "You make me sick," "I can't stomach what you're doing," "You haven't got the guts," "I really hunger for you." Also: our abdomen is our digestive ability, both physical and psychological. Through it we absorb information and experience. Stomach or abdominal dreams may refer to some disease in the actual organs. We might not be able to stomach something we have met in the everyday world. We may not be integrating our experience. To <u>vomit:</u> a discharging of unpleasant feelings resulting from ingesting, hearing, reading, being told, experiencing something unpleasant.

abscess <u>Abscess still swollen and unrelieved:</u> emotions still repressed and may be causing psychological infection, influencing views and decisions negatively. The dream abscess may also represent a site of physical illness that may or may not be obvious while awake.

ache Indicates where there may be blocked energy relevant to that part of the body. A man who dreamt of an ache in his throat later discovered in therapy that he had been holding back emotions about his father who had died suddenly. On release he was able to say how much he loved his father. <u>In chest:</u> withheld emotions. <u>Lower back:</u> blocked self-expressiveness, anger, or sexual energy. <u>Idioms:</u> my heart aches; a pain in the ass.

anus Basic and perhaps rejected feelings. Also, your will inability to hold on or let go. <u>If relaxed:</u> easy self-expression. <u>If tense:</u> not letting go of feelings you might be judging as "shitty." <u>If playing with or being entered by penis or finger:</u> introverted sexuality; self-pleasure; narcissism. <u>Excrement:</u> the negative emotions and ideas we might not want to let go of; sometimes money; worry over something judged unclean; a cleansing or need for cleansing of inner feelings, such as guilt, inhibitions, resentments, hate, worry, or fear. <u>Holding or letting go:</u> how we give of ourselves; whether we can "let go"; generosity or lack of it. <u>Idioms:</u> talking out of ass; pain in the ass; an asshole; head up the ass; disappears up; all tits and asshole (no ability to reason). See **control, controlling; excrement.**

appendix Something within yourself that may become a problem; an internal problem; possibly referring to the appendix itself. <u>Having appendix out:</u> inner pain or problem needing attention or being attended to.

arms   Ability to love, give, take, create, defend, reach out. <u>Injury to:</u> loss of confidence; not able to reach out or create; loss of or psychological trauma regarding abilities. Left is the supportive feelings. Right is extroverted activity. <u>Tied up:</u> sense of restriction to activities. <u>Bicep:</u> strength; sense of being capable. <u>Idioms:</u> chance one's arm; give one's right arm; arm-twisting; keep at arm's length; with open arms; one arm tied behind back, babe in arms; strong-arm tactics.

back   Strength; particularly moral fiber; confidence physically; decisiveness, ability to stand in face of opposition; power to endure and face life's uncertainties without being overcome. <u>Somebody on one's back:</u> feeling dominated by someone else; carrying one's parents' wants and decisions instead of one's own. <u>Idioms:</u> backbreaking; back to the wall; back against the wall (and what it implies); behind one's back; get off my back; put somebody's back up; rod for one's back; pat on the back; stab in the back; turn one's back on; scratch my back.

beard   See *hair* below.

blood   One's energy and sense of existence; link with one's family, such as feelings of connection or bonding, inherited tendencies—what we now call genes, but also includes inherited strengths and weaknesses of character; universal life or power, therefore connection with humanity; pain or struggle; injury; death. In ancient times blood was used as the first ritual sacrament. Later this was symbolized by wine or red ochre. It was noticed that at times of great change, such as birth or death, blood often preceded the change. Blood was seen as the carrier of the spirit of life and character that lived in a person or animal. If we think of what genes now are known to carry, the untold generations of human experience, with all its pain, tragedy, and wonder, then blood can represent this collective human experience. Blood is sometimes felt as a link with the unconscious forces and subpersonalities within. It is a doorway to the subtle world of the unconscious. When we see blood on the earth or on someone's clothes, it suggests great injury or death. So this aspect of blood in dreams, must be remembered. In cultures such as the Macedonian, where symbols were often thought of in terms of good or bad luck, *light blood* represented good news, *dark blood* bad news. For women there is obviously a strong link between bleeding and menstruation. Therefore in women's dreams involving blood, the blood may depict whatever feelings, pleasure, difficulties are associated with menstruation for the dreamer.

Blood flowing from a crack: possibly menstruation or loss of virginity. Blood on the ground: someone hurt or dead. Bloody clothes: personal emotional hurt or injury, perhaps even death of someone. In sexual dreams: may refer to loss of virginity, menstruation, or fertility; or hurt to sexual feelings. See *blood* under **archetypes.** Idioms: after one's blood; blood brother; blood is thicker than water; bloodletting; blood money; blood on one's hands; blood relative; bloodsucker; blue blood; draw blood; fresh blood; blood out of a stone; cold/hot blood; in the blood; blood boil, run cold; out for blood; sweat blood; taste blood; young blood; bleed someone white; one's heart bleeds.

bone Strength; a broken bone can be a loss of strength and ability; the structure and support in yourself. Burying a bone: hiding something from someone. Or storing something for the future. Digging up bones: remembering something from the long past.

brain Intellect; thinking; insight; creativity; what someone really thinks. Idioms: brainstorm; brainchild; pick someone's brains; harebrained; scatterbrained.

breasts Self-giving. In woman's dream: in many women's dreams the breasts figure prominently in a generally sexual way. <u>Woman's breast in a man's dream:</u> return to infant dependence; sexual desire.

breath   See **breath.**

chest   A place to store emotions; our emotions; pride. <u>Man's dream:</u> sense of social confidence. <u>If healthy:</u> positive sense of social recognition. <u>Woman's dream:</u> ability to give of oneself; good feelings about womanhood. See **breath.**

ears   Subtle information; rumors; intuition. <u>Idioms:</u> an ear for; all ears; reach one's ears; flea in the ear; gain the ear of; ears burning; long ears; lend an ear; hear from; will not hear of; hearing things.

eyes   How we see the world and ourselves. Eyes are used in many ways in dreams. They can represent the soul or psyche in its many moods—dark deep eyes; desperation in its eyes; shining eyes; impersonal eyes; staring eyes; eye to eye. <u>Lack of eye contact:</u> avoidance of intimacy. <u>Closed eyes:</u> introversion or avoidance of contact; not wanting to see. <u>Loss of sight in right eye:</u> not seeing what is going on in the outside world. <u>Loss of sight in left eye:</u> not seeing what you are really thinking or feeling; not aware of self, motives, behavior; no "in-sight." <u>Idioms:</u> I see; can't you see; you must be blind; I saw it with my own eyes; all eyes; eye-opener; evil eye; sheep eyes; one in the eye; turn a blind eye; keep your eyes open; easy on the eyes.

face   Self-image; concerns about how others see you, or what image you have of yourself; expression of or hiding of inner feelings and attitudes. <u>Blushing:</u> embarrassment, probably about how you feel; feelings you do not want other people to see. <u>Something wrong with face:</u> sense of not being adequate; fear of how others see you. <u>Changing one's face or head:</u> changing one's attitudes or decision about something; being uncertain or "two-faced." <u>Hiding</u>

one's face: being ashamed of something; low in confidence; being afraid of how others see you; hiding your motives or feelings. Idioms: face the facts; face the music; face value; flat on one's face; face-lift; long face; poker face; blue in the face; two-faced. See *head* below.

feet Foundation; balance in life; to have "one's feet on the ground"; to be well or badly "grounded"; fundamental issue in your life. Barefooted: to be in contact with reality. Might also suggest rough going if walking is hard. Of course, in some cultures it could suggest poverty. Loss of foot or feet: incapacitated in making moves, or in being independent or self-motivated; in the *Oneirocriticon*, c. A.D. 350, it says that to lose one's feet points to a barrier in regard to a planned journey. Idioms: put one's foot in it; feet of clay; grass grows under.

hair Thoughts; self-image; attitudes. See *Washing hair* under **washing.** Baldness: aging; feeling obsolete; lack of thought. Beard: depending upon feelings in the dream, it can suggest masculinity, deceit, wisdom, or some kind of cover-up. Brushing hair: clarifying attitudes or thoughts. Changing hairstyle: changing attitudes; a change of mind. Chest hair: masculinity, virility. Cutting off beard: making a change; feeling more certain about one's manhood; or uncertainty about manhood. Cutting right off: less thinking; denial of sensual and physical drives, as monk. Dark hair: unconscious area of thoughts and attitudes; "dark" thoughts or attitudes. Disheveled hair: mental confusion. Fair hair: awareness; "light-headed." Genital or armpit: sexuality. Hair on chest of female, even child: the male side of the woman; might be parents' desire for a boy, generating male characteristics. Long and matted: not caring about social image or self; dropout. Long: freedom; permissiveness; girlhood with woman. Plaited or ponytail: girlhood; socialized thoughts and feelings. Tight style: discipline; self-restraint. Very long beard: sense of eternal. White beard: wisdom or experience. Wig: false attitudes or thoughts; an assumed social front. <u>Woman's dreams—armpit or leg hair:</u> social expression of sexuality or physicality. <u>Idioms:</u> keep your hair on; hair-raising; have us by the short hairs; let one's hair down; make your hair curl, stand on end; didn't turn a hair; put hairs on your chest; tear one's hair out; split hairs. See **shampoo.**

hand Most frequently dreamt-of part of body. Self-expression; grasp—of life, of ideas, of opportunities; our hold on people, our children, situations. Extension of our power—to give, take, wound, heal, support, or do. <u>Fingers:</u> fingers can be expressive of your feelings. It can be the finger of scorn; accusing finger; finger of suspicion; beckoning finger; to put your finger on it. Fingers represent your grasp on things, your method of materializing yourself, or leaving your mark upon matter. Therefore, your personal skills. The finger can represent the penis, as is common use in sex-play; your means of sensing, or fingering, things. Fingers can, as the wedding ring finger, suggest something like marriage. The fingerprint also denotes your uniqueness. <u>Fingernails:</u> weapons; personal condition—i.e., dirty or cared for. <u>Handshake:</u> contacting an aspect of self; friendship; nonverbal communication. <u>Fist:</u> anger; restrained anger; threat; graspingness, selfishness, arrogance, aggressiveness, tension. <u>Dirty hands:</u> dirty work; unclean activity. <u>Rough hands:</u> Marks left by difficult experience; roughness in handling others. <u>Clawlike hands:</u> clawing, wounding ability. <u>Idioms:</u> secondhand; in the hands of; bite the hand that feeds; hands are tied; soil one's hands; hand to hand; hand-to-mouth; hands off; hard hand; helping hand; openhanded; lend a hand; upper hand; burnt fingers; at one's fingertips; snap one's fingers; green fingers; have a finger in; itchy fingers; sticky fingers; fingers crossed; lay a finger on; point the finger at; get one's finger out; fingers to bone.

head Thoughts; opinions; intellect; decisions; intentions; self-image. Fairly understandable from the huge number of idioms about head and face, such as "lose one's head/face," so one might literally dream of a headless figure. Dreams may also use the head as an image to show how one is "of two minds" about something, or is changing one's mind. This might be shown by having two heads, or changing one's head. <u>Idioms:</u> above one's head; enter one's head; get something into one's head; go off one's head; over one's head; swollen or big head; head above water; head in sand; egghead; square head; off the top of my head; hold your head up high; come to a head; head over heels; over your head; get it through your head; turn one's head; heads up.

heart Emotions; pity; sympathy; likes and dislikes; one's actual physical heart. Being stabbed, shot, or in any way injured in the heart may depict deep emotional hurts, but also may be a warning of physical heart problems. <u>Idioms:</u> lost your heart; have a heart; have no heart; heart like stone; change one's heart; done one's heart good; from bottom of heart; sick at heart; don't let your heart run away with your head; wearing your heart on your sleeve; the heart of the matter; heavy heart; after your heart; break your heart; my heart's in my mouth; openhearted.

internal organs Often to do with concerns over health. Could be a sense of illness in that part of body; mostly anxiety about illness. See *separate organs*.

jaw Your strength to stop anyone getting into you—through your mouth. Your power to hold on to emotions—by clenching your teeth. The jaw can also represent being swallowed up—in other words, a fear of losing your identity or will.

legs Support; motivation; the emotional and physical strength you use to get about in life. To "have one's legs knocked out from under one" means loss of confidence and urge to carry on with life. Although you may depend upon someone like partner or parent for support—or work or position—for self-value, ultimately the legs represent your emotional or conceptual support system. So you may be considering, in your leg dream, what sense you have of your value. When trying to understand legs in your dream see **left, right; lame.** <u>Idioms:</u> legless; didn't have a leg to stand on; my legs went to jelly; my legs were paralyzed; I couldn't stand up for myself; felt like I had a ball and chain on my legs.

lungs Might relate to tension, feelings of being "suffocated" in a relationship or situation, as one may have been with one's mother or home life. Often to do with smoking or such. <u>Idioms</u> as relate to breathing, such as: catch one's breath; bated breath; hold one's breath. See **breath.**

mouth Pleasure area; your hungers, sexual pleasure. Also, because we speak with our mouth and tongue, they can represent what we say. A dream of our mouth being buttoned—button your lip—or sewed up, could suggest that inwardly we regret having said certain things, and need to hold our tongue. <u>Chewing:</u> considering; mulling over something. <u>Pulling something out of mouth:</u> trying to clear emotions or attitudes not properly expressed. Perhaps one is not admitting something. <u>Idioms:</u> all mouth; a big mouth; nasty taste in the mouth; mouthwatering.

muscles Your strength, therefore confidence and sense of adequacy; your ability to act on decision; sense of being outwardly forceful; masculinity in its physical side. Also may refer to physical muscle.

navel Connection with mother or another person; feelings of dependence; needs for nourishment at a basic baby level. See *umbilical cord* below.

neck Connection between body (feelings and sexuality) and head (thinking and willing); weak point. Often refers to attitudes as in idioms. The neck is also the point up to which we can be easily immersed in water. Beyond that point there is danger. So it can depict what we can take in life, and what is more than enough. <u>Idioms:</u> breaking one's neck; up to one's neck; risk one's neck; stick one's neck out; dead from the neck up/down.

nose   Curiosity; intuition—as with "smell a rat"; penis. <u>Malformed nose:</u> might relate to the idiom "nose out of joint"; sense of not appearing good to others. <u>Idioms:</u> have a nose for; nose out of joint; rub nose in it; up one's nose.

ovaries, uterus   For many women, represents their sense of validity or adequacy just as testes do for men; ability to have children, so could represent fears or feelings about this; creativity. See **vagina; individuation.**

paralysis, paralyzed   Feeling a lack of confidence; fear; a sense of not being able to cope; feelings of hopelessness, or that there is no way out of a present situation. Dreaming one is paralyzed may depict the paralyzing effects either of fears we have, or what we have imagined as real in the way described in the entry on **paralysis—while asleep or trying to wake;** we may be "paralyzed" by feelings of guilt or inadequacy; internal conflict paralyzes us.

pelvis   The sexual function as a whole. So not simply sex, but reproduction and how you handle this power of life and death. The pelvis may also link with the way you merge into another person, or if you can allow that merging and emerging. Some dreams show the pelvis as connected with lizards or snakes, and this shows the powerful instinctive drives and energy that can either flow out in sexual activity, or flow up the spine as expanding consciousness. Our unconscious often connects sex with giving oneself, a death of self, and making connections or bonds—obviously reproduction also.

body

penis For a man the penis represents more than simply his sexual appetite. It depicts the whole drive of life through his glandular system, which develops the body type he has. It is therefore often depicting a sense of his own power of self-expression, his potency in expressing himself and capability in the world. The positive aspect of the penis/masculinity is for him to demand his woman meets his maleness, his caring aggression, his sexual desire, with her own fiery energy and strength. <u>In a woman's dream:</u> your relationship with desire for a mate; relationship with your male characteristics, such as ambition, work capability, aggression, intellect; depicts the relationship with genital sexuality with your partner. <u>Penis replaced by vagina:</u> could be feeling inadequate as a man; contact with the female receptive in oneself; loss of male drive in sexuality. <u>Loss of penis:</u> see **castrate.** <u>Penis turns into a snake:</u> feeling the intense instinctive drive of sexuality. This is a realization of the drive as existing beyond one's personality; an expression of what the sex drive is doing, depending what is happening to the snake. <u>Bleeding from penis:</u> emotional hurts or fears that are interfering with expression of healthy sexual feeling. See **castrate;** *bed* under **furniture, furnishings; knob.**

rectum Children often see this as the place from which one is born, the place from which things come out; one's deeply personal self, therefore acceptance or rejection of intrusion; discharge of unneeded feelings and experience; deeply sensual and fundamental feelings; feelings of dirtiness. See *anus* above.

shoulders Ability to bear or to carry what life brings. <u>Idioms:</u> have broad shoulders; shoulder to the wheel; shoulder to cry on; rub shoulders; chip on shoulder.

skin One's contact with the world; what tactics we use to deal with others; strength or vulnerability in feeling the impact of other people, their remarks and actions. <u>Rough skin: rough exterior. Burnt skin: hurt in relationship with outside world or people. Shed skin: like a snake, changing one's old way of life; old attitudes. Spots, blemishes, moles: feelings about personal failings or some sense of not being as good or acceptable as other people; a feeling that other people see you as unattractive or can see failings in you; shyness; difficulties about facing or being in the company of other people. Idioms: under one's skin; a thick skin; skin-deep; skin alive.

spine   Strength; moral power; support.

teeth   Aggression; defense; ability to "chew things over"; our "bite" on life, or the ability to get what we want; words we say or swallow; our social appearance, often a sign of our age, as suggested by such idioms as long in the tooth, milk teeth, etc. If we see someone with few or no teeth, it often arouses a feeling in us that the person has lost their effectiveness in life, their strength—they have "lost it." This may be exactly what we are portraying in losing our teeth in a dream—the feeling, even temporary, of "losing it." This may be felt as the sense of not being able to get what one deeply wants, and so is experienced as a sort of death, or a loss of self in some degree. In some cultures the loss of a tooth often depicted the death of a family member. Bad tooth: a painful or rotten part of one's feelings, life, or relationships; angry or regretful words. False teeth: lies told; false face; not keeping spoken promises; the aging process and loss of good looks. Spitting out lots of teeth: something you want to "spit out" in the sense of admitting, saying, or expressing emotionally. Teeth falling out: often a sense of loss, such as death of family member or loved one; the aging process as it relates to maturity, so worries about getting older and one's changing image. When our first teeth fall out at around seven, it is probably our initial experience of losing something from our body, something weird happening—we might even fear other bits of us could drop off or out. Feeling the loss of something, or fears of looking peculiar and aging. <u>If single tooth:</u> this may suggest loss, change, or death of someone. <u>Tooth being pulled out:</u> Jung felt this dream represents giving birth if dreamt by a woman. In general it probably has associations with loss or painful loss. <u>Toothless:</u> loss of effectiveness; feelings about aging. <u>Idioms:</u> show one's teeth; get one's teeth into; gnash one's teeth; grit one's teeth; teething troubles; long in the tooth, milk teeth, cutting one's teeth.

testicles This depicts the male capability to become aroused, or to have sexual drive. So loss of testicles, small testicles, would suggest anxiety about being capable sexually with a woman. They also represent virility in the sense of male confidence, strength, and energy. See *penis* above. A <u>woman's dream:</u> her feelings about sex with a male; feelings about wanting to conceive, or wanting the man deep in herself. What she is doing to a male or the male in herself. See *vagina* below; *penis* above. In <u>a man's dream:</u> what he is doing with his sexual urge; his battery of energy and self-worth; sense of maleness; the life process beyond personality; one's genetic connection with ancestors.

tongue Speech, expression of what we feel; saying what is deep inside us, perhaps unknown to oneself; penis. <u>Idioms:</u> find one's tongue; tongue in cheek; lose one's tongue; sharp tongue; hold one's tongue; forked tongue.

umbilical cord Dependence; connections and emotional ties of dependence or need with other people.

vagina, uterus The vagina refers to much more than a woman's sexual feelings and drives. It depicts the urges and processes of her being that are the foundations of her waking personality. The ability to procreate; the glandular bias that connects with what the conscious personality faces in emotional, mental, and physical disposition; the caring, nurturing feelings that emerge out of sexual mating when healthy; the desire for a mate; the sense of connection and identity with other women, other female creatures and female aspects of nature. In its positive aspect it may represent the sure confidence with which a woman may demand from her man that he treat her womanhood with the respect it deserves. This means meeting the full flood of her sexual need with its desire for a child, a caring and supportive nest to rear that child in, and her female creativity that may rise from that basic reproductive drive into social creativity and personal demand for respect. If the dream is directly about the uterus, this suggests an immediate connection with the ability to reproduce in some way, with pregnancy, with nurturing a child. <u>Bleeding vagina:</u> fears about one's sexuality and femininity; hurts to emotions connected with sexual relatedness. <u>In male dreams:</u> fears about meeting a woman's full sexuality; the deep experience of the relationship with one's mother; birth and how mother met one's emerging male sexuality; one's desire for sexual expression.

bomb   Explosive situation; sudden events producing anxiety—as when we say something occurred out of the blue; one's own aggression; fear of death; remembered anxieties of war experience; social bombshells—such as being criticized in the press. See **airplane; air raid; mine; war.** <u>Idioms:</u> I feel blitzed; come as a bombshell; go down like a bomb; go like a bomb; put a bomb under someone; earn a bomb.

book   Memories; things you have learned or are learning from experience; attitudes toward learning; other people's opinions; the world of imagination and escape. <u>Old books:</u> inherited wisdom; learning; greater awareness.

boot   See *shoes* under **clothes;** for boot of car, see *car boot, trunk* under **car.**

border   See **frontier, border.**

bottle Vagina; feeling bottled-up. If <u>something in it</u>: resources you have. Of <u>wine, spirits, or beer</u>: sometimes an influence entering your life to change it; relaxation. If <u>red wine</u>: you may have felt there is more in life than your ego, its worries and desires; sense of sharing life. See **alcohol.**

bottom This is sometimes used in England to suggest the posterior, the behind. So it might be wordplay for that; if about the bottom of a garden, hill, or hole, it can suggest something at the back of your mind known but pushed to the back; If you are at the bottom, it suggests difficulties, or a long climb, effort to get to the top; isolation; or even back to where you were; being at the bottom can also be despair. The <u>bottom of a bucket or box</u>: the power to hold, to contain something. So when we say "the bottom fell out of the world for me," we mean that we no longer feel held up or sustained by the world.

box In general the box suggests contents, what you have or hide inside yourself. Depending on the size of the box, it can represent memories, or treasured experiences. It might, like "chest," represent the way you store feelings in your chest. <u>Closed box</u>: often represents the womb/uterus and its connection with childbearing; memories; the unknown.

boy *Male Under the Age of Thirteen* <u>If known</u>: what you feel about that boy, but referring to yourself—i.e., you might think the child cautious and anxious, so it depicts your childhood feelings of caution and anxiety. <u>Male dream</u>: yourself at that age; the difficulties faced, habits acquired, attitudes imprinted on you by experiences at that age—circumstances may not have permitted parts of you to mature, so your relationship with a woman and the world might still be conditioned by that age mode. So, could be part you need to "father" toward maturity. Also, the eternal potential for growth, openness to the new and enthusiasm about tomorrow. <u>If older than yourself</u>: your potential or how you feel about maturing. Female dream: your developing ability to express in outer action. Feelings about a son. See *son* under **family.**

boyfriend   Your emotional feelings, attachment to, the boyfriend; the difficulties, struggle with feelings and sexuality felt in connection with boyfriend or other males; your insights into his behavior. Ex-lover/boyfriend: any feelings or hopes still connected with him; the ex-boyfriend or lover often becomes a symbol for all the hopes for love that are not being satisfied at the moment, or in the present relationship; occasionally the past. It may occur in some dreams that the ex-lover is seen as a dead body, or a murder is involved. This is usually because we are killing, or have killed some of our longings and love.

brain   See *brain* under **body.**

bread   Fundamental nourishment; your basic emotional and biological needs; substance in the sense of wealth or possessions. In an overall sense it represents your experience of physical or bodily life, so connection with others; sometimes represents a baby/pregnancy, especially if uncooked and being put in an oven. See **food.**

break   Broken promise; shattered idealism, hope, or faith; feeling broken in spirit; changes as we "break" with the past; feelings of loss or damage. Idioms: lucky/bad break; break a habit; break down/up; break new ground; broken heart; break the ice; break the news; break through; break with.

breasts   See *breasts* under **body.**

breath   Being alive; pace of life; emotional state—i.e., peaceful or disturbed. Breathing in: taking in something; absorbing an influence; absorbing life. Holding the breath: expression of will; we breath-hold when repressing

113

breath

emotions and anxiety. <u>Fast breathing:</u> excitement; emotional release; experience of fear. <u>Underwater and not breathing:</u> womblike state; experience of level of awareness without sexual, biological drives, and without opposites; return to deep relaxation—healthy if you can easily emerge. Might be an escape from waking reality if you cannot. See *lungs* under **body.**

bride Feelings about or desire for marriage; love; receptivity and fertility; integrating parts of personality previously not expressed. <u>Female dream:</u> your marriage and what it means to you; feelings, fears, or hopes about marriage; feelings about daughter. If <u>getting married:</u> integration of inner feelings and unconscious, especially if bride/groom is oriental or black. <u>Male dream:</u> frequently depicts one's relationship with your feelings and nonrational nature.

bridegroom Desire to be married or find a partner. <u>Female dream:</u> feelings about marriage or getting married; integration with intellect and exterior capability. <u>Male dream:</u> feelings about marriage; attempt to integrate conscious and unconscious.

bridge Crossing from one phase of life, activity, or emphasis to another; can represent leaving youth behind and meeting old age; the connection between yourself and another person, a relationship, a link between self and opportunity, self and change in life; another possible meaning is a way of passing over obstacles or difficulties, as the song "Bridge Over Troubled Water" suggests. <u>Fallen bridge:</u> lost opportunity; broken bonds and connections; parting in relationship; broken opportunity or a way of dealing with obstacles lost. <u>Building a bridge:</u> creating a way to deal with difficulties; building a link with others or another person; overcoming problems or hesitations. <u>Idioms:</u> burn one's bridges; cross that bridge when I come to it; water under the bridge; bridge builder; bridge the gap.

brother   See *brother* under **family, family relationships.**

bubble   Illusion; delicate and easily lost; daydreams; sometimes the transitory human existence or identity.

bud   Vagina; the penis; the unfolding of the world of sexuality, full of emotional and physical levels of experience and richness.

Buddha, buddhist   Depends a great deal on personal associations with Buddhism, but may represent what you feel or realize about existence beyond your ego; often in Western dreams associated with the denial of, or loss of, ego; liberation from thinking and desiring; in a Christian person's dream, may be a threat to their belief system. See *the self* under **archetypes; buddhism and dreams.**

Buddhism and dreams   The story of Gautama Buddha's life (567–487 B.C.) starts at preconception when his mother, Queen Maya, is said to have dreamt that a six-tusked elephant pierced her side with one of its tusks. This produced an immaculate conception. She understood the dream to mean the resulting child would become a monarch whose domain was the world. The Buddhist scriptures contain mention of five of the Buddha's dreams, and also include dreams of his father, King Cudhodana, and his wife, Gopa.

   The fundamental aim of Buddhism is to find liberation from the things that bind consciousness to illusory concepts of oneself and the world. This goal, called Liberation or Nirvana, is sometimes described as the blowing out of the sense of self or one's ego. This should not be thought of as a killing of oneself psychologically, but rather an untangling of our fundamental self from the many influences it is usually enmeshed in. Part of this is the illusory view we have of the world. Buddhism does not see the world itself as an illusion, but the emotions and concepts

Buddhism and dreams

we hold that provoke responses to the world are seen as the illusion. Therefore, dreams are not thought of as being illusions, but depict the illusions of everyday experience of life. The very nature of dreams are expressive of the complicated realm of fears, longings, and mental concepts we are deeply enmeshed in. Nightmares especially show how deeply involved our waking self is with the internal world of passionate feelings and imagery.

building   See **house, buildings.**

bull   See *bull* under **animals.**

bullet   Sexual impregnation; aggression; penis; desire to hurt; pain. See **shot; war.**

burden   See **knapsack.**

burglar, intruder   Fears or difficult emotions arising from the unconscious; neglected parts of yourself that if met could change your viewpoint to a more mature or inclusive one; feelings to do with intrusion. <u>Female dream:</u> sometimes repressed desire for or fear of male partner or sex; or desire for a better sexual relationship.

burial   Letting go of the past as we knew it, and opening the way to a meeting with what we gained from it; repressing experience that may be painful or we do not wish to meet; feelings about death or loss. <u>Buried alive:</u> memories of difficult birth and its fears. See *rebirth, resurrection* under **archetypes.**

burning   Burning emotions; release of emotions or energy. See **fire.**

bus   Experience, undertaking, or relationship with a group of people; direction taken in company with others; trying to get somewhere but depending on others; overweight problem. <u>Bus stop:</u> waiting for events to take you somewhere; being involved with strangers or other people in a direction you are taking; depending on social events to get you to where you want to go; trying to get somewhere in life; trying to leave something or someone behind. <u>Idioms:</u> miss the bus; big as a bus.

business and dreaming Although the world of business and the world of dreams are often considered to be incompatible, this is not so. When we see dreams as a "printout" of the most shrewd and capable computer we have access to, your brain, we can see them as a source of useful information. If you are in business, there is information in your memory, along with considered projects, questions about problem areas, that have never been put on an electronic computer. There is no computer program outside your mind that can handle and manipulate all the variables, the integrating of different information sources—written words, feeling hunches, spoken information, personal observation and experience—and then sift, explore different combinations, and reach into pure creativity by leaping into the new. Dreams should not be seen as oracles, but if we take their information into account along with other sources, we find them a real addition to our business equipment. See **creativity and problem-solving dreams.**

buying See **purchasing.**

C

cab   See **taxi** and **car**.

cafe   Easygoing source of relaxation and sustenance; meeting point of different parts of your nature. See **food; barroom**.

cage, cell   If the <u>dreamer is in the cage:</u> frustration arising from a sense of social pressures restraining expression—or from one's moral restraints imprisoning one; feeling caged by economic situation, lack of opportunity, or lack of developed abilities. The cell often depicts how we imprison ourselves within anger, resentment, or depressed feelings; or we may be trapped by childhood trauma. <u>Something or somebody else caged:</u> desire to restrain whatever is represented by the thing, person, caged. See **escape; fence; holding;** *hospital* under **house, building; prison**.

cake   See *cake* under **food**.

calendar   Passage of time; reminder or suggestion of something important arising.

calf   Because it is a baby animal, a calf may link with your childhood, and your dependent link with your mother. The calf might also be associated with food or money if you are a farmer or in the food industry.

calf, leg   This represents your physical ability to get about in the world.

camel   See *camel* under **animals.**

camera   Taking notice; memory; sometimes what we may have noticed out of the "corner of our eye" but not processed into waking awareness. See **photos.**

canal   Most often the way we direct, socialize, or control emotions—therefore depicts relationships and goals.

cancer   Fear of this illness; a part of our personality or being that is out of harmony with our wholeness; expression of how we feel about other people's—especially our mother's—emotional influence. This influence might be eating away at our sense of well-being. Occasionally awareness of illness in part of body suggested.

candle   Male sex organ. <u>Lighting a candle:</u> a birth; prayer. <u>If lit amid darkness:</u> finding understanding or courage amid doubts, fears, depression; hope. Occasionally, measurer of how much time we have left in life. <u>Idioms:</u> burn the candle at both ends; not fit to hold a candle. See **flames; light.**

candy   See **sweets.**

cane   Aggression; sadistic or masochistic sexuality; authority. See **walking stick.**

canyon   See **valley.**

cap   See *hat* under **clothes.** <u>Idioms:</u> cap in hand; thinking cap.

capital   <u>Capital cities such as London, Tokyo, Moscow, unless the home of the dreamer, depict:</u> material opportunity;

central issues in dreamer's life; the central sense of self, around which other issues revolve. If <u>somewhere like Jerusalem or Mecca:</u> one's central religious drives and ideas. See **city, town.**

captain   See *captain* under **roles.**

car   Your motivating drives; sex drive; ambition; sense of failure; whatever is driving you in life; means of or desire to "get somewhere" in life; independence; personal choice and freedom, therefore decision-making; personal space into which you can invite other people to share your life; privacy in which you can be yourself; feelings about the particular car in dream; your body. Cars are such an enormously important and frequent part of modern life, they represent all manner of things. But they are particularly representative of ability to move around or power to direct our life, to achieve results, and make choices. They also depict the ambitions, attitudes, and care, or lack of it, that drive us. The manner in which we make our way through life of course involves us in countless relationships of various sorts. So the car is again a symbol of such meetings and partings. But car dreams may also relate to the business of driving our actual vehicle in everyday life, and the manner in which we do so. Therefore some car dreams may warn us of attitudes we have that are dangerous not just in relationships, but actually on the road. See **ESP in dreams.**

<u>Accelerator:</u> ability to govern one's expression of energy. If <u>pressing down on accelerator:</u> desire to reach one's goal or desire quickly; frustration; ability or "drive" to succeed. <u>Lack of response from accelerator:</u> no inner enthusiasm for tasks or goals. <u>Alone in vehicle:</u> independence; making decisions alone; feeling alone. <u>Another driver:</u> being passive; being influenced by the opinions or emotions of someone else, or one's own secondary characteristics—i.e., anxiety or emotional pain may lead us to make many decisions, so be the driving force in life, rather than what might be more satisfying; dependence on another person. <u>Brakes not</u>

working: might suggest high anxiety or losing control of a situation or events, thus may indicate a fear of taking chances or initiating things in case they get "out of hand"; difficulty in controlling sexual desire or emotions. Brakes: one's ability to be in control of a situation. This might be control of anxiety or sexuality or emotions. Car body: dreamer's body; oneself. Car boot/trunk: the memories, the karma, or influences from past actions and experiences we still carry with us; the "baggage" of anxieties and thoughts that might not be necessary; tools for dealing with difficult life situations. Car on fire: stress of some sort causing "burnout," either physically or emotionally. Car parts: body parts, but also the function in oneself they might suggest—steering wheel, for instance, could suggest control over one's direction or emotions. Car torn apart or dismantled: stress; failure to care for one's body; self-destructive attitudes. Collision: possible conflict of opinions with another person; careless behavior leading to problem in relationship; painful encounter; careless driving in waking. Crashing vehicle: self-desired failure—perhaps to avoid stress or responsibility and change; fear of failure; failure in relationship; argument—you may be on collision course with boss or partner; occasionally psychological or physical breakdown threatened. If the vehicle crash has a sense of death in it, then the dream may be exploring the anxieties or feelings around death. This is not a prediction of death, but a meeting with whatever values and fears one has about it. It may, however, be warning you about activities having a negative effect on your life or health. See **ESP in dreams.** Doors: your way of letting other people share your life. The passenger door in particular refers to the people you let near you. Driver's seat: the attitudes directing how you live your life. Whoever is in the seat is influencing your life, either through your permission, through dependence or dominance, perhaps even fear. Driving carelessly: lack of responsibility socially or sexually; need for more awareness. Driving without license: feeling guilty about your way of life or social conduct; not daring to test out your quality against social standards, therefore may hide sense of inadequacy. <u>Drunk driving:</u> not in control of your life; occasionally refers to an influence that uplifts or changes you; alcohol is dominating you. <u>Engine:</u> energy; heart; central drive. <u>Fuel:</u> feeling drives; motivation; whatever has "fueled one's drive." <u>Headlights off:</u> loss of awareness. <u>Headlights:</u> being able to see what is happening in your life; what lies ahead; insight. If <u>dreamer driving:</u> being independent; self-confidence; being responsible for one's own life direction. <u>Mirror:</u> looking back on what is "behind" you, what you have left behind, or what is approaching you from the past. <u>Not being able to see through windshield:</u> avoiding seeing something that is important to you. <u>Not in control of car:</u> usually a warning that we are not living life with due awareness or care. In some way we are either not watching what we are doing, or are feeling anxiety about not being in control of events. <u>Old car, scrapped car:</u> sense of old age; feelings about death; outmoded way of dealing with life. <u>Overtaken:</u> feeling of being left behind or not competing. <u>Overtaking:</u> getting ahead; immersed in rat race. <u>Passengers:</u> people important in your life; feelings about how you relate to others; people influencing your direction in life. <u>Parking lot, car park, parking:</u> a socially acceptable place to rest, to meet, to make some sort of change or exchange. The parked car might also mean you have stopped "going anywhere" in life, or that you have changed to walking—getting somewhere through personal effort. Or even that you have stopped "driving yourself"—relaxing. <u>Can't find parking place:</u> perhaps you are finding it difficult to relax, to get out of the demands of the "traffic" of your life. <u>Puncture:</u> see <u>Flat tire</u> under **car**. <u>Reversing:</u> sense of not getting anywhere; feeling that one is slipping backward; reversing a decision; change of direction. <u>Running over someone:</u> "killing" some part of self through misplaced drive or ambition; aggression. <u>Seat belt:</u> sense of safety; caution; obeying or disobeying the rules. <u>Sports car:</u> self-image to do with being free, daring, unconventional, and high-powered; perhaps single. <u>Steering wheel:</u> decision-making; being in control; ability to choose. <u>Towing, being towed:</u> dependence if being towed. Looking after a dependent or needy part of oneself. <u>Traffic jam:</u> things in your life not flowing well; frustration; blocked emotions or finance. <u>Tire:</u> the attitudes and skills you use to smooth out the rough patches in your life. <u>Flat tire:</u> physical problems or injury; let down by something unexpected; unexpected delay in some area of your life; frustration or irritation. <u>Windows, windshield:</u> protection and your view of the world and other people. <u>With one other person:</u> relationship with that person. <u>Idioms:</u> backseat driver; drive at; drive away; drive somebody mad, round the bend, round the twist, to drink; what are you driving at?; taking someone/being taken for a ride.

cards, playing Opportunity; personal skill; sociability; competition; a gamble; sense of fate. The different suits depict different things. <u>Hearts:</u> emotions; relationships. <u>Diamonds:</u> riches; intellectual. <u>Spades:</u> one's body; movement; sensuality. <u>Clubs:</u> instinctive drives, such as fear, sex, hunger. <u>Ace of clubs:</u> wealth, health, and happiness. <u>Ace of diamonds:</u> financial good fortune. <u>Ace of hearts:</u> love and good relationship. <u>Ace of spades:</u> feeling of success in work. If <u>business card:</u> identity or opportunity. <u>Greeting card:</u> hoping for news; thoughts about sender. See **games, gambling.**

cards Greetings; feelings about or received from others; reminder.

carpet See *carpet* under **furniture, furnishings.**

carriage Similar to car, but because drawn by an animal or engine, more suggestive of a direction brought about by biological drives such as sex and aging. Can depict how you are dealing with such drives.

carried, carry An ability being used; what one is "carrying" in life, such as carrying a grudge or taking responsibility.

carried, carry

<u>Being carried:</u> a desire to drop responsibility; a return to childhood relationship; needing help. <u>Carrying person:</u> treating someone else, or some part of yourself, as a child or invalid; feeling you are "carrying the load" in life, work, or a relationship; something from the past you are still "carrying"; overzealous, as depicted by idiom "carrying things too far." <u>Idioms:</u> carried away; carry a torch; carry the can.

carrot   See *carrot* under **food.**

case   See **bag.**

cassette   See **record, cassette, CD, computer disc.**

castle   See *castle* under **house, buildings.**

castrate   Trauma and/or fear regarding sexual drive, possibly leading to "cutting off" full sexual flow; fear of the responsibility that develops with sexual maturity; the difficulty in facing the pains and adjustments that come with rejection by the opposite sex, competition for work and wealth, standing without parental support, making decisions, discriminating in the world of ideas, and exercise of will.

cat   See *cat* under **animals.**

cataclysm   See **end-of-world dreams and fantasies; atom bomb.**

catacomb, crypt   Usually refers to feelings connected with death. It suggests, even in this, a womblike condition and birth, so a child may also figure in the same dream. Also, a place of power or hidden forces, where there might be a connection to the unconscious; inner link with other people and the energies of our body.

caterpillar Male sexuality; prenatal forces of growth; bacteria. If <u>moving to chrysalis stage:</u> urge to find environment in which to make life changes. <u>Chrysalis:</u> major change going on within yourself; a new aspect of yourself getting ready to emerge; desire to retreat from the world.

cave Prenatal life; the vagina; the process of reproduction and birth. Also, an entrance to our unconscious; the void we face at the end of individuation. We <u>may find in the cave:</u> a fear of the irrational or being lost; a sense of meeting the divine; our traumas or destiny; a meeting with death and rebirth. See **catacomb, crypt; unconscious.**

Example: "I am in a large, airy cavelike room. I am pregnant and wearing a white gown. I am lying on my back on a flat slablike surface with my legs drawn up." (Barbara A.)

Cayce, Edgar Born in Hopkinsville, Kentucky, on March 18, 1877. Died, Virginia Beach, January 1945. Cayce was an uneducated man who found he could put himself into a sleep state in which he had access to a collective mind or universal consciousness. Cayce was a very Christian man and couched his statements in a biblical manner. In his sleep state, however, he could verbally respond to people's questions, and using medical terms he did not know consciously, diagnose illness in people, even at a distance. He could speak foreign languages he had never learned and get information he had no conscious access to. Because of this he was asked to the White House twice. At one period a hospital was built in which he worked with six doctors, diagnosing from his sleep condition. In this state, when asked how he could get information about the past, about people at a distance, he replied that every person has access to what he called the cosmic mind—Jung's collective unconscious—while they sleep, but few people can bring this contact through to conscious expression. He also maintained that prolonged working with one's dreams gradually made conscious this contact with cosmic life. The information garnered from Cayce's unconscious in this manner suggested that humans are cosmic beings. A lifetime is a brief interlude of learning in an eternal pilgrimage through time and space. The conscious personality we so often raise so high is but a temporary experience assumed by an older, larger being, the Individuality, or Self, as Jung called it. The ego dies at death, but the Individuality absorbs its experience. Dreams are the meeting point between this older self and the personality it assumes but briefly. The phenomena of Cayce's life are not unique. Other men and women in the past have exhibited a similar faculty. Cayce was a modern example of the practical possibilities connected with the collective unconscious. Cayce's biography is *There Is a River* by Thomas Sugrue, or *Seer Out of Season: The Life of Edgar Cayce*, by Harmon Bro. Cayce dictated 14 million words from his sleep state. A record of these is kept at the Association for Research and Enlightenment, Virginia Beach, VA. See *http://www.are-cayce.com.*

CD   See **record, cassette, CD, computer disc**

ceiling   See *Ceiling* under **house, buildings.**

celebrity   See **famous people.**

cellar   See *basement, cellar* under **house, buildings.**

cellular phone   See *cellular phone* under **telephone.**

cemetery   Depicts your thoughts and feelings regarding death; your family heritage of attitudes or traditions; contact with the dead; things in your life you have "buried"; melancholy about life or feeling "different" to other people; a relationship, that you think is "dead and buried."

center, middle   See *center, middle* under **shapes, symbols.**

ceremony, ritual   Similar to initiation. In the example, the girl is with her boyfriend. She may thus have been "initiated" into sexual activity. Sex with her boyfriend has changed her image of herself. A ritual depicts: important change, such as entrance into puberty; deeper levels of one-self; new attitudes or skills, just as marriage is an entrance into a new type of life and social situation. From the wider sense of self our unconscious has, things are seen as important that we consciously feel are trivial. A ceremony in a dream brings such things to our attention.

Example: "A ritual began whereby a large knife was drawn and a few deep cuts were made to both our faces. I put my hands to my face and saw them covered with blood, crying and crying." (D.A.)

chain Restriction; strength; dependence. We might feel "chained" to our marriage partner or work, or we may be chained by mental attitudes or habits; connection as suggested by the links in the chain—a connection broken by breaking any one of the links; sometimes the image may suggest a series of events—links—that lead to the present situation.

chair See *chair* under **furniture, furnishings.**

champagne See **alcohol.**

chapel See **church.**

chased We are, in a real sense, pursued by what we have created with our thoughts, emotions, action, and inaction. What we are avoiding might be sexual feelings, responsibility, expressing what we really feel in public, fear of death, sense of failure, guilt, emotional pain, or grief. But it might be our creativity, love, or a passionate response to living, our deepest wisdom and oneness with things. We can never escape from ourselves, so such feelings may pursue us through life unless we meet them. By animal: one's passions; anger; natural feelings. By thing or shadowy creature: usually past experience or trauma; a hurt from childhood. <u>Chased by opposite sex:</u> afraid of love or sex; haunted by a past relationship. <u>Chasing:</u> something you are pursuing in life; something or someone you want; aggression. See **follow.**

cheat, cheated Being dishonest with yourself. Not living up to your real feelings. Feelings about being betrayed or your trust abused in some way.

check Something being asked of you that you might not like; past actions catching up with you; a reminder of something you need to do or attend to.

chemist Usually health concerns; what the body needs; healing; can be similar to doctor—wisdom about self, insight into self. See *doctor* under **roles.**

check Money check: A promise; unredeemed value or potential; something you have earned. See **money.**

chest, box May refer to one's physical chest; more often the way we keep hidden or hide our emotions; our most valued ideals and hopes; our best insights; the best in us.

chew To think something over. To analyze or break it down in order to absorb it. To sample something, or take it into yourself as a feeling or idea. See **eating.**

chicken See *chicken* under **birds.**

chicks See *chicks* under **birds.**

child Your feelings about your childhood; feelings of growth or vulnerability, such as dependence. What is happening to the child in the dream will give a clue to what sort of feelings. If the dream child is one of your children, look up *son* or *daughter.* See **boy; girl;** *daughter* and *son* under **family, family relationships.**

choke Conflict; indecision, as when we choke on words; repression of emotion; an emerging emotion or memory.

Christ See **Jesus;** *Christ* under **archetypes; religion and dreams.**

christening Traditionally, the rite of christening represented the acceptance into the community of a new being. The name was given by the parents and recognized by the community. This may still be the meaning in some dreams. But it may also depict a change, a new beginning. The unconscious uses water and immersion to show how we, as a conscious person, may allow the unconscious process of life to wash through and transform us. See **baptism.**

chrysalis See **caterpillar.**

church Religious feeling or beliefs, including moral code; your feelings about organized religion; a sense of your relationship with the forces of life within you, and the world outside of you. A church may depict this sense and what you do with it; your sense of what is holy or fundamental to all life, and therefore eternal, such as the urge to exist; the cycles of life and growth; reproduction and interdependence; the qualities or functions you have developed or built in your personality that transcend the limitations of your identity; the physical structure of the church particularly represents these inbuilt qualities. See *Christ* under **archetypes; compensation theory; religion and dreams.**

cigar, cigarette Masculinity; penis. <u>Cigarette:</u> anxiety or release from it; dependence; feeling of having a support, a friend, or help to meet stress; may associate with feelings about cancer; feeling part of a group.

cinema Films often portray on the screen elements of our inner world, with its fantasies, fears, trauma, and passions. Looking at the screen is like looking at a mirror in which you see portrayed your inner life and drama. Therefore the cinema can depict these aspects of yourself; sometimes a place of romance, of sexual contact, or fantasies about it; films enlarge the area of your experience, just as dreams do, so some dreams might use this image to suggest vicarious experience. The cinema may also be a dream environment in which you can have an objective view of parts of your personality, as if they were film characters. See **film.**

circle   See **shapes, symbols.**

circus   The arena or area of awareness in which we can watch the instinctive drives and see how well they are socialized or brought under control. All the instinctive, physical, passionate sides of one's nature.

city, town   One's relationship and interaction with society, therefore the many choices you make or can make about direction, relationships, activities; one's sense of community; the mental and emotional environment in which one lives. <u>In some dreams:</u> work and opportunity. <u>Hometown or town of birth:</u> the familiar way of life; the way you usually go about things, or did in the past. <u>Strange town:</u> the new; different attitudes or way of life; new choices or opportunities. <u>Alone in a town:</u> feeling isolated and out of touch. <u>In a deserted town:</u> outmoded social attitudes or way of life. <u>Lost in a town:</u> feeling uncertain regarding your place or direction in society. <u>Idioms:</u> go to town; ghost town; man about town; paint the town.

cliff   On edge; danger; decision; taking a risk; a barrier; or the unknown, depending on dream content; a wider view of life, one that includes death; an uphill struggle in life; looking back or down, out of which one has wisdom; the test of self-trust, facing fear.

climb   We climb to avoid something; to get away; to climb out of some mess we are in, in which case it expresses effort on our part; we climb to get something, to reach it, so this can be ambition or motivation. But climbing has risks. Attaining new heights in work or relationship, we reach the new and face anxiety, so may have a fear of failing/falling. Climbing may also depict the first half of life, and going downhill middle or old age. We climb to see what is there, beyond, above, out of sight. <u>Idioms:</u> climb down; social climber. See **hill; mountain.**

clock   <u>Clock, watch:</u> the restrictions we place upon ourselves; sense of duty and timing; realization of urgency or having "lots of time." <u>Ticking clock:</u> might be the heart; life ticking away. <u>Big clock:</u> one's life—how much time is left. <u>Clock-watching:</u> tension; being bored or lacking satisfaction; feelings about aging. <u>Clock with hands still:</u> death. With <u>hands racing:</u> time running out; sense of urgency. <u>Alarm clock ringing:</u> message to wake up to something happening in your life, or to remember something you had set yourself to do; warning. See **time of day.**

close   To <u>close a door, etc.:</u> to be closed emotionally; decision; protectiveness. For close as in near, see **positions.** See *door* under **house, buildings.**

closet   See *closet, wardrobe* under **furniture, furnishings.**

clothes   Clothes can be the stance or attitudes we use to meet other people or special situations, such as work or danger; self-protection, such as might arise from one's feelings of reserve, shyness, anxiety, or aggressiveness used in fending off sexual or other advances; clothes can depict self-respect and how we see ourselves in society—the difference between what we want and what we feel others want of us; when we consider their color, our clothes can also express our emotional condition and moods. Constance Newland gives the example of dressing in violet symbolizing being inviolate sexually.

clothes

Clothes situations

<u>Armor, protective clothing:</u> defenses against internal anxieties, past hurts, and external intimacy. <u>Changing clothes:</u> altering one's mode of behavior, role, or mood. <u>Children's or teenage clothes in adult's dream:</u> youthful or immature attitudes or behavior. <u>Clothing inappropriate to dream surroundings:</u> attitudes or behavior inappropriate to one's situation. <u>Dirty or untidy clothes, if the dreamer's:</u> difficult or grubby feelings; one's inner condition, such as an untidy mind, or grubby-feeling values. <u>Man in woman's clothes:</u> unacceptability of male role, with its connection with breadwinning, aggression, being cannon fodder in war; homosexual tendency; desire for mother. <u>Naked or see-through clothes:</u> desire to be attractive and noticed or enjoying an acceptable form of intimacy; being open about what you really feel; fear of other people seeing what you really feel, think, and desire; anxiety about not being adequate socially; lacking ability to conform to social norm. See **nude.** <u>New clothes:</u> change in attitudes; new feeling about self. <u>Old but comfortable clothes:</u> aspects of self we may not express in public, but who we are when relaxed. <u>Other people's clothes worn by dreamer:</u> the social attitudes and responses we have adopted from others. <u>Overdressed, unable to get clothes off:</u> too cautious in relationships; difficulty in changing attitudes or self-image; self-protectiveness; avoiding intimacy. <u>Ragged or inappropriate clothes:</u> feelings of inadequacy; depressed feelings; rebellion against authority or society. <u>School clothes:</u> See **school.** <u>Tight clothes:</u> being too restricted in attitude; being tight emotionally. <u>Undressing:</u> revealing one's real character; move toward intimacy. <u>Woman in male clothes:</u> unacceptability of female role, motherhood, housewife; lesbian tendency; desire for father figure. <u>Worn out or old clothes:</u> attitudes ready to leave behind; old habits no longer useful; feeling worn-out, old, or tired. <u>Idioms:</u> dress to kill; dress up.

Types of clothing

apron　Mother role; household world; getting to work on a family situation.

belt　Often tightly restrained sexuality or emotions; protectiveness. <u>Idioms:</u> belt up; tighten one's belt.

blouse, shirt　Feelings and emotions; your public image. <u>Idioms:</u> stuffed shirt; shirtsleeves (informal).

coat　The general "self" we use in public—we might be shy in public but very warm with a single friend. *Overcoat:* usually protectiveness; not giving any secrets away; not showing intimacy or vulnerability; our belief system, political or religious, that we use to meet the world. Such systems may be a way of allaying anxiety about decisions and self-responsibility, and without them we may feel vulnerable and exposed; no display of intimacy. <u>Idioms:</u> dragged by one's coattails; up one's sleeve; coat of many colors.

dress　Femininity; exteriorization of feelings; how you present yourself to others. <u>Wedding dress:</u> see **marriage, wedding.**

gloves　Protection, as in wearing rubber gloves; keeping "one's hands clean," as in the sense of avoiding "dirty business"; being out of touch. Also, can represent someone's hand—holding their glove would be holding their hand. Picking up a dropped glove: similar to picking up a handkerchief dropped by a woman—an invitation to a relationship. <u>Idioms:</u> hand in glove with; iron fist in velvet glove; with kid gloves; with the gloves off.

hat　Opinions, beliefs, mental attitudes—for instance, a Jewish skullcap would represent the religious beliefs of the wearer; a role, such as would be suggested by a chef or

clothes

policeman's hat; protection, such as helmet. Idioms: at the drop of a hat; brass hat; eat one's hat; hang on to one's hat; under one's hat; old hat.

jacket   Feelings with which you clothe yourself. Particularly to do with degree of formality you present yourself with.

raincoat   The attitudes used to meet difficult emotions or events; often appears in dreams about dead spouse, suggesting tears or the release of emotions. See **rain.**

shoes   Position in life; life situation; one's character or chosen way of life; the character traits developed to deal with rough life situations; the condition of one's chosen direction—i.e., formal dancing shoes in a discotheque would suggest outmoded approach; a way of life. Some shoes are worn by particular social groups. Shoes from different roles—i.e., nurses' shoes: may indicate our need for the qualities of that role. Taking off shoes: leaving the past behind; dropping a long-established role; being open to change. See **nude.** Walking without shoes: going through a rough patch in life if walking is difficult; letting go of the everyday duties and responsibilities; contact with nature. Idioms: be in someone else's shoes; don't criticize your brother until you walk a mile in his moccasins; if the shoe fits, wear it; the shoe is on the other foot.

skirt   More particularly sexual than dress. Colors and length say a lot about what is being done with sexuality in a social sense.

socks   These are often used in dreams to represent the personal quality, cleanness, or untidiness of the person. They therefore depict some sort of judgment about what sort of person you are, or how you see someone. Socks also can represent particular roles, such as a footballer's socks, or special quality socks for business or social ritual. The strange idioms surrounding socks also show other associations, like "pull your socks up," "knocked my socks off" (suggesting a powerful experience). Socks can also be associated with warmth or protection from a difficult situation.

suit   The image you or other people have of you; the way you present yourself to others; formality; work; different suits—wet suit, bathing suit, etc.—represent different attitudes or feelings.

swimsuit, bikini   Relaxation; revealing your feelings.

tie   Sometimes represents something that chokes back feelings; formality; if colorful, it might represent creativity or a new approach to situations.

trousers   Maleness; protection; socialized sexuality. Idioms: wears the trousers; with their trousers down.

underclothes, underpants, briefs   Intimate sexual feelings. If *black:* restraint, or unconscious sex drives. Dirty or grubby: sex attitudes we are not proud of; difficult feelings about biological side of self.

work clothes   Working at something; attitudes concerning work.

clouds   If bright: usually feelings of upliftment or religious feelings. If dull: depression, feeling overshadowed by something.

coach   See **bus.**

coal   Money, good luck, energy; ancient unconscious knowledge you have brought to the surface. Such wisdom needs to be unfolded from the symbol by exploring the feelings and ideas connected with the image.

coat

coat   See *coat* under **clothes**.

coffee   Social contact; something stimulating; a dependency; health risk. <u>Offering, being offered:</u> friendship, intimacy; what we thirst for or desire.

coffin   Nearly always a reminder of one's own mortality. Thoughts and feelings about death are often in the background of our mind, and dreaming of a coffin suggests you may be exploring how you relate to death. Sometimes, if the coffin is linked with someone you know, it may show a hidden desire to get them out of your life. Perhaps worries about the health of the person, or fear of losing them. The coffin can also depict death and rebirth. Also, death of a relationship and the feelings of loss; one's feelings about the death of someone, such as husband. See **funeral**.

coin   This may represent something you value, so can have a very wide significance. For instance, two gold coins in one person's dream represented his twin sons, who were of great value to him. If the money is dirty, it may be a suggestion that you are living beneath your best motives, earning money in a grubby way. Because we call loose money "change" in English, sometimes the coins might represent change in your life—small changes. See **money**.

cold   Held-back emotions, especially fear; feeling neglected or "left out in the cold"; sometimes connected with feelings about death. <u>Idioms:</u> cold shoulder; cold storage; cold feet; in cold blood; cold refreshing; cold murderous rage.

collective unconscious   Jung describes this as the "inherited potentialities of human imagination. It is the all-controlling deposit of ancestral experiences from untold millions of years, the echo of prehistoric world events to which each century adds an infinitesimal small amount of variation and differentiation. These primordial images are the most ancient, universal, and deep thoughts of mankind."

Jung tried to explain his observation of a strata of consciousness in which individual minds have their collective origin in a genetic way. This seems unlikely, and Rupert Sheldrake sees it as a mental phenomena. Dr. Maurice Bucke called it Cosmic Consciousness. J. B. Priestly saw it as "the flame of life" that synthesized the experience of all living things and held within itself the essentials of all lives. If we think of it as a vast collective memory of all that has existed, then the life of Edgar Cayce exhibited a working relationship with it.

Language can be seen as a physical expression of this collective mind. Within language lie all the ideas, feelings, and struggles of untold generations. We live it and express it in daily life, yet it existed prior to birth and will survive our death. See **Cayce, Edgar; religion and dreams; sea.**

collision   This may be telling you that a conflict of opinions with another person or careless behavior leading to problems in relationship is happening.

colors   In many dreams where color predominates, there are usually strong feelings, as in the example. This suggests colors depict emotions and feeling tones. Where a dreamer is largely intellectual or out of touch with their feelings, the color would stand in the place of the emotion, instead of alongside it as with Elise D.

Example: "I was standing in a very beautifully carved chapel or religious place. There seemed to be shadowy nun- or monklike figures around. But it was the exquisite coloring of the place that filled me with a sort of ecstasy. Everything was in the most delicate shell pink." (Elise D.)

White is the most frequently mentioned color in the collection of dreams used for this book. Black is next, then blue.

black   The Unconscious; unknown; hidden or avoided; evil; the unaccepted side of self; not being aware; depression;

negative; secrecy; fear; death. Also, the earthy, or source of life and growth. What is hidden in the unconscious or body can be powerfully transformative. <u>Black animals:</u> unconscious drives and urges. See **dark.** <u>Black clothes or undergarments:</u> hidden or unconscious feelings or sexuality.

blue   <u>Dark blues:</u> in many women's dreams, threatening men appear dressed in dark blue or navy blue overalls; depression; negative thoughts or intuition. <u>Light blues:</u> our sense of intuition; having a wide awareness of life; religious feelings. Also, coolness of nature. Often seen in visions of the womb as a blue grotto or woman with halo of blue, so connects with prenatal and infant relationship with mother. <u>Idioms:</u> blue film; blue funk; blue pencil; blue-stocking; feel blue; out of the blue; vanish into the blue; blue-blood; true blue; once in a blue moon.

brown   Depression; dullness; earthiness; excrement; concealment. <u>Idioms:</u> brown study; browned-off.

gold, golden   Something that is valuable or of deep significance; very attractive.

gray   Unhappy or colorless dull existence; the daily round without color; morbid or serious thoughts; officiousness.

green   Potential for growth; healing or positive change. Often found in dreams about heaven. <u>Dark greens:</u> evil intentions; growth of negative attitudes; sickness; envy; jealousy. <u>Idioms:</u> green fingers; green light; green (naive).

indigo, violet   Mostly religious feelings; intuition.

orange   Blending or balance of emotions and intellect. Sometimes, warmth; religious feelings or insight.

pink   Softness; femininity; a baby girl; tender love rather than passionate love, the sort one might have for a child. See *red* below.

red   Even where red appears quite casually in a dream, there is frequently fear, screaming, horror, or a sense of danger in the same dream; red also represents one's basic emotions, earthy nature, and sexuality. In these senses it depicts one's strength or vitality and down-to-earth health and power. Because of the modern association with traffic lights and warnings such as brake lights on cars, it may sometimes be used as a warning, or a way of saying "stop" or "no." See *blood* under **body;** *blood* under **archetypes.** Less frequently: blood; menstruation; the biological life-force; conception; reproduction; death. Pale pink: baby feelings; weakness. Red and gray often appear together: emotions connected with depression. Red brick building: homeliness; warmth. Red clothes, motif: sexuality; passion; strong emotions. Red earth: fertility; richness; the healing power of the body; the collective memory of past human struggles and discoveries that we now inherit as personal or social skills, or ease of performance of things that would have been difficult or impossible for our ancestors. Red face: anger; high emotion. Red flowers: love; passion; dangers of passion. Red furniture, decor; plush: richness; comfort. Rose pink: love. Idioms: see red; in the red; red carpet; red-light district; red-faced; red tape.

white   Awareness; clearness of mind; purity; cleanness; light feelings. In certain dreams white is very threatening. Perhaps we have connections with hospitals in these dreams. Maggots, mold, dead or sick people, and shrouds can also be white, so white can depict death or sickness. White clothes: a sense of wholeness; purity or marriage. White animals: urges and sexuality that has been accepted or integrated with conscious activities. Example: "There was a huge white kitchen. I was scared when I entered it and there was a door leading out of it into a white corridor with a turquoise carpet that scared me even more." (H.H.)

colors

yellow Lightness of feeling; intellect; extroversion; cowardice; intuition; caution or quarantine; hopefulness for the future.

comb Something you are doing or thinking about doing to tidy up your thoughts or self-presentation. <u>Idioms:</u> fine-tooth comb.

comet Sign of coming changes, new influences from within, birth of a new self.

compass Your attempt to find a direction or activity you feel confident about.

compensation theory Jung, Hadfield, and several other dream researchers believe the dream process is linked with homeostasis or self-regulation. See *Man and His Symbols,* Jung; *Dreams and Nightmares,* Hadfield; *Mind and Movement: Liberating the Body,* Crisp. This means that the process underlying dream production helps keep psychological balance, just as homeostasis keeps body functions balanced by producing perspiration when hot, shivering when cold, and the almost miraculous minutiae of internal changes. Despite self-regulation or homeostasis being an obvious and fundamental process in the body, in nature and the cosmos as a whole, it still appears difficult for many people investigating the mind to accept a similar function psychologically.

Put bluntly, dreams are said to compensate for conscious attitudes and personality traits. So the coldly intellectual man might have dreams expressive of feelings and the irrational as part of a compensatory process. The ascetic might dream of sensuous pleasures, and the lonely unloved child dream of affection and comfort. But this is only the most basic aspect of compensation.

Jung's view of compensation was far more inclusive. He quotes as an example the dream of an elderly general he met while sitting opposite him on a train journey. The general told Jung that he had dreamt he was on parade with younger officers while being inspected by the commander in chief. On reaching the general the commander asked him to define beauty. This surprised the general, as he expected to be asked technical questions regarding his service. He was embarrassed and could not give a clear answer. The commander in chief then asked a young major the same question and received a clearer answer. The general experienced feelings of failure and his grief woke him. Jung's questioning led the general to realize that the young major who successfully answered the query about beauty actually looked just like himself when he was that age and a major. Further questioning led to the information that at that age the general had been interested in art, but the pressure of work and the rigidity of the military life had eroded the interest. Jung goes on to suggest that the dream in his late life was helping to compensate for the one-sided development necessitated by his army career. The dream, in fact, reminded the general of this neglected side of himself.

This concept of wholeness, linked with the Self, which such compensatory dreams connect with, is best seen in the collection of many years' dreams by an individual undertaking their own personal journey to self-acceptance and integration. Through an overview of dreams gained in this way, the two aspects of compensation become much more clearly drawn. The dream work, aimed at meeting the neglected or hurt parts of oneself, opens the way to more pronounced compensation. See **computers and dreams; gestalt dream work; movements during sleep; science sleep and dreams.**

compost   The irritating, useless, outgrown parts of yourself, the energies of which can be reused once the habitual methods of expressing them have broken down; the extraction of fertile ideas and insight from digesting old experience.

computer Powers of the mind; rational unemotional mind; personal potential or abilities; memory; looking into the unconscious or activities of the mind; perhaps the extended faculties of the mind. See **email; internet; modem; record, cassette, CD, computer disc.**

computer, dream process as a The brain is not a computer, but it has the power to compute. The word *"computare"* is Latin, and comes from *"putare,"* to think. Neither is a computer anything like a human brain. But there are parallels. Christopher Evans, a psychologist, computer scientist, and world authority on microprocessors, said the brain and computers are both information handling devices—taking impulses that in themselves mean nothing, like sound waves, and processing them. It was also his theory that both computers and the waking brain function are taken "off line" to reprogram. Our behavior responses and information bases need bringing up-to-date with new experience and information received. In the case of the computer, "off line" means having modifications made to programs. In the human it means sleeping and dreaming—the dream being the powerful activity of review, sifting, and reprogramming. Furthermore, the brain and computer use "programs." In humans, a program means a set of learned responses, values, or activities, such as walking or talking, but including more subtle activities such as judging social or business situations.

If, as Christopher Evans believes, dreaming is partly a period of revising and updating responses, insights, and skills, then by working with the process one can make it more efficient. The background for this statement is that many people have recurring dreams that change very little. Looking at this from the "programming" view, the attempt to revise is thwarted. But individuals can free such "stuck" dreams by using dream processing. See **gestalt dream work; processing your dreams.**

computers and dreams Because of the ease with which computers can file, sort, cross-reference, and present information, a great deal of work has been done in analyzing the content of thousands of dreams. As computers are an everyday part of many homes, we can easily use them to gain insight into our dreams. Three areas of helpfulness are:

1. We can enter many dreams, then with a program such as dtSearch or Alchera can easily scan through them to see the frequency of dream themes. Also, one can link one section of the dream record with another section. If you categorize your dreams with labels—such as "work," "relationship," "anxiety"—you can easily find all the dreams in any category. See *http://www.dtsearch.com*.

2. Most modern word processors have a word search facility that easily locates words or phrases. Thus you can easily look back over past dreams to find where a particular symbol occurred, and what you said about it at the time. This approach to dreams—insight through a series of dreams—is explained by Hall in *The Meaning of Dreams*. Important issues in your life and development occur as frequent dream themes, and are easily seen using a computer. See **series of dreams.**

3. The program Alchera *(http://mythwell.com/index.html)* is specialized software for recording and gaining insight into your dreams. It has ready-made comments on dream symbols, much as this book does. But it is possible, for instance, to dream of a tree, write your associations with the dream image, and develop your symbol information. If you then dreamt of a tree six months later and entered this, the program instantly reminds you of the past reference to tree and can display it. Gradually a reference base of your dreams and comments can

be built up and quickly scanned. Such comparisons help you to form a personality profile of yourself or others. See **Hall, Calvin.**

conditioned reflex   Although we are used to thinking of animals showing conditioned reflexes, we seldom realize what a large part they play in human life. This is obvious in the problems we would face in going against social conditioning. When we move against an implicit social conditioning, we feel the pressure or pain of that—whether it is sexual, clothing, or whatever it is. If we go against such conditioning we may discover the underlying feelings and forces that have created the conditioning in the first place. Dreams often reveal to us what our conditioning is, and how it was imprinted.

conformity   One of the most powerful, and largely unconscious, urges we have is to conform to the way of life, beliefs, clothing, and styles lived by the people around us. Even if we are an unconformist, there are still huge areas of our mind, beliefs, and views of the world that conform to well-established patterns. So if there are elements of your dream in which you do not conform, or you are aware of yourself conforming, it marks great change. This is because you are becoming aware of your conformity, and might thus change it if you wished.

confused   Confusion and perhaps conflict in your life. There are usually good reasons why we feel bewildered, and such feelings may arise from an intuitive level where there is memory of past experience informing us about the present. The confusion may also arise from opposing inner feelings or external differences. See **emotions, mood.**

conjurer   See *magician* under **roles.**

contraceptive   See **birth control.**

control, controlling   There is a huge area of learned skills given over to various sorts of control. This starts from a very young age when we learn not to mess our pants, and later to ride a bike and drive a car. Being out of control can arouse a great deal of fear, or even terror. Yet learning to be out of control is tremendously important. Many things in life are beyond our control—even our heartbeat and life processes. Many things, such as a relationship, confront us with areas that are also difficult to control. The spontaneous and creative becomes less frequent if we are too controlled or rigid. Therefore it is important to define what your dream is describing if questions of control or lack of control are portrayed. See if you can discover what you are meeting, and what a wise stance might be.

convict   This may be depicting antisocial urges, or feelings of being trapped, perhaps by your undirected emotions and reactions to events. It may also show how you are holding back some of your feelings and urges. See **prison.**

cook   See *cook* under **roles; cooking.**

cookie   See *cookie* under **food.**

cooking   As in the example below, ways we transform "inedible" or "unpalatable" aspects of life; nourishing ourselves; satisfying a hunger; creativity; our ability to make something new of the varied opportunities or experiences we have; giving of oneself. See *cook* under **roles; food;** *kitchen* under **house, buildings.**
    Example: "I saw piles of French loaves. On picking one up I saw that although the crust was crisp, the inside was runny wet dough. I wondered if cooking would make them edible." (Derek L.)

cord   May be similar to chain or rope—restriction. But often depicts the feeling bonds we have with another person or situation; the umbilical, in the sense of dependency that holds us. <u>Breaking the cord:</u> becoming independent of parents or authority figures—often anger or resentment is directed at the person we are dependent upon. Also, might be a play on words, as in "struck a cord"; in accord. See *umbilical cord* under **body; rope.**

corn   Whether this is corn on the cob or wheat, it probably links with a harvest, a reward from work done. It also suggests fertility, nourishment, and a sense of fullness. In some dreams it may represent sustenance or strength in times of need or trial.

corner   Feeling trapped or restricted; or as in the second example, a hidden or little admitted aspect of oneself. Occasionally such boundaries or restrictions might produce a sense of snugness or security. When a <u>street or projected room corner:</u> the unexpected or unseen; new experience; public gaze; indecision or the act of making a decision; turning point. <u>Idioms:</u> drive somebody into a corner; in a tight corner; knock the corners off someone; turn the corner; hole-in-the-corner affair.
   Example 1: "I was afraid the thugs would corner and attack me." (Sasha) Example 2: "I went into an obscure corner of the cloakroom and hung up the coat—then I went through the pockets." (Ms. Williams)

corpse   See *dead body* under **body.**

corridor   See *corridor* under **house, buildings.**

cosmetic   Desire to attract attention; our public traits; cover-up; an attempt to improve oneself.

coughing   In many cases this links with emotions that have got trapped and are trying to be expressed. Sometimes, if you are coughing up lumps of something, then it is probably past experience and the feelings attached to it that are irritating you and seeking release.

Talk the dream and the feelings over with a sympathetic friend to see if you can touch your feelings more fully. Occasionally the word is used as a suggestion of coffin. This would be indicated by the tone of the dream.

cousin Probably represents your opinions or feelings about that person. See *relatives* under **family, family relationships.**

country See **abroad** or specific country; **countryside.**

countryside One's natural spontaneous feelings; a relaxed state; the forces of "nature" in us; moods—a rainy countryside would be a more introverted mood than a lively sunny scene. Country lanes: meeting what is natural in us—this may disturb the dreamer, perhaps being in the form of a wolf or animal. See **road; landscapes;** *farmer* under **roles; settings.**

couple See *couple* under **people.**

cover This has many possibilities, but the most frequent are to do with protection, concealment, or inclusiveness—i.e., including something, as when two people cover themselves with a sheet, suggesting togetherness. It might also be used to mean a creation of an atmosphere. Another possibility is that it means some sort of situation—when someone is covered by flies, suggesting an impressive and perhaps unnerving situation.

crab See *shellfish* and *crab* under **fish.**

crack A flaw in one's thinking; a weakness in the attitudes or defenses we use in meeting life; the unexpected; the irrational breaking through into consciousness; the vagina. Idioms: cracking up; crack of doom; paper over the cracks.

crane   See *crane* under **birds.** <u>Mechanical crane:</u> you might be undergoing powerful changes, or making major decisions.

crater   Memory of old hurt, old emotion or pain, or a frightening situation. If it is volcanic, a crack in the outer self through which inner repressed passions might pour out.

crazy   Being mad or irrational in a dream, or meeting a person or animal that is mad or insane, usually shows us facing urges to behave, or emotions, that feel very threatening, or we cannot understand rationally. Perhaps they are drives that were sane in a past environment. The dream madness is often a partial expression of feelings that might be sane if we could allow them expression in their fullness. Pains and inhibition tend to twist and malform what might otherwise be healthy, or prevent us from properly understanding them. <u>Being confronted by mad person, people:</u> meeting parts of oneself that have not been integrated with our present situation; cultural fear we have about meeting the unconscious. <u>Being mad:</u> feeling threatened by the irrational and perhaps disintegrated aspects of the unconscious. See **anger.**

cream   Best of life; luxury; special treatment; affection.

creativity and problem-solving in dreams   Few dreams are by themselves problem-solving or creative. The few exceptions are usually very clear. When they occur the problem-solving can apply to a wide range of human experience. For instance, the problem might be personal or psychological. It might be a mathematical problem. It could be an insight that produced a creative idea, thus solving a problem to do with questions being asked or something being attempted.

   Although in any collection of dreams clear-cut problem-solving is fairly rare, nevertheless problem-solving appears to be a basic function of dreams. The proof of this lies in research done in dream withdrawal. As explained in the entry **science sleep and dreams,** subjects are woken as they begin to dream, therefore denying them dreams. This quickly leads to disorientation and breakdown of normal functioning. Therefore, a lot of problem-solving is occurring in dreams even though it may not be obvious. In other words, the factors that lead to the breakdown when dreams are withdrawn is being dealt with. This feature of dreaming can be enhanced to a marked degree by processing dreams and arriving at insights into the information they contain. This enables old problems to be cleared and new information and attitudes to be brought into use more quickly.

To approach your dreams in order to discover their creativity, first decide what problematical or creative aspect of your life needs "dream power." Define what you have already learned or know about the problem. Write it down, and from this clarify what it is you want more insight into. If this breaks down into several issues, choose one at a time. Think about the issue and pursue it as much as you can while awake. Read about it, ask people's opinions, gather information. This is all data for the dream process. If the question still needs further insight, before going to sleep imagine you are putting the question to your internal store of wisdom, computer, power center, or whatever image feels right. For some people, an old being who is neither exclusively man or woman is a working image. In the morning note whatever dream you remember. It does not matter if the dream does not appear to deal with the question. Investigate the dream using the techniques given in the entry **processing your dreams.** Some problems take time to define, so use the process until there is a resolution. If it is a major life problem, it may take a year or so. After all, some resolutions need restructuring of the personality, because the problem cannot disappear while we still have the same attitudes and fears. See **gestalt dream work; processing your dreams.**

149

creatures Sometimes we dream about creatures that are not like any animal we know—perhaps ancient, mixtures of plants and animals. These can represent our fear of things like bacteria, or illness due to microorganisms. Occasionally they may even represent what such an illness is doing in the body.

credit card The feelings you have about money; the opportunities, power, and pleasures it brings, or the stress and uncertainty involved with it; ability to get what you want, or to feel secure. <u>Having or getting a credit card:</u> a sense of gaining greater ease and opportunity with money; finding an easier feeling about relating to the world and having the power to move around in it; temptation to spend. <u>Loss or destruction of credit card:</u> uncertainty about your financial future; feeling of stress or struggle to get your needs in life; loss of power. See **money.**

creeper Doubts, insinuations, stagnancy, vegetating.

cripple Difficulty in fulfilling your potential. The parts of your body usually represent the psychological functions they play. So a leg would represent your ability to stand up for yourself, to be independent, etc. Therefore, being crippled suggests psychological hurt to whatever limb or part of body is crippled. See **body; left, right.**

crocodile See *alligator* under **animals.**

cross See *cross* under **shapes, symbols.**

crossing A change, but often with much vulnerability; an obstacle, usually of a feeling nature, to overcome. Maybe fear or uncertainty causes you to be unable to make the change, then you might dream of a bridge giving way. Such changes are often to do with major life junctures, such as from youth to adulthood; prepuberty to adolescent; single to married; young to middle age. Sometimes, a trial or test, such as initiation. <u>Crossing a river or chasm:</u> apart from change, sometimes depicts the death of someone. See **bridge; river; road; individuation.**

crossroad   Decision—as in the example below; union of opposites; conflict. Crossroads also have a certain amount of anxiety involved, as with crossing.

Example: "I keep in touch with an old boyfriend who I have not seen since I was eighteen, that is fourteen years ago. In my dream I was on holiday on a coach that stopped at a crossroads. I met my old boyfriend, who had come from the other direction, and we walked together. I felt enormous pleasure being in his company again. A hearse passed us slowly with a child's coffin." (P. B.) In trying to decide what direction to take, P. B. still finds emotions tie her to the past, but the dead child shows she really knows the relationship has ended.

crow   See *crow, raven, rook* under **birds.**

crowd   Feeling crowded out; public opinion; your feelings about people in general; anonymity; camouflage. <u>Lost in a crowd:</u> feeling without personal direction; confusion on meeting many opinions; desire not to stand out. <u>Attacked by crowd:</u> fear of public opinion; feeling one's own angry urges as threatening. <u>Talking to, leading, or part of crowd at a central event:</u> an impulse or idea that unifies many parts of one's own nature—as the many aspects of our being, such as visual impressions, sensuality, thoughts, musical sense, religious feelings, sexual drive, intuition, fear, ambition, hunger, desire for acclaim, the sadist in us, and so on constitute a crowd. <u>How we relate to the crowd:</u> suggests our relationship with our inner community and the external public. Being unable to tolerate parts of oneself leads to intolerance toward external people with those traits. See *group* under **people.**

crutch Substitute, sense of incapacity. Something you use or do because the real thing is not functioning. For instance, alcohol or cigarettes might be a crutch.

crying The release of sorrow, grief, misery that has been held back, knowingly or unknowingly, during the day. It may be an intuitive knowledge of another person leaving, or dying; or sorrow over something we have done. Or else they might be crocodile tears in an attempt to convince ourselves that we feel badly over an attitude, desire, or action.

crystal Sense of the eternal; the self; rigid views or emotions; crystallized opinions, thus habits. Crystal ball: intuition.

crypt This often depicts your unconscious memories or feelings. But it may be connected more with repressed parts of self, or family influences from the long past. It may also link with feelings about the unconscious, or fear of death. See **cave;** *basement, cellar* under **house, buildings.**

cuckoo See *cuckoo* under **birds.**

cuddly toy See **teddy bear; toys.**

cul-de-sac Sense of efforts leading nowhere; a woman's legs—vagina at the end; a sexual relationship leading nowhere.

cup Offering oneself; a woman offering herself and sexuality; a receptive state of being that can receive intuitively from the unconscious.

curse Autosuggestion. That is, inner results of fears entertained such as negative fears we carry within; the inheritance of past actions; past lives, or hereditary traits or taints; the power of material values to influence decisions and life; an intuition of someone wishing you ill.

curtains   The ability to reveal or hide something, such as we do with feelings or thoughts, perhaps even memories; privacy; homemaking; luxury or poverty, depending on the curtains; the ability to shut the world out, or to remain withdrawn in sleep.

cutting   To sever connections, to become independent, to cut off sympathy or affections; to injure, or desire to injure; sexual desires that express as the desire to hurt, to cut, to enter through pain through experiences of being let down, scorned, ill-treated; can also mean reducing in importance or impact.

cyclone   See **tornado.**

cyst   A morbid collection of memories, emotions, energies, that are not harmonizing or adding to your life in general.

D

dagger   Aggressive urges, hatred, expression of force—whether intellectual, moral, or physical; the ability to cut through difficulties. Can denote penis. See **weapons.**

dam   Bottled-up emotions and drives, such as ambition or sexuality. There is often tremendous power or energy waiting to be used or directed. So it can depict the controlled release of such emotional energy.

dancing   Feeling at one with someone, or with aspects of yourself; unity, as seen in the cells working as a harmonious whole; happiness; sexual mating dance; getting closer or more intimate. If the <u>dance is awkward:</u> lack of harmony connected with what is depicted. <u>Animals dancing:</u> harmony with unconscious drives and sexuality. <u>Skeletons or dark "things" dancing:</u> developing a relationship with what we fear, meeting it; dancing with death—in life we always dance with death, meaning we have an intimate relationship with it, but might not be ready to recognize who our partner is.

Example: "We were both shy of each other but as the dance went on I found I could move so well to his steps that we felt like one. It was so effortless that it felt like floating." (Andrea)

dark   What is unknown; not defined by the intellect or conscious self; things you are unaware of; depression; confusion; feelings of evil; secrets we hide from self or others, or things we don't want to know about ourselves; things we do "under cover of darkness"; old or worn-out; the womb; death. <u>Dark water:</u> emotions that are felt and powerful but have not been defined or their source understood. <u>Dark colors:</u> feelings emanating from unconscious sources; depressed or unhappy feelings. <u>Idioms:</u> a dark horse; in the dark; keep it dark.

date

calendar date   This needs to be considered in connection with the other parts of the dream. It can relate to something that happened on that date in the past, and is still important to you in some way. If not that, try looking for what you associate with the month, year, and numbers in the date.

romantic "date"   Hopes about a relationship. Release of pleasurable feelings about yourself.

daughter   See *daughter* under **family, family relationships**

day and night

day   Mostly our mood; being conscious; "seeing" what we are doing; waking experience. See **light; time of day.**

night   Similar to dark. Usually the unconscious; dark or little sensed areas of oneself; loneliness; areas of subtly felt urges or feelings. Sometimes, freedom. We may be constrained by the social or moral rules we apply to ourselves during the "day" or waking consciousness. But on the edge of consciousness, or in sleep, we find a wonderful freedom that allows us escape. Sometimes shown by escaping from a house at night and running away. See **dark.**

dead end   See **cul-de-sac.**

dead people dreams   People we know who have died. Most dreams in which dead people appear are expressive of attempts to deal with our memories, feelings, guilt, or anger in connection with the person who died; or feelings about death. When someone close to us dies we go through a period of change from relating to them as an external reality, to meeting and accepting them as alive in our memories and inner life. <u>Dead husband or wife:</u> many dreams of dead people come from women who have lost their husband. It is common to have disturbing dreams for some period afterward; or not to be able to dream about the husband or wife at all; or to see the partner in the distance but not get near. In accepting the death, meeting any feelings of loss, grief, anger, and continuing love, such dreams gradually become happier and resolved.

dead person or body   Usually represents some area of your life that has "died." This can refer to death of feelings, such as hopelessness in connection with relationship and the loss of feelings about someone; the depression that follows big changes in life, such as loss of a loved partner, job, children; a sense of one's life in general being without the stimulus of motivation and satisfaction, as when one feels oneself in a "going nowhere" relationship or life situation; repressed anger killing positive expression. The dead person in the dream may link several of these feelings together, as symbols often represent huge areas of experience. So the dead person may be a part of yourself you want to leave behind, to die out.

death and dreaming   In every moment of our life we face the possibility of death. It is not surprising then that the subject of death figures in many dreams. As with any major life event, in our dreams we meet death in various forms as part of our attempt to develop a working relationship with it. Such dreams enable us to become aware of what our deepest fears or feelings are regarding our own death, or the death of someone we love or know. In the example below, for instance, the dreamer does not face any great fear of death itself. The strongest feelings are of loss. Over a period of time the dreamer may move beyond such feelings of loss into exploring other possibilities of death.

Example: "I was due to be executed—what for I don't know. I was not especially afraid of this, but my most vivid feelings were of great sadness at the people I was leaving behind, and for all the things I wanted to do in life, but would not now be able to. Then at the end I was watching myself being hanged."

Examining many dreams dealing with death, it is noticeable that some dreamers are stuck in fearful or grief laden feelings, while others move on into a positive relationship with the ending of life. The difference appears to be centered on what level of emotion the dreamer can tolerate and accept, and how daring they are. Many people, on meeting death in their dream, awake with feelings of pain, fear, or dread. If they could fully meet those feelings they would pass on to develop a very different experience of death in their dreams. The following waking dream illustrates this.

I knew I was dying and it was incredibly real. So real I wept deeply because I knew this was the end of everything and I would lose my children. All that I had created in life would be at an end too. But there was nothing I could do about that and I died. Then I seemed to be at a slight distance watching my dead body, and I saw my father, who had died some years before, come and carry the body over a threshold into a heavenly meadow. There a resurrection took place. I was given new life. And the new life came from all that I had given to others, and all I had received from others, during my life. That was my spiritual life.

As can be seen from this beautiful experience, the dreamer meets the depth of feeling connected with the final ending of life, then moves beyond it. So the last part of the dream is not an avoidance of pain, but an acceptance of the finality of death and how it is transcended by giving ourselves away to others, and receiving from them.

decay Something in your life not being alive and expressive; something you are not proud of, or you feel "rotten" about; something not working well in your body or feelings.

deep Usually we live on the surface of our mind. In sleep we dive down deeper but lose sense of self. If we maintain some awareness in these "deeps" of the mind, it is somewhat like snorkeling in deep sea. We realize what immense and unbelievable depths lie beneath us. Dreams often portray this as depth—a hole; deep water; a chasm; space; also nonverbal life in the womb, or early childhood, which is remembered as patterns of feeling reaction rather than verbal utterance. In the depths we may find gems, skeletons, archaeological objects, and these relate to the memory of our evolutionary past, family influences we carry within us unknown. Deep cuts: suggests a hurt that penetrates us; or emotions that affect us powerfully. Idioms: in deep water; in the deep end; deeply troubled; deeply hurt.

deer See *deer* under **animals.**

defecate Self-expression; release of tension; getting rid of negative experience or emotions; creative expression; permitting the natural in oneself. See **excrement.**

defense Any sort of defense system, such as a castle, a shield, weapons, fighting, may depict one of the basic ways of dealing with life—being defensive. Defensiveness means that in some way one wards off the impact of life experiences. In this way the influence of these experiences, negative or positive, are kept from being taken in and absorbed or integrated. For instance, a person may have very rigid religious beliefs and defend themselves from hearing anything that enlarges or questions these beliefs. They may do this by arguing away any other ideas or experiences, or by holding a sense of righteousness and difference between themselves and other people. Similarly, one can defend using clever intellectual argument that yet has no open doors to allow new ideas, feelings, or experience. See **castle; defense mechanisms;** *anima* under **archetypes.**

defense mechanisms   Although the dream process attempts to release difficult emotions, trauma, and past experience, most people have built-in mechanisms that prevent this spontaneous healing activity. It is natural to pull our hand away from a hot surface because of the pain. We do this "without thinking"—unconsciously, in fact. Similarly, we unconsciously pull away from any painful or frightening emotions, even though it may be in our best interests to release or integrate them. The nonrelease leads to physical tension, a massive use of energy to contain such emotions, and even development of physical illness. Resistance may also be in the form of not wanting to change, fear of the new, feeling threatened by fresh views of life, or any questioning of the values one has long lived by. To free oneself from such resistances needs a positive motivation and the learning of new psychological and even physical skills, as presented in present forms of self-help and psychotherapy.

deformity   Part of your nature that due to fear, repression, or ignorance has not been able to grow in its natural beauty. This often happens from traumatic childhood experience; something you do not like about yourself.

déjà vu   Many dreamers say they find a connection between a place they dream of—especially a house—and a place they later see while awake. Most of these descriptions appear to be attempts to find connections obvious to no one but the dreamer. A strong desire to have the inner world connect with the real world seems to be the motivation. This may be through a need to have meaning and connection with a wider, invisible life. "Déjà vu" literally means "seen before." The valid cases of it are rare. Nevertheless, people do have dreams and experiences in which they can demonstrate they have been to a place before, yet not physically. The most common explanation is that of reincarnation. The Bralornes, for instance, on tour to India, stepped off their tour boat into Bombay for the first time. Within minutes Mr. Bralorne knew what street they would shortly arrive at, giving its name. This continued, until he had a memory of a house that he thought should be at the foot of Malabar Hill, with a big banyan tree in front of it. The couple asked a policeman if such a house existed. He said such a house had been on that very spot. His father had been a servant in the house, and it had belonged to the Bhan family. This really amazed the Bralornes, as they had called their son Bhan Bralorne.

demolition Major changes in your inner or outer life have been, or are being, undertaken; breakdown of old attitudes and approaches.

demons See **devil**; *devil* under **archetypes.**

dentist See *dentist* under **roles.**

departing A breaking away from old or habitual patterns of behavior; leaving a situation, such as a relationship, a financial setup, or work; the struggle to become independent, as in leaving home; change. Sometimes, desire to get away from responsibility or difficulties. Can also refer to death, perhaps when we see a spouse walking away from us, or departing on journey. This is not necessarily a prediction, but confronting the situation. Idioms: new departure; the departed dead; leave in the lurch; leave someone to it; left holding the baby.

depression and dreams One hundred forty dreams were collected from a group of patients suffering depression. The same number of dreams were collected from people similar in age and social background, but not suffering depression. The dreams were given code numbers, mixed, and given to an independent judge. He was asked to look for any evident themes of self-punishment—such as "I was waiting for my friends all night but they never turned up," "My fiancé married somebody else." Such self-punishing themes occurred with greater frequency in depressive's dreams. These self-punishing themes can be changed using such techniques as outlined under **processing your dreams.**

descending, down Something below us: can depict past trauma that is not being faced, literally run away from; something we have left behind or we feel "above." Descent, going down stairs or in an elevator: getting more down-to-earth or practical; a return to difficulties after living in fantasies or escapism; depression; sexual restraint; a return from meta conception. See **aura.** Descending into cave, cellar, or hole: meeting repressed wisdom or fears carried unconsciously from family or culture; experience of womb existence. Going down a hill: can mean loss of status; aging; failure, illness, or death; fear of being out of control; positive sense of exhilaration. Idioms: feel down; down-and-out; down in the dumps; down-to-earth.

desert or wilderness Loneliness—literally being deserted; lack of emotion or satisfaction; no creativity or growth in one's life; dry intellectualism; social isolation; sexual barrenness. Occasionally, as the symbol in the Bible of wandering in the wilderness, depicts both the human sense of having no real meaning or direction and of being a wanderer in the infinity of time and decision. It shows the difficulty of being self-responsible and making decisions in the infinity of choices.

desk Work; authority; discipline; communication; a project you are dealing with.

destination Because the unconscious has a powerful faculty for synthesizing experience, it frequently arrives at a sense of what we most wish for, or want to create through life. Yet we may not have become aware of what is realized unconsciously. This may be depicted by a place we are heading toward, or a goal; a destination we do not remember; our conscious ambition and desire; hopes; what we have struggled long for. See **direction.**

devil The devil in your dreams usually represents the parts of your urges and emotions you have repressed or do not feel in control of. The angers or urges may even feel to us as if they are strong enough to control us, so we represent them as an external force pushing us to some sort of evil. In each of us there is the potential for creativity or destruction. This is especially noticeable in connection with fears, such as fear of illness. Such a fear, if based on imagination rather than a real cause, can still cause illness. In this sense our mind can turn against us. This enemy—our undirected fear—may be pictured as the devil or an evil entity. See *devil* under **archetypes; evil; aboriginal; active/passive.**

devour, devoured <u>Being eaten by dogs or creatures:</u> losing your sense of identity, or what you think or want, in meeting other people's will, anger, or ideas; being "consumed" by fear, pain, emotion, or a drive; fear of death. <u>Swallowed by large creature or fish:</u> opening to awareness of unconscious content. <u>Devouring:</u> being possessive; hungering for something.

diamond See **jewels.**

diary Memories; insights into yourself; looking within and discovering things you might not otherwise know.

dice Fate, chance, luck, a gamble.

digest To absorb, to make use of, to understand and incorporate into your way of life. To accept. See **eating; food.**

digging, excavation   Delving into hidden or buried areas of ourselves. We may uncover feelings from childhood, creative realizations, features of the unconscious, even dead bodies or ancient creatures. Digging can also represent work on renovating our attitudes, personality structure, or habits. See **garden.**

dimension   See **world** for other dimensions.

dinner   See *meals* under **food.**

dinosaur   In terms of evolution, our personality is a young, new thing. It grows throughout life, but its roots reach into the ancient processes of life and consciousness active in us. These processes are as old as life on this planet. Life on the planet is also only an extension of processes active in the cosmos. So in dreams we often sense this primordial past out of which our present self has grown, and frequently depict this meeting as a prehistoric animal. Also, extinct; outmoded; clumsy; instinctive.

dirty   Actions or feelings that we feel are grubby or immoral. The unconscious has a natural morality based on its sense of connection with the universal principles of mating, birth, growth, and death. Where social or sexual life does not align with this or our consciously accepted principles, we may dream of being dirty.

disappearance   Depicts the way our conscious self relates to the unconscious. Memories, emotions, or ideas suddenly appear in awareness, but can disappear just as rapidly, sometimes never to be seen again. See **amnesia; vanish.**

dissection   Intellectual inquiry that lacks feeling and sympathy. But it can also show a deep self-analysis that might be painful, a sort of tearing oneself apart to discover why or what is happening.

ditch

ditch   Obstacles; things you might get caught or trapped in, therefore a hazard; a drainage or release for your feelings; a way of getting rid of something—"ditching"; feeling discarded or thrown away.

diving   Taking a chance; facing anxiety. <u>Diving underwater:</u> delving into your mind or unconscious. Exploring the meaning of a dream, or an eventful meditation, might be depicted as diving underwater in dreams. See **swimming.**

divorce   May be an expression of anger toward one's spouse; fear, intuition of or hope for breakup of marriage; parting of a relationship, such as in work or community; breakdown of something. <u>Male dream:</u> difficulty with one's feelings. <u>Female dream:</u> difficulty with social extroversion and intellect.

doctor   See *doctor* under **roles.**

dog   See *dog* under **animals.**

doll   Many "doll" dreams are, as in the example below, using the doll as a target for violence. This may refer to how the dreamer felt as a child when smacked or attacked emotionally—like a helpless doll. Also, childhood states of feeling; a means of displacement for anger or feelings the dreamer would like to discharge on another; a feeling of wanting to be a precious "doll" to someone; wanting to be loved. See also **toy.**

   Example: "She continues to attack him, and to my horror and feeling of helplessness, his head comes off. But the neck is made of some sort of material with a string hanging off it, and I realize it is a doll's head." (Simon T.)

dolphin   See *dolphin* under **fish, sea creatures.**

door   See *door* under **house, buildings.**

dragon Because the part of our mind we name "the unconscious" is so ancient and huge, we sometimes depict contact with it as a dragon or monster; an aggressive woman or man. In myths the hero is often shown doing battle with a dragon, serpent, or some other monster, to get a treasure. This is probably because the dragon depicts the massive and irrational forces of the unconscious, the life urges and untamed fears and sexuality that one must face and deal with in order to gain the treasure of potential locked in sexual, mental, and emotional energy; the untamed or unsocialized sexual drive that can overpower or trap a girl emerging into womanhood, or threatens a youth facing manhood. The overcoming of it means facing one's fears of the vast power of such natural drives, and finding satisfying expression.

drama See **film; theater.**

drapes See **curtains.**

dreamer Your "self-image" is displayed by what you do in your dreams. If you are the active and central character in your dreams, then you have a positive, confident image of yourself. The role you place yourself in is also the one you feel at home with, or one that is habitual to you. If you are constantly a victim in your dreams, you need to consider whether you are living such a role in everyday life. Dreams may help you look at your self-image from a more detached viewpoint. You can look back on what you do in a dream more easily than you can on your everyday waking behavior. This helps you understand your attitudes or stance, a very growth-promoting experience. It is important to understand the viewpoint of the other dream characters also. Although they depict views not habitual to you, they enlarge you through acquaintance. See **analysis of dreams; identity and dreams; processing your dreams; individuation; interpretation of dreams—influence of.**

dress

dress   See *dress* under **clothes**.

drink   To absorb or take something subtle into yourself. This may be taking in feelings such as pleasure; absorbing a mood; "drinking in" our surroundings. When <u>connected with thirst:</u> suggests needs or longings being met. If in company <u>with someone of the opposite sex, or a group:</u> taking in the pleasure or otherwise of the relationship or group. Sometimes connects with childhood emotional need. See **alcohol.**

driving   See **car**.

drowning   Because of the water, drowning depicts a feeling of being overwhelmed by difficult emotions or anxieties. <u>Dreamt about someone else:</u> may occasionally show your apprehension about their health or well-being, having the suggestion of death or breakdown.

druggist   See **chemist**.

drugs   In general, they relate to whatever you associate with the particular drug. For instance, aspirin might connect with your attempts to deal with pain; hallucinogens to the meeting with unconscious feelings and intuitions, or the attempt to avoid reality. Drugs usually change the way you feel, so the drug in the dream may be indicating this change of feeling. Of course, some drugs may be associated with illness, so you must see if you have this association with the dream drug.

drugstore   See **chemist**.

drum   May represent the heart, sexual tension, intercourse, masturbation, depending on context in dream. Can be awareness of the natural rhythms of our life processes, such as heartbeat; menstruation; the belly; circulation; and the feelings arising from our depths, such as primitive urges. See **music; musical instruments.**

drunk   Loss of control; lack of reason; having no soul or self-control; abandonment to the irrational or natural urges. Thus, freedom from the burden of self-awareness, responsibility, and decision-making. Occasionally means we are filled with power from beyond the limitations of waking awareness. See **alcohol.**

dwarf, malformed figure   A part of your personality left undeveloped or not integrated. For instance, you may have musical ability that was suppressed by the need to bring up children. A part of self malformed by painful childhood experience or lack of emotional nourishment. It may therefore be a link with your unconscious.

E

eagle   See *eagle* under **birds.**

ear   See *ears* under **body.**

earth   The things you take for granted that act as the supportive background to your life and activities, such as parental love, your reality as a person, social order, the thousands of things that constitute "reality" for you; the basic "taken for granted" aspects of your nature; the "ground you stand on"; attitudes and relationships you have taken for granted; everyday life; the past. The ground, like earth, holds in it all past experience, summarized as it is in culture and language. <u>Soil:</u> the material from which things can grow; the environment for something new to grow. <u>Soft earth, fields:</u> mother; the fundamental processes of life out of which we have being and which continually nurture us. <u>Under the earth, swallowed by the earth:</u> the unconscious habits, drives, and psychobiological processes that existed before our emergence as a conscious self, and in which we might lose self in death. <u>Off the ground:</u> losing connection with one's roots of family or culture. This may also be occasionally shown as being on a high building. <u>Idioms:</u> down to earth; go to earth; like nothing on earth. See **unconscious.**

earthquake   Insecurity; the breakdown of opinions, attitudes, or relationships that seemed so dependable; breaking down or relaxing of old body tensions. May also show great inner change and growth that makes you feel uncertain of your "ground." The growth from youth to puberty may be felt as an earthquake, as also maturity to middle age. See **earth.**

east   Personal connection with source of life; birth; the mysterious or religious aspect of self; the unconscious and the mysteries it holds; the Self.

eating   Satisfying your needs or "hunger." This can be any area of need, such as emotional, mental, sexual, depending on dream context; information about actual nutritional needs or physical allergies. <u>To eat:</u> to continue involvement in the fundamental processes of life, a celebration of interdependence. <u>To not eat:</u> shows a conflict with the physical reality of one's body and its needs; an avoidance of growth or change; an attempt to be isolated from others, reality, the whole. <u>Avoiding certain foods:</u> expression of decision-making in dealing with needs; food allergy. <u>Fasting:</u> withdrawal or turning away from natural urges. Not taking in what society, the world is offering. <u>Giving food to others:</u> giving of oneself to others, or nurturing some aspect of oneself. <u>Eating objects or repulsive food:</u> meeting objectionable experiences; trying to "stomach" things that make you "sick." <u>Idioms:</u> eaten away; eat dirt; eat humble pie; eat like a horse; eat one's heart out; eat one's words; eat out of one's hand; eat out of house and home; what's eating you?; proof of the pudding is in the eating; dog-eat-dog. See **devour, devoured; food.**

egg   Potential; parts of self as yet unrealized or not fertilized by conscious action or quality; the female ovum; a sense of wonder regarding life; prenatal life; feelings about wanting to retreat from life.

ejaculation/emission during a dream   Our sexual needs attempt to satisfy themselves even though we may

169

make a conscious attempt to deny them. The ejaculation, male or female, shows the sexual nature of one's dream, even if the symbols seem to have no obvious connection. The attitudes in one's dream also show something of the relationship to sex. This may be mechanical, fearful, loving, guilty, etc.

elastic   The ability to adapt. It may also show feelings to do with things that rebound.

electricity   Energy and emotions. The drama in the dream will suggest whether the energy or emotion is being met or used constructively or destructively. For instance, in some conditions of anxiety or excitement one can "burn oneself out." It is this self-destructive power of feelings and drives that electricity in dreams refers to. See **emotions, mood.**

elephant   See *elephant* under **animals.**

elevator   See *elevator* under **house, buildings.**

email   Principally about communication, or connection. This connection may be through one's thoughts or intuition, not only through physical links such as the telephone line. See **letter; telephone.**

embryo   An extremely vulnerable aspect of us; prenatal experience; or feelings connected with our prenatal life—for instance, we may have been told our mother tried to abort us. Even if this is not so, the idea acts as a focus for feelings of rejection and infantile pain. The embryo or fetus would therefore symbolize such feelings. In a woman's dream may connect with conception or pregnancy. See **baby.**

emerald   See *emerald* under **jewels.**

emigration   The changing of habits, ideas. The search for self. A change of direction in life.

emotions, mood There is a level of your experience that is typified by intense emotional and physical response to life. The intense response to pleasure and pain seen in babies is still alive in you, though perhaps buried. Such emotions and bodily drives may remain almost entirely unconscious until touched by exploring your dream content in the right setting, or revealed by dramatic events in your life. When such feelings and bodily movements arise, as they do in dreams, we may be amazed at their power and clarity. See **processing your dreams; movements during sleep.** Whatever feelings or emotions we meet in dreams, many of them are bound to be habitual responses we have to life. Where these habits are negative we can begin to change them by working with the dream images as described in *carrying the dream forward* under **peer dream work.** See **love; anger.**

empty Lack of pleasure, enthusiasm, good feelings; loneliness; lack of relationship; sense of isolation; something dead. Or one's potential; opportunity; space to be oneself. Depends on feeling quality in the dream. Empty house, buildings, shell: outgrown habits or ways of life; old attitudes; death; and/or potential. See **house, buildings.**

enclosed, enclosure The defenses we use, such as pride, beliefs, anger, to protect ourselves from deeply feeling the impact of the world, relationship, love, anxiety, or pain. These are often felt as traps or restraints, even though they are parts of our personality. For instance, one may feel trapped by one's own feelings of dependence upon family.

encyclopedia Memory, inner knowledge; collective human wisdom, so may depict connection with the collective unconscious. See **book; collective unconscious.**

end Used in many different ways, depending on context. Goal; point of change; release; death. End of path or road:

the end of one's life; the boundary of what one already knows or has done; end of a relationship, especially if walking with person. <u>Exit of tunnel or cave:</u> finding the way out of a difficult or depressed stage of life. <u>End of table or line:</u> feeling left out, unconsidered, forgotten; putting oneself last. <u>End of garden, room, passage, or road:</u> can be used to show polarity or opposites, as in the following example, in which the end of the tunnel suggests an opposite to the fear she is experiencing.

Example: "I'm trapped in a long passageway or corridor. I can't get out. I'm feeling my way along the wall—there is a small light at the end of the tunnel, I can't get to it. I'm very frightened. I wake up before I get to the end. Then I feel afraid to go back to sleep." (Petra W.)

end-of-world dreams and fantasies   Depicts the powerful and threatening inner and outer changes that accompany major life transitions and social changes. The transition from childhood to adolescence, for instance, is the end of the world that existed for the whole lifetime of the individual up until that point. Such points of transition occur several times in the life of anyone who dares to grow and adapt. Menopause for women, the leaving home of children, the loss of a job, retirement, loss of partner or health, can all be represented by the end of the world, or a world.

enemy   The person or group you are pitted against represent something, probably within yourself, that you are in conflict with. Such dreams show parts of yourself you struggle with. Jung called this the Shadow, the aspects of oneself you are frightened of, or repress for one reason or another. But it may simply depict something you are struggling with, a relationship, for instance, or feelings about work. See *the Shadow* under **archetypes.**

engine   One's motivating drive or energy; the body's energy and mechanical or automatic functioning; the sexual or natural urges; sometimes the heart. See **machine.**

enter, entrance   New experience or new area of experience. A <u>secret entrance:</u> an attitude or psychological "stance" that opens a new experience of self, or allows access to parts of oneself usually inaccessible. See *door* under **house, buildings.**

eruption   A breaking into consciousness of repressed urges, fears, terrors, or even insights and healing. Basically a healing process, but it can be disturbing.

escape   Finding a way of moving beyond restrictions, perhaps caused by anxiety or past pain. We often use "escape" to avoid difficult feelings. This is like reading an exciting novel because it distracts our attention from feeling alone or depressed. The problems remain. <u>Something escaping from us:</u> a realization, emotion, or opportunity eluding awareness. See **enclosed, enclosure.**

ESP in dreams   Many dreams appear to extend perception in different ways.

dreaming the future   Just before his title fight in 1947, Sugar Ray Robinson dreamt he was in the ring with Jimmy Doyle. "I hit him a few good punches and he was on his back, his blank eyes staring up at me." Doyle never moved and the crowd was shouting, "He's dead! He's dead!" He was so upset by the dream, Robinson asked Adkins, his trainer and promoter, to call off the fight. Adkins told him, "Dreams don't come true. If they did I'd be a millionaire." In the eighth round Doyle went down from a left hook to the jaw. He never got up, and died the next day.

The problem is that many dreams felt to be predictive never come true. Often dreamers want to believe they have precognitive dreams, perhaps to feel they will not be surprised by, and thereby anxious about, the future. When the baby son of Charles Lindbergh was kidnapped, and before it was known he was murdered, 1,300 people sent "precognitive" dreams concerning his fate, in response to newspaper headlines. Only seven of these dreams included the three vital factors—that he was dead, naked, and in a ditch.

dreaming together   The Poseidia Institute of Virginia Beach, VA, has run a number of group "mutual dreaming" experiments. Although the institute suggests very positive results, a critical survey of the dreams and reports reveals a lack of hard evidence. Like other areas of ESP dreaming, it can seldom be willed. But the dreams did show themes related to problems regarding intimate meeting. Also, some of the dreams were directly about the goal of dream meeting. See **meeting in dreams.**

the dream as extended perception   Even everyday mental functions such as thought and memory occur largely unconsciously. During sleep, perhaps because we surrender our volition, what is left of self-awareness enters the realm where the nine-tenths of the iceberg of our mind is active. In this realm, faculties can function that on waking seem unobtainable. A list of these would include:

1. Extending awareness to a point distant from the body, to witness events confirmed by other people. This is often called out-of-body experience or OBE. Some of these experiences suggest the nature of consciousness and time may not be dualistic. We do not have to be either here or there. See **out-of-body experience.**
2. Being aware of the death or danger of a member of family. Kinship and love seem to be major factors in the way the unconscious functions.
3. Seeing into the workings of the body and diagnosing an illness before it becomes apparent to waking observation. Dr. Vasily Kasatkin and Professor Medard Boss have specialized in the study of such dreams.
4. Access to a computerlike ability to sort through a massive store of information and experience to solve

problems. These dreams are often confused with precognitive ability. Prediction does occur from these dreams, but it arises, as with weather prediction, from a massive gathering of information, most of which we have forgotten consciously. Morton Schatzman, in an article in *New Scientist,* showed how subjects can produce answers to complex mathematical problems in their dreams. See **computer dream process; creativity and problem-solving in dreams.**

5. Tapping a collective mind that stores all experience, and so is sensed as godlike or holy.

6. It seems likely that before the development of speech, the human animal communicated largely through body language. Some dreams suggest we still have this ability to read a person's health, sexual situation, intentions, and even their past, through body shape, posture, and tiny movements. See **postures, movement, and body language.**

See **Cayce, Edgar; collective unconscious; hallucinations.**

Evans, Christopher   In his book *Landscapes of the Night,* Dr. Evans puts forward a new theory of dreaming. He states that our brain has "programs" for dealing with survival. We have basic behavior programs for walking and talking, rather like a computer might have. We also have programs for social interaction and skills. In the different roles, such as lover, parent, breadwinner, employer, we need such different skills. But also, to deal with our process of change, our internal urges, anger, drive to succeed, we also need learned skills to handle them well. A person who doesn't handle anxiety or stress can easily fail in work or in relationships, despite being highly intelligent. Many people do not enter a relationship because of the problems it poses. Dr. Evans suggests that dreams are the means by which we both practice and update programs of survival. Our experience of the day may question or enhance behavior stratagems for work success or relationship. Without the reprogramming occurring in dreams, we would be stuck at one level of behavioral maturity. "As we gain in experience, as our input gets richer and more diverse, we modify programs rather than replace them with a completely fresh set." See **computer, dream process as a; gestalt dream work.**

evening   See **autumn; time of day.**

evil   Usually refers to urges that we have judged as wrong because of moral or social values, and thus denied expression. One's established values and beliefs may feel threatened by what is felt as evil. Whatever threatens our "I," or ego, is often felt to be evil, even if it is natural urges. The unbalanced and real evils in the world, such as terrorizing of individuals and minority groups, can of course be shown as the feeling of evil. When we conflict with our urges they often feel like external agencies—evil forces—attacking us. See **bewitched;** *devil* under **archetypes; devil.**

exams, being examined   Self-criticism or attempts to live up to moral or intellectual standards; habits of concern over accomplishments; worry about some coming test of self-value, such as a new job or new sexual partner. Examined by doctor: concern over health; desire for attention. See **tests.**

excrement   Feelings of repulsion; emotions or parts of experience that need to be let go of; infant level of self-expression and self-giving; physical need to have a healthy bowel; distasteful feelings or events; one's feelings about money. The Incan description of gold was "excrement of the gods"! Like digested food, feces can represent experience that was relevant and enjoyable at the time of consumption, but needs to be let go of, release of tension. Sometimes personal creativity; being able to let go of what you don't need—so can link with money and generosity; the primal level of being; sensuality, intense pleasure, and infant sexuality. Shit can of course produce wonderfully rich fertilizer. If <u>shitting on someone or something</u>: expressing desire to belittle them or to feel one's superiority; heaping unjust accusations on someone; bringing something that appeared powerful into perspective. <u>Idioms:</u> in the shit; feeling shitty; talking a lot of shit/crap; being shit on; being a shit. See **toilet.**

exit door   A way out of a situation; a way to escape; death. See *door* under **house, buildings.**

explosion   Anger; dramatic release of energy in making changes in self-expression; social upheaval; fear; orgasm.

eyes   See *eyes* under **body.**

F

facade   In some house dreams, great stress is given to the front or facade of the house. Sometimes it crumbles away, revealing what is within; sometimes it is painted or changed, and so on. The facade thus represents the front you show to the world, your social self that may hide quite a different interior. See **house, buildings.**

face   See *face* under **body.**

factory   See *factory* under **house, buildings.**

failure   Comparison; competitiveness; sometimes depicts alternatives—failure is the alternative to success. So the failure might be "because." See **falling;** *because factor* in **processing your dreams.**

Example: "I was in a race riding a horse but couldn't get to the starting gate in time. The others were way ahead of me, jumping the fences. I couldn't catch up, and one fence I came to grew to a huge height and was like a steel barrier. I couldn't get over it and felt a failure." (Peter D.)

Ron had not done well at school, had not taken any particular training, had no steady relationship and no children. In his late twenties, Peter looked at his friends with steady jobs, married with family, and felt a failure. From the dream he realized he was viewing life as a competitive race to succeed. This was stopping him from following his real interest, psychotherapy, which his family viewed as playing games. He chose to ride his horse into the fields and explore. He did, by going to America, training, raising a family.

fairground   One's public activity; the range of human fate—rich to poor, midgets to giants; "swings and round-abouts" of life. <u>Carnival, fiesta:</u> dropping social or moral restraints; letting go; creativity; social connections. See **market.**

fall   See **autumn.**

fall, falling   Loss of confidence; threat to usual sources of security—such as relationship, source of money, social image—such as loss of face or sustaining beliefs; tension; loss of social grace; moral failure—falling into temptation; coming down to earth from a too lofty attitude; sexual surrender. Occasionally, if we use fantasy and thought to get away from the "real" world, or if we use entertainment, alcohol, socializing to escape from inner pain and conflict, when these distractions are taken away and reality breaks through again there is a sense of falling and threat. So falling may depict this fear of being faced with inner feelings.

A <u>person falling:</u> wish to be rid of them; or anxiety in regard to what they represent. A <u>child or son falling:</u> See **baby;** *son* and *daughter* under **family, family relationships.** <u>House falling down:</u> personal stress; illness; personal change and growth due to letting old habits and attitudes crumble. <u>Falling into an abyss or pit:</u> fear of failure; fear of meeting one's own depths of feeling and the hidden side of oneself; anxiety about some form of death. <u>Going fast to an edge and falling:</u> could mean overwork and danger of breakdown of health. <u>Seeing things fall:</u> sense of danger or change in regard to what is represented.

During our development we "fall" from our mother's womb when ripe; being dropped by a parent must be our earliest sense of insecurity, and we fall many times as we learn to stand and walk. As we explore boundaries in running, climbing, jumping, and riding, falling is a big danger. At times it could mean death. Learning to walk down stairs is a great achievement for a baby, and has very real danger and fear of falling. See *stairs* and *home* under **house, buildings; abyss; chasm; flying.**

family, family relationships   The values, attitudes, and emotional or social responses we have absorbed from our family; the acceptance or tensions we feel in relationship with them; the support or pain we feel from parents and siblings. From our family we learn most of the positive and negative patterns of relationship and attitudes toward living that we carry into daily events. Father's uncertainty in dealing with people, or his anxiety in meeting change, may be the roots of difficulties in those areas. If our mother is unable to develop a feeling contact with us, we may lack the experience of being able to love.

Our maturing process calls us in some way to meet and integrate childhood patterns. This includes desire for the love of our parent of the opposite sex, and rivalry mingled with dependence with parent of the same sex. Even a missing parent, the mother or father who died or left, is a potent figure internally. An absence of a father or mother's love or presence can be as traumatic as any powerfully injuring event. Parents in dreams are images full of power and feeling, of the formative forces and experiences that helped forge our identity. They are the ground, the soil, and the bloody carnage, out of which our sense of self emerged. But our identity cannot gain any real independence while still dominated by these internal forces of our creation. Heraclitus said we cannot swim in the same river twice. Attempting to repeat or compete with the virtues or failings of a parent is a misapprehension of the true nature of our personality. See **individuation.**

family group   Our internal "family" of urges and values; the overall feeling tone of family life—security, domination, whatever it was; the unconscious coping patterns of the family. The background of experience that makes up our values and views. This background is made of thousands of different obvious and subtle things, such as social status, amount of books in the home, how parents feel about themselves, how they relate to life outside the family, whether dominant roles are encouraged, what nationality parents are, what unconscious social attitudes surround them. <u>Parents together in dream:</u> our general wisdom; basic values; background of information and experience from which we make important decisions or gain intuitive insights, negative or positive. Parents also depict the rules and often irrational disciplinary codes we learned as a child that still speak to us from within, and perhaps pass on to our children without reassessment. <u>Hurting, burying, or killing parent:</u> to be free of the introverted restraints and ready-made values gathered from parents. At some time in our growth we may kill or bury them in our dreams. Although some people are shocked by such dreams, they are healthy signs of emerging independence. Old myths of killing the chief so the tribe can have a new leader depict this process. When father or mother is "dead" in our dream, we can inherit all the power gained from whatever was positive in the relationship. <u>Seeing parent drunk, incapable, or foolish:</u> another means of gaining independence from internalized values, or stultifying drives to "honor" or admire father or mother. <u>Dead parent in dream:</u> perhaps the beginning of independence from parent; repression of the emotions they engendered in us; emotions regarding our parent's death; feelings about death. See **dead people.**

father   <u>General positive:</u> authority; ability in the external world; family or social conventions; how we relate to the "doer" in us; physical strength and protectiveness; the will to be. <u>General negative:</u> introverted aggression; dominance by fear of other people's authority; uncaring sexual drive; feelings of not being loved. See *father* under **archetypes; man.**

family, family relationships

mother   <u>General positive:</u> feelings; being given to, looked after, and fed; protection; feelings of dependence; ability in relationships; uniting spirit of family; how we relate to feelings in a relationship; strength to give of self and nurture; intuition. <u>General negative:</u> will based on irrational likes and dislikes; opinion generated by anxiety or jealousy; domination by emotions; lack of bonding. Each of us has a fundamental, perhaps instinctive, drive to bond with a woman at birth. This has generated from millions of years of survival strategy. If that bonding does not take place, much of what would have been natural unfoldment and growth, cannot, or does not, take place. So mother sometimes represents this whole difficult issue of survival and what happened in those early years of trying to become independent of such extraordinary needs. See *the Great Mother* under **archetypes; woman.**

brother, sister, daughter, son   The most general use in dreams is to depict an aspect of ourselves. It is almost universal to believe with great conviction that our dream is about the person in the dream. Most often the family member depicts the qualities in ourselves that we feel are part of the character of the person dreamt of. So the passionate one in the family would depict our passions, the intellectual one our mind, the anxious one our hesitations. Use the questions in **processing your dreams** to define this. Having done this, can you observe what the dream depicts? A mother seeing a son die in her dream often goes through great anxiety because there lurks in her a fear of it being a precognitive dream. Virtually everyone at some time dreams about members of close family dying or being killed. Lots of mothers dream this and their children live till eighty. But occasionally children do die. Is the dream then precognitive, or is it coincidental?

ancestors   The intricate web of cultural and family influences, physically and psychologically, that the dreamer's body and personality arose from. If it is a particular ancestor, then the personal associations with that person need to be explored. For instance, an uncle may have been renowned for womanizing, so would represent that tendency.

aunt To some extent an aunt is a role model. We gather from their success or failure strategies for our life. Whatever feelings we have about them, whatever we think of them, the dream will use this to illustrate something for you. So consider how you would describe your aunt, what sort of person she is, and how you feel about her. The dream will be using her image to illustrate the role you see her in. If she is a success, ask yourself what in yourself you are facing regarding success. If you feel she is a failure, ask yourself what of your feelings about failure you are facing.

brother Oneself, or the denied part of self, meeting whatever is met in the dream; feelings of kinship; sense of rivalry; the anger or pleasure from memories. In woman's dream, younger brother: outgoing but vulnerable self; rivalry. Older brother: authority; one's capable, outgoing self; feelings of persecution. In man's dream, younger brother: vulnerable feelings; oneself at that age. See **boy; man.** Idioms: big brother; brothers-in-arms; blood brother.

daughter One's relationship with the daughter; the daughter, or son, can represent what happens in the marriage of the parents. The child is what has arisen from the bonding, however momentary, of two people. In dreams the child therefore is sometimes used to depict how the relationship is faring. So a sick daughter might show the feelings in the relationship being "ill." In a mother's dream: often feelings of support or companionship; feelings of not being alone in the area of emotional bonds; or one's feeling area; responsibility; the ties of parenthood; oneself at that age; one's own urges, difficulties, hurts, that may still be operative; a comparison. The mother might see the daughter's youth, opportunity, and have feelings about that. So the daughter may represent her sense of lost opportunity and youth, even envy; competition in getting the desire of a man. <u>In a father's dream:</u> one's feeling self; the feelings or difficulties about the relationship with daughter; the emotional struggles you go through to mature; how sexual feelings are dealt with in a family situation—occurs especially when she starts courting; sister; parental responsibility; one's wife when younger. <u>Someone else's daughter:</u> feelings about one's own daughter; feelings about younger women.

grandparents   Personal feelings connected with the grandparent; family traditions, such as established values or unconscious attitudes; transcendent values; old age; death.

husband   Depicts how you see the relationship with your husband; your relationship with your sexuality; sexual and emotional desire and pleasure; how you relate to intimacy in body, mind, and spirit; habits of relationship developed with one's father. <u>Cannot find husband:</u> many middle-aged women dream of "losing" their husband while out with him, perhaps shopping, or walking in a town somewhere. Sometimes the dream portrays him actually killed. The greatest shocks occur when we have never even considered the event—such as a young child losing it's mother—an event it has never practiced, not even in fantasy, so has no built-in shock absorbers. As most of us know, men tend to die before women, and this information is in the mind of middle-aged married women and can lead to "losing" dreams in which the wife practices losing her husband. <u>Dead husband:</u> your memories and remaining emotions about your husband; the psychic bond you have with him. <u>Other woman's husband:</u> one's own husband; feelings about that man; desire for a noncommitted relationship with less responsibility. <u>Sex with husband:</u> the sexual dream is at best a wonderful indicator of how you, the dreamer, are feeling about your sexual and emotional relationship, or what you long for at the time of the dream. At worst it depicts all you fear might happen or be happening.

relatives   Including uncle, aunt, cousin, nephew, niece, etc. Usually an aspect of yourself relevant to the character of the person dreamt about. Sometimes represents your family traditions, unconscious attitudes, conventions, or even talents, that are part of the unique psychological and social environment a family provides.

sister   Feeling self, or the lesser expressed part of self; rival; feelings of kinship. In man's dream, younger sister: vulnerable emotions; rival for love of parents. *Older sister:* capable, feeling self. In woman's dream, younger sister: one's experiences at that age; vulnerable feelings; rival for parents' love. Older sister: capable, feeling self; feelings of persecution. See **girl; woman.** Idioms: sisters under the skin.

son   Extroverted self; desires connected with self-expression; feelings connected with son; parental responsibility; hopes or plans for their future. Mother's dream: one's ambitions; potential; hopes; your marriage. See first example below. Father's dream: yourself at that age; what qualities you see in your son; your possibilities; envy of youth and opportunities; rivalry. Someone else's son: feelings about one's own son; feelings about younger men. If dreaming of dead son: see **dead people.** Death of son: a mother often kills her son in her dreams as she sees him make moves toward independence. This can happen from first day of school on. See **boy; man.**

   Example: "My wife and I were walking out in the countryside. I looked around suddenly and saw my four-year-old son near a hole. He fell in and I raced back. The hole was narrow but very deep. I could see water at the bottom but no sign of my son. I didn't know whether I could leap down and save him or whether it was too narrow. Then somehow he was out. His heart was just beating." (Dan R.)

Dan had argued with his wife in such a way he feared the stability of their marriage. The son represents what they had created together—a child, a marriage. The marriage survived, as his dream assessed it would.

the triangle   Difficult conflict of interests; shifting feelings of relationship.

uncle   An uncle may be a role model. We gather from their success, or failure, strategies for our life. Whatever feelings we have about them, whatever we think of them, the dream will use this to illustrate something for you. So consider how you would describe your uncle, what sort of person he is, and how you feel about him. If he is a success, ask yourself what in yourself you are facing regarding success. If you feel he is a failure, ask yourself what of your feelings about failure you are facing.

widow   See **widow.**

wife   Depicts how you see the relationship with your wife; your relationship with your sexuality; sexual and emotional desire and pleasure; how you relate to intimacy in body, mind, and spirit; your feeling, intuitive nature; habits of relationship developed with one's mother.

the first wife   The past; competition for the second wife; possible sense of failure or pain for the man; past experience.

famous people   Desire to be noticed and acclaimed; your potential, often unacknowledged, and projected onto dream character; a parent; depending on how you relate to the famous person, your ability to accept yourself as respected; desire, ambitions, and efforts to become successful. Sometimes the person may, because of their life or role, represent a particular quality, such as courage, love, "ruling" drives in life, authority, etc. If you think of the person in a particular role or scene, this will probably be the major clue to what they represent—such as the lover who leaves, the father who sacrifices, etc.

<u>Actor/actress:</u> one is acting a role; wanting attention; deception. <u>Film/stage/TV star:</u> may be what is described above under famous people, but if the star has a particular quality, the dream may use them to denote this characteristic, such as love, treachery, courage, etc. <u>Pop star:</u> similar to what has been said about famous people, but might also carry feelings to do with intense teenage sexuality or need; what you hold as an ideal or idol; a role model; egomania. See **king; queen;** *actor/actress, acting* under **roles; theater.**

Famous people can be seen as social guinea pigs. Collectively we expose them to enormous amounts of money, sexual opportunity, drugs, alcohol, and tremendous social and commercial pressures. Then we examine every part of their life to see how well they cope. Millions identify with the image they portray of how to deal with reality at its best and worst. The famous person in our dream might therefore represent our coping mechanism.

fare The price one pays to achieve a goal; getting the right attitude or stance. See **ticket.**

farm, farmyard Care or expression of your natural drives, such as sexuality, parenthood, love of fellowship; the down-to-earth side of self; area of your animal propensities where territorial struggles, fighting over mate, etc. are expressed. See *farmer* under **roles.**

fat person Defenses used against anxiety or feelings of inadequacy; healthy, jolly feelings; sensuality. <u>Becoming fat:</u> pregnancy; carrying "more weight."

father See *father* under **family, family relationships.**

faucet Emotions—turning them on and off; tapping your resources; depicts how well you can get your needs.

fax machine, fax   May represent things, ideas, message, imagery, emerging out of the unconscious; the previously unexpected arising out of one's unconscious contact with other people and society; communication with someone. See **telephone.**

fear   See **anxiety; emotions, mood.**

feather   In many cultures feathers represent the quality or beauty of the bird from which they came. So an eagle feather would represent strength, pride, fierce protectiveness, transcendent insight, etc.; a peacock might represent beauty, self-aggrandisement—in India they symbolize awareness that transcends the senses; a black feather might depict the unconscious, or ability to explore it; a white feather in the past was associated with cowardice, but might also represent purity and wider awareness; ability to fly, to aspire, to lift up one's life from beliefs or fears that limit one; something easily blown by the wind—so nonresistance, insubstantial. See **colors** for possible meanings for other colors. Idioms: feather in one's cap; light as a feather; feather bed; feather one's own nest; birds of a feather flock together.

feces   See **excrement.**

feet   See *feet* under **body.**

fence   Your sense of social barriers, class barriers, or the attitudes used to segregate the sexes, races, or classes in work, opportunity, or relationship; need for privacy; territorial feelings; the social rules used to give each other respect; the defenses we erect to ward off what we fear as danger of hurt; also boundaries in relationship or society that might prevent us daring to express ourselves or be creative. Stretched wire-mesh fence: may represent the tension or stress that is holding one, or trapping one in anxiety. See **wall.** Idioms: rush one's fences; wrong side of the fence; sit on the fence.

188

ferry   Movement toward change; connections in a relationship; often associated with ferry across Styx and death. If <u>ferry you know:</u> consider why you use the ferry, what you associate with it. See **bridge.**

fiddle   As this is associated with music, or skill as a musician, it probably shows you expressing your innate potential with skill—or otherwise if the fiddle is not being played well. It might also relate to "fiddling about," and so suggest you are doing nothing constructive. Or you can be "on the fiddle," and so be attempting to cheat. You can "play second fiddle" or "first fiddle," and thus realize how you feel about a relationship or situation in which you are second best, or in the limelight. It can also represent sexual intercourse, or even masturbation. See **music; musical instrument.**

field   Fields often appear with animals, and suggest the dreamer's contact with what is natural in themselves; freedom from social pressure; sense of yourself when away from other people, with your natural inclinations; field of activity or study; feeling states, depending on condition of field—cloudy, bright, overgrown. <u>Field across river or very green fields:</u> the dreamer's concept of heaven. See **landscapes.**

fight   Usually your anger or frustration; may express difficulties in regard to independence or self-confidence; desire to hurt another person, or damage their reputation. A fight can also depict fighting for your space, your values, or honor; we may fight for survival—for our health, against crime or criminal impulses; we may also feel attacked by another person's opinions; assaulted by sexual desire; fight against depression; have a conflict over moral issues. See **attack; war.** <u>Idioms:</u> fight it out; fight like cats and dogs; look for a fight.

film   An aspect of your past or character that you do not wish to acknowledge; particular moods or realizations, depending on film; images of self and behavior projected

film

from the unconscious; one of your means of escaping from everyday life.

film star   See **famous people**.

find, found   Usually, as in the example below, to discover, realize, become aware of some aspect of oneself and gain access to or use of. One might be living with constant resentments about one's past or present situation, and then "find" release from this for a day, yet not be conscious how it was achieved. The dream might attempt to define this. Or it might be a new idea you realize unconsciously or in sleep. <u>Idioms:</u> find oneself; find fault; find out; find one's bearings.

Example: "I went into a cellar. It was rather cavelike. I had to scramble to get into it. The entrance was difficult to find, but I had discovered it many years before and been in lots of times. I found objects in the cellar and was looking for something." (T.C.)

finger   See *Fingers* in *hand* under **body**.

fire   Passion; sexuality; anger; desire; burning feelings such as resentment or frustration; desire to destroy; the process of growth or change in us that radically alters old dependencies and viewpoints; an emergency or calamitous change; your life process, often described as a flame that burns forever through different generations but leaves only ash behind; your vital energy; occasionally refers to physical illness or a warning of it. The <u>fireplace:</u> homeyness; the womb. <u>Underground flames:</u> unconscious emotions or desires that one may need to face for real growth; illness that has not yet come to awareness yet. <u>Fire in the sky:</u> great changes in viewpoint; meeting the next step in maturity. <u>Idioms:</u> too hot to handle; you burn me up; old flame; the burning bush.

fireman   See *fireman* under **roles**.

fish, sea creatures When we decide to speak or move, unconscious physical and psychological impulses and processes produce the response. Fish often depict these deeply unconscious processes. The fish can therefore represent something arising from within that could be nourishing or threatening, depending on the dream. For instance, a person might allow feelings to emerge that had been held back. As the feelings flow, a new sense of self might be realized, and be depicted as a fish; the attitudes and urges we have in common with humanity—the collective unconscious—and the impulses or insights arising; sexual drive in connection with reproduction, the many little fishes being sperm. In this sense we are the fish that swam the incredible journey and grew into a human. The fish may be the wisdom we have not yet brought to consciousness, regarding our personal journey in time and eternity. <u>Dead fish:</u> nonexpression of basic urges. <u>Eaten by fish:</u> feeling threatened by irrational urges or emotions; threat of losing conscious or rational direction of life. <u>Eating fish:</u> integrating inner realizations; feeling connected with society and the world, as in communion. <u>Fishing:</u> creating a receptive state of mind that allows the deep insights or processes to become known; trying to find one's connection with universal life; "fishing" for ideas; compliments or information; seeking intuition. <u>Many little fish in round container:</u> could be sperm, or depict becoming or wanting to become pregnant.

crab The shell of brittle emotions we guard ourselves with; grasping or hurtful attitudes. <u>Being nipped by crab:</u> physical or psychosomatic pain, or even illness caused by being too tight or self-protective.

dolphin, porpoise Because dolphins are wild creatures of the sea that actively develop a relationship with humans, they are often taken to represent the contact and relationship we have with the deeply unconscious natural forces within. Such dreams suggest life is not operating blindly, but reaches out to us if we reach out to it; powerful unconscious energies in us; conscious awareness of one's link with all life; contact with the one life within all things.

jellyfish Feelings arising from the unconscious that might be painful, sting the dreamer, bring a sense of helplessness/spinelessness, or are from a nonverbal level of memory.

octopus Feeling trapped by the influence of one's mother; dependence upon mother; one's own possessiveness or desire to cling to someone in a relationship. Hadfield, in *Dreams and Nightmares,* says that a baby often seizes upon its mother's breast with this feeling, so it may represent the desire to possess or devour others. The octopus can also symbolize any unconscious fear that may drag us into its realm of irrational terror, or any influence you fear will engulf you.

seal As the seal can emerge from the water entirely and live on land, the seal is sometimes used to represent the emergence from the womb and the pleasures or difficulties of life as a "land animal" physically independent of its mother. This is especially so if it is a baby seal. It depicts the emergence into your conscious life of your deepest instincts and life energies—in Eastern terminology, the *kundalini.* Otherwise the possible meanings are much the same as *dolphin, porpoise*—see above.

shark Fear of death; fear of the collective unconscious, or loss of self in the impersonal Whole or All; the power of the unconscious—so its protectiveness; someone who is a "shark," or unscrupulous.

shellfish Often the defensive shell we use to avoid hurt or sexual or emotional involvement; the female sexual organs. Oyster: also defensive shell, but may link with sexuality through common association; tight-lipped; secretive;

frigidity. <u>Lacking shell:</u> our naked vulnerability. See *crab* above; *Pearl* under **jewels.**

whale   The powerful evolutionary drive involved in reproduction, which lies behind individual male- or femaleness; the beneficent power of the collective unconscious. <u>Idioms:</u> big fish; big fish in a small pond; cold fish; fish for compliments; fish out of water; queer fish; smell something fishy.

fishing   See *Fishing* entry under **fish, sea creatures.**

fishing rod   Male sexuality; personal power, or feelings of impotence. <u>Getting a new fishing rod:</u> in a man's dream, might mean feeling anxious about his ability to "hook" a woman; or getting a better way of being receptive to intuition. For a woman it could mean a desire to "catch" a new man. In general, the rod suggests the means of pulling something out of the unknown of life or your mind. So it could suggest intuition or skill in acquiring the new, or something that nourishes.

five   See *five* under **numbers.**

flag   This can represent pride, either as one's connection with the group, as in nationalism, or as an individual. The flag is also used to depict occasions of rejoicing—such as marriage or victory, or mourning, as with someone's death.

flames   Life itself—our life as it moves through experience, leaving only memories; the mystery of consciousness underlying our personality; passion or anger. See **candle; fire;** *fireman* under **roles.** <u>Idioms:</u> baptism of fire; between two fires; fire up; go through fire and water; play with fire; under fire; add fuel to the flames; old flame; the old illness/love flared up.

floating   Often appears in dreams where the dreamer is getting close to someone of the opposite sex and some

floating

aspect of sexual feeling is present; an experience of awareness expanding beyond the usual boundaries of the person's beliefs or of their physical senses. <u>On water:</u> relaxation; opening to power beyond the ego; being indecisive; being carried along by events. See **flying.**

flood   Depression could be seen as an inundation of negative emotions; anxiety a flood of fear; an overflow of usually unconscious or uncontrolled feelings and urges into consciousness. The flood can of course be of positive feelings, like love. In any case, floods can be enriching to growth if handled well. In many flood dreams it is positive energy the dreamer is anxious about.

floor   See *floor* under **house, buildings.**

flowers   Sense of beauty; flowering of a feeling, quality, or ability; the sexual organs, depending on shape; transitory beauty of life or youth; the flowering of ripeness to live, love, and reproduce, and its passing; feelings of pleasure; youthfulness; time of flowering. <u>Bud:</u> penis or vagina, in the sense of growing male or female qualities. <u>Giving flowers:</u> giving love and tenderness. <u>Many flowers growing:</u> feelings of well-being and relaxation. <u>Dead flowers:</u> death or old age; dying love or abilities. <u>Giving dead flowers:</u> wishing someone dead or out of one's life; dead feelings. <u>Lotus and lily:</u> as these grow from mud, through water to the air and light, they sometimes represent wholeness and growth, showing our connection with the universal as we develop individually. *Rose:* love; the flowering of personal qualities, your soul or self. Sometimes the vagina. When the <u>shape or number of petals is featured:</u> a flowering of a new aspect of the self. See **colors; growth; plants; shapes, symbols.**

flying   A great deal of will, effort, and learning can be involved in flying dreams. This aspect of flying connects with the gaining of independence and the expression of one's potential. Adler saw flying dreams suggestive of confidence and the ability to solve present life problems. They portray the overcoming of obstacles, the gravity of life, or the things that pull down one's enthusiasm. The people who have them are often positively directing their life. Flying also expresses the dealing with other internal influences that hold us down, such as self-doubt, anxiety, and depression. There is a negative side to flying that depicts how we flee from internal trauma or fear by disassociating feelings and mind from reality. Flying alone occurs most frequently, showing the independent aspect of flying. But because it often involves positive feelings of pleasure, flying may depict our sexuality as in the example below, especially aspects of it expressing freedom from social norms and restraints.

Example: "I knew I could fly. I picked up one of the young women I felt love for and flew with her. Laughingly, I felt like Superman, and flew easily." (Simon W.)

Some researchers believe flying dreams often precede lucid dreams. See **lucid dreams; out-of-body experience.** Idioms: fly by night; flying high; send flying.

flying saucer   See **UFO.**

fog   Confusion; indecision; inability to see the real issues in yourself and your environment. Idioms: not the foggiest.

follow   To follow: to be influenced by, have an attraction to, pursue, seek something, look for. Nearly always suggests we are being led by an attitude, hope, or habit, and not consciously assessing present needs. Following animal: led by basic drives, intuition, or instinct. Following opposite sex: led by desire for satisfaction in love. Being followed: taking the initiative; pursued by memory, pain, guilt, ambition; a continued sense of hope; doom, hunch, instinct. Followed by opposite sex: memories of old love. Followed by animal: see **chased.**

food   There is food for the mind, food for thought, food
for the body, and nourishment that gives a sense of connecting with something eternal; we can digest information
or experience, the latter being food for growth as an individual. Food can represent any of these. We might also take
something into ourselves—such as experience of a relationship, qualities of another person, sexual pleasure, social
pleasure; warning about health in regard to what is eaten.
A meal: taking in life; absorbing experience and the world;
being enriched. If you are with others, then it might reflect
something about the way you relate socially to others. It
could also be a sharing of life and experience with others.
Being sick from eating something: see **vomit.** Food in
connection with a particular person: being nourished by
or hungry for relationship with them; enjoyment of sexuality with them. Frequent dreams about eating: suggesting a great hunger for something; perhaps a compensation
for dieting or problems with eating. Giving food: giving of
oneself, time, love, work, sex. Stealing food: dishonest
about needs in a relationship; feelings of being a parasite.

bread   Experience; everyday life. Given slice of bread: sex;
generosity.

cake   Sensual enjoyment.

carrot   Sometimes represents the penis. It can also depict
what you have to pull out of yourself through hard work,
or "digging." Promise of reward, as used with donkey.

cookie   Pleasure, perhaps connected with childhood. If
you are making the cookies, it might suggest caring for
your needs or those of other people.

fruits   Fruits of experience or effort and what emerges
from them. Soft, luscious fruits, such as fig or peach: may
represent female genitals. Long fruit, such as banana: may
depict male sexuality. Apple: Temptation; this links it with

the fruits of one's action, or the consequences of action, the fruit of one's labor; pleasure; food or sustenance; breast. <u>Grapes:</u> because grapes can be used to make alcohol, they often have a special significance, and are very ancient cultural symbols. They depict fruitfulness, fertility, but perhaps the opening of something that transcends one's personal life. So a woman dreaming of them, especially near her belly, can assume she is pregnant. But they also signify pleasures of the world, drinking, sex, wealth; conversely, in Christianity they signify the blood of Christ—the essence of human experience. <u>Lemon:</u> possibly symbolizes the feelings of bitterness, sourness. In some nations the lemon also has strong associations with health, so it might show a suggestion to use for your health. <u>Pineapple:</u> fruitfulness of soul. Quality or royalty. Self-confidence. Prickly exterior.

jam In a mess, a sticky situation; conserved ideas; fruits of labor; pleasure, perhaps childhood pleasure or feelings.

jelly or gelatin Childhood pleasure/needs; indecision through anxiety; feeling uncertain about oneself, perhaps through lacking a firm identity; something difficult to grasp, or feel certain about; potential that can be shaped by one's motivations and decisions. <u>Eating jelly:</u> taking in feelings of uncertainty or something that can be shaped, something that has potential; pleasure.

meals Social pleasure; acceptance; social intercourse. <u>If alone:</u> independence; loss of family ties; lack of social relationships or outside stimulus.

meat Physical or worldly satisfaction or needs; the best bit of life; nourishing; good fortune or good hunting in one's endeavors; sometimes refers to sexual behavior, suggesting it is lacking anything but a physical dimension. <u>If you are a vegetarian:</u> something to be avoided; feelings of guilt; death. <u>Raw meat:</u> instinctive or powerful emotions or drives.

food

milk   Self-giving; baby needs.

olive   Peace; kindness, because the oil can be pressed from the olive.

salad   Sometimes a direct reference to the body's need for such foods; lack of meaty—sexual—experience. Taking in feelings and influences that are alive and create personal growth.

soup   This might be sustenance, sustaining or strengthening emotions. But it depends what is happening to the soup. If spilt it can suggest making a mess of things, or feeling insecure about a social event. Offering soup depicts a giving of yourself, of your care and affection. The soup in a saucepan might be showing how you have gathered many things together to nourish yourself or someone else, so nourishment for body and soul.

sweets   Sensual pleasure; pleasures in life; special love.

vegetables   Basic needs; material satisfaction. If <u>long</u>, as carrot: male sexuality. If a woman's dream, feelings about sex with male. If male dream, his own sexuality. <u>Onion</u>: something to cry about; also the different layers of oneself—inner self, outer self. See **eating; restaurant; salad.**

foot   See *feet* under **body.**

foreign countries   Different attitude; different mental or emotional "climate" than one's norm; sometimes represents meeting an aspect of oneself that was previously unconscious, so unknown or foreign; the unfamiliar. One's personal associations or ideas about any particular country need to be explored. Use the questions in **processing your dreams.**

forest   Your natural feelings; the self you are underneath what you express through your needs for social and physical survival; the magical world of the unconscious, full as it is of strange forces, primeval creatures, and miraculous people. See **trees.**

forgetting   See **amnesia.**

fortress   See *castle* under **house, buildings.**

fountain   The process of life; flow of consciousness into awareness; joy of collective life; satisfaction of desire. <u>Drinking from and bathing in:</u> experiencing wider awareness arising from the unconscious.

four   See *four* under **numbers.**

fox   See *fox* under **animals.**

freeway   See *freeway/motorway* under **road.**

Freud, Sigmund (1856–1939)   When Freud, as a qualified doctor and neurologist, became interested in psychology, it was still a branch of philosophy. He gave to it a geography of the human mind, showed the influence the unconscious has upon waking personality, and brought dreams to the attention of the scientific community. His book *The Interpretation of Dreams* was a turning point in bringing concepts on dreaming from a primitive level to alignment with modern thought. With enormous courage, and against much opposition, he showed the place sexuality has in the development of conscious self-awareness. Freud defined dreams as being:

✳   "Thoughts in pictures." A process of thinking while asleep.

✳   "Ego alien." They have a life and will that often appears to be other than our conscious will. This led older cultures to believe they were sent by spirits or God.

Freud, Sigmund (1856–1939)

* "Hallucinatory." We believe the reality of the dream while in it.

* "Drama." Dreams are not random images. They are "stage-managed" into very definite, sometimes recurring, themes and plots.

* "Moral standards." Dreams have very different moral standards than our waking personality.

* "Association of ideas." In dreaming we have access to infant or other memories or experiences we would find very difficult to recall while awake.

Freud originally said that one of the main functions of a dream was wish fulfillment, and an expression of the "primary process of human thinking" unaffected by space, time, and logic. Later, in considering recurring dreams that reenact a traumatic incident, he agreed that dreams were not only an expression of the "pleasure principle." W.H.R. Rivers, studying dreams connected with war neuroses, saw such dreams as attempts to resolve current emotional problems.

Although there is still controversy regarding whether there can be a valid "dream dictionary," Freud himself saw dream symbols as having consistent meaning, so frequently one could attribute an interpretation to them independently of the dreamer's associations. See **Adler, Alfred; analysis of dreams; birds; Fromm, Erich; gestalt dream work; hallucinations, hallucinogens; hypnosis and dreams; Jung, Carl; lucidity; plot of dreams; unconscious.**

friend Your feelings about the friend. If the dream friend is no one you know, then usually represents the inner intuitive feelings that encourage and advise you. The character of this unknown person will tell you what aspect of yourself it displays. Or it may relate to your contact with friends.

frog   See *frog* under **reptiles, lizards, snakes.**

Fromm, Erich   A New York psychoanalyst, standing between Jung and Freud in his view of dreams. In his book about dreams, *The Forgotten Language,* he says they express both the biological drives and urges that are the substructure of self-awareness, as well as the wisdom that transcends waking thought. In his book *Escape from Freedom,* Fromm reveals how the process of social shaping of the individual personality developed historically. He was the first major psychiatrist who propounded a social and economic theory of psychological structure rather than an individual one based on relationship with parents and other individuals. See Bibliography.

front   Front of body, house, etc.: the more public or expressed part of one's nature, or attitudes used to meet "the world"; a "front" or facade, used to create an impression; the point of stress where we as a person contact others and meet impacts, and so are more vulnerable. Also, what is in front can mean the future. Sometimes, as with the front of a car, or the front door of a house, especially if hood or door is being opened, it depicts sexual nature. See **back.** Idioms: a lot of front; in front of; putting up a good front.

frontier, border   Making great changes in life; decisive changes; meeting a very different self, and thus a new experience of life.

frozen   See **ice.**

fruit   See **food.**

funeral   Feelings about death; very occasionally warning about health of person buried; wanting the buried person out of one's life. One's own funeral: may depict your feelings about your end. May also remind you of what you want to do while alive; desire for sympathy from family;

funeral

retreat from world; a feeling of deadness in life. <u>Burying yourself:</u> leaving an old way of life or old self behind. <u>Someone else's funeral:</u> a wish they were dead; a wish to be rid of them; fears about their death. <u>Parent's funeral:</u> difficulties with or move toward independence; exploring the feeling of their loss; repressing or letting go of the painful past. See **buried;** *rebirth, resurrection* under **archetypes.**

fungus   Feelings about decay or disease; sick ideas, emotions; unconscious activities becoming conscious.

fur   Your animal instincts breaking through into everyday life. These instincts are wholesome and strengthening, so needn't be repressed in most cases. If you have feelings about animal hides, then the fur could relate to this. See **animals.**

furniture, furnishings   Attitudes or habits developed from family or home life, especially if it is a piece of furniture from family home or past dwelling; the attitudes, beliefs we "furnish" our mind with; notions about self; self-image.

bed   Bed is an important symbol to understand. It often shows exactly what you are doing in the subtle areas of your relationship; intimacy; sexual pleasure; rest; the holy place in which you meet yourself and/or another person deeply; a desire to get away from the world, to withdraw into oneself; passivity; sensual rather than sexual contact; sickness; healing rest; privacy; the testing place of the relationship. Sometimes it represents sleep and meeting your unconscious—or torture, because in bed we may be tortured by insomnia, worries, physical pain. Also our life situation—you've made your bed, now lie on it. Bed is one of the most common symbols in dreams. <u>Idioms:</u> bed of nails; bed of roses; go to bed with; make one's bed and lie on it; test bed.

carpet Sometimes depicts your financial state, bare floorboards being poverty; can be the color or design that are important; comfort or lack of it in life—do you feel satisfied with self; a cover-up; feeling of being walked on. Idioms: sweep something under the carpet; on the carpet; roll out red carpet; rug pulled out from under one's feet.

chair Passivity; relaxed attitude; inactivity; receptivity or openness; escapism; rest; waiting. Placing of chair in group: sense of status. Wheelchair: an invalid situation; a sense of weakness. If pushing someone else: seeing self as carrying a weak person.

closet cupboard, wardrobe Memory; resources; different roles you play or attitudes and emotions expressed if wardrobe; hidden memories and emotions, such as skeleton in the cupboard; womb. Open, closed, or trapped in cupboard: whether we are "open or closed" to other people; trapped in old feelings; sense of isolation.

mattress See *bed* above.

rug See *carpet* above.

table Social connection with others; communal activity; everyday certainties that support your activities, such as confidence you will get paid at the end of the week; your attitude toward the inner and exterior community; an area of work or expression; an altar, or self-giving—if table is bare, perhaps not giving much of self. Quality of table: the quality of your relationship with others. Place at table: self-image of your status. Dressing table: one's attempts to create a good social image. Idioms: lay your cards on the table; tabling a motion; table talk; table-hopping.

fuse An electrical fuse represents your ideas, resolves, or confidence that may break down if pressure is brought to bear. Or it can be a wordplay to indicate unity.

G

gale   See **wind; tornado; whirlwind.**

games, gambling   Stances used to meet life; not taking life seriously—making a game of it; competitiveness; sense of winning or losing; teamwork; life skills. See **playing.** In some games there are real prizes, like money, but in many there is the sense of success or the feeling of defeat, so dreaming of games can indicate these. But in dreams games are often used to represent life, where chances we take can have very direct connection with real events. Such adult "games" as making a record, developing a business, starting a job bring us into direct interaction with the world, with an incredibly wide range of responses. Such games are extremely satisfying or disturbing because of these interactions, but like race-car driving, they can be fatal because of how real they are. What we do in our dream game will indicate how we are playing the "game" of life. We may be playing recklessly, by the rules, skillfully, caringly, etc. These indications can be seen as comments on real-life activities.

   Particular games suggest different "stances." Ball games and athletics: competitiveness; conflict within the dreamer—the two sides; sense of win or lose, success or failure; the game of love. Cards and chess: use of strategies and observation. Gambling: taking risks with your life, health, family; work, money—whatever is indicated in dream; desperate feelings. Games like darts, billiards, etc.: your aims and ambitions; aiming at a goal and trying to achieve it; the difficulties of achievement. <u>Opponents:</u> what you are meeting or in conflict with. This may be a part of your nature, such as self-awareness, sexuality, even your body. You might be in conflict with life itself or "God." <u>Id-ioms:</u> beat somebody at their own game; deep game; dirty game; fair game; game of chance; game to the end; give the game away; know what someone's game is; mug's game; name of the game; on the game; waiting game; game is up. See also *ball* under **shapes, symbols; doll; toy.**

badminton   See *tennis* below.

football matches, baseball, rugby   They may represent the strong drive to identify with a tribe, a group; a way the person gains identity and a sense of connection with people around them. In growing internationalism, such games may be of vital importance to maintaining a sense of identity within what may feel like being lost in a multitude.

tennis   Relationship and the sometimes battle for who is going to dominate that goes on in it; competition; the game people play in approaching sex—i.e., veiled remarks, casual telephone calls, verbal clues to readiness, etc.

gaol   See **prison.**

garage   <u>Personal home garage:</u> it may be a toolshed, workshop, frozen-food store, storeroom, as well as a car park. So you need to define how you feel while in it. Is it a quiet place to go; a functional store-area; a place to create? <u>Car repair garage:</u> need for personal attention or "repairs" to your ambition, drive, or ability to motivate yourself. Reserves of drive, energy, motivation; abilities, personal "tools" to meet life; resources; things you do not need but can't let go of. See **car.**

garbage   Experience and feelings you, or society, no longer feel are useful. Occasionally one discards, or considers as

garbage

useless, some aspect of self, or ability, that is actually valuable. We must realize, however, that all thought and feeling are expressions of inner energy. As such, while we discard an expression of the energy, we must not discard the energy, lest it leave us empty and unsatisfied. This is why garbage, or compost, needs to be thought of as material capable of being used in a new form.

garbage can The unwanted aspects of your memories or self; the things you want to get rid of in yourself; things you don't like or are ashamed of.

garden Your inner feelings and imagination; the soul/soil or psyche or the personal attributes and characteristics; the area of growth or change in you; what you are trying to cultivate in yourself; feelings of peace; being near to your natural self; meditative attitude. Beautiful garden: suggests satisfaction at time of dream; depicts the beauty and perhaps creativity or abundance of what you are doing with your life. Overgrown, or weeds in garden: awareness of particular parts of your personality that need working on. Perhaps negative habits need "weeding out." Square or circular garden: holds a lot of your gathered wisdom and insights that would be useful if made conscious. Garden pool: childhood, or early stage in the evolution of one's self-consciousness, during which there was a sense of communal awareness; sense of unity with life; one's feelings that may be observable if one's attention is turned inward—one looks under the surface. See *the self* under **archetypes; digging, excavating; processing your dreams.** Idioms: bear garden; up the garden path.

gardener See *gardener* under **roles.**

gas If referring to dangerous airy substance: harmful thoughts, insinuated evil masquerading as ideas or refined feelings. If referring to car fuel: See **gas/gasoline.**

gas/gasoline   Energy; what motivates you; your reserves; explosive or dangerous emotions.

gate   A threshold, like that between waking awareness and your total experience—such a gate needs to open and close; the gate can also portray the passage from one period of life, or level of maturity, to another. Therefore, to stand before adolescence, parenthood, death might be shown as facing a gate in a dream; a change, or leaving or arriving; similar to door—entrance to something different, or to someone else's life, as in marriage; change. See *door* under **house, buildings.**

gay   See **homosexuality.**

genitals   Direct reference to sexual aspect of self; often used to represent gender. In such dreams a man might dream of having female genitals, suggesting he is experiencing the female aspect of himself. See *penis* and *vagina* under **body; castrate; washing.**

germs   See **bacteria, germs, virus.**

gestalt dream work   Fritz Perls (1893–1970) was the main influence in an approach to dream work that was not interpretative. Unlike the Freudian or Jungian work, which includes a lot of interpretation on the part of the analyst, Perls encouraged the dreamer to explore and express their own sense of each character and object in the dream. This develops personal ability and insight in the dreamer. It enables the dreamer to arrive at direct perception of how they have unconsciously formed their dream. The insights into their own behavior arising from this enable them to more wisely make decisions about action. It also opens a door of direct experience regarding the enormously potent feeling content of dreams. Gestalt work lends itself to peer dream work, in which there is no external authority to judge the dreamer's insights, or to tell them how to work. This has great benefits in that dream exploration can be made by many people who cannot afford, or do not wish to undertake, psychoanalytic work. Its drawback is that the dreamer may avoid their own resistances to uncovering deeper material, and conflicts or fears. See **peer dream work; processing your dreams.**

gestures   See **postures, movement, body language.**

ghost   Memories, feelings, guilt that haunt us; parts of the wider awareness of the unconscious that attempt to communicate; the husks or influences from past traumas or events that have been emptied of hurt and real influence but still affect us as habit patterns; fantasies, hopes, longings we have given time to, and so filled with our life and sexual energy, and that now influence us. Ghost of a living person: a sense of their thoughts or presence influencing us; haunted by desire for them, or a resentment or feeling about them. A ghost that feels solid: the dreamer is "touching" aspects of their own mind or awareness existing beyond preconceived ideas and beliefs.

Robert Van de Castle points out that in his work with people, whenever he has helped them investigate a ghost dream, it has always led back to the childhood experience of a parent coming to the bedroom and lifting them or moving them to prevent bed-wetting. He says the ghost is invariably the mother, and the robber figure is the father. Some people believe the living can haunt a place while they sleep. This is possible, because a living person may experience an OBE and be seen as a ghost by someone in the area of the experience. Seeing a ghost while awake can still be considered as connected with the dream process. See **out-of-body experience; spirits; hallucinations, hallucinogens.**

giant   Childhood feelings about grown-ups, especially the frightening side of parents. If you are the giant, then it means you have excessive feelings of power over others, and being a big person. If someone else is the giant, then it may symbolize your relationship with them, such as feelings of inferiority, powerlessness, fear. If you take the trouble to understand what the other person signifies, apart from their size, it is often found that they represent one of your emotions, fears, or ambitions that has become too big for you to handle and has grown to giant proportions. A giant may also depict contact with an aspect of the collective unconscious.

gift Intuition; unconscious knowledge; what is received in a relationship—such as support, sense of worth, acceptance. <u>Giving gift:</u> giving of self; hoping receiver accepts or likes one. <u>Receiving unwanted gift:</u> difficulties in accepting someone, or something from within; pregnancy. See **giving**.

girl *female under the age of thirteen* Feelings; emotional self; young sexuality; vulnerability. <u>In male's dream:</u> emotions; sexual feelings; daughter. <u>In a female's dream:</u> oneself at that age—whether older or younger; feelings about sister or daughter; the aspect of oneself portrayed by the girl, as in example below. <u>Another girl with your man:</u> how you deal with your sense of being wanted; anxiety about not being attractive or lovable; suspicion; a side of yourself that relates you differently to your man. See **adolescent**.

Example: "I was watching, and at the same time I was a young girl sitting on a lawn." (Honey J.)

girlfriend Your emotional feelings for/about, attachment to the girlfriend; the difficulties, struggles with feelings and sexuality felt in connection with girlfriend of another male; your insights into her behavior. <u>Ex-girlfriend:</u> any feelings or hopes still connected with her; the ex-girlfriend or lover often becomes a symbol for all the hopes for love that are not being satisfied at the moment, or in the present relationship; occasionally the past.

giving Relatedness; the sort of exchange or give-and-take that goes on in a relationship, even the internal relationship

giving

with yourself, or the environment. <u>Giving:</u> one can give affection, support, sex, ideas, as well as wounds. One needs to see what the interaction is by looking at what is given. <u>Received:</u> consider what is received, to define what you are accepting or rejecting in yourself or from others. The idioms show the many ways this action can be used. <u>Idioms:</u> don't give me that; give-and-take; give as good as one gets; give away or giveaway; give oneself away; give somebody away; don't give a brass farthing; give place; give a piece of one's mind; give them enough rope; give someone the evil or glad eye; give someone the elbow; give one's notice. See **gift.**

glacier Emotional tension, repression; fear of living or expressing your feelings or emotions; frozen chunk of past experience.

glass The invisible yet tangible barriers we may erect or feel around others, such as natural caution, emotional coldness, disinterest, fear of being hurt, or pride; social barriers; invisible aspects of oneself that nevertheless may trap us, such as fear, lack of self-respect; self-doubt. <u>Frosted or smoked glass:</u> desire for privacy; keeping parts of oneself hidden; an obscure or unclear view of a situation; occasionally relating to death—the very real yet obscure experience we all face. <u>Breaking glass:</u> breaking through a barrier; shattered emotions. <u>Breaking something made of glass:</u> breaking a relationship; shattering an illusion; brokenhearted. <u>Stepping on broken glass:</u> glass is not very visible, so may represent hidden dangers; being careless about direction in life or present situation; or if it is being done without heed to injury, represents self-inflicted pain. See **break; glass—drinking; injury.**

glass—drinking <u>Empty drinking glasses:</u> past events; memories. <u>Full glasses:</u> present or future experience. See **cup.**

glasses—spectacles Ability to see—understand—or lack of it; a way of hiding oneself, as behind sunglasses. Terms like "shortsighted" or "longsighted" help to understand the use of glasses in a dream. <u>Sunglasses:</u> protectiveness or disguise.

glove   See *gloves* under **clothes.**

glue   One can be glued to the television, or a book. It can therefore depict emotional and intellectual involvement, empathy, dependence; sympathy or love; a "sticky" or difficult situation.

gnarled   The marks of experience and work. The difficulties and struggles of life, but often displayed as wisdom or inner power.

gnaw   Something may be eating away at you inside, such as conscience, worry. What is gnawing represents the source of worry. Gnawing can also mean attacking a problem or situation, or link with hunger for something. See **eating.**

goal   May refer to the external goals we have set ourselves, but dreams often use the image to refer to the internal sense of where we are going in life as a whole, and not just what job we might achieve. After observing the symbol-forming action of the unconscious, Jung came to the conclusion that the unconscious itself was purposive and had certain goals. Such goals arise out of the connection the unconscious has with all life, and its sense of wholeness.

goat   See *goat* under **animals.**

God   Jung says that while the Catholic Church admits of dreams sent by God, most theologians make little attempt to understand dreams in relationship to God.

<u>Being a god:</u> you are always the hero of your life. You are the central character of your drama of experience. As such, you are the deed-doer, the hero or fallen god, especially when the dream is portraying dramatic life events;

this may suggest dangerous overconfidence. <u>God in a dream can depict several things:</u> a set of emotions we use to deal with anxiety—i.e., our belief that a higher power is in charge, so therefore we are okay in the world and are not responsible, thus an escape from responsibility; a parent image from early infancy; a set of moral or philosophical beliefs one holds; self-judgment; something/someone we worship; a feeling of connection with humanity; an expression of the fundamental creative/destructive process in oneself; a sense of one's living interaction or relationship with all beings and the universe. The powerful emotions we sometimes experience about God may well be connected with tremendous childhood need for love and approval from parents. But equally as likely is that the immense feelings we have about meeting God in a dream may express the wonder and perhaps terror we experience in meeting the enormity of realizing we are an expression of the creative universe. As the ego melts and realizes itself as the One Great Life, undifferentiated, there can no longer be a real sense of separation. See *the self* under **archetypes; religion and dreams; individuation.**

goddess   <u>In a woman's dream:</u> the unconscious connection you have with all women, and all female creatures; the power of the collective psyche underlying your personality; the mysterious connections with nature and the forces of nature you are in tune with through menstruation, childbearing, and mothering. Also you are always the heroine of your life. You are the central character of your drama of experience. As such, you are the doer, the heroine or fallen goddess, especially when the dream is portraying dramatic life events. <u>In a man's dream:</u> your collective sense of women as a whole and not as individuals; personal fear of female power, usually relating to early experience of one's mother; your capacity to love in a transcendent way.

gold   The best or most valuable in yourself or in opportunity; the eternal; what stands the "acid test" or does not tarnish with time, in terms of personal qualities, such as love, patience, or care in work; something you value or want in your life. If <u>cheap or false:</u> something you valued but does not deserve respect. If <u>tarnished:</u> something beautiful and valuable in yourself, perhaps your spirit, that you have let become soiled. See *gold, golden* under **colors.**

government   Either the rules by which you govern your life, or exterior influences you feel governed or influenced by, or the inner forces that govern your health, well-being. In each case it would probably be wide influences, not from an individual.

grape   See *fruits* under **food.**

grass   Growth; sometimes can mean overgrown thoughts and feelings that need cutting; multiplicity, countlessness; the innumerable thoughts that can spring up.

grave   Feelings or concepts of death; feelings about someone who is dead; realization that a part of yourself is dead, buried, or killed. See **cemetery; tomb.**

graveyard   See **cemetery.**

gray   See **colors.**

Greece (ancient) dream beliefs   Antiphon, a Greek living in the fourth century B.C., wrote the first known descriptive book of dreams. It was designed to be used for practical and professional interpretations. He maintained that dreams are not created by supernatural powers but natural conditions. In the second century A.D., a similar book was written by Artemidorus, a Greek physician who lived in Rome. He claimed to have gathered his information from ancient sources, possibly from the Egyptian dream book dating from the second millennium B.C. He may have used works from the Assurbanipal library, later

213

destroyed, that held one of the most complete collections of dream literature. Artemidorus classified dreams into dreams, visions, oracles, fantasies, and apparitions. He stated two classes of dreams: the somnium, which forecast events, and the insomnium, which are concerned with present matters. For the somnium dreams Artemidorus gave a dream dictionary. He said *abyss* means an impending danger, a dream of warning. *Candle* to see one being lighted forecasts a birth; to exhibit a lighted candle augers contentment and prosperity; a dimly burning candle shows sickness, sadness, and delay. This latter is taken from folklore of the times, and because dreams tend to use commonly used verbal images, was probably true. He maintained that a person's name—that is, their identity, and the family, national, and social background from which they arose—has bearing on what their dream means.

Plato (429–347 B.C.) said that even good men dream of uncontrolled and violent actions, including sexual aggression. These actions are not committed by good men while awake, but criminals act them out without guilt. Democritus said that dreams are not products of ethereal soul, but of visual impressions that influence our imagination. Aristotle (383–322 B.C.) stated that dreams can predict future events. Earlier, Hippocrates, the "father of medicine," discovered that dreams can reveal the onset of organic illness. Such dreams, he said, can be seen as representing external reality.

Hippocrates was born on the island of Kos. On the island was the famous temple dedicated to Aesculapius, the god of medicine. There were about three hundred such temples in Greece alone, dedicated to healing through the use of dreams. Hippocrates was an Aesculapian, and learned his form of dream interpretation from them. In such temples the patients would ritually cleanse themselves by washing, and abstain from sex, alcohol, and even food. They would then be led into what was sometimes a subterranean room in which there were harmless snakes—these were the symbol of the god, and are the probable connecting link with the present-day use of snakes to represent the healing professions. Prior to sleep the participants were led in evening prayers to the god, thus creating an atmosphere in which dreams of healing were induced. In the morning the patients were asked their dream, and it was expected they would dream an answer to their illness or problem. There are many attestations to the efficacy of this technique from patients.

green   See *green* under **colors.**

greenhouse, glasshouse   Can represent either that one has been cosseted or over-cared-for in life, not exposed to difficulties or harshness—or vulnerable growing parts of oneself or others.

ground   See **earth.**

group   See **people.**

gun   See **weapons.**

guru   The wisdom of the unconscious. The essence of what one has learned from life, and the collective unconscious becoming known to your conscious self; the self. See **god; goddess;** *the self* under **archetypes.**

H

hair   See *hair* under **body.**

hairdresser   See **barber, hairdresser.**

half   Part of; divided; incomplete; in between; conflict. <u>Half open:</u> opposing feelings about whether to "be open" or not; can I, can't I—will I, won't I? <u>Halfway up/down:</u> indecision; faltering motivation; sometimes between the opposites, or outside of one's everyday experience. <u>Half full:</u> may refer to half one's life used up. <u>Cut in half:</u> conflict between intellect and body/sexuality. <u>Half buried:</u> something you are only partly aware of or is trapped.

hall, hallway   See *hall* and *hallway* under **house, buildings.**

Hall, Calvin   Author of *The Content Analysis of Dreams* and *The Meaning of Dreams*. Hall's work with content analysis—looking at the personality of the dreamer through a series of dreams rather than a single dream—is expressed in a popular form in his book *The Meaning of Dreams*. With the entrance into home life of computers, easy content analysis has become much more available. See **computers and dreams.**

hallucinations, hallucinogens   A hallucination can be experienced through any of the senses singly, or all of them together. So one might experience a hallucinatory smell or sound. Hallucinations are quite common without any use of drugs, such as alcohol, LSD, or cannabis. Everyone has the natural ability to produce hallucinations. One of the definitions of a dream, according to Freud, is its hallucinatory quality. While asleep we can create full sensory, vocal, motor, and emotional experience in our dream. While dreaming we usually accept what we experience as real. A waking hallucination is an experience of a "dream" occurring while we have our eyes open. The voices heard, people seen, smells smelt, although appearing to be outside of us, are no more exterior than the things and images of dreams. With this information one can understand that much classed as psychic phenomena and religious experience is an encounter with the dream process. That does not, of course, deny its importance.

Example: "I dream insects are dropping either on me from the ceiling of our bedroom, or crawling over my pillow. My long-suffering husband is always woken when I sit bolt upright in bed, my eyes wide open and my arm pointing at the ceiling. I try to brush them off. I can still see them—spiders or wood lice. I am now well aware it is a dream. But no matter how hard I stare, the insects are there in perfect detail. I am not frightened, but wish it would go away." (Sue D.)

Drugs such as LSD, cannabis, psilocybin, mescaline, peyote, and opium can produce hallucinations. This is sometimes because they allow the dream process to break through into consciousness with less intervention. If this occurs without warning, it can be very disturbing. The real dangers are that unconscious content, which in ordinary dreaming breaks through a threshold in a regulated way, emerges with less regulation, and without the safety factor of knowing it is a dream. Fears, paranoid feelings, past traumas can emerge into the consciousness of an individual who has no skill in handling such dangerous forces. Because the propensity of the unconscious is to create images, an area of emotion might emerge as an image, such as the devil. Such images and the power they contain, not being integrated in a proper therapeutic way, may haunt the individual, perhaps for years. Even at a much milder level, elements of the unconscious will emerge and disrupt the person's ability to appraise reality and make judgments. Unacknowledged fears may lead the drug user to rationalize their reasons for avoiding social activity or the world of work. See **ESP in dreams;** *Dead husband* in *husband* under **family, family relationships; out-of-body experience.**

hammer   See **tools.**

hand   See *hand* under **body.**

handbag   See **bag.**

harbor   See **quay.**

hare   See *hare* under **animals.**

harness   Directing your energy or potential; control; restraint.

hat   See *hat* under **clothes.**

haversack   See **knapsack.**

head   See *head* under **body.**

healing and dreams   There is a long tradition of using dreams as a base for both physical and psychological healing. One of the earliest recorded incidents of such healing is when "Pharaoh's spirit was troubled; and he sent for all the magicians of Egypt and all its wise men; and Pharaoh told them his dream, but there was no man who could interpret it." Then Joseph revealed the meaning of the dream and so the healing of Pharaoh's troubled mind took place—Genesis 41. The Greek temples of Asclepius were devoted to using dreams as a base for healing of body and mind. The Iroquois Amerindians used a social form of dreamed therapy also. Sigmund Freud pioneered the modern approach to the use of dreams in therapy, but many different approaches have developed since his work.

A feature that people who use their dreams as a therapeutic tool mention again and again, is how dreams empower them. Many of us have an unconscious feeling that any important healing work regarding our body and mind, can only be undertaken and directed by an expert. The expert might be a doctor, a psychiatrist, a psychotherapist, or even an osteopath. Witnessing the result of their own dream process, even if helped by an expert, people feel in touch with a wonderful internal process that is working actively for their own good. One woman, who had worked on her dreams with the help of a non-expert friend, said, "It gave me great confidence in my own internal process. I realized there was something powerful in myself working for my own good. It was a feeling of co-operating with life."

hearing   See *ear* under **body.**

hell   If threatening: fearful emotions, anxieties; one's self-created misery, perhaps arising out of such things as anger or resentment we cling to, or a sense of being different or unwanted; feelings that burn in us; pain from past trauma; memories of, or feelings connected with, a place or relationship we were deeply unhappy in. People who have suffered birth trauma often dream of this as hell. Sometimes people reverse the roles of heaven and hell. Hell becomes attractive, full of excitement, heaven an insipid place. See *devil* under **archetypes.** Hell also represents the projection of your inner state onto the world. If you are hateful, then the world also seems hateful; if you are depressed, the world appears depressing. In the unconscious, where the state of mind actually produces the surroundings, as in dreams, through your state of mind and feeling you literally create your heaven or hell.

herb   Healing, or some particular influence, such as drowsiness, stimulation, cleansing.

hero/ine   See *Christ* under **archetypes,** *hero/ine* and *the self* under **archetypes; compensation theory; religion and dreams.**

hiding   Hiding from feelings; avoiding awareness of something we don't want to see; being protective—hiding how we really feel about someone, or sexual feelings about someone; not knowing. <u>Hiding a body or object:</u> not facing difficult feelings connected with the body or a thing. See **dead people dreams.** <u>Hiding from something dangerous, or dangerous thing hidden:</u> feeling threatened either by unconscious contents or exterior situation.

high   <u>Being high:</u> can depict having a very wide view of one's situation in life; feeling isolated, alone, or away from the known and secure—as one might in starting a new job, losing one's job, or moving to a new town; apprehension; anxiety; one's aspirations and widest view of life, therefore a sense of connection with the world. <u>Looking at something high:</u> above one's head; feeling impressed or awed; challenge. <u>Being on a high building:</u> as with being high, but also being cut off from one's emotions and thus feeling isolated; achievement; fear of losing control; isolation from others. See **descending, down; hill; mountain; positions.** <u>Idioms:</u> high and mighty; high as a kite; high-flown; high flyer; high-minded; high places.

highway   See **road.**

hill   Difficulty, obstacle, something needing energy to deal with. A hill also symbolizes the climb to higher attainment, wider view of life or opportunities. You climb to success, or go down hill to failure, illness, death. You can see farther from above, or be overshadowed at the foot of a hill. A <u>hole at the bottom of a hill:</u> especially if surrounded by shrubs, depicts the vagina. <u>Going downhill:</u> feeling as if circumstances are pushing you; feeling you might, or have, lost control; the second half of your life, or old age. <u>Going uphill:</u> difficulties; hard work or effort; the first half of your life; or life itself if it feels like an uphill struggle. <u>Green sunny hillside:</u> feeling whole; a sense of heaven. <u>On a hill:</u> a clear view of your situation; achievement; something you have made an effort to attain; expanded awareness. Also hill or hills sometimes represent breasts or the belly. See **mountain; high; descending, down.**

Example: "I am riding through thick fog. I feel I should turn back. But then I see a pale golden white glow and know that if I continue to the top of the hill I will emerge from the fog into a most beautiful place." (Denny)

historic   In some dreams we find ourselves in the past, with the feeling of those times. This nearly always depicts not a past life, but our attitudes. So a cowboy scene might depict our pioneering spirit or sense of adventure. We need to define what feelings we derive from reading about or seeing films about such periods of history; our past; the person we were at some period in life.

history of dream beliefs   Based on the beliefs of early cultures such as the Australian aborigines and the Kalahari bushmen, we can be certain dreams were an important part of the life of early human beings. The earliest known record of dreams is recorded in the epic poem Gilgamesh, that is four thousand years old. The text includes an account of a series of dreams. See **American Indian dream beliefs; analysis of dreams; Australian aborigine dream beliefs; Buddhism and dreams; Greece (ancient) dream beliefs; religion and dreams; Islamic dream traditions.**

Hobson, J. Allan   In his book *The Dreaming Brain,* Hobson presents a well-researched theory of dreaming, based on biological and psychological processes. Through closely examining historical dream theories, and measuring them against present-day findings, he unfolds his new theory that dreams are not disguised urges, but transparent though sometimes scrambled hallucinations. In this theory, internally generated brain signals excite the visual and motor senses, but cannot be checked against external reality. This gives rise to bizarre imagery and discontinuities in the dream that are integrated into meaning by the brain. Hobson is not saying dreams do not hold information about the dreamer, but that such information is as straightforwardly expressed as is possible, given the nature of the brain's activity during sleep.

Another way of explaining the theory is to say that while awake the forebrain has the function of sorting and bringing meaning to the multitude of sensory impressions we receive. Most of us have observed this concerning half-heard words or indistinct images that we interpret as one thing, only to find later that what we "heard" or "saw" was not what actually existed. Hobson goes on to say that while sleeping, brain signals are generated that excite many areas of the brain. These signals, Hobson and McCarley say, produce random feelings, images, and motor impulses. The faculties that bring order and interpretation to the sensory welter of impressions go to work on these random impulses and give them some measure of meaning, perhaps order them into what we call a dream. In this sense a dream is created out of chaotic or random brain activities. The dreamer may impose particular sorts of order on these brain activities. Such personal dreaming arises out of predispositions, fears, etc. While this certainly explains something of the way the mind does work at times, it doesn't cover many of the aspects of dreaming. Things such as out-of-body experiences and gathered information beyond the ability of the senses are not covered by this approach. See the third example under *the dream as extended perception* in **ESP in dreams.**

holding   There are five aspects to holding. <u>One:</u> to control, as in controlling or "holding one's breath"; to be able to manipulate, kill, or do something with what is held; this includes holding on to something for support or protection. Two: ownership—this is mine to share or not. Three: in touch with; knowing; having a "grasp" of. Four: responsibility; left holding the baby; one's situation. Five: intimacy; taking to oneself, taking hold of oneself, holding an opinion or grudge. Idioms: get hold of; have a hold over someone; hold back; hold in.

hole   Difficulty or tricky situation in life; a situation you might "fall into"; a place to hide or feel protected in—therefore, womblike feelings; an escape route; a way of "seeing through" something; the vagina; death. Going in hole: meeting feelings, urges, or fears we usually keep unconscious; trying to avoid something; confronting aspects of self buried beneath our surface awareness; memories of womb existence; death—burial. Holes in clothes, objects: faults; weaknesses; illness; "full of holes." Holes in body: sense of weakness; emptiness in one's life, such as loneliness; illness; negative feelings about that part of self; see **body** for appropriate part. Hole in head: letting everyone know what you think; gossiping. Hole in road: danger, may represent illness, death, or death of person falling down the hole. Occasionally used as wordplay, meaning whole. See first example in *son* under **family, family relationships; tunnel.**

holiday   Sense of relaxation; being independent; satisfying one's own needs; reaching a period of one's life in which one can rest on one's laurels. See example in **crossroad.**

hollow   Feeling of emptiness in one's life; womb feeling or memories; feelings about the vagina. See **hole.**

homosexuality   Each of us has some element of homosexuality in us unconsciously. In one's dreams it may suggest a desire for the father's or mother's love, perhaps because they were not demonstrative. So one was led to

223

crave the love of a man/woman; conflict or anxiety about one's own gender; feelings of sexual inadequacy, or inadequacy in one's own gender; unconscious pain in regard to the opposite sex—this may be rationalized into reasons for being homosexual rather than being experienced and made conscious; depicting an introversion of one's sexual drive. Sometimes being the receptive partner in the same-sex relationship suggests in-turned or repressed sexual drive, possibly through trauma, fear, or inability to meet full woman/man.

honey   The essence of one's experience; pleasure; sweetness.

horse   See *horse* under **animals.**

hot   Pleasurable "warm" feelings; passion for someone. <u>Very hot, or burning:</u> potentially painful emotions or passions, which may leave their mark. See **fire.** <u>Idioms:</u> be hot on; hot and bothered; hot-blooded; hotheaded; hot stuff; in hot water; in the hot seat; make it hot for someone; get the hots; hot air.

hotel   See *hotel* under **house, buildings.**

house, buildings   A house nearly always refers to yourself, depicting your body and attributes of personality. Thus, if we take a large house with its many functional rooms, the library would represent the mind, the bathroom the cleansing or renewal of good feelings, the bedrooms one's sexuality or intimacy; the roof one's protectiveness or "coping mechanisms." But these parts of the building may also be seen as different parts of your body. See *home* and *house* below. Large public buildings, such as hospitals, factories, blocks of flats, depict particular functions suggested by their nature, such as work or healing. But, of course, if the house or building has a personal connection—the house you live in, or place you have worked—then you need to define what is the essential feelings about such. Or see **processing your dreams.** If a house or building has a quality of some other type of construction, such as a library feeling like a factory, or a house feeling like a church, both aspects should be accepted as important. Below are first listed general types of buildings and their situations, then after that the various parts of a house, with a larger description of *house* and *home*. <u>Falling-down or destroyed house or building</u>: something that is passing away or has passed. This can refer to a way of life or a particular personality style. This could be depicted as a building or house that has fallen or been knocked down; aging and the process whereby one loses some functioning or sexual attractiveness of the body in aging.

abbey, church, chapel, temple   The powerfully regenerative side of our inner life or feelings, as in the first example below; the world of experience we have created inwardly by thoughts, meditation, actions; our sense of contact with life; moral rules we make decisions from; moral authority; relationship with the community. Occasionally baptism, marriage, death, the mother, or refuge. <u>Walking past the church</u>: not entering into contact with the best in us—or anger toward dogma.

Example: "It was like an English church with several great spires. The whole building seemed to be built in a white and gold design. The gold parts shimmered in the sun. I gazed at this wonderful sight for some time and felt such a wonderful feeling of upliftment, my tiredness gone." (Johan E.)

Example: "The priest was going to question and assault my friend in connection with some opinion he had offended the church with. I went to stand near him to give him moral support, and physical help if necessary. I hated seeing anybody degraded. The priest saw my move and sent three thug-type men to shoulder me out. They surrounded me to knock me down. I went berserk and knocked them all over the place with kicks and punches."

house, buildings

(John P.) In this example, John sees the dogmas of the church as an assault and degradation of human qualities of love and moral support.

apartment, flat   In general, the same as *house* or *home* below, but may have a slightly different significance if you have lived in an apartment or flat. Therefore, the questions need to be asked as to whether you lived/live alone in the apartment. Did you share the apartment with others? What was living alone or sharing like? These form the associated feeling states connected with the dream apartment.

attic   The mind, ideas, memories, past experience. If <u>trapped in an attic:</u> a purely intellectual approach to life. <u>Finding an attic:</u> pleasure at new ideas, discovering potential or wisdom from past experience. <u>Threat from attic:</u> disturbing thoughts. <u>Window or turret looking out from attic:</u> our sense of connection with the cosmos; wider awareness; intellectual view. <u>Hiding in attic:</u> escape from other people; retreat from everyday life.

balcony, veranda   Relaxation; a wider viewpoint; away from involvement.

ballroom   See **ballroom.**

banister   Support; protectiveness.

bar   See **barroom.**

basement, cellar   Usually the things we have hidden from awareness in our unconscious. The example below shows how Mrs. K. has killed or repressed a part of herself. We might "kill" ambition, love, sexual drive, and these are pushed into our unconscious. But the basement or cellar is also the entrance to personal and transpersonal memories, biological "unconscious" functions, archetypal patterns of behavior, subliminal or psychic impressions, the collective unconscious. Frequently it is the place we keep memories of traumatic events in our life. So a dark shape or intruder might emerge from "downstairs." Our dark deeds or guilty memories are also in the basement. A <u>snake in the cellar or cave:</u> our psychobiological drive; the energy behind growth and motivation that includes sex drive. Often experienced as emotional or feeling drive or zest for life. This connects us with awareness of our evolution as a person. <u>Bad smell:</u> emotions that could cause depression or illness.

Example: "I know I have killed somebody and their body is walled up in the cellar. The strange thing is, I haven't a clue who this person is. Various people visit my home and I am terrified the body will be discovered. In one of these recurring dreams the police actually investigate the disappearance of 'the person' and go into the cellar. When I wake from these dreams I always have the most terrible guilty feeling." (Mrs. K.)

buying a house   See **purchasing a house** below.

castle   Feelings of security or insecurity; defensive attitudes; the way we defend ourselves against "attack"; past attitudes that may have been necessary in childhood to defend ourselves while strengthening our identity; our way of defending against the remembering or experiencing of childhood pain. See **defense; defense mechanisms.**

chimney   Smoking; the birth canal; sign of inner warmth. <u>Belching black smoke:</u> the grim mechanized side of culture centered on production instead of humanity.

church   See **church;** abbey, church, chapel, above.

classroom   See **school.**

corridor   No-man's-land; limbo; in-between state; the process of going from one thing to another. The example below may refer to the experience of birth in the birth canal. Such a corridor can also depict a sense of not being able to get out of a dissatisfactory situation. It may also depict a direction in life produced by circumstances, or even the female genitals. See *white* under **color.**

Example: "I'm trapped in a long passageway or corridor. I can't get out. I'm feeling my way along the wall—there is a small light at the end of the tunnel, I can't get to it. I'm very frightened. I wake up before I get to the end. Then I feel afraid to go back to sleep." (Sandra)

door   A boundary; the difference between one feeling state and another, such as depression and feeling motivated; the passing from inside oneself to exterior life; the feelings or attitudes, such as aloofness, we use to shut others out of our life, to remain independent or private; being open or inviting; a sense of leaving an environment or relationship—escape; entering into a new work or relationship situation. Freud felt that a door, a keyhole, a handle, a knocker, all depicted sex and sexual organs. Knocking refers to the sex act, the cul-de-sac is the woman's legs. But the image of a door has so many other ways of being expressed in dreams and is used very frequently. See **exit door.** <u>Back door:</u> our private, family life; our more secret activities; the anus. <u>Door to strange landscape or world:</u> finding entrance to unconscious or a new realization. <u>Doorknob:</u> See **knob.** <u>Front door:</u> public self; confidence; relationship with people in general; a vagina. <u>Shutting a door:</u> privacy; trying to find "space" for oneself; the dismissing attitudes or tension we use to shut others out of intimate contact; repressing memories or feelings; decisively ending something. <u>Side door:</u> escaping from a situation or being indirect. <u>Someone at a door:</u> opportunity; the unexpected; new experience or relationship.

factory   Work, for some people; the habitual, mass-produced reactions to life lacking individuality; conformity or cooperation with the group or society; productiveness, industry; inner physical activities, such as digestion.

first floor   Thinking and feeling. See *ground floor* below.

fortress   See *castle* above.

ground floor   Practical everyday life and its needs.

gymnasium   Challenges; meeting ways of gaining skills or strength; health issues. See **school.**

hall   <u>Public or dance hall:</u> how you relate to groups or the public; the attitude or function in oneself that connects the many different aspects of oneself; meeting sexuality; a place of initiation—maturing beyond old habits, ways of life, and views—perhaps because civic ceremonies such as marriage, trials, social rewards take place in hall-like environments.

hallway   The way one meets other people or allows them into one's life or intimacy; the receptive female reproductive function; connecting link with aspects of oneself.
    Example: "I find myself in the entrance hall of a very large house. The hall is very large with curved staircases, either side meeting at the top to form a balcony. There is nobody about and I am frightened. I start to walk up the stairs but then find myself hiding in the roof with very little space above my body." (Celia) The hall is probably Celia's childbearing ability and her image of herself as a woman. The words "little space above my body" suggest her main area of life has always been her childbearing function or physical attractiveness as a woman, and she has not developed her mental self. See **corridor;** *white* under **color.**

home   Your basic needs, such as shelter, warmth, nourishment—but usually in the sense of what you have created as your basic way of life, the structure of the way you respond to the world and relationships. This includes family attitudes and goals; the values, standards, goals you have accepted as normal, or are "at home" with; the situation or

house, buildings

feeling state in your home, which here means family atmosphere and attitudes; the state of feeling relaxed, being oneself, because you're away from other people and what you need to be in relationship with them. Thus a sense of being oneself, or absence of concern over other people's criticism. In clarifying this dream symbol, it needs to be defined as to what the state of feeling was or is in the home, and whether you share or shared the space with others, and what this was like. <u>In a past home:</u> depicts the parts of your character or experience that developed in that home environment. <u>Someone else's home:</u> what you sense as the attitudes and atmosphere—or the situation prevailing in that home. <u>Future home:</u> the direction you would like your life to take, or fear it might. See *house* below. <u>Idioms:</u> bring something home to someone; close to home; come home to roost; home and dry; broken home; home truth; home is where the heart is.

hospital   Hospital represents needing or being involved in a healing process of body or mind; worries about one's health. Example: "I was a prisoner in a hospital, although there were no locked doors or bars. It was a psychiatric hospital, but we were allowed to believe we had a physical illness. I had been very ill, but was trying to escape." (Lily) At the time of her dream Lily was feeling trapped in depression and also attending a therapy group.

hotel   Temporary attitudes or way of life; a short-term situation; relaxation; escape or separation from family or home situations; sexual activity outside home life; for people such as businessmen-women or media people, the hotel can represent work or the pursuance of work.

house   If the house is one you know, live in now or in the past, what is said about *home* applies. <u>Attackers/intruders from outside:</u> social pressures or response to criticisms. <u>Basement:</u> unconscious. See *basement, cellar* above. <u>Bedroom:</u> privacy; sex; intimacy; rest; feelings of wanting to retreat. See *bed* under **furniture.** Burning, falling down: big changes in attitudes; leaving old standards or dependencies behind; sickness. Ceiling: the attitudes or beliefs you use to protect your identity; the height or range of your imagination; your mental limit or boundary. Chimney: See *chimney* above. Cramped house: feeling of need for personal change; feeling restricted in home environment or in present personal attitudes. Damage, structural faults: faults in character structure; hurts, such as broken relationship; bodily illness. Dining room: appetites; social or family contact; mental or psychological diet. First and other middle floors: internal needs, rest, sleep, hungers; the trunk. Floor: basic attitudes and confidence; what supports you, such as health and goodwill of others. The floor often appears without much emphasis in many dreams. This suggests it is depicting the present situation or environment you are in. For instance, first floor or second floor would suggest a different situation in which the events of the dream are taking place. Front of house: our persona; facade; social self; face. See **facade.** Ground floor: practical everyday life, sexuality; hips and legs. If it is a house created by the dream: one's body and personality in all its aspects. Inside the house: within oneself. Kitchen: creativity; nourishing oneself; mother role; diet. Kitchen in woman's dream: may refer to pride in the ability to create a home and contribute something valuable to the family. Larder: hungers; sensual satisfaction; your store of memories or feelings that satisfy or nourish you. Living room: personal leisure; "space" to be oneself; everyday life. Nursery, child's bedroom: feelings about your children; one's own childhood feelings and memories. Other people in house: different facets of dreamer, or person or people involved quite deeply in your life. Therefore a stranger entering your house would suggest a new relationship. Other person's house: another person's life. If you go in the house, it shows you getting involved with that person, perhaps being a part of their life—for instance, entering a relationship. If you are watching someone else go in the house, it suggests an awareness of that person, or an aspect of self, being involved in another person's life. See entry below on seeing partner go into someone else's house. <u>Outside the house and garden:</u> extroversion or the relationship with environment. <u>People or things from upstairs:</u> influence of rational self. <u>Repairs, enlargement, renovation:</u> reassessment or change of attitudes or character; personal growth. <u>Row of houses:</u> other people. <u>Seeing your husband/wife/partner go in someone else's house:</u> this may suggest your partner has the tendency to move into another relationship. This may be only your fears, but it may show you sense a growing distance in your relationship, and the possibility of your partner going elsewhere. <u>Study, library:</u> mental growth; mind. <u>Things in the house:</u> aspects of one's feelings and makeup. <u>Toilet:</u> privacy; release of tension; letting go of emotions, fantasies or desires that we need to discharge. See **toilet.** <u>Top floor, attic:</u> thinking; the conscious mind; memory; the head. See *attic* above. <u>Windows:</u> one's outlook on life; how you see others. See *window* below. <u>People or things coming from downstairs:</u> influences, fears, impressions from unconscious or passions, or from everyday worries.

elevator Mood shifts or movement of attention—as when we move from being involved in physical sensation and shift to thinking; rise or drop in status or work situation; emotional highs and lows—the lift going out through the roof could show tendency toward being manic—going underground, meeting influences from the unconscious; being "uplifted" or feeling "down." <u>Trapped in elevator:</u> frustration; anxiety; feelings of restriction in trying to make changes.

Example: "I was in a lift with a young woman. She intimated there was some difficulty about getting the lift to work. I felt this was not so and pushed the button. The doors closed and the lift began to ascend. As it did, we moved close together and kissed. But the main feeling was of being accepted and liked. This moved my feelings so much I felt a great melting feeling in my abdomen, and a lot of body sensation against her body." (Anthony F.) Here the lift shows Anthony "being moved" emotionally and sexually—the lift can depict sex and the energy flowing up the trunk in love or meditation.

hut   Childhood family feelings; basic uncomplicated situation or relationship.

library   Memory; learning; memories of school. See **library; school.**

lift   See *elevator* above.

mansion   Although a house represents all the aspects of self in which our identity lives—body, emotions, creativity, etc.—a mansion is depicting the same thing with a different emphasis. It is ourselves as we are, plus features still latent, possibilities not yet developed or explored.

palace   A sense of importance, or privilege. In some dreams about a palace, there are evident feelings of something special happening. This probably links with the way palaces are used in fairy stories—as, for instance, the palace in which Sleeping Beauty lives. Such a palace represents the wonders of yourself, your amazing mind and qualities, that might be sleeping or overcome by enemies—i.e., disuse or ignoring them. The palace is also the storehouse of your culture and past, the treasure house of your family, social and racial inheritance.

plumbing   Internal organs, such as the digestive system or circulatory system; how you direct your emotions.

public house   Social, free-and-easy side of self; one's ability in relating to the public; alcohol dependency.

purchasing a house   In general, this may relate to making a decision to change, or wanting a change in your life or circumstances. Purchasing something in a dream also often involves the process of deciding or being uncertain. The decision-making is to do with clarifying what you want, what you would like. See **purchasing.**

roof   The philosophy, beliefs, or coping strategies we use to protect ourselves from stress. <u>Standing on a roof:</u> heightened awareness. <u>Mending a roof:</u> developing new coping strategies; feeling vulnerable. <u>Leaking roof:</u> need for new coping strategies. <u>No roof:</u> if not a threatening dream, suggests no barrier between personality and psychic or transcendent awareness; a sense of connection with life or wider awareness. If threatening, feeling invaded by forces outside oneself. <u>Roof garden:</u> mental growth or flowering of new ideas, insights, or abilities.

room   A particular feeling state—for instance, the room might feel sinister, warm, spacious, cold, etc.—so depicts such; womb. Sometimes a room, because of its spaciousness, represents the amount of potential or opportunity one has. The "containing" quality of a room may also depict involvement in one's mother or a particular situation. The <u>finding of extra rooms:</u> a common dream theme— recognition or discovery of previously unnoticed aspects, abilities, fears, or traits in oneself. If the discovery is distressing, this may reflect a feeling of a change in one's status quo that is disturbing. <u>Room without doors or windows:</u> may represent the womb and life in the womb. What is happening in the room may show the state of a pregnancy, or feelings about pregnancy; feeling trapped. Example: "There was a room in my house I had never been in before. It was filled with water and had three kittens submerged in it. While in the room I didn't need to breathe." (Zoe W.) The room here represents Zoe's childbearing function—her womb. The room can therefore depict mother or qualities of mothering. See description of various rooms under *house.*

ruins   An old and now useless way of life you led in the past; a particular personality structure that has now broken down; feelings you have about some aspect of your life. The ruins in many dreams are shown as a castle, and this suggests the defenses you used at one time to survive, but are now not necessary.

school   See **school.**

stable   The natural urges you have; birthplace of Christ—i.e., where we meet the influence arising from our innate link with all life.

stairs   Taking steps toward something; going up or down in life in your estimation, or in life; gaining a new skill, or facing a challenge—stairs are difficult and dangerous when we are children, and so probably remain as a symbol of challenge, danger, and achievement in adulthood. <u>Running up:</u> escaping from urges arising from lower down in the body, so a movement of attention toward the abstract or mental away from fears arising from unconscious or sexuality; lack of confidence, a fear of failing, or not being capable is also a common feeling in connection with stairs; if running up with pleasure, then it suggests exuberance producing a change in your feelings and situation. <u>Skimming down:</u> this is a dream often experienced by children. It is almost like flying down the stairs, the feet just touching the edge of the stairs every so often, creating an exhilarating sense of pleasure. The reason for the dream is most likely that going down stairs as a young child is a difficult and dangerous skill. Most of us have fallen at some point. As we gain greater physical control and can run down stairs, a sense of greater achievement arises. Not only stairs, but other areas of our environment that were dangerous are now a source of pleasure. The dream translates this feeling into the image of skimming the stairs.

house, buildings

wall Codes of behavior, belief systems, attitudes—often unconscious—you live within, or are protected by; the boundaries of behavior or thought you keep within, are fearful of extending beyond, or are trapped by—thereby, what one feels to be barriers or restrictions; one's feelings of confidence that protect against anxiety or social "knocks"; fears that keep you limited in your activities; the feelings or attitudes you keep people away with—the walls we put up between us to maintain privacy, stop being hurt, or to maintain a role or status; a special feeling situation that you have created, such as developing a sense of your own value; the "reality" you have accepted as the truth, either given you ready-made by your culture or one you have built personally. This reality is like walls you live within. Walls of a favorite house: might be your feelings of security in your marriage or family that give you defense against the "storms" of life.

warehouse Memories; past experience; aspects of self put in storage, such as ambition while bringing up children.

window In general, one is either looking out of, looking into, or going through a window. This makes them largely connected with what we see in the sense of perception or being aware of things, either within ourselves or in regard to other people. So they can depict our eyes or awareness. Looking out of a window: your "view" of or feelings about what you perceive in your environment or life; looking for a way out of a situation. Looking into a window: what you feel or "see" in regard to someone else if you see another person; what you are aware of when "looking" at or giving awareness to yourself. Climbing out of window: possibly your way of avoiding difficult feelings—i.e., by giving attention to exterior things—television, a book—rather than what you feel. Climbing in a window: looking within oneself or seeing what makes someone else "tick." Opening a window: letting others see your feelings or opinions; allowing other people's influence into yourself; letting in some new feelings. <u>No windows:</u> not seeing what is going on around you; introversion; attention held by internal feelings, thoughts, or concerns. <u>Height of windows—such as second floor:</u> suggests what area of your experience you are looking at the world through. You might only look at life through a basement window, which suggests being influenced by one's sexuality or unconscious feelings. See mention of levels of house above. <u>Domed window, window in roof:</u> depicts our head, or reach of our mind. <u>Idioms:</u> window dressing; window on the world; a room with a view.

housework   The cleaning out of nonfunctional—negative—attitudes, thoughts, and experiences; keeping our internal house in order, perhaps by taking time to clarify or define motives, opinions, and feelings about others; transforming yourself.

Humphrey, Nicholas   Humphrey sees human beings as needing to learn and modify strategies for social survival and interaction. He says of the human animal, "It depends upon the bodies of other animals not merely for immediate sustenance in infancy and its sexual fulfilment as an adult but in one way or another for the success—or failure—of almost every enterprise it undertakes. In these circumstances the ability to model the behaviour of others in the social group has paramount survival value." We know that cats while dreaming practice stalking and hunting. Humphrey speculates that in dreams humans practice and modify social behavior. See **Adler, Alfred; analysis of dreams; birds; Evans, Christopher; Freud, Sigmund; Fromm, Erich; gestalt dream work; Jung, Carl; lucidity; unconscious.**

hunger   Your needs or demands, physically, emotionally, and mentally. You may feel the need for success or fame just as acutely as the need for sex or food. See **eating; food.**

hunter/huntress The aspect of oneself that is either killing out your "animal" or gaining sustenance from it; the urge to get away from everyday responsibility; your breadwinning qualities.

husband See *husband* under **family, family relationships.**

hypnosis and dreams Many experiments have been done using hypnosis in connection with dreams. In the early part of the last century Carl Schroetter hypnotized Miss E., a pharmacist, in an attempt to test Freud's theory of symbol formation. He suggested Miss E. would dream of having homosexual intercourse with a female friend, L. The dream she subsequently reported was: "I sit in a small dirty cafe holding a tremendous French newspaper.... A woman with a strong Yiddish accent—L. is Jewish—asks me twice, 'Don't you need anything?' I don't answer.... She comes a third time ... I recognize her as my acquaintance. She holds a threadbare suitcase with a sticker on it that reads: 'For ladies only!' I leave the cafe with her ... she hangs on to me in a way I find unpleasant but suffer it.... Before her house she pulls out an enormous bunch of keys and gives one to me. 'I trust only you with it; it is the key to this case. You might like to use it. Just watch that my husband doesn't get hold of it.' " The dream contains several of the classical Freudian symbols of sex, such as the suitcase, the key, and the phrase "for ladies only." Miss E. had not, according to Schroetter, heard or read of Freud's ideas.

Roffenstein, suspecting Miss E. may have known something of Freudian ideas, chose "a 28-year-old, totally uneducated nursemaid of lower than average intelligence, who grew up and still lived in an uneducated milieu." He suggested she dream of intercourse with her father. She reported: "I dreamt about my father, as if he had presented me with a great bag ... and with it he gave me a large key. It was a very large key. It looked like the key to a house. I had a sad feeling. I opened the bag. A snake jumped out against my mouth; I shrieked aloud."

More recent experiments are reported by Ralph L. Woods and Herbert B. Greenhouse in *The New World of Dreams*. The suggestion was made to one subject that as a child she had wet the bed and her mother scolded her. That night she dreamt she fell into a pond in winter and her mother was angry. An interesting aspect of these experiments is that another subject under hypnosis was told the dream and asked what it meant. Without hesitation she said, "Oh, that girl must have wet the bed." This and other experiments suggest humans have an inherent, although perhaps unconscious, ability to understand the language of dreams.

I

I See **dreamer; identity and dreams; individuation.**

ice, iceberg Being cold emotionally or sexually. It depicts what is meant by the term "cold shoulder," where we shut off any display of warmth or compassion. It also therefore shows the dreamer as having "frozen assets" in a personal sense. <u>Icicle:</u> frozen male sexual feelings. <u>Iceberg:</u> similar to ice, but may suggest frozen potential. <u>Body locked in ice, perhaps dead:</u> deadening of all feeling reactions and enjoyment or motivation. <u>Idioms:</u> break the ice; cut no ice; put on ice; tread on thin ice. See **cold.**

identity and dreams To have a sense of personal existence distinct from others may be unique to human beings, and in large measure due to the learning of language. Jung's and Neumann's studies of the historical development of identity suggest that having an "I" is still a newly acquired function, in evolutionary terms. This makes it vulnerable. It is also noticeably something that develops during childhood and reaches different levels of maturity during adulthood. Although it is our central experience, it remains an enigma, a will-o'-the-wisp that loses itself in dreams and sleep, yet may be dominant and sure in waking.

In dreams, our sense of self—our ego, our personality or identity—is depicted by our body, or sometimes simply by the sense of our existence as an observer. In most dreams our "I" goes through a series of experiences just as we do in waking life, seeing things through our physical eyes, touching with our hands, and so on. But occasionally we watch our body and other people as if from a detached point of bodiless awareness. If we accept that dreams portray in images our conception of self, then dreams suggest that our identity largely depends upon having a body, its gender, health, quality, skin color, the social position we are born into, and our relationship with others. In fact, we know that if a person loses their legs, becomes paralyzed, loses childbearing ability, becomes blind, or is made redundant, they face an identity crisis. But the bodiless experience of self shows the human possibility of sensing self as having an identity not dependent upon one's body, one's state of health and social standing. In its most naked form, the "I" may be simply a sense of its own existence, without body awareness.

Dreams also show our sense of self, either in the body or naked of it, as surrounded by a community of beings and objects separate from the dreamer, and frequently with a will of their own. If we place the dreamer in the center of a circle and put all their dream characters, animals, and objects around them, and if we transformed these objects and beings into the things they depicted, such as sexuality, thinking, will, emotions, intuition, social pressure, etc., we would see what a diverse mass of influences play upon the ego. See **individuation; dreamer.**

illness If one has painful memories that are never cleared, or feelings of anger or resentment that are held within, these will often be shown in a dream as an illness or infection; a collapse of one's confidence, or the uprising of fears and depression can also be shown as illness; occasionally depicts the way we attempt to get love or attention, by being ill; sometimes relates to our actual physical body, but quite rarely; also may show intuitions about the physical condition of someone else. See **infection; body.**

imprisoned See **cage, cell; escape; trapped.**

incense An atmosphere you may be spreading by the way you think or feel.

incubating dreams As can be seen from the entry **hypnosis,** the dream process is quite amenable to suggestion and conscious influence. It is probably most helpful to think of this action as similar to the process of memory. In seeking information from memory we hold a question or idea in consciousness, the resulting associated memories or information being largely spontaneous. The question held directs what information is taken from the enormous pool of memory. A question might even call together scattered pieces of information that are then put together into a new composite, a new realization. So the process is not only recall of existing memory, but creative. It may also access skills, such as the ability to subtract one number from another. Because of these factors our conscious queries can influence the process of dreaming, causing it to respond. As dreams have access to our full memory, creative potential, as well as learned skills, such response to concerns or queries are often of great value.

To make use of this, first consider the query as fully as possible while awake. Look at it from as many viewpoints as you can. Talk it over with others. Make note of the areas that are already clear, and what still remains to be clarified. Just before going to sleep, use imagery to put your question to your unconscious resources. Imagine standing before a circle of gentle light—a symbol of one's total self—and asking it for the information sought. Then, as if you have asked a question of a wise friend, create a relaxed state, as if listening for the considered reply. In most cases, dreams that follow will in some way be a response to what is sought, though not necessarily in the way imagined. See **computer and dreams; creativity and problem-solving in dreams.**

Indian If you are not Indian, an aspect of your desires or needs that you do not usually identify with or acknowledge. See **aboriginal.**

indigestion An accepted idea or attitude that does not agree with you; the inability to "stomach" something; or may be actual indigestion; something you have taken in, perhaps something said to you, that you did not see at the time was a poisonous remark.

individuation One of Carl Jung's most interesting areas of thought is that of individuation. In a nutshell, the word refers to the processes involved in becoming a self-aware and independent human being. The area of being we refer to when we say "I," "me," or "myself," is our conscious self-awareness, our sense of self, which Jung calls the ego.

The journey of individuation is not only that of becoming a person, but also expanding the boundaries of what we can allow ourselves to experience as an ego. As we can see from an observation of our dreams, but mostly from an extensive exploration of their feeling content, our ego is conscious of only a small area of experience. The fundamental life processes in our being may be barely felt. In many contemporary women, the reproductive drive is talked about as something that has few connections with their personality. Few people have a living, feeling contact with their early childhood. In fact, many people doubt that a baby or young child remembers much. Because of these factors, the ego can be said to exist as an encapsulated small area of consciousness, surrounded by huge areas of experience it is unaware of. These unconscious areas direct our life to an extraordinary degree. Individuation means to emerge from unconscious dependence upon this hidden side of self. It means to become functionally more independent of the archetypes that dominate conscious life. In many ways it is similar to, and includes, becoming functionally independent of one's mother. See **Jung, Carl; love.**

infection Ideas or thoughts that cause irritability or negative internal states. Thinking one's job is not secure might create disinterest and loss of motivation in work, even if in reality the job is secure; taking in negative

infection

attitudes from others; warning about physical health; sexual impregnation. See **bacteria, germs, virus; illness; body.**

injection   Feeling other people's opinions or will forced on and influencing you; internal influence of something exterior; social pressure to conform or be obedient; sexual intercourse, or influences taken in during sexual relationship. If a <u>sedative is given:</u> return to nonresponsibility, as in infancy. See **syringe.**

insects   Irritations, or feeling something "bugging" us; feeling insignificant—the ant in the mass of other ants; the automatic, unfeeling processes of life; cold, unfeeling urges; sexual urges, especially with cockroaches—insects may also represent the sperm swarming toward the ovum, and therefore may deal with pregnancy; as Jiminy Cricket suggests, insects can represent conscience and guilt that remind us of feelings we might sooner forget—perhaps insects represent these areas because they live their life in our house and garden largely unseen, so depict thoughts and feelings occurring on the edge of consciousness. <u>Ants:</u> small irritations; stinging remarks; anxieties. <u>Bees:</u> collective activity; working as or within a community; hardworking or self-sacrificing. <u>Dead insects:</u> has been used to represent an unwanted baby in some dreams. As such, it shows the death of the fetus, or abortion of the fetus. <u>Glowworm:</u> intuition; inspiration in dark moments; the inner light. If <u>flying off:</u> one's children leaving home. <u>Lice, parasites:</u> thoughts or sexual habits that are purely selfish or carry a health risk; feeling others are parasitic. <u>Spider:</u> often the dependent emotions and conflicts one feels "caught in," connected with mother or family; any emotions you don't want to "handle," such as those surrounding a spouse leaving; wanting to ensnare or feeling trapped by someone; the basic survival instincts in us such as a spider might have—can I eat, or will I be eaten in this meeting/relationship? This level of sensory and feeling perception is important. Like a spider it keeps one foot/finger on the web or influences that connect you with other people and the world. Like the spider, if you are wise you thereby know something of what is coming your way— do you advance or run? See **web.** <u>Stung by wasps, bees, or hornets:</u> painful emotions; feeling stung by remarks.

inside   An inside pocket, inside a house, tree, car, most often represents your inner feelings or desires, perhaps usually unacknowledged. Inside a house, or other environment, means you are feeling, or involved in, what that environment represents.

internet   Life's unbounded possibilities, with all its variety and conflicting opposites; one's unconscious with its huge resources of experience and information; intuition; life—in the sense of the infinite possibilities of interaction and meeting with all the people, animals, and natural processes that are a part of everyday life; the exploring of the possibilities of interaction.

interpretation of dreams—influence of   Once you understand a dream, its images can be seen as a clear expression of personal information. For instance, a woman dreamt she was standing alone on a plateau and she could see two worlds hanging in the sky. In talking about the dream she said her husband had died and she had met another man. This new man was very different to herself and her past husband. The world he lived in was new to her and she was cautious. This helped her to see she had the choice between two worlds, and her dream was simply illustrating her situation—she was alone, on a plateau, facing choices. From this point of view, dreams are not strange or coded. They are not trying to hide information, but express it in much the same way we use imagery in everyday speech. In the above example "worlds" is the imagery used. But the words might also be "that was a close shave," "barking up the wrong tree," "got the sack" etc. Dreams also use other things that we take for granted as everyday parts of mental life. Wordplay and puns, for example, and the drama we understand so easily in films and plays but are mystified by in dreams. Such dream statements as "I was in a dark and lonely house," "The dark water moved slowly between the stones," "It was a beautiful bright sunny day and I was in a children's playground" are immediately understandable as expressions of mood.

What may confuse us in looking at dreams, especially our own, is that these factors are used all at once, and all put into imagery. Even so, if we look at them as if they were all a mime, where speech may occur but the main message is expressed by dramatic mood, substitution of action for words, wordplay and puns in image form, then we can grasp what the dream is communicating. A very simplified way of understanding your dreams is to disregard the imagery. Look at what feelings are involved and see if you can recognize the glimmers of such feelings in everyday life. If you can, then go back to the dream. Consider what the drama portrays, and see what comment it makes on the everyday events the feelings are connected with. See Introduction; **analysis of dreams;** key words under **discovering the meaning of your dream** in the Introduction; **language and dreams; peer dream work; processing your dreams.**

intruder   See **burglar, intruder.**

inventor   Creative aspect of oneself; personal insights; the self. See **roles.**

Iroquoian dream cult   The Iroquois (Huron and Seneca) American Indians, as early as the first European contact in the 17th century, had developed a deeper psychological understanding than the white races of the time. Father Fremin, who studied their customs, wrote that they had no divinity but the dream. They clearly described the conscious and unconscious, and said that through dreams the hidden or unconscious area of psyche makes its desires known. If it does not receive these desires it becomes angry. The Iroquois therefore developed a system of allowing the dreamer to act out their dreams socially. Although a moral and disciplined group, during such acting out the dreamer was allowed to go beyond usual social boundaries. This included receiving valuable objects or making love to another person's spouse. This was to allow unconscious desires to be expressed, thus avoiding sickness of body or mind. Such hidden desires were seen as the basis of social as well as individual problems.

Islamic dream traditions   Islam has a foundation in dreams, because of the *Lailatal-Miraj* or *Night Journey* of Mohammed's dream. In it he was initiated into the mysteries of the cosmos. In some Indonesian Muslim teachings, human consciousness is often dominated by forces of the animal and vegetable kingdoms, and forces resident in material objects. This means humans fail to recognize their true nature, and forever feel desirous of material goods, or are led by animal urges. The force behind dreaming is a means of being delivered from unconscious dominance by these forces. In early Islamic teachings, no distinction was made between sleeping dreams and waking visions. The world of imagery existent in dreams and visions was seen as having reality. This world, the *alam al-mithral*, exists halfway between the material world and the intellect. In today's language we might call this the world of the psyche, with its imagery. The Islamic teachings say this should not be seen as fantasy. The world of *alam al-mithral* can be entered by trained imagination and perception. Its imagery expresses truths of its nature. The reality of its landscape can be verified by others who explore its subtle territory—the territory of dreams and visions.

island   Feelings of isolation or loneliness—the loneliness could be as one might feel when retired from work, isolated from situations you once knew; feeling trapped; feeling safe from the world by introversion. <u>Swimming,</u>

island

getting to an island: move to independence. Desert island: attempt to "get away from it all." Island in stormy sea: personality traits that give strength amidst difficult emotions and turbulence. Large island, with other people: isolating oneself by involvement with a particular belief, group of people, or problem.

J

jacket See *jacket* under **clothes.**

jailer May be any of a range of attitudes—such as guilt, self-criticism, sense of alienation, intellect—restricting the expression of other parts of one's nature. So, attitudes or concepts you imprison yourself with, or hold yourself back with. See **prison.**

jaw See *jaw* under **body.**

jellyfish See *jellyfish* under **fish, sea creatures.**

Jesus The influence of the social norm as it acts on your decisions and feelings; a compensatory force in you to help meet difficulties; a point of truth from which you can see the quality of your life; your link with the living sentient universe, or the collective it. See *Christ* under **archetypes; compensation theory.**

jewelry May represent the giver of the piece, or one's feelings about them; love given or received; something valuable in a "quality of our life" sense, such as something we have learned through hard experience and ought to value; a woman's honor, self-respect, sexuality. If the jewelry has a particular history, such as a family heirloom, the first piece of jewelry given by spouse, then it represents what we feel about family tradition, spouse, etc. See **jewels; ring.**

jewels Things we, or our unconscious, treasure; integrity, or sense of wholeness; the lasting parts of our nature, even the eternal aspect of self or the essential core of ourselves. For instance, ability to creatively work with others is not just valuable in general, it also expresses the powerful symbiotic force in nature. It connects one with the universal. This might be depicted as a jewel.

Because of the different colors in jewels, and the different things socially associated with them, some jewels may have slightly different meanings. <u>Amethyst:</u> healing; influence of dreams. <u>Diamond:</u> human greed; hardness of nature; what one values; the aspects of one's life that are lasting and valuable, not only in an everyday sense but in a cosmic sense. <u>Emerald:</u> personal growth and awareness of connection with the natural in life. <u>Opal:</u> the inner world of fantasies and dreams; psychic impressions. <u>Pearl:</u> inner beauty and value that has arisen from the irritations or trials of life; tears, so can represent loss or mourning. <u>Ruby:</u> emotions, passion, sympathies; extending self to others. <u>Sapphire:</u> religious feelings; expansion of thinking boundaries. <u>Turquoise:</u> this jewel represents the mind as it goes beyond the boundaries of thought into intuition and wider awareness—awareness of connection with the essence of life. It is therefore sometimes connected with healing or wholeness, as the person moves beyond limitations into their own health or mind and body.

journey How you are feeling about your life, its ups and downs, goals and destinations, challenges and opportunities; undertakings you embark on, or experiences being met; what the overall tone of your life is may be depicted by the dream journey; the direction your unconscious is taking; your life and what it is achieving. The journey cannot be undertaken unless you are willing to travel, to move from one experience, one attitude, or way of life to another. So sometimes you meet hesitations or things to do before you can go. <u>Interrupted or difficult journey:</u> difficulties and anxieties of present life situation; symbol of the psychological journey of self-realization. In life we have lots of journeys, such as that through schooling; marriage and perhaps divorce; work; parenthood; and the overall journey of life and death. See, where applicable, **day and night,** for time of journey; **airplane; boat; car; hill; individuation; railroad, railway, train.**

judge   Sense of guilt or self-judgment; conscience; decision-making. May depict the "shoulds" and "should nots" we apply to ourselves, or our moral code. Sometimes the way we judge others becomes a harsh judge of ourselves. Feeling what a failure our parents were in raising us becomes a difficult judgment of our state as a parent. <u>Idioms:</u> judge not, that ye be not judged; sit in judgment.

jump   See *jump* under **postures, movement, body language.**

jury   Decision-making; conscience. See **judge.**

Jung, Carl (1875–1961)   Son of a pastor; his paternal grandfather and great-grandfather were physicians. He took a degree in medicine at University of Basle, then specialized in psychiatry. In early papers he pioneered the use of word association, and influenced research into the toxin hypothesis regarding schizophrenia. Jung's addition to modern therapeutic attitudes to dream work arose out of his difference of view with Freud regarding human life. Jung felt life is a meaningful experience, with roots in something that transcends birth and death. His interest in alchemy, myths, and legends added to the wealth of ideas he brought to his concept of the collective unconscious. The subject of symbols fascinated him and he devoted more work to this than any other psychologist. He saw dream symbols not as an attempt to veil or hide inner content, but an attempt to elucidate and express it. He saw dreams as a way of transforming what was formless, nonverbal, and unconscious into what was known and understood. In this way, dreams "show us the unvarnished natural truth." By giving attention to our dreams we are throwing light upon who and what we really are—not simply who we are as a personality, but who we are as a phenomena of cosmic interactions.

Jung recommended looking at a series of dreams in order to develop a fuller insight into self. In this way one would see certain themes arising again and again. Out of these we can begin to see where we are not balancing the different aspects of ourselves. See **active imagination; amplification; analysis of dreams; archetypes; Jung** under Bibliography; **black person; collective unconscious; compensation theory; creativity and problem-solving in dreams; Fromm, Erich; identity and dreams; individuation; lucidity;** *mandala* under **shapes, symbols; unconscious.**

jungle   Eruption of urges and feelings from the unconscious—could be negative or positive, depending on dream; confusion; area of "uncivilized" or unconscious, maybe nonsocialized feelings and urges, therefore may contain unmet anxieties (snakes and lions) or sexual urges (native men and women). <u>Idioms:</u> law of the jungle.

K

Kasatkin, Vasily Kasatkin was a Russian psychiatrist who spent over forty years researching the question of dreams in relationship to the body. He worked at the Leningrad Neurosurgical Institute. His study of more than ten thousand dreams was collected from 1,200 people. From these he developed a view of dreams other than the psycho-analytical view developed by Freud. He said dreams reflect the dreamer's internal physiological processes, and their sensory and social experiences and situation. His book, *Theory of Dreams,* published in 1967, summarized his findings.

key Any attitude, thought, or feeling that opens up areas of memory, experience, or motivation previously "locked up"; realization or information that allows solution to a problem; depicts an effective way of doing something; the penis, or sexual intercourse.

kidnap If the <u>dreamer is the victim of kidnappers:</u> the influence of fears and negative feelings are often presented as an external force or organized gang who victimize us. If such feelings are recognized for what they are, self-created emotions, they lose their power. Being kidnapped also suggests loss of security or feelings of security, or someone else forcing their will on you. <u>Kidnapping someone else:</u> influencing someone else against their will. This may, of course, be about yourself, referring to forcing yourself to do something against your feelings.

kill

kill   Being killed: an interior or exterior influence that you feel is "killing"—undermining, making ineffective, strangling, choking—your self-confidence, or sense of identity. Killing: repressing or stopping some aspect of oneself—as when we kill love for someone. Killing parents, animals: See **family, family relationships; animals.**

king   One's father; as the father the king may depict need for approval and loving acknowledgment; what you are ruled by; feelings of inferiority/superiority; in times past the king or queen represented the group, the overall collective psyche of the people. See *king* under **archetypes.**

kiss   Acceptance of what is being kissed; sexual agreement; tenderness; movement toward unity; occasionally a sign of betrayal or duplicity, as with Judas kissing Jesus. This would be depicted by the feelings in the dream. Idioms: kiss of life; kiss of death; kiss something/somebody good-bye.

kitchen   See *kitchen* under **house, buildings.**

Kleitman, Nathaniel   See **Aserinsky, Eugene**

knapsack   The resources and difficulties we carry in life; past experience or karma; a burden—perhaps of nursed anger or other negative feelings—we carry; if we feel parenthood a heavy load, we may see our child as a burden.

kneel   See *kneel* under **postures, movement, body language.**

knife   See *knife* under **weapons.**

knock   One's attention called to whatever is knocking. Some aspect of self, or a realization is asking to be let into consciousness. Knocking: trying to get attention; wanting to be allowed into someone's life; sexual act.

knot   Tangle of feelings or tension; relational tie such as dependencies, pain, or anger that knot us to another person; a problem; the ties we have to work; family; mother's apron strings or viewpoints—in this sense can be the umbilical cord, or tie to mother during prebirth life; through association with its sound, can mean "no" or "not." See **rope.**

Krishna   See *Christ* under **archetypes.**

L

label   Self-image; how you feel others see you; your view of what is labeled; definition of your feelings if labeled to someone else. If the label is obviously about an object, then it can be describing a quality you have, negative or positive; the label might be about information you hold unconsciously that is helpful.

ladder   Your feelings—whether anxious or secure—about reaching situations or opportunities in life that are new, presently out of reach, or not easily attained; attainment through effort and daring; the heightening of insecurity, anxiety, or feelings in life or sex—getting up, getting it up. <u>Rungs:</u> the separate steps or efforts necessary to "climb." <u>Idioms:</u> top of the ladder. See *stairs* under **house, buildings.**

lake, lagoon   The inner world of feelings and fantasies; the unconscious. <u>Sinking into:</u> becoming introverted; giving up on trying or expressing oneself. <u>Looking into depth:</u> self-awareness; looking into oneself. <u>Dirty water:</u> difficult feelings; being unsure of oneself; depression. See **water.**

lamb   See *lamb* under **animals.**

lame   Feeling uncertain about how one stands in life; loss of confidence or strength in expressing oneself or being motivated. <u>Left leg:</u> weakness in the feelings and ideas out of which we gain support. <u>Right leg:</u> weakness in external activities.

land   <u>Undeveloped pieces of:</u> potential; the opportunities to make yourself real in the world, to create something from within yourself. This might represent the undeveloped parts of your nature that need attention and cultivation or character-building. <u>Developed:</u> what you have created with your life energy.

landscapes   Moods and attitudes, but particularly the set of habitual feelings we meet life with. We create our surroundings in dreams, and landscapes depict what feelings we ourselves generate and live in. <u>Gloomy:</u> pessimism; self-doubt; depression; a gloomy view of life. <u>Sunny:</u> hopeful; optimistic; something to look forward to. <u>Recurring scenes:</u> habitual attitudes with which you approach situations. <u>Recurring scenes of past residence:</u> a stance you developed from that period of your life. <u>Recurring landscapes:</u> areas of our feelings or psyche we often return to. See **countryside.**

lane   See **road.**

language—foreign or strange   The unconscious often uses mysterious or foreign languages to express what lies within yourself that has never been thought about or put into words. Much of your most fundamental childhood experiences were preverbal, and so only accessible as powerful feelings and feeling responses. Even from babyhood we can make profound decisions about what we will reject or accept. These are formulated entirely as profoundly potent feeling responses. Dreams sometimes express these, and intuitions about your wholeness, as strange words or a mysterious language. If you play with the sounds and let them develop, what they contain can become verbalized. The unconscious, as in speaking in tongues—glossolalia—and, of course, in dreams, frequently moves toward clear awareness in stages. The strange language is a halfway house toward focused critical awareness. If we bring attention to these, as explained in **processing your dreams,** the next step, clear verbal expression, can be reached. <u>Speaking in language we are learning:</u> the language is becoming habitual, making it possible to think in it. See **speaking.**

large   See **size.**

late   See **time of day.**

laugh   Release of tension; attempt to put others at ease; ridiculing or feeling embarrassed by some aspect of self; taking things lightly; attempt to hide the truth; sometimes much laughter can hide tears or sadness. <u>Idioms:</u> don't make me laugh; laughingstock; laugh in somebody's face; hollow laugh; laugh up one's sleeve; laugh on the other side of your face.

Laundromat   This shows some way that you are changing attitudes, represented by the clothes. See **washing.**

laundry   Attitudes that need to be, or have been cleansed; experience that needs reevaluating. See **washing.**

lava   Deeply buried past experience that has pushed to the surface; heated emotions and sexuality; sometimes physical illness, such as fever.

lavatory   See **toilet.**

lawn   Part of yourself that needs frequent attention lest it becomes out of hand. If you have concerns about what the neighbors would think of an unruly lawn, then this would figure as your dream association; can also suggest feelings of relaxation or family life, maybe a play area; in some people's dreams it links with their feelings of being exposed to things like the rain, lightning, and birds, so suggests anxiety.

lawyer   See *lawyer* under **roles.**

lead   <u>Metal:</u> heavy-hearted; a weighty situation; feeling burdened; materialistic attitudes. <u>To lead:</u> to feel sure in a way that creates confidence for less certain parts of your thinking and feeling to be motivated; some strong feelings or ideas that motivate you. <u>Following leader:</u> an influence from something, such as a belief or even a need to feel confident. The leader might therefore represent either the confidence or the need. See *leader* under **roles.** <u>To be on a lead:</u> to direct something, as when you control your feelings, or give yourself certain boundaries to live within. To have a measure of control.

leaf   See **trees.**

leak   Wasted or lost energy; or something being allowed out or expressed. The energy leak might arise from any number of past hurts. <u>Idioms:</u> leak out (be revealed).

leather   Basic or instinctive responses, instinctive drives, or toughness. If wearing the leather as a coat, for instance, it might suggest feelings about fashion, animal welfare, or that you are expressing yourself in a fundamental way. See **animal.**

leaving   See **departing.**

left behind   Feelings of not being as good as other people; feeling burdened with things that prevent you from being accepted by others; feeling you can't keep up with what is needed.

left, right   <u>Left:</u> if you are right-handed, the left represents the less dominant, less expressed side of yourself, or the parts of your nature you try to hide or suppress. If you

left, right

write or knock in a nail using your right hand, you will hold the paper or nail with your left. So left leg or arm frequently has this sense of being the supportive but less dominant functions in you. Your confidence may support your activity as a salesperson, so may be depicted as being on the left. A few people might also find that in some dreams one side of their body represents the feelings and attitudes they absorbed from their mother, and the other side what they absorbed from their father. <u>Right:</u> the dominant, confident, conscious, exterior, or expressed side of self; rightness; correct social behavior; moral. <u>Dreams also use a play on what is right and left to illustrate polarity or opposites:</u> your internal world of feelings, memories, and values—the left; your external world of activity and environment—the right; a secondary choice—left; the "right" choice at the time—right; parts of self unconscious or shadowy—left; your conscious, known self—right; the immoral, selfish, wrong action—left; the moral, right action—right. <u>Idioms:</u> two left feet; keep on the right side of somebody; in one's right mind; in the right; Mister Right; set somebody right; right-hand man; right in the head; start on the right foot; give one's right arm.

legs   See *legs* under **body.**

lemon   See *lemon* under **fruits.**

length, long   The length of something in a dream usually signifies its importance. The size symbolizes its impact on you. If something is very long, it might also link with boredom or loss of interest.

lens   Focusing attention on an area of experience, realization, or intuition.

leopard   See *leopard* under **animals.**

lesbianism   See **homosexuality.**

letter Communication; feelings, intuitions, or hopes in regard to something received from another person, or a group of people. Hoping to have contact with or news from a person or company; opportunity, news, or love coming to one. Black-edged: news of or feelings about death. Letter from particular person: thoughts about or intuitions concerning the person letter is from; unrealized feelings about sender; hopes—perhaps to have contact with person. Opening letter: realizing something; receiving news; sexual intercourse. Unopened letter: feelings, thoughts, or intuitions that have not been made conscious or recognized; opportunity that has not been taken up or recognized yet; virginity. Sending a letter: the thoughts or feelings you radiate to others, perhaps unconsciously. A prompt to contact the person you are posting the letter to. Desire to be in contact. Idioms: French letter (condom); love letter; red-letter day.

library Life experience; wisdom and skills we have gathered; the intellect; research. Huge library: collective unconscious; vastness of the mind; cosmic mind. See **book; school.**

lice See **insects.**

lift See *elevator* under **house, buildings.**

light Being aware; being seen; waking as opposed to sleeping; to understand and have insight; to see; lightness of heart; hope; confidence; release from dark feelings and fear; becoming aware of how others might see you. Very bright light: intuition; the self; megaconcept. See **aura.** Spotlight, searchlight: focusing attention on what is shown. Flickering or dimming lights: uncertainty; anxiety; struggle to understand; loss of power or mental clarity; feelings about approaching death. Idioms: bright lights; cold light of day; come to light; hide one's light; in it's true light; lighter side; in a good light; see the light; light at the end of the tunnel; throw a light on. See **dark; day and night; flames.**

lighthouse Warning of danger of unconscious elements that may wreck areas of your life unless avoided. Use the light to become aware of what the danger is. See **light.**

lightning Unexpected changes, whether through unsuspected events or from sudden emerging realizations or emotions; discharge of tension, perhaps destructively; the power of your inner energies, such as pent-up emotions or sexuality, and how this discharge can threaten, destroy, or break down old attitudes or lifestyles, so allowing change; expression of wider awareness; intuition; conscience. Killed by lightning: life-changes occurring. These changes may be arising from within through the expression of aspects of oneself previously not released. The energy of the lightning may be repressed powerful drives—such as teenage sexuality—and may be felt as destructive. The repression of oneself in this way feels like death, or that one is not fully alive. Lightning-struck tree: death in some form—i.e., the loss of love, the ending of some part of one's personality, etc. Lightning striking someone: pent-up emotions or sexuality in connection with the person.

line Waiting for something you want; feelings about where you stand in relation to others; or whether you will get what you are seeking. There might also be feelings about what you deserve, or what you can allow yourself— i.e., maybe you feel other people deserve more. See *line* under **shapes, symbols.**

liquid Because feelings are often felt to flow within us, as when we listen to rousing music, or notice a feeling in the chest which moves to the throat, leading to crying or some other expressed emotion, they may be shown in a dream as fluid. Liquid in bottle: a change of feelings, as when we drink wine or medicine; influenced by exterior emotions; contained or withheld feelings or needs. <u>White liquid:</u> milk of kindness, self-giving, or sperm—the magic fluid out of which life emerges. See **water.**

little   See **size.**

liver   Irritability; suggestion for health or diet changes, perhaps in connection with alcohol. See *internal organs* under **body.**

lizard   See **reptiles, lizards, snakes.**

lock, locked   The emotions or physical tensions we use to keep others from "getting at us," or to prevent urges or fears from being experienced or expressed; desire to keep something safe or protected—such as one's honor or emotions; feeling trapped; vagina; sexual tension. Occasionally a problem that needs a specific solution—the key; ability to choose—whether to let someone into intimate relationship.

lodger   See **boarder.**

looking   Searching for something; realizing something, feeling impressions. See **seeing, saw, sight.**

lorry   See **car; truck.**

losing something   A lost opportunity; forgetting something that is important. Depending on dream might also suggest actual, or feelings about, loss of virginity; loss of health; losing a lover, partner; or whatever the lost thing depicts. If you dream often about losing things, like handbag, car, children, it could show that you are deeply uncertain about yourself. In other words you are feeling a loss of identity, wondering where you are going in life, who you are in the present situation, or what value you have. See *cannot find husband* under **family, family relationships.**

lost   Being lost depicts confusion; loss of motivation or ability to make clear decisions. Sometimes suggests issues in your life have arisen and not been noticed and you are being negatively influenced. In which case, consider the environment in which you are lost. If <u>lost in an unknown place:</u> it suggests you are in a new area of experience, a new situation or period of your life. You need to calmly take stock and get your bearings.

love   Like most emotions, love in a dream is usually a direct expression of that feeling, or a compensation for not receiving it. So one question to ask is whether you are trying to compensate for a lack in your life. Apart from that it may be helpful to see in what way the love is being expressed in the dream. The following stages of love may help in defining this. <u>Baby love:</u> completely dependent upon the loved person for one's needs—physical, emotional, and social. Great anger, jealousy, or pain if the loved one relates to anyone else or deserts you. Wants to be always with the loved one. Will have sex, but the emotional bond and cuddling is more important. <u>Adolescent love:</u> initial uncertainty or clumsiness concerning emotional and sexual contact. Desire to explore many relationships. Still finding out what ones boundaries are. Great sexual drive. Partner will probably be loved for one's own needs—for example, the dreamer wants a family and loves the partner to gain that end; the dreamer loves the partner because in that way they can get away from parental home. Great romantic feelings and spontaneous love that may not be maintained in face of difficulties. <u>Adult love:</u> growing sense of recognizing needs of partner yet not denying one's own. Ability to be something for the partner's sake without losing one's own independence or will. Becoming aware of the issues that color or influence relationship, and meeting them as partners. Independence and closeness together. Caring sexual partners through discovering each other's needs and vulnerability.

lover See *lover* under **archetypes; boyfriend, girl-friend.**

lucidity, awake in sleep Sometimes in the practice of deep relaxation, meditation, or sensory deprivation, one enters into a state akin to sleep. This is like a journey into a deeply interior world of mind and body, where your senses no longer function in their waking manner, where the brain works in a different way, and where awareness is introverted in a degree you do not usually experience. It can be a frightening world simply because you are not accustomed to it. In a similar way, a measure of waking awareness can arise while dreaming. This is called lucid dreaming. During it you can change or willfully direct what is happening in the dream in a way not usual to the dream state.

Lucidity also has the feature of enabling the dreamer to avoid unpleasant elements of the dream. The decision to avoid any unpleasant internal emotions is a common feature of a person's conscious life, so this aspect of lucidity is simply a way of taking such a decision into the dream. Some writers even suggest it as a way of dealing with frightening dreams. Avoidance does not solve the problem, it simply pushes the emotion deeper into the unconscious, where it can do damage more surreptitiously. Recent findings regarding suppressed grief and stress emotions connects them with higher incidence of cancer, and suggests that suppression is not a healthy way of dealing with feelings.

Another approach to lucidity is that it can be a sort of playground where one can walk through walls, jump from high buildings and fly, change the sofa into an attractive lover, leave one's body, and so on. True, the realization that our dream life is a different world and that it has completely different principles at work than our waking world is important. Often people introvert into their dream life the morals and fears that are only relevant to being awake in physical life. To avoid a charging bull is certainly valid for waking life. In our dream life, though, to meet its charge is to integrate the enormous energy that the bull represents, an energy that is ours but that we may have been avoiding or "running away" from previously. Realizing such simple differences revolutionizes the way we relate to internal events and possibilities. To treat lucid dreams as if they offered no other attainable experience than manipulating the dream environment, or avoidance of difficult emotions or encounters, is to miss an amazing feature of human potential.

It is now acceptable, through the work of Freud, Jung, and many others, to consider that within the images of the dream lie valuable information about what is occurring within the dreamer, perhaps unconsciously. Strangely, though, it is almost never considered that one can have direct perception into this level of internal "events" without the dream while lucid, or without dream interpretation. However, this is one of the major benefits of lucidity.

luggage   The habits of attitude, or the emotional environment we have created in life; the past we still carry with us; things we can't let go of in life; a baby, or feelings about being a parent. See **bag; knapsack.**

lumber   See **wood.**

luminous   Unity of many aspects of one's nature. See **aura; light.**

lungs   See *lungs* under **body.**

M

machine   The body's automatic functions and drives, such as breathing and aging; the mechanical forces of nature; habitual or mechanical behavior. <u>Intricate machine:</u> brain, or the thinking process in its mechanical, habitual form; the habitual, almost mechanical fantasies we have or things we do. <u>Idioms:</u> cog in the machine. See **engine.**

mad   See **crazy; anger.**

maggots   Impurities in body; sickness or sense of illness in the body; feelings about death. <u>Maggots in one's body:</u> The unconscious telling us that some of our attitudes are not wholesome or "well." So, repressed emotions causing tension in the chest might be represented as maggots. See **body.**

magician   See **bewitched; roles.**

magnet   The influence—to attract or repel—we have on others or they on us; repulsiveness; likes and dislikes; physical or personality charms, and the way in which they are used; the power resident in the body, which can be used for healing, or emotional psychic impact upon others, as in hypnosis, where one being has such an impact upon another that their suggestions are carried out to a greater or lesser degree. This is why hypnosis was often called magnetism.

magnifying glass

magnifying glass Making something conscious or clearer; becoming aware of something; making something bigger than it is.

mail See **letter**.

makeup The ability to change the impression we make on others; covering up our real feelings or situation; being like everyone else; feeling uncertain about oneself.

man An embodiment of what you deeply need, fear, hope for, or avoid. What the man is doing in the dream gives a clue to what the need or fear is. Therefore, a man trying to rape a woman would be her fears or pain about sex; a homosexual would depict those feelings; businessman, one's work or business abilities; loving man, one's feelings about love, and so on. In general, a person in a dream shows one of your character resources or problems, depending on how you relate to it. Each character trait is a part of your repertoire of behavior. If you are at odds with the person in the dream or threatened by it, then the trait dominates you rather than you directing it. An important point is that the dream image of the person or object summarizes the trait. Through the image you can access the resources of the trait. One can call this an image of power. <u>Bachelor:</u> feelings that are not involved in a relationship, or want to be free of a relationship; feelings about an available man. <u>Big man:</u> one's basic beliefs or attitudes to life that test out against reality. The bigness is the certainties that arise from this, and therefore the sense of strength. <u>Dreaming the man is looking at other women or leaving:</u> usually the fears about same. <u>Man in woman's dream—man she knows or loves:</u> feelings, worries about relationship; summary of what is happening, or what is feared will happen in the relationship. In either case, it is still information about the relationship. <u>Man in woman's dream:</u> fundamentally about your relationship strengths or difficulties, either with a particular man, or with men in general. Your ability to question conventional behavior and social habits; strength to look with insight into your own life and change it—but not your feeling values, emotions, and intuitions; creative or business ability in the world and power to be competitive and challenging; defense against "just knowing" out of the power of emotions and built-in prejudices; depending on how you deal with the male figure, it shows your ability to meet a male. So it may show you feeling the power of your womanhood and meeting the man with strength; or your lack of self-assurance, along with the difficulties this produces. <u>Older man:</u> father or one's accumulated experience and wisdom; perhaps even wisdom from the unconscious if man is white-haired or holy. <u>Two men:</u> might be triangle situation; different aspects of self. <u>Wild, ape, or half-animal man:</u> urges that have not yet been integrated and socialized, usually pertaining to sexuality in today's social attitudes, or natural social feelings at odds with present attitudes. <u>Idioms:</u> man-to-man; be a man; front man; hit man; make a man of; odd man out; right-hand man. See **family; woman;** and other entries pertaining to particular roles or age.

mansion See *mansion* under **house, buildings.**

manure In some ways our personality or identity is like a plant that feeds from the most unlikely material in order to grow. The plant can transform manure into living leaves and petals. We feed on experience and information—some of which may appear uninviting, painful, or unwholesome. In fact, the experience may be all of these, and be depicted by manure, and if not put to our roots—our process of becoming aware of things in an intensely felt manner, which links feelings with intellectual insight—remains a disintegrating influence; learning processes that pile intellectual information on children or adults without helping them to allow their deep, feeling responses are like piling manure on the psyche while cutting off its roots. Personal disintegration is the result.

map   Clarifying ideas of direction in life. Understanding of what one has or wishes to do, and how to do it. You might be wondering what direction you need or want to take in life, or where your present course of action is taking you.

marathon   See **race.**

market   Reality of everyday life; the push-and-shove, give-and-take of relating to people in general, but particularly "the public"; the wide range of experience one meets in exposing oneself to more than close family and friends; the buying and selling of things or self, therefore the self-interest in oneself or others.

marriage, wedding   Feelings about being or getting married; uniting two different aspects of yourself, such as intellect and feelings, practical and intuitive self; the "marriage" between conscious and unconscious self—any children of the marriage would be the flowering of new abilities or qualities; sometimes it refers to what your energy or drive is uniting with, such as a new business venture or creative scheme—any children of this marriage suggest your intuitive assessment of the likely outcome; in some cultures dreaming of a wedding signifies a death in the family. Dreaming of wedding if single: when single, one often dreams of marriage as a way of clarifying what it would be like, could one succeed in it, is the present partner okay, how shall one achieve it? Wedding dress: feelings and hopes about relationship and wedding; in a negative dream it represents anxieties about one's relationship or the future. Wedding dress given by mother: qualities and strengths absorbed from mother in regard to relationship; letting go of external mother by expressing her qualities in the present.

marsh, swamp   Feeling bogged down, held back, losing ground, perhaps due to lack of self-confidence or emotional support; may show the emotional dependence between child and parent one gets stuck in; or feeling unable to move because of relationship with an overbearing person; anxiety that undermines confidence.

mask — A different self we put on in meeting others; latent qualities we can express or don when needed—a mother might be a tigress when her children are threatened, but a meek person otherwise; her tigress would not be "false"; egoless.

masturbation This form of giving pleasure to oneself is often very necessary to bring peace and relaxation. This may be represented in a dream by such things as using a pump, beating a drum, or any rhythmic movement. If there is a tendency to repress the sexual need, it may happen that one masturbates during sleep, in an attempt to release sexual pressure. Because the person has consciously decided not to allow sexuality, this might give rise to a feeling of being possessed by another will. In fact, our unconscious will to express our needs has overridden the conscious decision during sleep. Out of such a split in the person, ideas about devils and possession probably arose. Although Christianity at a fundamental level appears to be teaching the love and acceptance of all sides of human nature—therefore integration through love thy neighbor as thyself, so love self—in practice it sometimes becomes tight morality that creates devils through rejection and splits in human nature. In many white Christians, there are enormous conflicts between sexuality, love, work, and transcendence. However, the sexual impulse can be irritated into excess by imagination.

mattress Similar to bed—the situation, comfortable or otherwise, one has created in life. You made your bed, now lie on it; comfort; sexuality; relaxed feelings. See *bed* under **furniture, furnishings.**

maze Confusion of ideas and feelings; conflicting urges and opinions; the difficulty in finding your way through

maze

the mass of apparently irrational emotions and images arising from within, or the variety of opinions and authoritative sources of information outside. This area of self is sometimes an area of seeming chaos. It needs some other level of yourself than the rational mind, such as the intuitive faculty, to guide you through. Sometimes you need to admit you are lost and need help. Occasionally the circuitous and often confusing route you take to greater maturity. In this sense the maze represents an attempt to find your way through conscious thoughts, opinions, doubts, and childhood traumas and fantasies, or the ever-shifting experiences of daily life, to an experience of your fundamental nature. At the center of the maze, however, instead of a treasure you may find emptiness. What is at the center—you are, reality, the unconscious.

meal See **food.**

measurement Might refer to wondering how long—days and weeks—something will be; comparisons; how "big" something is in life. How you measure up to your or other people's expectations.

meat See *meat* under **food.**

medicine Healing influence; meeting experiences we might not like but need in order to change a negative situation; positive changes that can be brought about; actual drugs we are taking. Idioms: taste of one's own medicine; take one's medicine.

meditation Being self-responsible for state of mind; listening to intuition and unconscious; introverting awareness, or escaping from external world. For people involved in any form of personal growth, they occasionally have a dream in which some form of instruction is given as an aid to their unfolding. Such dreams are worth following, as the unconscious has the ability to sift and consider our collective experience, and present what applies to our need.

medium   Intuition, but perhaps in an obscure way; contact with the unconscious or the dead in its symbolic form. See *the dream as extended perception* under **ESP in dreams; symbols, dreaming.**

meeting   As in <u>meeting someone:</u> this is usually about contact, about relationship, and especially about the factors governing the relationship. For instance, in one dream a man looking after children meets a man who he judges to be irresponsible. In fact, the man is ill and therefore not acting normally. So the factors governing the meeting are misjudgment or misinformation. Meeting is also about confrontation, or encountering challenge, the new, or about some sort of communication. There might also, in the communication, be questions asked. As in <u>a group:</u> activities, decisions, directions that are not simply yours; your involvement with other people. But also, at a more symbolic level, the bringing together of more aspects of yourself. Therefore a large group suggests a lot of energy, involving many different aspects of yourself.

Meeting in Dreams   Any two people, or group of people, who share their dreams, particularly if they explore the associated feelings and thoughts connected with the dream images, achieve social intimacy quickly. Whether it is a family sharing their dreams, or two friends, an environment can be created in which the most profound feelings, painful and wonderful, can be allowed. Such exposure of the usually private areas of one's feelings and fears often presents new information to the dreamer. It also allows ventilation of what may never have been consciously expressed before. In doing so a healing release is reached, but also greater self-understanding, and the opportunity to think over or reconsider what is discovered.

Herbert Reed, editor of the dream magazine *Sundance* and

resident of Virginia Beach, VA, initiated group dreaming experiments. It started because Reed noticed that in the dream groups he was running, when one of the group aired a problem, other members would subsequently dream about that person's problem. He went on to suggest the group should attempt this purposely and the resulting dreams should be shared, to see if they helped the person with the problem.

melt   A change; emotions softening.

menstruation   Emerging sexuality; procreative drive; mystery of life; acceptance of life working in yourself if menstruating—nonacceptance of basic life drives if not menstruating. Problems with menstruation: problems with relationship between what life needs of personality, and what personality wants of life; might refer to physiological problems that need attention. In man's dream: one's receptive, nurturing nature; the aspect of the male self that can "conceive" creative ideas. If ill: problems in sexuality, creativity, emotions, or in letting go of "I want." See **premenstrual tension.**

menstruation and dreams   In his book *Our Dreaming Mind*, Robert Van de Castle describes research he did on the subject of menstruation and dreams, with the help of nursing students in Miami. He found that the dreams changed their character with the different phases of the menstrual cycle. Prior to ovulation the dreams showed more male characters appearing. The dreamer showed interest in these males and found them appealing. Women appearing in the dreams of this phase tended to be pushed into the background of the dream events, and were often shown as competing with the dreamer. Following ovulation the dreams tended to depict men as less attractive, and the dreamers feeling some hostility toward them. The women in the dreams were people the dreamer tended to develop working relationships with. See **premenstrual tension.**

merchant   See *merchant* under **roles.**

message   Information to take seriously; a communication from your intuition or unconscious; information you need to know.

Mesopotamian dream beliefs   In considering the beliefs of another culture, especially in the distant past, we have to remember that individuals and cultures have vastly different mental worlds they live in.

The peoples of Assyria and Mesopotamia were animists—that is, they saw themselves surrounded by natural forces that linked with gods to be propitiated and devils to be feared. Anxious in the present, fearful for the future, feeling themselves the prey of powerful forces beyond their comprehension or control, they turned to a whole armory of devices for protection and reassurance—amulets and magic spells, prophecy, divination, and dream interpretation. There seems to be little doubt that in Assyria, as in Egypt, dreams were used in therapeutic processes. There are many rituals for dispelling the effect of evil dreams (i.e., dealing with anxiety): about 1700 B.C., a poem from Babylon describes how a noble had been made ill by demons coming from the netherworld, and how three dreams lead to his recovery. This is why the interpretation of bad dreams was more important than the deciphering of pleasant or obvious dreams—something had to be done about them. Anticipating contemporary psychoanalysis, the Assyrians believed that once the enigma presented by the dreams had been worked out, the disturbing symptoms or the affliction would pass. But whereas modern psychoanalysis uses the dream to reveal the hidden conflicts and repressed anxieties of the patient, the Assyrians believed either that a demon must be exorcized, or that the appropriate deity would reveal the means by which the sufferer could be treated. This means they dealt with the anxiety symbolically.

The Assyrians relied on dream books for help. This much we know from clay tablets found at Nineveh, in the library

Mesopotamian dream beliefs

of the Assyrian king Ashurbanipal, who reigned between 669 and 626 B.C. This library, the oldest directly known to us, was a repository of learning reaching back to the dawn of civilization—possibly to 5000 B.C. The Nineveh tablets, in fact, provide the link in a chain of dream theory that stretches from the most remote past to our time. It is believed that Ashurbanipal's dream book was used by the Roman soothsayer Artemidorus (about A.D. 140), whose work has in turn inspired almost every subsequent compiler of dream books. The Ashurbanipal tablets tell us, for example, that if a man flies repeatedly in his dreams, whatever he owns will be lost. In *Zolar's Encyclopedia and Dictionary of Dreams*, published in New York in 1963, we read: "Flying at a low altitude: ruin is ahead for you." Another idea that persisted is that dreams go by contraries. If an Assyrian dreamed that he was blessed by a god, he expected to experience that god's wrath; but "if the god utters a curse against the man, his prayer will be accepted." If you are cursed in a dream, Zolar tells us in 1963, "ambitions will be realized." Again, these are obvious ways to deal with anxiety.

metal   Hardness of feelings; the restrictions of the real world or of one's own imagination; strength of will or obstinacy; reality. See **iron.**

midget   See **dwarf, malformed figure.**

milk   Due to it being a product of a mother, it usually represents your feelings about how you related to your mother; it might also suggest the giving of sustenance, self-sacrifice, nurturing the young or needy parts of yourself or others; also motherhood, infantile sustenance, sympathy; it can be the symbol of something bland, harmless, mild, lacking the stimulus of alcohol, tea, coffee. Thus one can be called a milksop, which is another name for childlike, unmanly, cowardly; on occasions, milk can also represent sperm. <u>Idioms:</u> milk and water; milk of human kindness; milk somebody; cry over spilt milk. See **food; drink.**

mine, mines   Underground mine: for many a place of work; otherwise the unconscious and its resources; bringing to consciousness one's potential and innate wisdom.

mirror   Concern over one's "image" or how others feel about one; self-examination; self-love, negative only if the love is not shared with others; anxiety about changing or aging; one's view of oneself; being absorbed in oneself; self-awareness in the sense of insight into behavior or character traits; the mirror is similar to water and can depict looking into the unconscious to see who one is.

miscarriage   May be an attempt to heal the experience, if dreamer has had miscarriage or abortion. From the point of view of the unconscious it is at times important to name the baby; fear of or warning about miscarriage; loss of new idea, project, or growing aspect of self.

mist   See **fog.**

modem   This, like telephone, is about communication with others. But it is probably less personal. It is more about contact in general—how you manage to keep in contact with the world via technology, with business activities, and especially with your intuition and wider awareness. See **telephone.**

money   What we value; being valued by others; one's potential, energy, or personal resources; power to change things or do things; or having power, even over someone else; personal potency, therefore links with sexuality and self-giving; what we pay for our desires or actions—"I told my husband a few home truths last night, but he certainly made me pay for it"; opportunity, because money buys time to explore or try the new. Finding money: realizing something valuable; gaining power; release from stress or "down" feelings, in that we feel excited and uplifted upon finding money. Losing money: losing power or

money

opportunity. <u>Not enough money:</u> sense of being inadequate or failing potency. <u>Stolen money:</u> feelings of guilt about gaining power; feeling cheated; loss of power if money is stolen; feeling others are taking us for granted; giving oneself cheaply in sex or relationship. See **credit card.**

monk   See **roles.**

monkey   See *monkey* under **animals.**

monster   Internal emotions or drives you are frightened of; dread of death; a monstrous deed done or lie lived; your negative relationship with your life energy. Use the approaches in **processing your dreams** to change the monster into usable personal resources.

moon   Love; romance; intuitions arising from the unconscious; one's inner world of fantasy, imagination, the psychic, or one's inner soul life; menstrual cycle and the female mysteries. Because of its connection with the tides, the deep inner movements caused by the subtle side of our nature, the tides of feeling, even madness; the pull and attraction of mysterious dark desires; a woman's strange, sensual, overpowering attraction; desire to escape life; a world you live in, such as the world of crime, love, etc.

Morena, Jacob   See **psychodrama.**

morgue   See **mortuary.**

morning   See **time of day.**

mortuary   Feelings about death; parts of self dead but not buried, may be brought to life by being used.

moth   A compulsive urge toward something, perhaps the search for the light of understanding; the self you assume in your dreams or fantasy; the unconscious urge your being has to survive personal death; the hidden side of your mind. See **insects.**

mother   See *mother* under **family, family relationships.**

motorbike   Youthful drive and motivation; physical energy; restlessness, sexual drive; daring; independence.

mountain   Something big in your life; reaching a wider awareness of your life or situation; something that stands above the commonplace; beyond the fears and anxieties of everyday life; separation from others or from everyday life or society; isolation; attainment achieved by facing the difficulties of life. If one is <u>climbing the mountain:</u> the struggle with oneself, such as facing lack of confidence and forging on; meeting the difficulties of life and trying to move on. See **hill.** Example: "I was on top of a mountain with my sons, but was terrified I was going to fall." (Francis H.) Francis feels alone in a high position and fears failure.

mouse   See *mouse* under **animals.**

mouth   See *mouth* under **body.**

movements   In general, the quality of your movements depicts your feeling or mental state, your confidence or lack of it, your ability to make changes—move easily—or difficulty in facing change; the quality or lack of it that you express in your life; what you are creating or "giving off" in everyday life. <u>Agility:</u> coping well with one's situation; adaptability; mental quickness. <u>Easy-flowing movement:</u> self-acceptance and thus easy expression of oneself; feeling in harmony with emotions and sexuality. <u>Getting stuck, unable to move:</u> often being held back by anxiety or fears, such as fear of failure. See **postures, movement, body language.**

movements during sleep   Adrian Morrison, at the University of Pennsylvania, investigating narcolepsy, a condition producing sleep in the middle of activity, found that a small area of the brain, the pons, suppresses full muscular movement while we dream. If this area is damaged or suppressed, humans or animals make full muscular movements while they are asleep in connection with what is dreamt. He observed that cats would stalk, crouch, and spring at imaginary prey. These very important findings suggest:

1. The unconscious process behind dreaming, apart from creating a nonvolitional fantasy in the dream, can also reproduce movements we have not consciously decided upon. This shows we have at least two centers of will that can direct body and mental processes. The waking will decides movements using voluntary muscles. The "dream will" leads to spontaneous movements while we sleep and dream, but also while awake and passive, in the sense described under the entry **active/passive.**
2. Christopher Evans, linking with the work of Nicholas Humphrey at Cambridge University, sees the movements of the dreaming cats as expressions of survival "programs" in the biological computer. These programs or strategies for survival need to be replayed in order not only to keep in practice, but also to modify and improve them in connection with the influx of extra experience and information. In the human realm, our survival strategies and the way we relate to our social, sexual, marriage, and work roles may also be replayed and modified in our dreaming.

Such movements are not linked simply to survival or social "programs." Important agendas in dreaming are: a) releasing painful emotions or trauma, and b) moving toward psychological growth. Also, the process producing these movements does not keep strictly to the realm of sleep. That such "dream" activities as spontaneous movement or spontaneous verbalization should occur during waking would appear to suggest that a dream must occur with them. Research shows this is unlikely. However, it does show that a dream may be imagery produced to express this mental, muscular, emotional "self-regulation." The imagery may not be necessary if the process is consciously experienced. See **compensation theory; paralysis; science, sleep, and dreams.**

movie, movie theater   See **cinema.**

mud   The fundamental, primordial, sensual, slimy basis of life and how we relate to it; emotions that cause us to feel bogged down; past experience that may hold us back, but has enormous growth potential in it; the healing possibilities of our body and its minerals; feelings of hopelessness or despair; one's health, if on body. Idioms: mudslinging; drag somebody through the mud; one's name is mud; stick in the mud.

mummy—Egyptian   The dead; feelings we have buried about a dead person; emotions about death; our mother; a part of self that might be reborn; attempt to preserve a way of life that is dead—mummification—instead of facing change and the new.

murder, murderer   Each of us are implicated in killing—by denying, repressing, controlling—some part of our nature. These denied areas of our sensitivity or potential can fortunately be resurrected through self-awareness of our deed. If we flee from a murderer, it depicts a fear that is threatening our confidence, or something we feel threatened by. Murderous rage in dreamer: it is observable that repressed sexuality or traumatized childhood love leads to feelings of murderous rage that may not be expressed socially, but do appear in dreams; may also express childhood anger linked with emotional bond with mother being damaged. In this case the dreamer will be the murderer—even if in the dream the murderer appears to be someone else. The murder will then be the killing of any love or emotional connection or bond between child and parent. The child often thus murders its own feelings of love for the parent in order to survive apparent or real desertion—as, for instance, a child being put in foster care. The bonds are so instinctive and strong, to survive parting, the child may have to hack away any emotional links. See *father* under **archetypes**.

muscle   See *muscle* under **body**.

museum   Memory; family and cultural heritage; the living past within us.

mushrooms   Feelings or realizations that arise without warning from within; perhaps there is a question here of whether a situation or relationship is nourishing or poisonous, due to the possible association of poisonous or even consciousness-changing mushrooms; something fragile and strange emerging into your life. <u>Mushroom cloud:</u> See **atom bomb**.

music   The play of subtle feelings and forces in our being; realizations difficult to define; the influence of wider awareness in our life. <u>Playing music:</u> self-expression; expressing our essential self which might be overlooked in general activities. <u>Idioms:</u> music to one's ears; face the music. See **music; musical instrument**.

musical instrument   Often one's sexual organs; one's skills or lack of them in self-expression. A <u>musical instrument being played:</u> this depends upon what feelings the music produces. Whatever the feeling—whether sad, uplifting, haunting, wistful, stimulating—take it as expressing that in yourself, and see if you can connect the feeling with everyday issues in some way. A <u>large, complex instrument:</u> the mind and its influence in the rest of our being. See **drum; organ**.

N

nail Bonding; holding power, male sexuality. If <u>nail is in body:</u> consciousness painfully bound to physical reality; pain of bonds. <u>Idioms:</u> hit the nail on the head; tough as nails; nail biting; bed of nails; nail in one's coffin.

naked See **clothes; nude.**

name of person or place Your name represents your sense of self, your essential "I." If the <u>name is altered:</u> suggests a sense of change in the way you see yourself. <u>Other people's names:</u> feelings for that person; the quality you feel in regard to someone else with the same name; or wordplay or associations with the name. Names also suggest qualities—as in Peter, the rock; or one's friend Pat may be pleasure-loving—so we use the name or person to represent that quality. See **wordplay, puns.** <u>Place names:</u> these can represent your feelings about the place, or be similar to personal names in their suggestion of something. <u>Idioms:</u> Call someone names; clear someone's name; have a bad name; not a thing to one's name; in name alone; in the name of; make a name for oneself; name-dropper; one's middle name; name is mud; somebody who shall be nameless; or my name's not . . . ; worthy of the name; name in vain; lend one's name to; name the day.

narrow Narrow-minded; limited choices or view; feeling restricted.

natives Natural feelings; being uncivilized, feelings without too much social restraint. See **aboriginal; black person.**

navel Dependency—especially upon mother; the way we connect our deepest self with the outside world.

near The nearer something is to you in a dream, the closer it is to becoming conscious in a direct way rather than as a symbol. See **positions.**

near-death experience See **analysis of dreams; out-of-body experience.**

neck See *neck* under **body.**

necklace Display of special qualities; richness of feelings; feelings connected with the giver; social position; may represent "millstone" around neck.

needle Penetrating insight; male sexuality; power to mend ills; irritations. Needle in body: sickness in body. Needlework: what one has made of oneself. Idioms: get the needle; needle in a haystack.

neighbor Your relationship with other people; the qualities you see in your neighbor, or the conflict you have with them.

nest Emotional dependence upon parents; home life; not being independent; female sexuality; nest egg. Idioms: foul one's own nest; hornets nest; feather one's own nest; cuckoo in the nest.

new Whatever is new in one's life—a relationship, opportunity, scheme. If contrasted with old, an attempt to decide, contrasting what we already know from the past/old and what is arising.

newspaper Something that is news to you, or you have just become, or need to be, aware of; something conscious rather than unconscious; something publicly known about yourself.

Nietzsche, Friedrich Wilhelm In his book *Human, All Too Human,* Nietzsche said of dreams, "I hold that as man now still reasons in dreams, so men reasoned also when awake through thousands of years.... This ancient element in human nature still manifests itself in our dreams, for it is the foundation upon which the higher reason developed and still develops in every individual; the dream carries us back into remote conditions of human culture, and provides a ready means of understanding them."

night See **day and night; time of day; dark.**

nightclub This depicts the feelings that might lead you to visiting or avoiding a nightclub. See **barroom.**

nightmares Many dreams lead us to feel an intensity of emotion we may seldom if ever feel in waking life. If the emotions felt are frightening or disgusting we call the dream a nightmare. Scientists find this definition too vague and so use two categories to define different types of anxiety dreams. The first definition is "REM anxiety dreams," and the second is "night terrors." The REM anxiety dream is one that occurs during REM (rapid eye movement) activity, in other words, during a normal dreaming period. These are reported to occur most frequently during the last part of the sleep cycle—that is, just prior to waking. One usually remembers the imagery and feelings of these dreams clearly. Night terrors occur during the first two hours of sleep, mostly in stage-four sleep, and the dreamer has either no recall of imagery at all or it is a single impression, such as a physical sensation of heaviness or difficulty in breathing. After waking from such a dream experience, the person feels disoriented for some time. See **science, sleep, and dreams.**

nightmares

One of the common features of a nightmare is that we are desperately trying to get away from a situation, feel stuck in a terrible condition, or meet fear or disgust in almost overwhelming degree, so that on waking we feel enormous relief it was just a dream. Because of the intensity of a nightmare we will remember it long after other dreams—remember it even if we seldom ever recall other dreams. We may even worry about what it means for a long period of time, perhaps even years. Many people on waking find the feelings, or sometimes even the imagery, continuing for some time. So, for instance, they may feel so much fear they have to switch all the lights on in the house.

Because many dreams have been investigated in depth—using such varied approaches as hypnosis, exploration of associations and emotional content, and LSD psychotherapy in which the person can explore usually unconscious memories, imagery, and feelings—we can be certain we know what nightmares are. They arise from several causes.

1. Unconscious memories of intense emotions—such as those arising in a child being left in a hospital without its mother. Many people who have been trapped in an awful situation—whether that is a dreadful marriage, a political or war prison, or a life situation one yearned to get out of—frequently dream they are back in the situation, unable to get out.
2. Intense anxiety produced—but not fully released at the time—by external situations, such as involvement in war scenes; sexual assault; being attacked and one's life threatened; involvement in a natural disaster, such as flood or fire; car accident, etc. The nightmares of Vietnam veterans have been extensively studied, for instance. Their nightmares closely parallel their actual combat experiences.
3. Many nightmares in adults arise from fear connected with internal drives such as aggression; sexuality; and the process of growth and change, such as a youth meeting the changes of adolescence,

loss of sexual characteristics, old age, and death. So this is fear of change, the future, and imagined events. Sometimes nightmares show themselves as a terror of being discovered as the perpetrator of some awful crime, such as a murder. Again, this is usually connected with one's own internal relationship with feelings and urges.

4. Serious illness shown in the dream symbols.
5. Precognition of fateful events.
6. Threats to self-esteem. We may either be faced by, or fear, the loss of something important to us, such as the failure of our relationship, loss of a child, being seen as stupid at work, or not coping with life in a way others approve of. Many professional people I have spoken to report dreams in which they experience themselves involved in some sort of critical situation at work. For instance, a regular nightmare for radio presenters is that they dream the equipment fails, the CD player refuses to work, or they miss their prompt. Sometimes a deep sense of inadequacy haunts a person. This may be in terms of their sexual performance, their physical attractiveness, but may not be based on such obvious factors. In some cases it is rooted in their general but unconscious assessment of themselves measured against others. This may arise out of a family attitude of inferiority, or something like premature birth, where the baby/child feels some steps behind others, or is led to feel so by an anxious parent. See **recurring dreams.**

Example: "A THING is marauding around the rather bleak, dark house I am in with a small boy. To avoid it I lock myself in a room with the boy. The THING finds the room and tries to break the door down. I frantically try to hold it closed with my hands and one foot pressed against it, my back against a wall for leverage. It was a terrible struggle and I woke myself by screaming" (Terry F.). When Terry allowed the sense of fear to arise in him while awake, he felt as he did when a child—the boy in the dream—during the bombing of the second World War. His sense of insecurity dating from that time had emerged when he left a secure job, and had arisen in the images of the nightmare. Understanding his fears, he was able to avoid their usual paralyzing influence.

Understanding the causes of nightmares enables us to deal with them. The things we run from in the nightmare need to be met while we are awake. We can do this by sitting and imagining ourselves back in the dream and facing or meeting what we were frightened of. Terry imagined himself opening the door he was fighting to keep closed. In doing this and remaining quiet he could feel the childhood feelings arising. Once he recognized them for what they were, the terror went out of them. The reason this change can occur is that when the fearful emotions originated, it was at an age, or within a circumstance, during which there was not the ego strength, security, or viewpoint to meet and deal with the fears. If they cannot be met at the time, they are encapsulated in a way to push them out of consciousness, and surrounded with layers of anxiety or psychosomatic symptoms. As an adult we may have matured to the point where we can now meet these powerful emotions in a transformative way. The new confidence and concepts brought to the old experience are the transformative agents. Of course, sufficient ego strength must be developed first in order to do this. We may have learned to meet our emotions and redirect them in a satisfying way. Therefore, many people find strengthening dreams occurring first in their exploration of dream content. It is often only later they start meeting nightmares. But nightmares sometimes start simply because we are now strong enough to deal with them.

nightmares—abstract According to the collection of dreams used as data for this book, these usually occur to children. They often appear as a dot, small object, or shape that is, or becomes, threatening and increases in size. The examples below suggest there is some relationship between the dream and feelings connected with a parent or parents.

It may be the dream portrays unspoken moods felt by a parent that the child feels anxious about. Very often we sense something going on that is not spoken about or visible externally. Such hidden things are picked up by our unconscious, which attempts to communicate them as a dream or intuition. We often feel very uneasy until we realize the situation—perhaps the person it refers to might even deny it if asked.

Example: "When I was a child of about eight years I often used to have an abstract nightmare. It consisted of (a soft wavy line) being attacked by the enemy (a pointed, zigzag line). As the enemy (zigzag) overcame him (soft waves), I would wake up in terror. The nightmares ended when my father died unexpectedly from a heart attack." (E. B.) Example: "I am eighteen years old, and ever since I was eight I have been having the same dream and I cannot understand why. I dream of a small black dot that rotates in a spiral, and as it goes around it gets bigger, and as it gets bigger it gets faster, until in the end it laughs or glares at me and then it blows up. I used to have this dream about twice a week. I don't know why it keeps coming back." (Simone D.)

noon   See **time of day.**

north   The head, as opposed to south, the genitals. <u>In the northern hemisphere:</u> darkness; unconsciousness; coldness, suggesting a situation that leads us to seek the light and warmth; death; frozen emotions. <u>In the southern hemisphere:</u> light; warmth; life and growth. See **directions.**

nose   See *nose* under **body.**

nuclear explosion   Anxiety about the future; great change in the dreamer's life. See **atom bomb.**

nude   Dropping the facade, attitudes, or feelings we may mask our real emotions with in everyday life—for instance,

nude

a child may scream if someone it dislikes gets near it, but an adult will probably tolerate the nearness, or refrain from expressing displeasure; expressing things that are not usually accepted socially; desire to be seen for what one is; expression of natural feelings or desire to be intimate; revealing one's true nature. <u>Anxiety about being nude:</u> fear that others know what you really feel and desire; revealing desires and acts that are considered socially unacceptable and therefore one feels guilty or shocked about being seen doing or feeling, such as being caught making love with the husband's/wife's best friend; feeling vulnerable and having one's weaknesses exposed; guilt about being a human animal with sexual characteristics and urges. See **clothes.**

numbers   Numbers can have a personal or symbolic significance. For instance, we may have had three children, so the number three in a dream about children could be connected with our feelings or fears about them; but three has generally been seen as the troublesome triangle in love—or the child, mother, father threesome. So a number may refer to a particular year of one's life; the number of a house; the months or years that have passed since an important event; your family group; or have a general significance such as indicated in language—i.e., three's a crowd; seventh heaven; nine days' wonder, etc.

zero   The female; unconscious; the absolute or hidden; completeness. The circle or zero also represents the most profound aspect of human nature and the cosmos, that of the hidden, the invisible within all phenomena. It is the silence or void in which all feeling, thought, sound exist—the space between the notes of music that allows it to be heard. It is the nothingness that essentially allows existence.

one   Oneself; a beginning; the first; unity; being alone; independence. <u>Just one left:</u> near the end. <u>Idioms:</u> it's all one to me; one up; at one with; one and only; one off.

two   Duality; relationship; indecision or making a decision; balance; male and female; two sides to an argument—or a way of comparing; opposition; opposites, such as light and dark, harmony or conflict; parents, and reproductive possibility. <u>Chased by or fighting with two people:</u> two-against-one feeling, as may have happened with child and parents; feeling odds are against one. <u>Idioms:</u> put two and two together; two's company; two-timer; in two minds.

three   Triangle; mother, father, child; synthesis; creativity—the child springing from the two opposites—therefore sometimes represents the solution to opposition. <u>Confronting three people, or out with two others:</u> facing collective will of others; nonsexual friendship. <u>Idioms:</u> three's a crowd.

four   Physicality; the earth; stability and strength; the home or house; reality; down-to-earth, yet at the same time the transcendent within the physical; the four sides to human nature—sensation, feeling, thought, intuition; earth, air, fire, and water. <u>Four or more people:</u> feelings about meeting group decisions and feelings; someone's opinion or will backed by others; supportive feelings. <u>Idioms:</u> foursquare; on all fours; four-letter word.

five   The human body; human consciousness in the body; the hand; sometimes called the number of marriage because it unites all the previous numbers-1+4 and 2+3; the five senses.

six   The symbol of this is the double triangle, or circle divided in six. It represents symmetry, unity of spirit and body, the visible and invisible. It is the harmonious relationship between man and God, spirit and body, the eternal and the transitory. Its sign is Virgo, which expresses as craftsman or critic. It is a sign of service, and rules the intestines. The sixth house rules health. It may also be wordplay for sex. <u>Idioms:</u> sixes and sevens; six of the best; hit for six.

seven   Cycles of life—7,14,21, etc.; a week; transcendent meanings—seven candles, seven churches, seven chakras, seven colors, seven notes in music—so represents human wholeness. <u>Idioms</u>: seventh heaven.

eight   Death and resurrection; infinity; old fonts and baptisteries are octagonal because of the association with regeneration.

nine   Pregnancy; childbirth; the end of a cycle and the start of something new; cycles. <u>Idioms</u>: nine days' wonder; nine times out of ten; nine-to-five; cloud nine; nine points of the law.

ten   A new beginning; the male and female together—ten to one.

eleven   Eleventh hour.

twelve   A year; time; a full cycle, or wholeness, as in the Zodiac or the twelve disciples.

thirteen   Bad luck.

big numbers   A lot; impressive; much of oneself involved.

million, billion   Beyond the personal; often associated with riches of some sort.

nun   Sexual restraint; religious feelings or morals; idealism.

nurse   Healing process; someone you know who is a nurse; work situation for many; sister.

nut   Feeling a "nut"; inner nourishment or wisdom that needs work to get at its kernel.

O

oak   See *oak* under **trees**.

OBE   See **out-of-body experience**.

obsessed   We are each obsessed in some degree. Few of us could walk down our road nude, or maybe even without shoes and socks. We take such obsessions for granted and accept them as norms, so we do not feel mentally unbalanced. When a similar power of feeling leads us to behavior outside the norm, we face doubts about ourselves. Obsession in dreams may illustrate some anxiety, drive, or desire that is leading us beyond our accepted norm; or the obsession may be used to escape the real feelings, such as childhood pain or adult conflict and entrapment. In past cultures, the ideas or fears that obsess us would have been described as an evil spirit or ghost taking over the person. This is because the irrational obsession takes hold of us against our will, so is quite an accurate image. The obsessing factor may still appear in present-day dreams in the form of a spirit or demon.

obstacle   Depicts something that causes uncertainty, or withdrawal of enthusiasm, creativity, or love. Such might be produced by someone's criticism, which evokes our self-doubts; indecision; our inhibitions or anxieties; maybe even a hidden form of not wanting to succeed because it would confront us with the new—we might fail. The

obstacle

obstacle, obstruction, barrier, or interference can be a person, a wall, a river, an animal—or it might be an internal thing, like paralysis or a lump in the throat. Refer to the entry on the appropriate subject to define what it is acting as an obstacle to. See first example in **failure; fence; wall.**

ocean   See **sea.**

octopus   See *octopus* under **fish, sea creatures.**

odor   See **perfume, scent, smell.**

office   Feelings about or relationship with work; feelings about authority.

officer, official   Relationship with authority or officialdom; one's father; how we authorize our own activities; our sense of right and wrong; a coordinating or directing function in ourselves; a sense of sureness out of wider awareness or experience.

oil   Attitude that removes friction in oneself or in a relationship; flattery; unctuousness; fat in one's diet. <u>Idioms:</u> well-oiled; oil the wheels; strike oil; oil on troubled waters; burn midnight oil.

old, ancient, antique   The past; the different lives we have lived—baby, youth, lover, parent, provider, what is established and well-worn; tradition and wisdom of folklore. <u>Old building:</u> past way of life; former life with family or another person. <u>Old people:</u> wisdom; mother or father; past experience; traditions; old age or feelings about aging; death. <u>Old things or furniture:</u> past or outworn ways of life or activities.

ancient   Usually suggests contact with parts of our being older than the development of the conscious self, such as cellular wisdom; life processes; accepted traditions or ways of life; wisdom of the unconscious.

antique Elements of our past experience that might be worth keeping; wisdom of unconscious. See **age.**

onion See **food.**

opal See *Opal* under **jewels.**

operation Memories regarding actual operation; a sick inner attitude that needs attention; fear of illness; physical illness.

orange See *orange* under **colors;** *orange* under **food.**

orchard Fruitfulness, the results of labors. The sort of fruitfulness of a long life well spent. Or if an orchard in bloom, it can depict youth or female fertility. Also peace and personal growth. See **garden.**

orchestra The working relationship between the different aspects of oneself—mind, body, spirit; one's sense of social cooperation or harmony in the cosmos. <u>Conductor:</u> the self; whatever is directing one's life. See **music; musical instrument.**

ore One's potential; new ideas or energy potentials you are bringing to consciousness from your unconscious resources. These potentials are probably to do with innate processes from the long past, or aspects of yourself you have never dealt with before; resources needing work to make usable. See **mine, mines.**

organ The different aspects of self, different ideas, feelings, abilities, weaknesses, and strengths that can be played or called upon; the whole range of our being as it responds to decisions and activity; sexual organs. See **music.**

orphan Feeling abandoned or unloved; feeling rejected or misunderstood, or part of yourself is being rejected and misunderstood; vulnerability in independence and consciousness. Sometimes this reflects difficult events in your childhood, leading to you feeling abandoned or unwanted. If so, there is often a link with feelings of belonging—whether you feel you belong to anyone, or anyone belongs to, or really links with, you. See **abandoned.**

out-of-body experience Because out-of-body experiences occur while the person is apparently asleep, they can be considered as manifestations of sleep phenomena, but they do not have the same characteristics as a typical dream. Dreams are seldom verifiable observations of external events occurring at the same time as the dream. Out-of-body experiences (OBEs) frequently display an accurate observation of external events not available to the sleeping person except by extraordinary means. This suggests that human consciousness is not limited to the smaller range of awareness the body senses give.

OBEs have been reported thousands of times in every culture and in every period of history. A general experience of an OBE might include a feeling of floating or rushing along a tunnel, or release from a tight place prior to the awareness of independence from the body. In this first stage some people experience a sense of physical paralysis, which may be frightening. Their awareness then seems to become an observing point outside the body as well as the sense of paralysis. There is usually an intense awareness of oneself and surroundings, unlike dreaming or even lucidity. Some projectors feel they are even more vitally aware and rational than during the waking state. Looking back on one's body may occur here. At this very first stage of complete independence some people experience intense fear. This is most likely due to the fear that one is dying. I believe there is an unconscious connection between the exteriorization of one's awareness and death. Example: "Then I looked down on my sleeping body. Suddenly I was terrified. I didn't at the time understand this terror, but the thought came to me in a flash that this was what I had read about—i.e., people leaving their body in projection. The fear immediately vanished, to be replaced by uncontrollable laughter. Looking back I think the terror arose because I was certain I was dying. The laughter came at the realization this was not so, and was a release of tension brought about by the terror." (T.C.)

Once the awareness is independent of the body, the boundaries of time and space as they are known in the body do not exist. One can easily pass through walls, fly, travel to—or immediately be in—a far distant place, witnessing what may be, or appears to be, physically real there. Sir Auckland Geddes, an eminent British anatomist, describes his own OBE, which contains many of these features. Example: "Becoming suddenly and violently ill with gastroenteritis, I quickly became unable to move, or phone for help. As this was occurring I noticed I had an 'A' and a 'B' consciousness. The 'A' was my normal awareness, and the 'B' was external to my body, watching. From the 'B' self I could see not only my body, but also the house, garden, and surrounds. I needed only think of a friend or place and immediately I was there and was later able to find confirmation for my observations. In looking at my body, I noticed that the brain was only an end organ, like a condensing plate, upon which memory and awareness played. The mind was not in the brain, the brain was in the mind, like a radio in the play of signals. I then observed my daughter come in and discover my condition, saw her telephone a doctor friend, and saw the doctor also at the same time."

As OBEs often occur at times of stress, a near-death experience, great pain, or in deep withdrawal, they may have a link with such human and animal situations. In other words, OBEs may have developed as an evolutionary or survival method to deal with death, near-death, pain, or stress. For instance, many cases of OBE occur in a near-death situation, where a person has "died" of a heart attack, for instance, and is later revived. Because of this there are attempts to consider the possibility of survival of death through study of these cases. In fact, many people after experiencing an OBE have a very different view of death than prior to their experience. From the opposite point of view, that of the external observer who is not asleep, many OBEs have been witnessed by relatives of people actually dying through war or accident. During the two world wars, many cases were reported, and later corroborated, of seeing the dying person appear, and of them telling of their death, or silently communicating it. I believe this points out the deep connection between an OBE and dying, pain, and stress. I have felt that the OBE is, in fact, the remains of something that existed in primitive animals as a survival mechanism. It was a way of communicating the cause of death to those with genetic bonding. This awareness would help in avoiding the same death.

In a nutshell, the world of the OBE is created by the concepts of the "dreamer." This world is experienced as physically real, in a similar way to the world of dreams. Yet it is neither a dream in the usual sense, nor a dream in which the person is highly lucid. There is a different quality about it than either dreaming or lucidity. The difference is that during an OBE the physical world can also be experienced and witnessed. So in trying to analyze events during an OBE, we must discover what aspects are created out of unconsciously held concepts, and what are witnessed physical world events or objects. Whatever the answer, this view of the OBE suggests there is no need for a person to travel to a site, or to have a silver cord—or, in fact, any sort of body at all. What emerges is that consciousness can at certain times completely go beyond the limitations of space, location, and time that we usually accept. For instance, it is very real for us to accept that if we wish to personally experience the streets of Tokyo or New York we will have to transport our body to those locations. If we go to New York we cannot at the same time experience Tokyo. With an OBE these rules do not apply. Consciousness does not have to travel. See **paralysis—while asleep or trying to wake** for an explanation of this; **altered states of consciousness**; *rebirth, resurrection* under **archetypes; ghost; hallucinations, hallucinogens.**

oval   The womb; female qualities or sexuality.

ovaries, ovum   Fundamental feelings about sex, reproduction, fertility, and therefore womanhood.

oven   May depict pregnancy or the womb; the human ability to transform character qualities. From being a sulky, irritable person, one can change to being self-giving and open. Depicts this because the oven transforms inedible substances or objects into delightful food.

overcoat   See *coat* under **clothes.**

owl   See *owl* under **birds.**

oyster   See *oyster* under **fish, and sea creatures.**

P

packing   Leaving home; becoming or wanting to be independent; making changes; wanting to get away. <u>Already-packed case:</u> readiness to meet change. <u>Packing and wondering what to take:</u> decisions about what stance or attitudes are suitable to meet present situation or change; sense of an end in sight; attempt to be independent. <u>Can't pack in time:</u> anxiety about details; feeling unready for change. <u>Idioms:</u> pack off; pack up; send somebody packing; pack one's bags.

pain   If in parts of body, this depicts tensions arising in yourself from living in conflict with your basic needs or feelings. See **body,** *Parts of body.*

painting   <u>A painting:</u> the unconscious frequently senses things, or synthesises out of our experience, views of things we have not been consciously aware of. A dream may depict this as a painting; subtle feelings or realizations; a view we have of or about something. <u>Any form of artistic expression:</u> self-expression; expressing one's feelings or intuitions; one's inner situation; creative ability. <u>Painting, as in decorating:</u> making changes in the way we live or feel about ourselves; expressing feelings; the impression we give to others; what "color" we are painting things, in the sense of painting a very black picture; a cover-up. We can paint the town red; paint too rosy a picture. Or we might be working at changing our appearance or lifestyle. See **photos.**

pajamas   Being casual or intimate; sexuality; difficulty in facing life. In <u>street or public in nightclothes:</u> revealing one's sleep, perhaps honest self, to others; inappropriate attitudes. See **clothes.**

palace   See *palace* under **house, buildings.**

pan, pot   <u>Cooking pot or pan:</u> receptive state of mind and feelings, perhaps connected with creativity (cooking), family life, or providing for one's needs; everyday life. <u>Chamberpot:</u> feelings and values connected with excretory functions; female sexuality. <u>Idioms:</u> flash in the pan.

pants   See *underclothes, underpants, briefs* or *trousers* under **clothes.**

paper   <u>Blank writing paper:</u> unexpressed sentiments or ideas; opportunity; feeling a lack of communication with someone else. <u>Wrapping paper:</u> depending on the color and quality, how you feel others see you; the exterior impression of what you are getting or giving in a relationship; the outward appearance of your potential. <u>Idioms:</u> Commit to paper; not worth the paper it's written on; on paper; paper tiger; pen to paper; paper over the cracks.

parachute   Depicts whatever life skill one uses to deal with anxiety about failing/falling; achieving a more down-to-earth, practical attitude after flying high, or retreating into flights of fancy.

paralysis   See *paralysis, paralyzed* under **body.**

paralysis—while asleep or trying to wake   Many people complain of feeling paralyzed while they are partially awake but dreaming. This may be due to the fact that voluntary movements are inhibited during periods of the dream process. All brain signals to the voluntary muscles are stopped. Therefore, if we become slightly awake and attempt to move at that time, we feel paralyzed. This is not sensed as a problem if we are unconsciously involved in a dream. If enough self-awareness arises in the dream state, then awareness of the inability to move may occur, along with the anxiety this can arouse. In fact, this is probably only a problem to people who are frightened of the paralysis. For most people, active dreams manage to break through the inhibition enough to cause mild movements and vocal sounds.

Another factor is illustrated by what Elsie says in the example below—the harder she tries to move, the worse it gets. Our unconscious is very open to suggestion. If this were not so, we would lack necessary survival responses. In a dimly lit situation we may mistake a shape for a lurking figure. Our body reactions such as heartbeat react to the mistake as if it is real until we gain fresh information. Whatever we feel to be real becomes a fact as far as our body reactions are concerned. The fear that one cannot move becomes a fact because we believe it. When Elsie relaxes, and thereby drops the fear of paralysis, she can be free of it. This applies to anything we feel is true—we create it as an internal reality. Example: "It starts as a dream, but I gradually become aware that I cannot move. The harder I try to move the worse it gets, and I become very frightened. I can neither move nor wake myself up. Sometimes I feel as if I am leaving my body. But to deal with the fear I have learned—it's a recurring thing—to stop struggling, knowing that I will eventually wake." (Elsie)

The excellent description in the following example was given by Roy Herbert. It was taken from a feature he wrote. Unfortunately the news cutting did not have either the name of the paper or the date with it. Example: "In this condition, I can hear what others are saying to make me come to. The bedroom is the one I am in, though sometimes altered in layout, and the real persons in it may be joined by dream ones. I can speak and even offer suggestions on how to bring me awake, such as cold water on my head, though I am told that the words are not intelligible. I am aware that my mouth is dry. My brain is working on some levels that are far from asleep. I have been able to censor swear words from anguished advice I am offering the rousers, for fear of offending them, though I am not awake. The worst thing of all is that I have almost no power in my limbs while the struggle is going on. The prospect of sinking back into deep sleep, unable to move, is terrifying—so dreadful that I finally burst fully awake with the sensation of shooting up through water into the air. I don't think that I can be unique in floating halfway, half awake and half asleep, paralyzed but speaking and thinking in a half-real world. It might be interesting to hear from other sufferers."

Other strange phenomena occurring either during or on the edge of sleep probably have similar causes, or are linked in some way. Roy Herbert's description vividly portrays the experience of being locked halfway between the "real" world and the "dream" world, and perhaps that is part of the fear experienced. But the threshold of waking that Roy is trying to approach need not be the one that leads to a loss of the dream state. What I mean is that Roy's dream imagery stops when he wakes. For many people their dream imagery persists when they wake, and they have to travel further into waking than Roy does to lose the sense of having no control, or of being invaded by experiences from "outside" themselves. See **hallucinations, hallucinogens.** Much of the problem felt by people in these states arises from their relationship to what is being experienced. People actually seek the state Roy describes through self-hypnosis or meditation. Understanding that the paralysis is caused by the dream process inhibiting voluntary muscles, can rob it of its terror. See **awake, difficulty in awaking sleeper; movements during sleep.**

parasites   Lice, fleas, bugs: things said, thought, or done that make you feel uncomfortable or ashamed; feelings that one is, or someone else is, a parasite in a relationship.

parcel, package   Something we have experienced but not explored the import of. A parent may die, for instance,

parcel, package

but we may not "unwrap" the feelings evoked enough to see we have taken something to heart. If we did we might find a regret of not expressing the love we felt while Mom or Dad was still alive, and we now want to be more daring in giving love; one's potential or latent skills; impressions or "gifts" received from others—such as support, love, their example—but not made fully conscious.

park Your public self and how it is growing, or how you see your growth and endeavor from a public viewpoint. It might also associate with relaxed feelings, or even romance. National park: meeting your natural self as opposed to the self you may have to be to survive socially or economically.

parking lot See Parking lot, car park, parking under **car.**

parrot See *parrot* under **birds.**

party Our feelings about groups; social skill or lack of it; social pleasure; search for sexual partner. Dreamer as the host of the party: our relationship with the different aspects of self; exploring social relationships or our feelings about groups. Dreamer as main guest, at birthday party: wanting family or social acclaim and love, or feeling loved.

passage A sense of being "in-between" regarding work, love, or life; change as in a "rite of passage"—so the movement between stages or phases of life; the back passage (rectum) or front passage (vagina, and so the birth passage). See **corridor.** Idioms: work one's passage.

passenger Being a passenger: feeling that circumstances are carrying you along, either because you are passively allowing them to, or because you feel powerless to change; sense of being carried along by the process of life, such as aging; a joint direction you are taking, as in a business venture or relationship. Someone else driving: being motivated or moved by someone else's viewpoints, opinions, or enthusiasm; being dependent, perhaps on who is driving the car; allowing a secondary part of self, such as indecision, pride, or stubbornness, to direct decisions. <u>Carrying passengers:</u> feeling you are taking the responsibility in work or family. See **car.**

passport   Your sense of identity, with its connections with racial, national, and family background; feelings about travel; authority or confidence, especially regarding your identity.

past   See **historic.**

path   The approach or attitudes one uses regarding life in general, or in relationship or work; the direction one has decided on or is following; the way a relationship or marriage is going; a line of thought or inquiry; the path sometimes represents one's overall direction or experience of life within the process of growth and change. If <u>well-worn path:</u> a well-established or habitual way of doing something; the way other people do it, so following the norm. <u>Losing a partner on the path:</u> fear or intuition that the relationship will end or partner die first.

pay   In nearly all the dreams studied that refer to pay, the action is to pay for something, like a fare or goods. None of them are about being paid. This suggests that pay and paying depict concerns about wanting to, or having to, give something of value, either to get something or to feel a situation is dealt with. The payment can therefore refer to what you have to bring to a situation to make it work, or get positive results. <u>Being paid:</u> results of previous effort or experience. Reward for what you have done or been.

peacock   See *peacock* under **birds.**

pearl   See <u>Pearl</u> under **jewels;** *oyster* under **fish, sea creatures.**

peer dream work   The way of working known as the Peer Dream Group came about from the author's experience that dreams are largely self-explanatory if approached in the right way. An exterior expert or authority is not necessary for a profound experience of and insight into dreams if certain rules are respected and used. You are the ultimate expert on your own dream, and when treated as such, and supported in your investigation of your dream drama, you can powerfully explore and manifest the resources of your inner life.

Fundamentals of practice

The suggestions that follow have arisen from forty years of dream work. They have been particularly tested with many small groups, and are usually employed with groups of three to five people, but sometimes with just two people working together.

find a partner you can relax with who can give sympathetic and nonintrusive support   Agree with the partner that any confidences disclosed during the dream exploration will not be told to others.

the dreamer tells the dream; it is sometimes helpful for them to tell it in the first-person present, as if they were experiencing the dream as they are telling it   The telling of the dream can include any relevant information, such as immediate associations, or events directly linked with the dream. Example: "This is my dream. I am driving my car, alone. I can see a female friend and stop to offer her a lift. I partly want her to be impressed by my new car. She looks at me. Now she tells me she doesn't want a lift and I am watching her walk off with a man I do not know. I have recently bought the car I am driving in the dream. I like it very much and like to have my friends ride in it." (Joel)

the helpers now ask the dreamer questions to clarify for themselves the imagery and drama of the dream   The questions at this point should not be to explore the dream, but simply to gain a clear image of the dream.

Q: You didn't describe the street you were driving along. Was it a shopping center or quiet place?

A: It was quite a crowded road, with people, not so many cars. I think this was also connected with my feeling of wanting to be seen in my new car.

Q: Are you attracted to your female friend?

A: Yes.

the dreamer next chooses one of the characters or images in the dream to explore   The character can be themselves as they appear in the dream, or any of the other people or things. It is important to realize that it does not matter if the character is someone known or not, or whether they are young or old. The character needs to be treated as an aspect of their dream, and not as if they were the living person exterior to the dream. In choosing an image to work with, such as a tree, cat, place, or an environment like the street in the example dream, it must again be treated as it appears in the dream, not as it may appear in real life. One can take any image from the dream to work with.

the dreamer stands in the role of the character or image they are using   So if they choose to be the car in the example dream, they would close their eyes, enter into the feeling sense and *imagery* of the dream, and describe himself or herself as the car.

Example: "I am a car. Joel has recently purchased me, and he is driving me, largely because he feels I will help him gain respect from other people. I am quite a large car, and have a lot of power. But even with all this energy, I do not make my own decisions. I am directed by Joel's desires and wishes, and enable him to fulfill them more readily."

From this short description it can already be seen there is a suggestion the car represents Joel's emotional and physical energy, directed by his desires and decisions.

*the helpers now ask questions of the dreamer, who stays in the
role of the dream character or image*   The questions must
be directly related to the role the dreamer is in. So Joel, in
the role of the car, could be asked: Are you a secondhand
or new car? Who was driving you before Joel? Do you feel
that Joel handles you well? What does it feel like to be directed where to go all the time? Do you have places you
would like to go?

Joel should be helped to remain in role. If he slips out of
it and stops describing himself as the car, gently remind
him he is speaking as the car. Also, the questions should be
asked with an awareness of time necessary for the
dreamer's adequate response. So do not hurry the questions to the point where the dreamer cannot properly explore his or her associations and feeling responses. If
emotions are stimulated by a question, allow the dreamer
to feel the emotion. An emotion is usually a response to
something, and therefore gives information concerning
what is moving us deeply. If a line of questioning is producing promising results, do not lead the dreamer off in
another direction. For instance, Joel may have been asked
if he wants to get out of his car and follow the woman, and
he shows some feelings about this. A question such as "Are
there any shops in this street?" would take him completely
away from such feelings. To ask relevant questions, it is
useful to be interested in the dreamer and their dream.
Have a questioning mind in relationship to the dream. So
do not have already fixed opinions about it. Be like a de-
tective gradually unfolding the information and emotions
behind the dream. As the dreamer answering the questions, let your helpers also know what you feel in response
to their questions, or what memories or associations occur
when a particular part of the dream is being explored. Example: Joel: "When you asked me if I want to follow the
woman, I immediately realized that in real life I am holding myself back from letting my feelings about her show."

When you have come to the end of what you can ask
about the dream image, the dreamer should be asked to

summarize what they have understood or gathered from what they have said or felt in response to the questions. To summarize effectively, gather the essence of what you have said about the symbol and express it in everyday language. Imagine you are explaining to someone who knows nothing about yourself or the dream. Bring the dream out of its symbols into everyday comments about yourself. Example: A man dreamt about a gray, dull office. When he looked at what he said about the office, he rephrased it by saying, "The dream depicts the gray, unimaginative social environment I grew up in after the second World War. It shaped the way I now think, and I want to change it toward more freedom of imagination and creativity."

Work through each of the symbols in the dream within the available time.

A dream that leaves the dreamer unsatisfied, or in a difficult place, can usefully be approached by using the technique of carrying the dream forward. The following techniques describe how to carry the dream forward and how to use the body in dream exploration. These are extremely useful tools to occasionally use in peer dream work.

carrying the dream forward   Imagine yourself in the dream and continue it as a fantasy or daydream. Alter the dream in any way that satisfies. Experiment with it, play with it, until you find a fuller sense of self-expression. It is very important to note whether any feelings, such as anger or pleasure, are in the dream but not fully expressed. If so, let yourself imagine a full expression of the feelings. It may be that as this is practiced you are more openly expressive in subsequent dreams. This is healthy, allowing such feelings to be vented and redirected into satisfying ways. In doing this, do not ignore any feelings of resistance, pleasure, or anxiety. Satisfaction occurs only as we learn to acknowledge and integrate resistances and anxieties into what we express. This is a very important step. It gradually changes those of our habits that trap us in lack of satisfaction, poor creativity, or inability to resolve problems.

peer dream work

Example: "When my husband died, for quite a few times I had this funny dream. I was walking along a field and saw a lot of sheep guiding me, and I followed them. Suddenly they disappeared into a cave. I went in the cave and a row of mummies were there. One was wearing a medallion on a chain round its neck. The dream recurred quite often. One day Tony came to me and I told him the dream. He asked me to sit in a chair and relax, which I did. Then he said for me to go to the cave, and in my relaxed state I went and walked to the mummy with the medallion. Then he asked me to take off the bandage from the top. As I unwound it, the face of my husband was uncovered. I screamed and screamed and came out of the relaxation. Tony then said, 'now let him go.' I have never had that dream since." (Betty E.)

use the body to discover dream power   The brain sends impulses to all the muscles to act on the movements we are making while in the dream. This is observable when we wake ourselves by thrashing about in bed, or kicking and shouting. A part of the brain inhibits these movements while we sleep. The important factor is that a dream is more than a set of images and emotions, it is frequently also a powerful physical activity and self-expression. If we explore a dream while sitting and quietly talking to a friend, even if we allow emotions to surface, we may miss important aspects of our dream process. Through physical movement the dream process releases tensions and deeply buried memories that are stored in our body. These may not release and heal by simply talking about them. It is often enough to realize this aspect of dream exploration for such spontaneous movements to emerge when necessary. By being aware of the body's need to occasionally be involved in expression of dream content, we may catch the cues and let these develop. Frequently all you need to do is to let the body doodle, or to fantasize, while exploring a dream. Jung suggested this technique for times when the person was stuck in intellectual speculation. To practice it you can take a dream image and let the hands spontaneously doodle, watching what is gradually mimed or expressed. When you have gained skill doing this, let the whole body take part in it. This can unfold aspects of dreams that the other approaches might not help with. See **movements during sleep.**

pelvis   See *pelvis* under **body.**

pen, pencil   Desire to communicate; occasionally male genitals, because of shape.

penis   See *penis* under **body; castrate.**

people   People in your dreams depict your human attitudes, strengths, and anxieties. They show the way you relate to yourself and to others. They are among the most important characters in your dream life. The dream image of a person is like a holographic presentation of what you feel, think, desire, or fear about the person whose image it is. This holographic image usually contains massive memories linking with the person dreamt of. You, the dreamer, manipulate this image for a variety of reasons. But the image is in no way the person it appears to be. In fact, the memories and feelings involved may be from years past. Meanwhile the real person may have changed enormously. They are getting on with their life, going through change, perhaps even have died. But the image is like a magical thing that can present you with past pains, gratify your needs, and enable you to explore further reaches of the relationship.

As social relationship is one of the most important factors outside of personal survival—and survival depends upon it—such dreams help you to clarify your individual contact with society. Human beings have an unconscious but highly developed sense of the psychological social environment. We are all involved in relating to other people individually and collectively. Are we in conflict with group behavior and direction? Do we conform, but perhaps have conflict with our individual drives? Do we find a way

people

between the opposites? Much of our response is laid down in childhood and remains unconscious unless we review it, but becomes visible in dreams.

<u>Couple:</u> depending on the context of the couple in the dream, they can represent the dreamer's parents and the family situation and environment at the age of the couple portrayed; if the dreamer has been married, it can depict the dreamer's marriage situation at the age of the couple; hopes for a relationship; possible outcomes of a relationship; friendship; partnership; some sort of relationship. <u>Dead people:</u> the influence those people still have in your life—i.e., you are still influenced by them, or your relationship with them, even though they are dead. Feelings about death. <u>Group of people:</u> a group of people can depict how you meet the pressure of social norms; public opinion. <u>Large crowds:</u> enormous involvement of yourself in issue; your relationship or feelings about the social environment you live in; in groups we have a feeling of being looked at or on view—how we relate to that may be depicted by what you are doing in the dream group. See **party; roles.** <u>Old person:</u> See **age.** <u>People from our past:</u> considering that the major part of our learning and experience occur in relationship to other people, such learning and experience can be represented by characters from the past. For instance, a first boyfriend in a dream would depict all the emotions and struggles we met in that relationship, and what we learned from it or took away from it. Therefore, dreaming often of people we knew in the past would suggest the past experiences or lessons are very active at the moment, or we are reviewing those areas of our life. A woman who had emigrated to Britain from a very different cultural background frequently dreamt, even twenty years afterward, of people she knew in her native country. This shows her still very much in contact with her own cultural values and experiences. <u>Several people in a dream</u> suggest: not feeling lonely, involvement of many aspects of oneself in what is being dreamt about; social ability.

pepper   Warming up one's emotions; livening up the situation; irritation.

perfume, scent, smell   A smell can remind us of a particular situation or person; odor attracts, repulses, relaxes, or offends; so it can depict feeling responses or intuition, and may summarize what you feel about a person or situation; frequently in dreams a smell expresses an intuition of something rotten in one's life if the smell is bad; the rotten smell might mean "bad" emotions felt in a relationship; a hunch or feelings about something, as in the example below; memories. Good smell: good feelings; nonverbalized intimations or love.

Example: "I went back in time in circles, almost as if going unconscious. I went back and back, and then there came this awful smell, such as I've never experienced. I always felt it was the smell of death. I would wake terrified. One night my husband, a practical and down-to-earth man, said he would read me to sleep to see if it helped me not have the dream. It made no difference, I still had the nightmare. Imagine my surprise, though. He said, 'I knew you'd had the dream again, for there was an awful smell in the room for a minute.' " (Mrs. R. S.)

Also explainable by the large number of idioms regarding smell. Idioms: on the right scent; throw someone off the scent; in bad/good odor with; odor of sanctity; smell a rat; smell of greasepaint; smells fishy; something stinks to high heaven; like stink; raise a stink; what you did stinks. See *nose* under **body**.

Perls, Fritz   See **gestalt dream work**.

perspire, sweat   Mostly fear. As we get near to experiencing areas of our memory or inner feelings that disturb us, rapid heartbeat and perspiration are some of the first signs; excitement; feeling we are repulsive to others if we feel the perspiration is obnoxious; occasionally, pleasurable exertion. <u>Idioms:</u> in a cold sweat; no sweat; sweat blood; sweat of one's brow; old sweat; sweat it out.

pet   Very often depicts feeling of responsibility or caring; feelings of affection, such as we might feel for a pet; natural drives, such as procreation or desire to be "petted." These feelings may have been "house-trained" or caged, or not fed, depending on dream. Therefore, the action in the dream will indicate what one is doing with this side of one's nature; feelings of being like a pet—only being able to do what the person you are dependent upon wishes. An <u>unfed pet:</u> feelings of responsibility toward caring for someone else, or caring for one's own basic needs. Maybe the children have grown up and left, and there is no one to spend one's caring and affection on. Or else we are so busy we forget our needs. <u>Baby pets:</u> if in a woman's dream, may signify her maternal drive, her desire for children; one's own dependent self and feelings. <u>If we have kept a pet such as we dream about:</u> what the pet in the dream depicts rests very much on what the dreamer's relationship with the pet was. For instance, a woman whose daughter kept a rat that was well liked would have completely different associations and feeling responses in connection with rats than many people. <u>In the dream of a child:</u> may refer to the child's feelings of being dependent; affection and unconditional love; caring feelings of responsibility. See **animals.**

petrol   See **car; gas, gasoline.**

petticoat   See **clothes.**

pharmacy   See **chemist.**

philosophy of dreams   In attempting to summarize the information gathered from viewing thousands of dreams—not simply at face value, but explored in depth through the emotions and direct associations of the dreamer—a philosophy or view of life arises. The synthesis of the information gathered suggests that our birth as a physical and psychological being is a paradox. We are unique, and at the same time a common undifferentiated process. Psychologically we have our identity out of the lives of thousands of humans who preceded us and left the gift of language, of music, of art, of concepts and information. Our mental life, our consciousness, is in some very real way formed out of what they left from their life, just as our body is formed out of what we eat, and genetic material. Our consciousness has been whittled out of the rock of possibilities by the love, the struggle and pain, the endeavor and wit of other people's lives. Particularly our psyche has been shaped or modeled by our parents, and the traces in their life, unknown though they may be, of their parents, backwards for many generations.

Our identity is given to us by the humans who raise us. This sense of self arises because we are treated as if we were a self. This, with language, is the creative matrix of our self-awareness. The giving of a name is therefore a miracle that acts as a nucleus around which the many mental connections can be made that form our self-image. Perhaps this is why giving the name in baptism is seen as a holy rite in Christianity.

Our conscious personality can live without ever becoming aware of its connections with other lives except as it meets them in everyday affairs. That its existence has depended upon what was given by countless other lives—that humans constantly create each other through the dynamic flux of communication, consciously and unconsciously—might never be realized. That one's own life is also a part of this creative process, this sea of living consciousness, might never be known. Nevertheless, each individual life constantly takes part in the collective, negatively or positively. This is not a mystical thing, but is plainly observable. Language, for instance, is not something we created alone. The clothes we wear, the food we eat, the house we live in, and the materials it is made of are all a part of collective skill, effort, and knowledge. We exist in this collective creativity all the time. We depend upon it but perhaps seldom acknowledge it. Our unconscious, however, is vitally aware of it and communicates to us as fully as it can what it sees of our relationship with this collective life process and social activity, although we frequently ignore it.

From the point of view of dreams, if our life has given nothing in deed, in love, in rearing of children, in ideas or art, or in common humanity, we are dead—during life and afterward. Giving and receiving, kinship and symbiosis, growth and decay are the fundamentals of the living process, according to dreams. Life is action within the whole. At death, we face a very real end, a real death. There is no magical escape from this. All that we have been, all we have become, all we gathered and won is lost—finished. But the paradox occurs again. Dreams suggest that out of all we gave of ourselves, out of all we received from the being of others arises a new existence re-created in a realm of consciousness that does not depend upon the body. This may mean that we continue as living influences in the lives of those who still live. But the suggestion is that something more than this occurs.

phoenix   See **birds.**

photos   Memories; wanting to be remembered or noticed; looking at some aspect of oneself. <u>Developing photos:</u> bringing to consciousness what was latent or unrealized before. <u>Looking at family photos:</u> realization of past influences in your life; family environment, mentally and emotionally. <u>Photo of oneself:</u> one's self-image; need to look at oneself or get an objective view. <u>Photos that come to life:</u> the living influence of past experience, our continuing involvement in what the picture depicts; something that we held as a thought, which is taking shape and becoming real. <u>Taking photos:</u> capturing a realization; taking notice of something; remembering.

physician   See *doctor* under **roles.**

piano   See **musical instrument**.

pictures   See **painting; photos**.

pig   See *pig* under **animals**.

pill   An experience you need, or are making yourself meet because you think it is good for you; something we "swallow" because we think it is right—we may "swallow" lies or excuses; an attempt to deal with internal feelings by external means. A <u>pill we are actually taking:</u> may link with feelings or physical reactions to the drug being taken. <u>Idioms:</u> sugar the pill; bitter pill.

pillow   Comfort; support; may represent someone we rely on or want to be close to. <u>Hugging pillow:</u> feeling alone and needing contact.

pimple   Character blemishes if on face; worry about how you appear to others; sense of not being inwardly clean; feelings about one's spots.

pin   Small ideas, actions, or information that help create something or hold things together; one's connection or emotional bond with things. If <u>stuck in:</u> irritation or hurts; irritating or painful sexual intercourse. <u>Idioms:</u> for two pins; don't care two pins; on pins and needles; pin back one's ears; pin one's hopes on; pin someone down; pin something on someone; pin money.

pipe   Unconscious connections with others; emotions, or things that you feel are "on tap"; a difficult way out of a situation; sometimes refers to the experience of being born, especially if accompanied by panic or fear; the "pipes" in one's body—see *the dream as extended perception* under **ESP in dreams**. <u>Crawling into pipe:</u> sexual intercourse—sex creates unconscious links with partner; experiencing unconscious connection with others. <u>Sewage pipe:</u>

pipe

the group feelings or ideology, the collective negative or hidden aspects of society or one's relationship with others.

pit   Feelings or situations one finds it difficult to get out of; feelings about death; feeling trapped or forgotten. Often relates to a mass of unconscious assumptions that have been taken in from our family and culture. These assumptions create a view of the world and life in which we can easily become entrapped, and thus are depicted by the pit. See **abyss; fall, falling; void.**

place, environment   See **setting.**

placenta   Dependence; being depended upon; how one gains nourishment from another.

plait   Plaited hair: girlhood. See *hair* under **body.** Plaiting rope, etc.: weaving different influences in one's life together; uniting conflicting feelings or people; a triangle situation.

plane   See **airplane.**

plank   Depends what they are used for in dream. Can be security in life if flooring—or sense of losing basic support if rotten floor. See *floor* under **house, buildings.** If for making something: potential; the materials you have for undertaking a project or "making something of oneself." If nailed above one: feeling of being trapped, fear of death; setting up one's own death, in the sense of killing one's chances in work or relationship. See **fence; coffin; wood.**

plants   Areas of progressive change in one's life; emerging personal qualities; occasionally one's children being helped in their growth. Dead or dying plants: loss of vital enthusiasm; dying pleasure; lost love. See **flowers; weeds.**

318

plate   If <u>food on plate:</u> what one has a sense of ownership about; what one has received or hopes to receive from others, or from one's own efforts; what you have created and now face. <u>Communal plate:</u> what is available to you but you may have to compete for or share—in work, relationship, life. <u>Empty plate:</u> one's needs; appetites; receptivity; perhaps status, as in the past only the rich had plates. <u>Idioms:</u> handed to one on a plate; on one's plate. See **food.**

plateau   Reaching a plateau in one's life—a place where things remain the same, where there is little change; a wider and calmer viewpoint of life, where one is neither climbing ambitiously or descending and losing what one has gained.

play   See **film; theater.**

playing   Depends what the "game" is. Whatever we "play" at in a dream might just be fun or suggest great seriousness. As humans we use an enormous number of strategies to gain our ends, as explained in the book *Games People Play.* So play in a dream can depict a sense of relaxation; a way of practicing something without responsibility; not taking something seriously; a game can also be a way of playing creatively, exploring feelings, ideas, and approaches in a safe way before trying them out in life. This sort of self-allowing, of letting oneself "want" something without too many serious overtones can be very creative and the beginning of new developments in life. The enormous number of idioms on play define some of these "games." <u>Idioms:</u> come into play; fair play; foul play; make a play for; make play of; play a part in; play along with; play at; play cat and mouse; play dead/possum; play down; played out; play fair; play false; play for time; play hard-to-get; play it cool; play no part in it; play on words; play safe; play people off against each other; play something down; play the field; play up; play upon a weakness/fear; play up

playing

to someone; the state of play; play somebody at their own game; child's play; play ball with; play it by ear; play fast and loose; play gooseberry; play havoc with; play merry hell; play into their hands; play one's ace; play one's cards right; play second fiddle; play the fool; play the game; play the white man; play to the gallery; play with fire; two can play at that game. See **games, gambling.**

plot of the dream   In attempting to understand our dreams, it is important to honor their drama or plot. Dreams appear to be very specific in the way they use the characters, objects, and environs occurring in them.

Example: "I was walking up a steep hill on a sunny day when my husband came running down the hill with blood pouring from his right arm. He couldn't stop running. As he passed me he called to me for help. I was happy and peaceful and ignored him. I calmly watched him running fast down the hill, then continued on my way." (Denise T.) Out of the infinite number of situations Denise could have dreamt about, this was the one produced. Why? There are many factors that appear to determine what we dream. How events of the day influenced us, what stage of personal growth we are meeting, problems being met, relationship situations, past business—such as childhood traumas still to be integrated—are some of them. If Denise had dreamt she and her husband were walking up the hill, the whole message of the dream would have been different. If we can accept that dream images are, as Freud stated, a form of thinking, then the change in imagery would be a changed feeling state and concept. If the language of dreams is expressed in its images, then the meaning stated is specific to the imagery used.

In processing our dreams, it is therefore profitable to look at the plot to see what it suggests. It can be helpful to change the situation, as we have done with Denise's. Imagining Denise walking up the hill on a sunny day arm in arm with her husband suggests a happy relationship. This emphasizes the situation of independence and lack of support for her husband that appears in the real dream. Seeing our dreams as if they were snatches from a film or play, and asking ourselves what feelings or human situations they depict, can aid us to clarify them. As a piece of drama, Denise's dream says she sees, but does not respond to her husband's plight.

Our internal "dream producer" has an amazing sense of the subtle meanings of movement, positioning, and relationship between the elements used. A way of becoming more aware of what information our dream contains is to use visualization. Sit comfortably and imagine yourself back in the dream. Replay it just as it was. Remember the whole thing slowly, going through it again while awake. As you do so, be aware of what it feels like in each scene or event. What do the interactions suggest? What does it feel like in the other roles? We can even practice this with other people's dreams. If we imagine ourselves in Denise's dream, and replay it just as she describes it, we may arrive at a feeling of detachment from the husband. If we stand in the husband's role we may feel a great need that is not responded to as we go "down hill fast." In this way we gather a great deal of "unspoken" information from dreams.

Looking at our dreams in this way can be more difficult, simply because we do not always want to see what is being said about ourselves. See **amplification; peer dream work; postures, movement, body language; processing your dreams;** key words in the Introduction; **settings.**

plumbing   The way we direct emotions or the flow of feelings; our internal "plumbing"—intestines, colon, bladder, kidneys, etc. See **pipe; water.**

plunge   Taking a risk; facing uncertainty; going into something unknown or untried.

pocket   One's personal secrets or thoughts; self; sense of ownership or possession; vagina. <u>Trouser pocket:</u> can refer to sexuality; your intimate space that you only allow

pocket

certain people to enter. <u>Idioms:</u> be in somebody's pocket; in/out of pocket; pocket one's pride; burn a hole in one's pocket; dip into one's pocket; line one's pocket.

pocketbook   See **wallet.**

poem, poet   I have virtually no record of people dreaming about poetry or poets. Where it does happen the poem seems to sum up profound feelings that summarize the dreamer's best or worst view of life. So it seems a poem is a form of self-expression of subtle content or impressions, probably like a gestalt.

point   Anything pointed can refer to male sexuality; reaching a point—arriving at a culmination or change; a meaning; a decision to be made; something powerful or focused enough to penetrate. This can refer to an idea or an experience that can enter us or get through any defenses we may have.

pointing   Drawing one's attention to something; feeling at the receiving end of someone's emotions or suggestions; directed power. <u>Pointing hand:</u> drawing your attention to something. <u>Pointing stick or gun:</u> aggressive or defensive sexuality or emotions.

poison   Warning to avoid something; something that will not be good for us; attitudes, emotions, or thoughts that can harm or frighten us; warning against business deal or relationship; possibly related to foods we are eating that are not suitable. <u>Idioms:</u> what's your poison; poison one's mind; poison pen letter; avoid it like poison.

pole   The penis; male sexuality; self-expression in its positive extending aspect. Anything upright—like this can also represent the spine, with its connotations of strength or "spinelessness." So a pole with flag flying high could show the mood of well-being and rejoicing. The pole thrown down or broken could be a sense of defeat or low spirits.

policeman/woman   See *policeman/woman* under **roles.**

politics, politician   Sometimes symbolizes interests in how you govern your outer life as distinct to inner life. Naturally, if you have strong political feelings, it would symbolize the underlying attitudes that produce these feelings or ideas. It also links with shrewdness, or attempts to maneuver or influence; or perhaps to do the thing that others will support.

pollen   Sperm, fruition, fertility, as from new ideas.

pond   See **pool.**

pool   Our inner world of thoughts, fantasies, and feelings; sometimes a sense of unity with living beings—collective consciousness or the influence other people have on us in a social or group interaction—as, for instance, when public opinion or condemnation influences us. Being underwater in the pool: looking at what is happening deep within your mind and feelings; an aspect of yourself that is submerged, in the sense of being unconscious. Particularly links with looking into yourself and becoming aware of what you are feeling or daydreaming. See **water; swimming pool.**

pop star   See *pop star* under **famous people.**

Pope   Father figure; code of behavior arising from religious beliefs; God.

positions   One's stance or position in life; the way one is relating to what is depicted—or the way we feel we are relating to it.

positions

above   What is superior or has a wider view or possibility than our present standpoint; sense of inferiority in relationship to what is above us; what we strive for. If we are standing above or high up: having a wider viewpoint; being intellectual; feeling superior or in a position of advantage. Idioms: above all; above and beyond; above asking; above oneself; aboveboard; above one's station; risen above oneself. See **high; hill; mountain; flying.**

adjacent, adjoining   Suggests a strong connection with the dreamer, or what is wanted or being worked toward. For instance, in Japan, rocks or trees that are close together are sometimes seen as married or linked. Dreams use the same sort of symbology to suggest a more than surface connection with someone or some aspect of life. There could also be the suggestion of confrontation or discovery—being near something, in this case, meaning that we can no longer escape meeting it, or it is near at hand—in the sense of being discovered or experienced.

behind   The past; what you have chosen to or want to forget—left behind; what one is unaware of—as talk behind one's back; what has been learned or dealt with. People behind dreamer: taking the lead in relationships; being decisive. Idioms: behind the scenes; behind the time; fall behind; put something behind me.

below   Something you feel is "beneath you"; what is "below" in the body—so the nonintellectual aspects of self; something one can now look back on from a detached viewpoint. If below something else, see *above*. Idioms: beneath my contempt; it's below my standards.

beside   See *adjacent, adjoining* above.

close   Intimacy; being made aware of; what one feels connected with or has ties with; near to, in the sense of making a decision—near to leaving home; close to, as "close to finding the solution"; a situation that is near at hand or being confronted or realized now. <u>Idioms:</u> at close quarters; closefisted; close on; close to home; that was close.

distant　Barely conscious of; a longtime off; something one does not identify with strongly.

in front　The future, what is seen and understood; what is being confronted.

opposite　Meeting or "facing" a situation; opposition or resistance to decided direction.

side　Supportive feelings, as "by one's side"; as well as; indication of choice, as "what side are you on?" or "who's on my side?" <u>Idioms:</u> from all sides; let the side down; on every side; on the wrong side of thirty; on the right/wrong side; on the side; pass by on the other side; pick sides; put to one side; side by side; side with somebody; take sides; take to one side; the other side—death; safe side; bit on the side; seamy side. See *adjacent, adjoining* above.

post, postman/woman, post office　Communication; delivery of hopes, change, reward, or disappointment. See **letter.**

poster　Something the unconscious is trying to show you.

postures, movement, body language　Even in everyday life, the way we hold and position our body, the inclination of chest and head, the movement of hands are a means of communication. The apparently intuitive information in some dreams, when investigated, can be traced to an unconscious insight into the language of the living body. We all have this ability to understand body language, but it seems to be something that is inherited from our ancient forebears, perhaps developed to an intense degree as a survival need prior to the growth of verbal language. It therefore remains a largely unconscious ability. In our dreams, however, it is a major factor in how the dream is structured.

If you cannot find a satisfying description below, imagine yourself making the movement or posture in the dream, to see if you can define what the feeling quality is, or what you are saying nonverbally. It can often be of value to make the movement or take up the posture physically instead of in imagination. By comparing the movement/posture with another one, it can help to clarify its quality.

jump Jumping to: daring; taking a risk; sometimes connected with **flying.** Jumping to avoid: feeling of threat; anxiety; evasion tactics. Jumping off: getting out of a situation. Jumping at dreamer: unexpected; irritations. Idioms: one jump ahead; the high jump; jump at; running jump at yourself; jumping down one's throat; jumping off place; jump out of one's skin; jump the gun; jump the place in line; jump to it; jump on the bandwagon; jump to conclusion.

kneel Humility; acknowledgment of dependence or co-operation; sense of awe; defeat.

prone Relaxation; letting go of activity; introversion; sex; retreat from the world; feeling injured; afraid to stand up for oneself; noninvolvement; negative introversion; weakness; death. Idioms: lie low; lie at one's door; lie in wait; take it lying down. See: *squatting down* and *standing* below.

run Exuberance; flowing life-energy; strong and easy motivation. One can run to or run away, so it is important in some dreams to define which one it is. Running away: avoiding something; trying to get away from something—one's own emotions or sexuality, for instance; not meeting problems in a way that will resolve them; anxiety about what you are running from; feelings of guilt. Running to: trying to reach a goal; energetic attempt to reach a goal; anxiety; responsibility and self-giving; sometimes running toward danger. <u>Running with great pleasure, a sense of unhindered energy and potential:</u> Held back by one's own hesitations. See *paralysis, paralyzed* under **body.** <u>Idioms:</u> Run for one's money; run of the house; out of the running; on the run; run along; feeling run-down; run for it; run out of steam; run out on someone; run up against; run wild. See **chased; emotions; mood; nightmares; processing your dreams; lucidity.**

sit   One's situation at time of dream; status, depending where one is sitting; being relaxed; inactive waiting. *Sitting up:* becoming more involved. <u>Idioms:</u> sit back; sit for; sit in on something; sit on; sit out; sit something out; sit tight; sit at someone's feet; sit in judgment; sitting target; sit on the fence.

squatting down   sleep; rest; withdrawal; noninvolvement. *Idioms:* Feel down; down and out; do someone down; down at heel; downhearted; down with. See *prone* above.

standing   Our involvement in the exterior world of change, opposites, and needs that require expenditure of effort; our "standing" in society; what one "stands" for; being active; confrontation; cooperation with others. <u>Idioms:</u> know where one stands; left standing; make a stand against; stand alone; stand aside; stand by; stand corrected; stand down; stand firm; stand in someone's way; stand up for; stand up to; stand one's ground; stand on ceremony or dignity.

turn   A change; making a new decision.

walk   Motivation and confidence; where you are walking is what you are meeting in life, or where you are going; personal effort in trying to get somewhere; changing one's relationship with things; a period of experience you are passing through. <u>Walking up a lane:</u> as above, but may be memory lane. <u>Idioms:</u> walk over somebody; walk away with; walk off with; walk on air; walk tall; walk the streets; walk out on; walk out with.

potter   The drives, creativity you are shaping your life with, or being shaped by; the self.

poverty   Feelings of being inadequate; negative emotions depriving you of well-being; sense of deprivation; being tight emotionally and sexually.

prayer   Depending upon feelings in dream, looking for certainty in face of anxieties; seeking approval or authority for one's desires; expression of pleasure and thanks; seeking cooperation of unconscious faculties to aid one's everyday activities; attempt to channel the forces of the unconscious; feeling at one with life.

precipice   If <u>at the top:</u> fear of failure; on the edge of losing confidence; near to a leap into the unknown or great change. If <u>precipice drops into a void:</u> death; the unconscious or unknown. If <u>at bottom:</u> sense of insurmountable obstacle in life.

precognition   As a part of the human survival ability, the capacity to predict the future is a well-developed, everyday part of life. So much so, we often fail to notice ourselves doing it. When crossing a road we quickly take in factors related to sounds, car speeds, and our physical condition, and predict the likelihood of being able to cross the road without injury. Based on information gathered, often unconsciously, we also attempt to assess or predict the outcome of relationships, job interviews, business ventures, and any course of action important to us. If a detailed observation were made of the habits of ten people, one could predict fairly accurately what they would be doing for the next week, perhaps even pinpointing the time and place. For instance, some would never visit a bar, while others would frequently be there.

Because the unconscious is the storehouse of millions of bits of observed information, and because it has a well-developed function enabling us to scan information and predict from it, some dreams forecast the future. Such predictions may occur more frequently in a dream rather than as waking insight, because few people can put aside their likes and dislikes, prejudices, hopes and anxieties sufficiently to allow such information into consciousness. While asleep some of these barriers drop and allow information to be presented.

Ed Butler's dream is about his work scene. Each detail was real and horrifying. Shortly afterward, Rita was burnt, just as in the dream. Example: "I was startled by the muffled but unmistakable sound of a nearby explosion. While unexpected, it wasn't entirely unusual—the high-energy propellants and oxidizers being synthesized and tested in the chemistry wing were hazardously unstable. When I heard the screams I froze for an instant, recognizing that they could only be coming from Rita, the one woman chemist in the all-male department. I rushed to the doorway of her laboratory. Peering through the smoke and fumes I saw a foot sticking out of the surrounding flames. I was only in my shirtsleeves, unprotected, not even wearing my lab coat, but I had to go into the flames. I grabbed Rita by the foot and noticed with horror that her stockings were melting from the heat. I pulled her back into the doorway and tugged at a chain that released gallons of water on her flaming body. When satisfied the fire was quenched, even though my own clothes still smoldered, I ran for the emergency phone." (From *Dream Network Bulletin,* June 1985.)

Some precognitive dreams, as Ed's dream of the explosion, do not seem to predict from information already held. So far, there is no theory that is commonly accepted that explains this. A not too bizarre one is that our unconscious has access to a collective mind. With so much more information available it can transcend the usual limitations when predicting from personal information. The speculative side of modern physics suggests an extension to this in saying the

precognition

origins of our life lie beyond space and time. If we touch this aspect of ourselves, we may transcend our usual timebound self, and see things in new ways—one of which might be precognition. See **ESP in dreams; prophetic dreams.**

precognitive dreams   See **ESP in dreams.**

pregnancy   A new area of your potential or personality developing; a deepening relationship with your unconscious producing a new area of experience—still unexpressed but developing; a new scheme or creative idea "hatching." In a woman's dream: may refer to desire for a child; fear of being pregnant—i.e., in a relationship but not wanting to be pregnant. If pregnant at time of dream: anxieties regarding pregnancy and birth. Carolyn Winget and Frederic Kapp researched the dreams of seventy pregnant women. Those women whose dreams included a high percentage of anxiety themes were the ones who delivered their babies in the shortest time—less than ten hours. The conclusion was that by allowing feelings of anxiety in our dreams, we are less influenced by anxiety in waking, and we can deal with situations more confidently. Someone else pregnant in dream: an aspect of oneself about to bring forth new characteristics; an intuition about that person. See example under **girl; cave; birth dreams during pregnancy; birth.**

pregnancy dreams   See **birth dreams during pregnancy.**

prehistoric   Primeval urges and drives, such as fear, territorial aggression, mating rituals, survival; urges that have not been integrated fully into present social situation, perhaps because they were repressed during childhood. Many of our social rituals—such as the father giving the daughter in marriage, which possibly arose out of the need to allay aggression between males, and break the father's sexual bond with the daughter—arose from these basic drives; our babyhood or prenatal life.

premenstrual tension   Dr. Ernest Hartmann carried out studies in connection with people who have stable sleep patterns. His aim was to define whether waking events influenced people's need for sleep. For instance, a loss of boyfriend or a stress situation caused many young women to have an increased need for sleep. Some people who had undergone successful psychotherapy for their emotional difficulties, and some meditators, found their sleep need was decreased.

Wanting to know more about why these situations changed sleep need, Hartmann went on to study dream sleep in a group of women who suffered premenstrual tension. This group were prone to depression and irritability during PMT. Records show there is an unusually high rate of murder, suicide, and admission to psychiatric hospitals during this time. Although Hartmann found this group needed a little more sleep time than a control group, the main feature of change was their increased need for dreaming. Their length of time spent in dreaming increased in relationship to their depression. The conclusion reached was that one of the functions of dreaming is to help deal with difficult states of emotion or anxiety. See **menstruation and dreams.**

presents   Receiving: being affirmed; feeling recognized or loved; gaining something from a relationship. Giving: giving of self—negative or positive; making love; if it is a present actually received in life, probably relates to giver and circumstances of giving. See **parcel, package.**

priest, priestess   One's religious beliefs; one's relationship with religious beliefs; a sense of sin; sympathy; a sense of community; a nonsexual relationship.

prince   The best aspect of the dreamer if male; one's brother or lover/boyfriend if female. It can represent the animus in a female dream. Conscious (or in a woman may be unconscious) intellectual, masculine qualities. Sometimes it depicts the attitudes and qualities in us that search

prince

for truth, try to find a way through personal difficulties, or attempt to direct or use the physical and mental heritage. It is also often used to represent the best in a man, and an ideal male in a woman's dream. See *anima,* and *animus* under **archetypes.**

princess   The best aspect of the dreamer if female; one's lover/girlfriend if male. It can represent the anima in a male dream. Sometimes represents the inner self, the receptive, gentle, sympathetic nature. A sense of beauty and love in alignment with life. The princess in a woman's dream can depict her strength to search for meaning and ways to positively deal with difficulties and personal problems. See *anima* and *animus* under **archetypes.**

prison   Traps we create for ourselves out of our anxiety, patterns of behavior, and concepts such as right and wrong, good and bad. See *wolf* under **animals; cage, cell; escape; holding; trapped.**

prize   May reflect people having praised dreamer, and so the dream reflects a different or more positive viewpoint or appraisal of oneself; feeling rewarded; occasionally intuition about a coming acclaim; feeling good about oneself, therefore self-congratulation; can also be compensatory in that the dreamer wants or needs praise and recognition.

problem-solving dreams   See **creativity and problem-solving dreams.**

processing your dreams   Below are simple techniques that make it possible to quickly gain information from your dreams. They have been put as a series of questions.

What is the background to the dream?   The most important aspects of your everyday life may have influenced the dream or feature in it. Briefly consider any aspects of your life that connect with what appears in the dream.

Example: "I have a plane to catch. I get to the plane but the suitcase is never big enough for my clothing that I have left behind. I am always anxious about stuff left behind. I wake, still with the feeling of anxiety." (Fiona) When asked, Fiona said plane flights had been a big feature of her life. She had moved often, traveling to different parts of the world, leaving friends and loved ones behind.

What is the main action in the dream?   There is often an overall activity—such as walking, looking, worrying, building something, or trying to escape. Define what it is and give it a name—such as those listed, or something like "waiting," "searching," "following." Activities, such as walking or building a house, need to be seen as generalizations. Walking can simply represent taking a direction in life or going somewhere, and building can be seen as creating something new or developing what already exists in your life. When you have defined the action, look for further information under the headings in this book, such as **swimming.** Having considered the general meaning of whatever your dream action is, consider if it is expressive of something you are doing in waking life. See key words in the Introduction.

What is your role in the dream?   Are you a friend, lover, soldier, dictator, watcher or participant in the dream? Consider this in relationship with your everyday life, especially in connection with how the dream presents it. Where possible, look for the entry on the role in this book. See **dreamer.**

Are you active or passive in the dream?   By "passive" is meant not taking the leading role, being only an observer, being directed by other people and events. If you are passive, consider if you live a similar attitude in your life. See **active/passive.**

What do you feel in the dream?   Define what is felt emotionally and physically. In the physical sense, are you tired, cold, relaxed, or hungry? In the emotional sense, did you feel sad, angry, lost, tender, or frightened anywhere in the dream? This helps clarify what feeling area the dream is dealing with. It is important also to define whether the feelings in the dream were satisfyingly expressed or whether held back. If held back they need fuller expression. See **emotions, mood.**

Is there a "because" factor in the dream? In many dreams something happens, fails to happen, or appears ... because! For instance, trapped in a room you find a door to escape through. All is dark beyond and you do not go through the door, "because" you are frightened of the dark. In this case the because factor is fear. The dream also suggests you are trapped in an unsatisfying life situation through fear of opportunity or the unknown.

Am I meeting the things I fear in my dream? Because a dream is an entirely inward thing, we create it completely out of our internal feelings, images, creativity, habits, and insights. So even the monsters of our dream are a part of ourselves. If we run from them, it is only aspects of ourselves we are avoiding. We can never escape ourselves, so we might as well find a way of internal ease. Through defining what feelings occur in the dream, you may be able to clarify what it is you are avoiding.

It is also helpful to replay the dream several times while awake and relaxed, and imagine facing or meeting the things one fears or is running away from. It is of enormous help also to rephrase, or rescript the underlying messages attached to one's fears. For instance, you may have had very reasonable fears as a baby/child that your mother would abandon you—perhaps because you went into hospital and felt abandoned. So the original message might have been, "The person I love and utterly depend upon can leave me and I am powerless to make her love me in a way to bind her to me." The new message might be, "I am not a baby any longer, and can actually survive alone, though I love having a partner to share life with. So I don't need to feel complete panic when there is any sign of them with-drawing or getting emotionally distant."

This needs to be done over and over to develop a new habit of relaxed relationship or response to a life situation. Sometimes it is a shift of attitude we need. The following dream illustrates this. Example: "I ran away from home be-cause I was found out for skipping school. I ended up in a chip shop with some friends. I saw my brothers and a friend out of the window. They told me my older sister had died of a heart attack. Then with my sister's boyfriend, who told me she was already buried, and only my mom had been at the funeral." (Brenda) Brenda makes the move of being independent, but does so to avoid problems rather than face them. Being independent—running away from home—means making decisions and being strong enough to live them. If Brenda did leave her family behind like this, she would worry if any mishap occurred. It's a big step to sink or swim by yourself, and let others do the same. So Brenda could try being independent using an-other attitude than "running away." See **nightmares;** *car-rying the dream forward* under **peer dream work.**

What does the dream mean?   We alone create the dream while asleep. Therefore, by looking at each symbol or as-pect of the dream, we can discover from what feelings, thoughts, or experiences what drive or what insight we have created through the drama of the dream. In a playful relaxed way, express whatever you think, feel, remember or fantasize about when you hold each symbol in mind. Say or write it all, even the seemingly trivial or "dangerous" bits. It helps to act the part of each thing if you can. For in-stance, as a house you might describe yourself as "a bit old, but with open doors for family and friends to come in and out. I feel solid and dependable, but I sense there is some-thing hidden in my cellar." Such statements portray one-self graphically. Consider whatever information you gather as descriptive of your waking life. Try to summarize it, as this will aid the gaining of insight. See **peer dream work.**

processing your dreams

Can you amplify the dream?   You will need the help of one
or two friends to use this method. The basis is to take the
role of each part of the dream, as described above. This
may seem strange at first, but persist. Supposing your
name is Julia and you dreamt you were carrying an umbrella, but failed to use it even though it was raining, you
would talk in the first person present: "I am an umbrella.
Julia is carrying me but for some reason doesn't use me."
Having finished saying what you could about yourself,
your friends then ask you questions about yourself as the
dream figure or object. These questions need to be simple
and directly about the dream symbol. So they could ask:
"Are you an old umbrella? Does Julia know she is carrying
you? What is your function as an umbrella? Are you big
enough to shelter Julia and someone else?"—and so on.

The aim of the questions is to draw out information
about the symbol being explored. If it is a known person or
object you are in the role of—your father, for instance—the
replies to the questions need to be answered from the
point of view of what happened in the dream, rather than
as in real life. Listen to what you are saying about yourself
as the dream symbol, and when your questioners have finished, review your statements to see if you can see how they
refer to your life and yourself. If you are asking the questions, even if you have ideas regarding the dream, do not
attempt to interpret. Put your ideas into simple questions
the dreamer can respond to. Maintain a sense of curiosity
and attempt to understand—to make the dream plain in
an everyday language sense. Lead the dreamer toward seeing what the dream means through the questions. When
you have exhausted your questions ask the dreamer to
summarize what they have gathered from their replies. See
postures, movements, body language for an example
of how to work with body movement to explore a dream
meaning; **peer dream work.**

Summarize   To summarize effectively, gather the essence
of what you have said about each symbol and the dream as

a whole and express it in everyday language. Imagine you are explaining to someone who knows nothing about yourself or the dream. Bring the dream out of its symbols into everyday comments about yourself. See **amplification; associations of ideas with dreams; compensation theory; dreamer; peer dream work; plot of the dream; postures, movement, body language; series of dreams, working with; settings; symbols and dreaming; wordplay, puns.**

propeller   A driving force or interest.

prophetic dreams   See **ESP and dreams; precognition.**

prostitute, prostitution   Dire sexual need unconnected to feelings of care or respect; sexuality breaking out of deadening moral restrictions; feeling you have "sold out" or betrayed your real self or real feelings in order to survive or for money; on the game, or playing sexual games. Woman's dream: unacknowledged sexual longings; feelings of "cheapness" or guilt in sex; desire to be more free sexually. Woman dreaming another woman is prostitute: one's own hidden desires; feeling the other woman is promiscuous, or might be in competition with her; uncertainty about one's own sexual value. Man's dream: wishing a woman was more available; wish that sexual relationship were as simple as an exchange of cash; being ill-at-ease about his sexual practices; feeling unable to break free of sexual dependence on partner/mother.

prowler   See **burglar, intruder.**

psychodrama and dreams   This was developed by Dr. Jacob Moreno. In psychodrama there is no "interpretation" of a dream. The dreamer unravels the meaning of the dream by acting it out with the help of others. The dreamer acts the main role of him- or herself, and directs the helpers in the other roles. Roles can later be changed to explore other aspects of the dream. In dramatizing and exploring the dream in this way, the obvious as well as the hidden meaning, associations, and emotions are made clear. To finish, the dreamer is encouraged to take the dream forward, altering it to what feels more adequate and satisfying. This gives the person opportunity to express and enact what was absent in the dream, and provides release from recurring dreams, and catharsis where necessary.

psychologist, psychiatrist, psychoanalyst. Often used as a dream symbol of your attempts to understand self, to release self from problems, to find one's true being. In these dreams the analyst usually depicts your strength or character brought to bear on the difficulties you are trying to redeem. If you are undergoing therapy, it can represent the dynamics and the personal responses you are feeling about what is happening. The psychoanalyst represents the part of yourself effecting change, mental and emotional growth, insight. It may also be used as a symbol of a fear of mental illness, or the difficulties you experience in meeting the irrational part of yourself. See *analyst* under **roles.**

pulling Doing something about a situation; positive action or expression of will. Being pulled: being influenced by someone or something else; being pulled by your emotions—perhaps attracted to someone; going along with something, as when "going with the flow." Pulled against one's will: being influenced by aspects of your nature that you feel at odds with; influenced by someone else against one's own inclinations. Idioms: have pull; pull one's socks up; pull out; pull through; pull something off; pull strings; pull the women; pull together; pull up one's roots; pull rank.

pulse The state of your enthusiasm or energy; feelings about health; anxiety about death.

puncture See Flat tire under **car.**

punishment, torture Depicts the internal pain or fear of retribution that occurs inside us due to conflict between our social training and internal drives. The more rigidly moral we are, the more hell and punishment we dream about; a means of allaying guilt out of childhood feelings of responsibility for such things as being unloved by parent (we must have done something awful or be awful), death of parent, abused by adult. See **hell.**

puns See **wordplay, puns.**

puppet Manipulation or feeling manipulated; feeling powerless against what feels like an external influence—the power of alcohol or drugs.

puppy See **animals; pet.**

purchasing This often indicates some level of choices being made, decisions faced; there may also be elements of how much or little you are being influenced by internal desires or external sales pressure; one dreamer says when she feels good at work she immediately goes out to buy a new dress. This suggests confidence and social power are involved in purchases. But sometimes we make purchases when things go wrong, as a means of counteracting the down feelings. In some dreams the question of your financial status arises, so purchasing may be dealing with how you are feeling about your money situation. See *purchasing a house* under **house, buildings; sell, selling; shop, shopping.**

purse Something in your nature you value and try not to lose; your sense of identity and power to be socially acknowledged as an effective person; a woman's sexual feelings; the vagina. See **bag.**

pushed, pushing Pushing: being positive in what you want; exerting your will or effort of will; manipulation or

pushed, pushing

control of something. If you are forcefully pushing some-one, then it is usually your anger that is involved. Ask yourself why you might have feelings of anger in regard to that person or what that person represents. Pushing back at someone might not be about anger, but about holding your ground. <u>Being pushed:</u> feeling coerced or taken for granted. Feeling bullied or attacked. <u>Idioms:</u> give someone the push; when it comes to the push; push off; push/press on; pushover; push one's luck.

pyramid   The self; wider awareness; integration of self; death.

Q

quadrangle   See *oblong* under **shapes, symbols.**

quarrel   Conflict within yourself or with exterior situation or relationship. See **people**—it describes some of the main areas of human conflict.

quartz   Deep internal processes, such as those shaping the body—consciousness can influence these, so the dream may show what relationship exists; the self. See **jewels.**

quay   Departures; meetings and partings; leaving a phase of life behind, or meeting a new one, and how we encounter such changes. See **beach.**

queen   One's mother; a figure we use in dreams to illustrate our need for acknowledgment and personal and public acclaim; also represents one's culture, language, and traditions. In some dreams the king or queen is dreamt about as the dreamer is becoming acclaimed externally, and the dreams may precede this. See **king;** *king* and *queen* under **archetypes.**

queue   Waiting for something you want; feelings about where you stand in relation to others; or whether you will get what you are seeking. There might

queue

also be feelings about what you deserve, or what you can allow yourself—i.e., maybe you feel other people deserve more.

quicksand   Feelings of insecurity; emotions that take away our confidence or sense of value or adequacy.

R

rabbit   See *rabbit* under **animals.**

race   Taking part in life and the human race—perhaps acknowledging one's position in the "race"; competitiveness, or feelings of competition. Being in the race and the feelings you have about it show your inner assessment of how you feel you are doing in your passage through life. <u>Racing car/bike:</u> competitive drive; sexual energy; daring. <u>Running the race:</u> exerting oneself; expressing oneself; the struggle or contest of life; participating or being involved; the course of one's life. The <u>finishing line:</u> one's goal, or a goal one is aiming for or has reached, perhaps like a point in one's life. Achievement of something in life—for instance, achieving confidence; the end of life. See **bicycle;** Example in **failure.**

radar   Intuition; one's subliminal sense of other people, or of what feelings or "signals" other people are giving out.

radio   Our sense of what is "in the air"—messages we are picking up from other people or our environment. <u>Being on the radio:</u> feeling valued; having a sense of something worth communicating; communicating.

radioactive   The effect on oneself from other people's thoughts or feelings. A subtle influence from other people, or one's surroundings. Usually other people's negative attitudes or ill wishes.

raft

raft Something lifesaving; feeling adrift without control or direction.

railroad, railway, train Opportunity or choices in life; your life direction if on train, or the direction the events in life are taking you. <u>Carriages:</u> the compartments of your life. <u>Leaving someone behind or being left behind:</u> feelings about loss of spouse, or breakup of relationship; being left; change of some sort. <u>Lines, tracks:</u> a communal or generally accepted direction; habitual pathways of thought or action; rigidly fixed to certain attitudes or way of life; inflexibility. <u>Missing the train:</u> feeling left out of opportunity; sense of inadequacy; held back by one's own hesitations; hidden desire to avoid change or to make one's individual journey. <u>Railway station:</u> moving toward something new; changing scenes—i.e., from family to work environment; leaving something behind—a relationship, one's youth; one's ability to change; effort to get somewhere in life or experience something new; parting or meeting, saying farewell or waiting for someone; changes in a relationship or work. The <u>train journey:</u> the aspect of your journey through life that has connections with other people and has a predetermined end, limiting your individual will, and passing through certain stages; journey into self-awareness; can refer to aging and death, especially where there is a feeling of "departing" or "time of departure"; the train of thought or experiences that carry us through life. <u>Train engine:</u> the energy that takes us through life; libido. <u>Idioms:</u> go off the rails; lose track of something; make tracks for; on somebody's track. See **airport; ticket.**

rain Depending on dream setting, depressed feelings or difficulties; emotions that take away enthusiasm and act as a barrier to action; tears and emotional release—an outpouring; other people's emotions "raining" on one; return of feelings after a dry, intellectual, or unfeeling period; something that gives life or heals. <u>Idioms:</u> come rain or shine; it never rains but it pours; saving for a rainy day.

rainbow   A sense of better things to come; illusion; an awareness of the beauty and value of life in the midst of difficulties. Before his assassination, Henry IV dreamed he saw a rainbow over his head. This was seen as suggesting a violent death. <u>Idioms:</u> chasing a rainbow.

raincoat   See **clothes.**

ram   See *ram* under **animals.**

rape   This can mean you are overcome by events, by other people dominating you, or by your internal rejected emotions. Rape in dreams is very different from rape in real life, as we create our dream, so why introduce rape? Perhaps in the example below Liz W. discovers her own power in the situation as she realizes the weakness of the male.

Example: "I tried to turn, but my legs were like lead. The man caught me and I fought. He tried to rape me but couldn't do it. As I talked to him I began to feel sorry for him and not frightened. I realized that inside he was a nice person. In the end, I found I liked him so much I began to kiss him myself." (Liz W.)

Example: "A man is trying to make love to me and at the last moment I repel him, as I know it will cause a pregnancy. When I was about ten I was raped and for many years had a fear of men." (Anonymous)

This is the other side of rape. Rape in this dream may be memories, the effects of which are still visible in the life of this dreamer, causing her pain in warm sexuality.

rat   See *rat* under **animals.**

raven   See *crow, rook, raven* under **birds.**

reaching out   The desire for something; attempt to grasp, control, or manipulate something or someone, depending on dream; extending or giving oneself. <u>Being</u>

reaching out

<u>reached toward:</u> feeling of being asked for something; demands of other people; someone extending to you.

reading   Realization; recall from memory; scanning internal memory for information.

receive   This is usually about a straightforward receiving of something, like feelings from a relationship, or ideas that are helpful.

record, cassette, CD, computer disc   Can simply be the sort of pleasure we feel on listening to music; the impressions left on us by events, people, and therefore memory, but often memory integrated by the unconscious into insights; information we have gathered; the impression we might leave behind at death—what remains of us; the impression we would like to give others. <u>Idioms:</u> for the record; track record.

records   <u>Paper or filmed:</u> usually memory or information you may have forgotten or not accessed before.

recurring dreams   If you keep a record of your dreams it will soon become obvious that some of your dream themes, characters, or places recur again and again. These recurrences are of various types. A certain theme may have begun in childhood and continued throughout your life—either without change, or as a gradually changing series of dreams. It might be that the feature that recurs is a setting, perhaps a house you visit again and again, but the details differ. Sometimes a series of such dreams begin after or during a particular event or phase of your life, such as puberty or marriage. The theme of the dream can incorporate anxious emotions, such as the example below, or any aspect of experience. One woman, an epileptic, reports a dream that is the same in every detail and occurs every night. In general, dreams recur because there are ways you habitually respond to your internal or external world. Because your attitude or

346

response is unchanging, the dream that reflects it remains the same. It is noticeable in those who explore their dreams using such techniques as described under **processing your dreams** that recurring themes disappear or change because the attitudes or habitual anxieties that gave rise to them have been met or transformed.

Example: "This dream has recurred over thirty years. There is a railway station, remote in a rural area, a central waiting room with platform going round all sides. On the platform mill hundreds of people—all men, I think. They are all ragged, thin, dirty, and unshaven. I know I am among them. I looked up at the mountainside and there is a guard watching us. He is cruel-looking, oriental, in green fatigues. On his peaked cap is a red star. He carries a machine gun. Then I looked at the men around me and I realize they are all me. Each one has my face. I am looking at myself. Then I feel fear and terror." (Anonymous)

A recurring environment in a dream where the other factors change is not the same. We use the same words over and over in speech, yet each sentence may be different. The environment or character represents a particular aspect of oneself, but the different events that surround it show it in the changing process of our psychological growth and experience. Where there is no such change, as in the example above, it suggests an area of our mental, emotional self is stuck in a habitual feeling state or response.

Some recurring dreams can be "stopped" by simply receiving information about them. One woman dreamt the same dream from childhood. She was walking past railings in the town she lived in as a child. She always woke in dread and perspiration from this dream. At forty she told her sister about it. The response was, "Oh, that's simple. Don't you remember that when you were about four we were walking past those railings and we were set on by a bunch of boys. Then I said to them, 'Don't hurt us, our mother's dead!' They left us alone, but you should have seen the look on your face." After she realized the dread was connected with the loss of her mother, the dream never recurred. Another woman who repeatedly dreamt of being in a tight and frightening place found the dream never returned after she had connected it to being in the womb.

Recurring dreams, such as that of the railings, suggest that part of the process underlying dreams is a self-regulatory homeostatic one. The dream process tries to present troublesome emotions or situations to the conscious mind of the dreamer to resolve the trauma or difficulty underlying the dream. See **nightmares; processing your dreams; serial dreams.**

red   See *red* under **colors.**

red Indian   See **American Indian.**

red Indian dream beliefs   See **American Indian; American Indian dream beliefs; Iroquoian dream cult.**

reflections   Present view or opinion of oneself—because few of us define how we really see ourselves, the self-image may be largely unconscious, therefore shown as a face that might be different to what we are used to seeing; how we feel others see us; may also be aspects of ourselves the unconscious is showing us that we may not have been aware of.

refrigerate   To cool down our emotions or sexuality; to be cold emotionally or sexually; a romance that is cooling off; something we have put on "cold storage."

relationship and dreams   Most dreams depict relationship in one form or another. However, some dreams specifically show us in a particular relationship. Such dreams are usually highly significant in that they reveal aspects of what we are doing in the relationship that we may not admit or realize consciously. It can therefore be transformative to gain insight into any dreams that show us in relationship with present partners or lovers.

Example: "I was with Lorna and she told me she was pregnant. I said to her this was impossible and it couldn't be my child. She looked at me and shrugged, saying, 'Okay, I'm not pregnant.' " (Sinclair) On exploring the dream Sinclair realized the enormous feelings involved. He had not realized consciously that Lorna had completely offered herself to him in their relationship. The dream shows him rejecting this complete offering of her sexuality and womanhood, and her turning away rejected. This had actually happened, but Sinclair had not been conscious of what was occurring between them. The dream enabled him to realize how he pulled away from a woman's full flow of self-expression, and he began to change this.

relatives   See **family, family relationships.**

religion and dreams   In most ancient cultures, consideration and even veneration of dreams played a great part. Some groups felt that dream life was more real and important than waking life. Not only were dreams looked to for information about hunting, as in Eskimo and African groups, but also for ways of healing physical and psychological ills, such as the Greek Dream Temples of Asclepius; insights into the medicinal properties of herbs, barks, and clays with African tribal witch-doctors. Common to most of these groups, and evident in the Old Testament, was also the sense that through dreams one had awareness of the transcendental or supersensible. St. Peter's dream of the sheet and unclean animals was a turning point in the history of Western society—as was Constantine's dream of his victory if he used the symbol of Christianity.

At its most fundamental, the human religious sense emerges out of several factors. One is the awareness of existing amidst external and internal forces of nature that cause us to feel vulnerable and perhaps powerless. Such natural processes as illness, death, growth and decay, earthquakes, the seasons confront us with things that are often beyond our ability to control. Considering the information and resources of the times, one of religion's main functions in the past was the attempted control of the "uncertain" factors in human life, and help toward psychological adjustment to vulnerability. Religions were the first social programs offering people help and support toward emotional, mental, physical, and social health and maturity. Even if primitive, such programs helped groups of people gain a common identity and live in reasonable harmony together. Like a computer program that is specific to a particular business, such programs were specific to a particular group, and so may be outdated in today's need for greater integration with other races.

Dreams also portray and define the aspect of human experience in which a person has a sense of kinship with all life-forms. This experience gives us a sense of connection with the roots of our being. While awake we might see the birth of a colt and feel the wonder of emergence and newness; the struggle to stand up and survive; the miracle of physical and sexual power that can be accepted or feared. In looking in the faces of fellow men and women we see something of what they have done in this strange and painful wonder we call life. We see whether they have been crushed by the forces confronting them; whether they have become rigid; or whether, through some common miracle, they have been able to carry into their mature years the laughter, the crying, the joy, the ability to feel pain that are the very signs of life within the human soul. These things are sensed by us all, but seldom organized into a comprehensive view of life and an extraction of meaning. For many of us it is only in our dreams, through the ability the unconscious has to draw out the significance of such widely divergent experiences, that we glimpse the unity behind phenomena. This sense of unity is an essential part of transcendent experience. See **angel; Christ,** *rebirth, resurrection* and *devil* under **archetypes; buddhism and dreams; church; compensation theory; evil; fish, sea creatures; heaven; hell;** *sweets* under **food.**

rent   Interpersonal responsibility; what we "pay" for what we have or want. <u>Collecting rent:</u> what we want from others, or what we are getting from them in the way of feelings, influences.

reptiles, lizards, snakes   Our basic spinal and lower-brain reactions, such as fight or flight, reproduction, attraction or repulsion, sex drive, need for food, and reaction to pain. This includes the fundamental evolutionary ability to change and the urge to survive—very powerful and ancient processes. Our relationship with the reptile in our dreams depicts our relatedness to such forces in us, and how we deal with the impulses from the ancient part of our brain.

   Modern humans face the difficulty of developing an independent identity and yet keeping a working relationship with the primitive or fundamental parts of their nature, thus maturing and bringing the primitive into an efficiently functioning connection with the present social world. The survival urge at base might be kill or run, but it can be transformed into the ambition that helps an opera singer meet difficulties in their career. Also, the very primitive has in itself the promise of the future, of new aspects of human consciousness. This is because many extraordinary human functions take place unconsciously—in the realm of the reptile/spine/lower brain/right brain/autonomic nervous system. Being unconscious, they are less amenable to our waking will. They function fully only in some fight-or-flight, survive-or-die situations. If we begin to touch these with consciousness, as we do in dreams, new functions are added to consciousness. See *the dream as extended perception* under **ESP in dreams.**

frog   The deeply unconscious psychobiological life-processes, which transformed us from a tadpole (sperm) into an air-breathing frog (adult)—therefore, the process of life in general and its wisdom. The enormous information such symbols hold if we explore them gives them their

351

power; meeting with what we find difficult or repulsive in life and ourselves, which if we can accept transforms into personal potential and power—the frog-into-the-prince story. It is often a form of love that transforms the dark sides of oneself, the toad or beast, into something that is life-enhancing; subpersonality, an aspect of one's character that is usually unconscious, but occasionally shows itself in behavior; the frog has also been associated with the power of resurrection and renewal. <u>Frog spawn:</u> sperm, ovum, and reproduction.

lizard   Very much the same as snake, except it lacks the poisonous aspect; awareness of unconscious or instinctive drives, functions, and processes. <u>Chameleon:</u> either one's desire to fade into the background, or adaptability.

snake   The Hebrew word for the serpent in the Garden of Eden is *"Nahash."* It can be translated as blind, impulsive urges, such as our instinctive drives. The snake can represent many different things, but usually the life process. If we think of a person's life from conception to death, we see a flowing, moving event, similar in many ways to the speeded-up films of a seed growing into a plant, flowering, and dying. The snake depicts the force or energy behind that movement and purposiveness—the force of life, the latent energy or potential within matter—that leads us both to growth and death, along with the passionate emotions and urges that drive us so powerfully. That energy—like electricity in a house, which can be heat, power, sound, and vision—lies behind all our functions. So in some dreams the snake represents our sexuality; in others the rising of that energy up our body to express as digestion—the intestinal snake; or as the creative or poisonous energy of our emotions and thoughts. In the destructive aspect the snake represents the poisonous thoughts and emotions that can destroy us. We tend to depict this snake attacking us, even though we have ourselves given rise to such poisonous emotions as fear, hate, and guilt. Because our life-energy flows into thinking and emotions, we are in this way directing the creative force of life. Directing it negatively has the power to bring illness and death, for we are dealing with the power of life and death itself. The opposite is also true. The power of life and death can be directed creatively. Then the snake is seen in its healing role in dreams, and in ancient times was shown in the form of the staff with two snakes coiling up it—caduceus—still used today as a symbol of the medical profession.

In coils of snake: feeling bound in the "blind impulses" or habitual drives and feeling responses. Instincts and habits can be redirected, as illustrated by Hercules' labors. Sitting on snake: mastery of the instinctive nature and transformation and the making conscious of the wisdom and power resident in the unconscious. Snake biting you: unconscious worries about your health, frustrated sexual impulse, your emotions turned against yourself—as when internalized aggression poisons us, causing very real illness, so may be shown as the biting snake. It may also suggest an influence in one's life—the venom—that takes away one's identity and perhaps opens one to a life beyond self, the spirit. Snake biting others: biting remarks; a poisonous tongue; emotional energy turned against oneself or someone else. Snake colors—green: our internal life-process directed—perhaps through satisfied feelings, love, and creativity—into a healing process or one that leads to our personal growth and positive change. White: eternal aspect of our life process, or becoming conscious of it. Blue: religious feelings or coldness in relations. Snake in connection with any hole: sexual relatedness. Snake in the grass: intuition of talk behind your back; danger; sneakiness. Snake with tail in its mouth: the circle of life—birth, growth, reproduction, aging, death, rebirth; the eternal. See **colors; anxiety dreams;** *death* and *rebirth, resurrection* and *the self* under **archetypes; Greece (ancient) dream beliefs;** snake in cellar or cave in basement, cellar under **house, buildings; hypnosis and dreams; jungle; paralysis.**

toad   Deeply unconscious drives and processes, such as the biological activities to do with intestines and cells, so what we might feel squeamish about—might therefore connect with abortion; the power of life in us; a cold-blooded or ugly part of ourselves. See: *frog* above.

tortoise   Our vulnerable feelings or hurts that hide behind a defensive shell—perhaps of shyness, introversion, or withdrawal—could be anger; in ancient China the tortoise represented the cold dark of north and death. See **crab; shell; snail;** *shellfish* under **fish, sea creatures.**

rescue   Intervention in your life by someone else's action or emotions; something that changes the situation you are in, or changes mood. Rescuing someone else, or animal: the effort we make, or what we have put into dealing with a relationship difficulty or an internal feeling state. Rescued by animal: the supportive and loving action from the unconscious "animal" level of oneself; can relate to one's desire to do something admirable or noble, such as saving souls, helping someone in distress, and thus having power in life. Rescuing someone of the opposite sex: breaking the bonds of emotion, sexuality, or dependence that tie us to parents or others.

restaurant, cafe   Sociability; search for emotional or sexual satisfaction; hunger for company or sexuality; because one's sociability might at times be a fear of being alone, might represent this. See **food.**

riding   Idioms: along for the ride; a rough ride; ride something out; let it ride; ride roughshod; take somebody for a ride; riding high. See **car;** *horse* under **animals.**

rifle   See *guns* under **weapons.**

right   See **left, right.**

ring   Wholeness; one's essential self; connection with the All. <u>Wedding, engagement ring</u>: the state of the relationship, as in example below, where Mary is "choking" on or "can't swallow" her relationship. <u>Heirloom, parent's ring</u>: Psychological influence of the family or parent, even if dead. <u>Idioms</u>: have a hollow ring; have a true ring; run rings round someone. See *circle, round* under **shapes, symbols.**

Example: "If I swallow I am going to swallow and choke on my engagement ring. I seem to be trying to stop a ring going down my throat." (Janice P.)

ritual   See **ceremony.**

river   The feelings that flow through us or we are immersed in; the process of life in our body, connecting with emotions, sexuality, and changes of mood; the flow and events of our life or destiny. The images of rivers used in literature and films helps us understand their symbolism. The river can be calm, in flood, or even dried-up—representing our state of feeling about our energy, sexuality, and emotions—the energy that as anxiety can cause illness, or as pleasure sustain health. Similarly we can drown in the river (drown in despair), float on it, be carried along by prevailing feelings, or cross over, suggesting change or even death. <u>Being in river</u>: being influenced by or immersed in one's internal flow of feelings and energies. For instance, one may have fallen in love and never developed a relationship with that person. Years later in an unsatisfying life situation one might be haunted by memories and longings for the love that might have been. Thus one would be immersed in such feelings. <u>Crossing a river</u>: making great changes. If one is in the water to cross, it means meeting a lot of emotions in the process of change. <u>Seeing someone cross a river</u>: feelings about death, as with falling in the river. <u>Going against the current</u>: resisting one's own feelings; going against prevailing influences or attitudes; going back to the womb. <u>Directing a river</u>: channeling one's emotional or sexual energy.

river

<u>Stagnant river:</u> restrained feelings or sexuality; holding oneself back.

road   Your prevailing direction in, or approach to, life—this direction/approach can be either self-created out of one's own actions or decisions, or arise out of other people's or social influence; the norm in social behavior, therefore the direction in life taken by many people; one's predispositions; any direction you are taking, such as a love affair, a business, a new attitude; one's public activities. <u>Crossroads, deciding which road to take:</u> many choices; the size, richness, cleanliness, amount of people, situation of the road shows how you inwardly see either the direction chosen, or the choices confronting you. <u>Alley:</u> limited possibilities or horizons; present limited possibilities will be overcome with effort and initiative. <u>Alley with dead end:</u> concern about a tight situation that appears to have no way out. <u>Crossroad:</u> change; decision; indecision. See **crossroad.** <u>Cul-de-sac, dead end:</u> feeling or intuition that your direction will not be rewarding or lead to openings or opportunity. <u>Detour:</u> problems about your present life-direction or relationship. <u>Fork in the road:</u> something to decide; parting from accustomed way or relationship. <u>Going out from house into road:</u> how others see you; being in public view. <u>Going the wrong way up a one-way street:</u> going against prevailing attitudes; defying public opinion. <u>Known road:</u> feelings associated with that road; what you have already done; the past; habits. <u>Lane:</u> individual direction. <u>Freeway/motorway:</u> a major direction and quick route to where you want to go in life. For some dreamers it will represent facing more power or threat than they feel relaxed about. <u>One-way road:</u> lacking choice; conformity; no turning back. <u>Road ahead:</u> the future; aspects of self not yet expressed; new areas of endeavor. <u>Road behind:</u> the past; what you have already achieved or done. <u>Unpaved road, track off to one side:</u> going off the beaten track or being sidetracked. <u>Idioms:</u> on the road to recovery; road hog; end of the road; take to the road; middle of the road; the high road to. See **track.**

robot Responses that are automatic or not thought out, acting purely on social or imprinted responses, perhaps through pain. The robot in some dreams is linked with the future and how we feel about it. It also can suggest being defended, in the sense of armor defending against hurt, so having no feelings. This might be expressed as being a zombie.

rock Reality, but not just physical reality; the physical world; the eternal as it is met by our waking self; stability; a remembrance of something or someone important to us; a source of power, or the spirit—in ancient times rocks were thought to be the dwelling places of gods. The symbol of the rock may therefore link our conscious personality with innate unconscious archetypal forces or strength. If the rock is sculpted: what our life has expressed to enrich our eternal nature. A small rock/stone: the unconscious sees our personal existence as a part of the material the cosmos is made of—another pebble on the beach. The rock portrays how we shape the material of our nature through our life, similar to the parable of the talents. See **stone.**

rocket Male sexuality; feeling threatened from relationship with male; energy directed in a way to gain greater awareness of yourself.

roles The different people in our dreams—such as doctor, lawyer, businessperson, or tramp—in general represent the different abilities, weaknesses, or interests we have ourselves. Even if we know the "role model," it still depicts that person's quality or skill in ourselves. The only difference might be that our personal reactions to that particular doctor or schoolteacher will also play a part. Roles often play an important part in our self-image. Without an appreciated social role we may feel uncertain and ineffective. Maturity might require the acceptance that we are nothing, but can be many things.

roles

actor/actress, acting Depending on context, can represent yourself wanting public acclaim, or not expressing real self—acting a role. Just as someone's life may be "acted out" onstage or in a film, so actors may represent a showing of facets of your life, especially inner life; the false image we may be expressing; our attempt to impress others, or act a part; one's inflated opinion of oneself. In some dreams when we see ourselves on the stage, or are watching a film or show, it denotes the examination or contemplation of some special situation in one's life. Idioms: act a part; act on impulse or information; acting up; caught in the act; as the actress said to the bishop; get in on the act. See **theater.**

advocate See *lawyer* below.

alchemist The magical and transformative aspect of mental and emotional action within us. It depicts the ability we have to transform our feeling state, and in fact our nature, by changing our experience and body. The symbol particularly points to the ability to change what we consider useless, painful, or worthless into great value. This links with the process in us that can present childhood trauma or negative family attitudes to consciousness, and in doing so transform them into insight and useful energy.

analyst An analyst, psychologist, psychiatrist in our dream depicts our self-assessment. Depending on the dream, the self-assessment may be supportive or self-destructive. Our mind can transform itself in a number of ways. Sometimes one new piece of information, or a new mental discipline, can change the quality of all mental life. The analyst represents such power to transform, as well as the often avoided self-awareness. Can also suggest fear about one's own mental strength and health; a source of wisdom; insight.

artist The aspect of oneself that is in contact with the irrational, creative side of the unconscious; the desire or ability to be creative; the drive to express something of one-self that may be repressed; desire for public recognition, or a chance to demonstrate your skill or quality; the impractical aspect of self. <u>Meeting an artist:</u> becoming aware of a creative idea or an aspect of self that is creative. <u>Watching an artist at work:</u> recognizing artistic or creative ability, but being passive about it. See **painting.**

ascetic   Conflict with natural drives; desire to be less dominated by same; avoidance of sex; an attempt to find the transcendent, which may be an inverted fear of one's unconscious or a bid for power to control; development of will. See *ascetic* under **archetypes; religion and dreams.**

astrologer   Intuitions, thoughts or concern about your future; intuition concerning your innate abilities or qualities, and where they might lead.

authority figure   Might depict what has arisen in your life out of relationship with father; one's relationship with authority; a view of how one uses power of authority.

backer   Support; confidence; energy; another person's influence in your life.

baker   Creative ability; ability to alter one's approach to make experience more acceptable—such as when comments, instead of being taken as criticism, are taken as information; creator of bread, so the provider of basic needs; may be connected with money, because of the term "bread" or "dough" being used for money.

bartender   This depends whether male or female. Also depends on your relationship with alcohol. If you drink frequently, then it possibly relates to the feelings that lead to drinking. Other possibilities are sociability, loneliness. See **woman; man.**

roles

bus driver/fare collector   How we give someone authority in a group situation, although we may be more capable than they; the part of self concerned with paying our way; feelings helping or standing in the way of reaching our goal.

butcher   Expresses some form of aggression, either directed to others or from others toward yourself. May also relate to dealing with parts of your life that are dead but hold useful experience.

captain   The daring, doing, positive side of self; how we relate to father figures or dominant male authoritative men; the side of our nature that is capable or is in touch with the wider issues in our life, and makes decisions out of comprehensive awareness.

captive, prisoner   Many emotions, anxieties, moods or ideas "captivate" us, or act as means of denying free expression to our talents, sexuality, or well-being. Fear of illness might stop us going on holiday; thoughts that only the privileged can make it in business might stop us developing ideas we have. In this sense we, or areas of our potential, can be imprisoned or made captive. Using **processing your dreams** and the allied methods can help to define what is restraining us and find freedom from such restraints. See **imprisoned;** *wolf* under **animals; cage, cell; escape; holding; trapped.**

carpenter   The creative but practical part of us; the side of us that tends to create with old ideas and attitudes—the wood—but perhaps is not very radical; sometimes the self. See *Christ* under **archetypes.**

clown   See *fool, clown, trickster* under **archetypes.**

conjurer   Depending on dream, might be the ability to easily change our moods or attitudes, which is a commonplace yet at the same time magical ability humans have—in this way we might pull out of a deep depression and suddenly become creative; or perhaps the youthful side of self that forever wants magical or idealistic answers to life situations and relationships; trickery.

cook   The active and practical side of our nature that can transform inedible aspects of a relationship or situation into something that satisfies us; the sense of responsibility that "feeds the family"; female reproductive ability—puts one thing in the oven (sperm and ovum) and out comes something else (baby); need for or ability to nourish oneself and provide for physical, emotional, mental, and transcendent needs. <u>Idioms:</u> cook the books; cook someone's goose; cook up; what's cooking.

cripple   Emotional hurts; parts of us injured by trauma or twisted by such withheld feelings as anger or jealousy.

dentist   Depends on your relationship with dentists—fear of being hurt; the courage and ability to deal with painful areas of experience; father's distressing sexual attentions—or rape feelings; need for care of what comes out of our mouth, such as things we say, opinions, criticism.

doctor   Our dependence upon authority figure for a sense of wholeness, or to deal with anxiety; the healing process within us, or the unconscious wisdom we have concerning our needs and well-being. The doctor might give us advice, for instance; anxiety about health; desire for intimacy or to be looked at; the presager or supportive agent in the process of dying. In some dreams the doctor appears to represent intellectual curiosity or rational thought, but perhaps with an open mind; fear of illness or of being hurt/damaged by an operation or medical procedure. <u>Idioms:</u> doctor something; have an animal doctored; doctor the accounts.

farmer   Feeling easy with sexuality and material world; practical, down-to-earth feelings; care of "animal" side of

self; earthy wisdom; the easy reversion to earthy or instinctive behavior—such as hunting to kill, or unrefined sex. See
farm, farmyard.

fireman   How we deal with our passions or outbursts of
emotion or anger; dealing with misplaced energy or personal
emergencies involving passion, burning pain or fiery feelings.

fugitive   See *fugitive* under **archetypes.**

gardener   The down-to-earth but wise aspect of self; the
wisdom or insights gathered through life experience, from
which we can direct our growth and life to integrate the
many parts of our nature; the process in each of us—the
Christ—that synthesizes our life experience, and considers
what love, what resonance with all life there is in it. See
compensation theory; digging, excavation; garden.

halfwit   See *idiot* below.

hermit   Sometimes symbolizes a desire to escape the demands of the world. Or a hermit is the representative of
your inner feelings.

hero   See *hero/ine* under **archetypes; individuation.**

idiot   See *fool, clown, trickster* under **archetypes.**

jockey   Ability to direct energy and instincts. The drive to
win at what you are attempting. So being a jockey might
link with success or failure.

judge   Feelings of guilt; self-criticism or judgment; how
we are relating to someone whose judgment means a lot to
us; social condemnation.

king   See **king.**

lawyer   Often links with feelings of uncertainty or difficulty involving another person or group of people. You may be trying to clarify action to take in the dream, or sort out your feelings about an issue. The lawyer may also represent inner certainty or confidence, an authority figure, maybe even a desirable lover.

leader   Our relationship with authority figures, or the generally accepted ideas that people take to guide their life; the relationship with the leader might show how much responsibility we are taking for our life; feelings of being responsible, as in parenthood or professional capacity.

lover   If <u>one's lover:</u> your present feelings or fears about the relationship. If <u>dream lover, someone else:</u> your sexual desires or needs; sexuality that is either not accepted or not expressed in present relationship. See **affair;** *lover* under **archetypes.**

magician   Sometimes the self—the magical abilities the unconscious has that are seldom tapped; one's potential. <u>Black magician:</u> the negative or selfish ways we might use our power or internal insights and wisdom; the shadow or unacknowledged side of self.

masseur   Healing influence, loosening up of rigid attitudes, tensions, preconceptions, repressions.

matador   This might show sexual tensions, or the killing of the fundamental drives.

mechanic   Your means of dealing with habitual reactions to life; your skill at dealing with problems; when you can't get started in the mornings, or on a project. The mechanic might also point to a physical problem, depending on the dream content. See **car; engine.**

roles

merchant The business, commercial side of self. Desires for profit in some area of your life.

monk Influence of religious teachings; difficulty in meeting sexuality and emotional and financial independence; awareness of the transcendent; an attitude toward life that is not so bound to material things, worldly achievement, or sexuality.

nun Sexual purity; fear of sex; religious feelings; one's sister.

pirate Our piratical or plundering urges, or what we feel plundered by; sense of having someone else take what is important to us.

policeman/policewoman Sense of what is socially right or wrong—our feelings of what others would dislike or punish us for; our social rules of conduct rather than our innermost sense of rightness, therefore inhibitions; feelings of guilt or shame. <u>Policeman/woman at one's door:</u> anxiety about bad news; traditionally a sign of trouble arriving at one's doorstep. <u>Policewoman:</u> as general, but more emphasis on moral issues connected with feeling values.

sailor One's ability to meet the storms and calms of life.

salesman Someone seeking to influence you; opportunity; one's business sense. <u>In a woman's dream:</u> perhaps a hint of things you want—a lover, a new romance—that you are not admitting to yourself; the man in your life trying to get what he wants at your expense.

scientist Creative, rational mind; intellectual curiosity; in some dreamers, the fear of rational, critical people or looking at oneself analytically; insight into the unconscious through rational investigation.

secretary   The other woman; practical, business side of self-supporting creative action.

seductress, seducer   Sexual desires; sexual drives that have not been matured into satisfactory expression in relationship with real person; sexual longings unattached to present partner; fantasy of being loved.

servant   Social roles—*top dog* under dog feelings; feeling you are treated like a servant, or treating someone else as; class distinctions.

shepherd   Being in contact with instinctive or feeling reactions in self; the self. See *farmer* above; *Christ* under **archetypes.**

shopkeeper   May relate to work if dreamer works in shop or store; relates to how one supplies one's needs, or who supplies one's needs—therefore, might show feelings about parents. It might throw light on how you gain your needs from other people, or decisions about what you want from life or others.

soldier   If <u>in opposition with:</u> things we feel in conflict with; our internal conflicts and involvement with the "wars" or trauma we have experienced. If <u>soldier or united with soldiers:</u> willingness or ability to face internal conflicts and hurts; daring to confront the difficulties of life. <u>In woman's dream:</u> inner conflicts; feeling threatened regarding relationship with a male. <u>Military service:</u> feeling bound by social or personal disciplines or restrictions; learning strengths and self-discipline to meet internal conflicts.

solicitor   See *lawyer* above.

stranger   Unknown aspect of oneself; part we avoid "meeting" in everyday life, or may not have met before.

roles

tailor   Your ability to shape a project or idea out of raw materials or basic concepts; an influence that can help you change your public image.

teacher   Relationship with authority figure; learning situations; something to learn or teach.

thief   Fear we might lose something, or that what we have gained will be taken; unacknowledged desires; desire to take from others; conflict of will; feelings of having been induced into a sexual encounter or fear of sex. See **stealing.**

victim   Being the victim: feeling victimized; often depicts the chip on our shoulder. We may have been hurt sometime and go on bemoaning our fate. The "chip" may be useful in avoiding real responsibility or in hiding from trying out one's positive creativity or sexuality. Thus we avoid possible failure or further hurt. Other person as victim: may still be as above; the hurts and damage received from relationship with others; passive anger—by being the victim we get someone else to be a bastard and can thus sneer at them because we have manipulated them; hidden desires to avoid success, perhaps as a way of hurting parent. See **victim.**

waiter/waitress   Wanting to be waited on; feeling you are being made to wait on others; wordplay for waiting around for someone else.

roof   See *roof* under **house, buildings.**

room   See *room* under **house, buildings.**

root   See Roots under **trees.**

rope   If tied by rope: what is holding us back from expressing; strength turned against oneself. Tying someone

<u>else:</u> restraints we use to hold back particular parts of our feelings or drives; sometimes sexuality. See **knot.**

row, rowing   Making personal efforts to get somewhere. If there is someone in the boat with you, it suggests efforts in a relationship. It might link with fitness if you use rowing for exercise. Or competition or cooperation if you are in a rowing team. If this is <u>row, as in arguing:</u> See **argue.**

round   See *round* under **shapes, symbols.**

rubbish   See **garbage.**

ruby   See Ruby under **jewels.**

rug   See *rug* under **furniture, furnishings.**

ruins   See *ruins* under **house, buildings.**

running   See *run* under **postures, movement, body language.**

rust   Negligence; sense of aging; seeing how transitory worldly things are.

S

sack The womb; death; getting the sack.

sacrifice May refer directly to feeling someone is or will make you a scapegoat; sometimes connected with decision-making—we cannot have all things at once, so we are willing to sacrifice one thing for another; occurs in some dreams where a change is occurring in one's personality—parts of our nature we once identified with can now be allowed to die to the process of growth. Sacrifice depicts a strange fact of human psychology—some aspects of oneself grow in strength and maturity when we let them "die." While we maintain a behavior pattern or belief, it stays in its habitual form. When we let go of it, a new approach can emerge.

saddle Influencing something or somebody by your will; feeling constrained to support someone else; in control; secure relationship with natural urges. If thrown from saddle: out of control.

sadism Anger from childhood hurts; sometimes the inability to face the real emotional pain of one's own hurts as a child; lack of real sexual satisfaction, perhaps because of lack of emotional development. See **satanism.**

safari Coming face-to-face with your instincts or unsocialized urges.

sailing   How you are handling or feeling about your life. The images in sailing lend themselves to depict human endeavors to work with the tides and influences of life. <u>Dealing well with wind, waves:</u> suggests being able to meet internal and external pressures, emotions, and drives, and using them to advantage. <u>Being overwhelmed, sinking:</u> finding emotional and sexual drives, anxieties too much to cope with. See **boat, ship.** <u>Idioms:</u> plain sailing; sail against the wind; sail close to the wind; sail into something; sail under false colors; set sail; trim one's sails; take the wind out of someone's sails.

sailor   See *sailor* under **roles.**

salad   See *salad* under **food.**

saliva   One's soul or spirit; the emotional or feeling energy of your being. Ancient people said the saliva carried mana, which might be translated as life energy. <u>Spitting:</u> projecting one's emotional energy. The mood or attitude with which one does this gives the clue to what you are "putting out" to others or the world, or "spitting up" of your feelings.

saloon   See **barroom.**

salt   The subtle qualities you bring to your activities that transform them from empty trivialities into meaning or savor; zest; may sometimes refer to the body's reaction to salt. <u>Idioms:</u> above/below the salt—in or out of honor; salt a mine; salt something away; with a pinch of salt; worth one's salt; salt into a wound; salt of the earth.

sand   Lack of security; a shifting situation; passage of time; lack of emotion or nourishment; abrasiveness or irritations. See **desert or wilderness.** <u>Idioms:</u> built on sand; sands of time are running out; bury one's head in the sand.

Satan   The things in self, or in the world, that we feel frightened of, or feel we cannot control; the influence of

Satan

dry intellectualism or materialism. See *devil* under **archetypes; evil; satanism.**

satanism   Directing your feelings and energies in a way that is against your innate needs and feelings.

satellite   Communication between the more global or cosmic awareness of the unconscious and your everyday waking self. If in satellite: might suggest loss of a down-to-earth attitude; global view. Being attacked from satellite or UFO: thinking and feeling have been split from realistic evaluation, perhaps because internal pain is scrambling communications. See **UFO.**

sausage   Penis or male sexuality; down-to-earth experience. Idioms: not a sausage.

savings   Sense of security; what we have not expressed; one's potential.

scald   To tell off, or be told off, or criticism; pain, a deep hurt.

scales   Justice; conscience; trying to make a decision—weighing the information; fairplay; trying to find a balance.

scar   Influences and unconscious pains still remaining from past hurt.

school   The learning process; what we learned at school—not lessons, but interrelationships, class structure, competitiveness, authority, mortification, group preferences, etc.; habits of behavior or feeling reactions developed during those years—puberty occurs at this time, and confronts us with many new feelings, choices, and drives. Can sometimes refer to feelings of rejection or aloneness due to the stress faced by many children on leaving their mother for the first time to attend school. <u>Classroom:</u> study; relationship with authority; whatever sense of oneself engendered by school. Maybe you need to ask yourself what you actually learned at school. <u>Graduating:</u> the tests you meet in life and relationships; entrance into a new life; the sense of achieving adulthood, or the skill leading to adult independence; probably also associates with your sense of value. <u>Gymnasium:</u> taking risks in learning something new; daring; physical health. <u>Library:</u> knowledge, and learning ability; stored information. <u>Places in school:</u> particular abilities or difficulties you have. <u>School clothes:</u> social attitudes or moral rules learned at school. <u>School friend:</u> your attitudes developed in school, as you are "meeting" them in the present.

science, sleep, and dreams   In 1937, through the use of the electroencephalograph (EEG) measuring tiny electrical brain impulses, Loomis and his associates discovered that the form of brain waves change with the onset of sleep. The next leap forward in understanding came when Aserinsky and Kleitman found rapid eye movements (REM) in 1953. In 1957 the REM were linked with dreaming. This defined sleep into two different observable states, REM sleep and NREM (non-rapid-eye-movement, pronounced non-REM sleep). Within NREM, three different stages have been identified. These are defined by the different EEG patterns of electrical activity in the brain. They are measured by their height amplitude, and frequency of up-and-down movement. There are also electrical changes occurring in the muscles (measured by an electromyograph, or EMG) and in movement of the eyeballs (measured by an electro-oculograph, or EOG).

While awake, the height is low and the frequency fast. As we relax prior to sleep, the EEG shifts to what are called alpha waves, at 8 to 12 cycles per second (cps). Stage one of sleep is the transition between this drowsy state of alpha waves to sleeping, in which theta waves occur, with 3 to 7 cps. In this first stage we experience random images and thoughts. This lasts about ten minutes, followed by stage two, in which "sleep spindles" occur that have 12 to 14 cps on the EEG. These last from a half to two seconds, with K complexes following, which are slow, large EEG waves. About half our sleep period is spent in this second stage of sleep. Deep sleep is reached when our brain exhibits delta waves, when "autonomic storms" occur, during which large erratic changes occur in heart rate, blood pressure, breathing rate, and in other autonomic nervous-system functions. These are the changes accompanying our dreams.

If we slept for eight hours, a typical pattern would be to pass into delta sleep, stay there for about seventy to ninety minutes, then return to stage two and dream for about five minutes. We then move back into delta sleep, stay for a short period, and shift back to level two, but without dreaming, then back into level three. The next return to stage two is longer, almost an hour, with a period of dreaming lasting about nineteen minutes, and also a short period of return to waking. There is only one short period of return to stage three sleep, which occurs nearly four hours after falling asleep. From there on we remain in level two sleep, with three or four lengthening periods of dreaming, and returns to brief wakefulness. The average amount of body shifting is once every fifteen minutes.

Facts and Figures   In undergoing 205 hours of sleep deprivation, four healthy males showed various physiological and psychological changes. Some of these were headache, lack of concentration, hallucination, memory loss, tremor, and in some, paranoia. In all cases one night's sleep restored normal functioning. One in ten people who complain of excessive daytime drowsiness suffer from sleep apnea, which is a stoppage of breathing while asleep. A condition called narcolepsy causes sufferers to fall asleep at inappropriate times—while making love, walking, playing tennis, working.

As we age we usually sleep less. Our REM sleep in particular decreases sharply. See **movements during sleep; paralysis—while asleep or trying to wake.**

scientist   See *scientist* under **roles.**

scissors   Cutting remarks; cynicism; sharp tongue; anger; fear of or feelings about castration (female castration expresses in cutting off breasts)—the cutting off of developing sexual characteristics in body and mind; sometimes refers to separation, independence—as in cutting umbilical cord—or death; cutting something or someone out of one's life; cutting off or cutting out feelings.

screw   Male sexuality; intercourse; security. Idioms: got a screw loose/missing; put the screw on someone; have a screw; screw you.

scurf   Thoughts; ideas; opinions.

sea   The sea may depict a strange environment in which we might have no skill in surviving; something new or strange that confronts us; the boundary between unconscious and conscious; our processes of life and the origins of our life; the wisdom, still unverbalized because locked in process rather than insight, of our existence; source of the huge life-drives, such as that urging us toward independence, mating, and parenthood; a symbol of infinite energy or consciousness, in which human existence is only a tiny part; the waves of experience we face in life, some acceptable, some threatening. Although some writers say the sea may represent one's mother, and the situation one meets in becoming independent of her, it is probably better to think of the sea representing the state of being and awareness we emerged from in our mother's womb. That is, a nonstriving, nondemanding existence in which our needs were usually met without a personal struggle or without any defined sense of self. Therefore a sinking into the sea could be seen as a sinking back into this loss of personality, or personal striving and independence. A struggle to survive could be partly a difficulty with existing by one's personal effort and work—the difficulty of "keeping one's head above water" in life and being independent.

Going under the sea: bringing internal contents to consciousness; remembering the womb experience; letting our ego surrender a little; looking at death. If there is a sense of hugeness or depth: going beyond the boundaries of experience usually set up by our conscious self, or ego. Learning to swim: learning to survive in a new environment, such as happens when we emerge from childhood into adult sexual drives, or the school or work environment. See **swimming.** Rescued from the sea: see **air-sea rescue.** Tide: rising and falling of feelings such as love, pleasure, or sexuality; may refer to aging when going out; tide in our affairs. See **beach; fish, sea creatures; water.** Tidal wave: any release of emotional or sexual energy. The reason this image is used is that when we feel enormous release of emotions such as might happen when we fall in love, have a baby, or are publicly condemned, our ego often feels carried along by the experience rather than in control. We may have learned how to ride such waves as surfers do. This requires confidence, daring, and balance. If we can do it we can open ourselves to a much greater range of feeling or change than if we felt threatened. Even happiness may be repressed, due to feeling threatened. Anxiety or depression is one of these enormous waves, which may threaten to engulf us, and so is one of the human conditions the tidal wave represents. Waves: impulses, feelings, and emotions, such as sexuality, anxiety, anger. Dealing with waves might therefore be about letting go of controlling things; flowing with life and yourself; riding the spontaneous moment. Idioms: all at sea; plenty more fish in the sea; lost at sea.

seal For seal as in a stamp or design, it suggests authority or permission. It can also represent a person or their influence, power, or lack of it. See *seal* under **fish, sea creatures.**

séance Meeting the unconscious as if it were spirits; concern about death or the dead; intuition; a condition in which intuitive knowledge, repressed desires, or unconscious wishes can express, but perhaps in the guise of spirits of the dead; the unknown; the irrational; the dead.

searching   Usually indicates an attempt to find: a past way of life—like wanting to have childhood absence of responsibilities; a lover from the past; an answer to a pressing problem; one's identity or sense of value in a particular setting. May indicate a feeling of having lost something—youth, sexual appeal, creativity, motivation. See **looking.** Idioms: searched high and low; a searching look; search me.

searchlight   Focused attention; concentration; insight.

seasons   Times or periods of one's life. See **spring; summer; autumn; winter.**

seaweed   Developments, ideas, or concepts that have formed in the unconscious, and have come to mind ready-made. An intuitive answer to a problem. Inner tangle of feelings. It can also suggest being able to move with the tide of events and feelings.

sedative   Attitudes we use to stop ourselves feeling anxiety or emotions. This may be dangerous to our health if feelings such as guilt or grief remain unfelt. Something, an influence, that is putting you to sleep.

seed   Sperm or ovum; one's children, or feelings about one's children; hopes for children; the collected influence and experience of the past; a new idea arising out of past experience; a suggestion; a possibility or potential; something that can emerge in your life.

seeing, saw, sight   Looking at something implies our attitudes or response to what is seen. Being looked at by someone else in the dream suggests seeing oneself from a viewpoint that is not our norm. By actually attempting to stand in the role of the other person, as described in **processing your dreams,** we can become conscious of this different viewpoint. By standing in our role in the dream, and actually taking time to consider what it is we are "seeing," and the impressions involved, we can "see" or become aware of what the dream is getting us to look at regarding ourselves. The view a person has in their dream, the environment they see, reflects how they see life and themselves at the time of the dream. It shows the narrowness or wideness of their "vision." Idioms: from the look of things; look after; look askance at; look at; look before you leap; look blue; look down on; look for; look forward to; look into; look out; look over something; look small; look the other way; look up to; look for a fight; don't like the look of; as far as I can see; as I see it; do you see what I mean; I'll see about that; I see; see over something—overseer; see eye to eye; see life; see red; see which way the wind blows; catch sight of; get out of my sight; in sight of; lose sight of; out of sight, out of mind; second sight; at first sight. See **searching.**

sell, selling   This sometimes links with a difficult parting or loss—as, for instance, selling a house. In this case it might point to change, or feelings about change. It can also reflect business or financial concerns, positive or negative; letting go of past links. See **purchasing.**

semen   Essence of masculinity; the sense of one's personal identity, but also the potential one has as an individual. Thus the withholding of sperm in the dream might be the nongiving of self, warmth, emotion, bonding.

sequential dreams   See **recurring dreams; serial dreams.**

serial dreams   Many people report recurring dreams, but these are of two types. One is the dream that recurs much the same in every feature. The other—serial dreams—are those that slowly change and evolve. Serial dreams might be about something like learning to fly, in a long series of dreams; or exploring territory or a house that you only slowly penetrate. Sometimes they are about a relationship that is at first difficult, but gradually becomes more accessible and enjoyable. Such dreams usually reflect changing attitudes and skills in yourself. For instance, a man who was confronting his own fears concerning sex experienced a series of dreams in which he at first had difficulty getting close to and loving a woman. The dreams evolved into ones in which he satisfyingly made love. The theme of these serial dreams usually gives a clue to the area of our personality the changes refer to. Common themes are: gaining of confidence; learning skill in relationships; developing courage to go beyond usual boundaries of anxiety, and thus take risks such as starting one's own business; discovering latent potential in oneself. See **recurring dreams.**

series of dreams, working with   Looking at a series of our dreams often gives you insight into aspects of yourself that would be missed considering only single dreams. For instance, there may be a theme running through the dreams, or a character or animal. So noting the changes in the dream series in regard to the animal or person gives information about what changes are occurring in connection with that aspect of your life.

settings   The environment in which the action of the dream takes place signifies the background of experience that supports the situation dealt with in the foreground.
  Example: "I was near a lake in the countryside. Everything was frozen. I saw some horse droppings still steaming and this seemed to be the only living thing around." (Kevin K.) Kevin's comments on this are that the frozen lake and countryside express his feelings about the world around him. He sees it as cold and uninviting. It is frozen and there is no life in it for him. That is, he cannot find anything in life to excite him or have meaning. The horse dung, he realized, is the resources he can use to change his

life. The dung can be manure or food for growth, or fuel to burn for energy and heat. This made him feel as if there is a way to transform his old unsatisfying patterns of "frozen" emotions into something growing and satisfying. So Kevin's dream setting illustrates his view of the world— that it is a cold, uninviting place. It is the feeling state he lives within most of the time.

Therefore the background of the dream points to the environment in which the main action of your life is happening. For instance, parents provide a background of support for their children to go to school or to the movies. A different background would change the whole feeling of the foreground. So it represents the things we might take for granted, but which give enormous color to our life and activities. If one dreams of going for a walk in the country on a sunny day, that background gives a completely different "color" than walking between traffic in a busy town street.

If possible, define a feeling and functional quality to the background of the dream you are considering. A city background might have the feeling of high activity and hurry, and the function of providing work opportunity. The country background might have the feeling of nondemanding quietness, and the function of relaxing you. When you have defined a feeling and function, consider what part those things are playing in your life, and what the details of the dream suggest about them.

seven   See *seven* under **numbers.**

sewing   Creating a new attitude; changing old habits; healing a hurt or tear in a relationship if mending.

sex and dreams   Although sex is symbolized in many dreams, where it appears directly it shows that the dreamer is able to more easily accept their sexual urges and hurts. What is then important is to attempt an understanding of what setting or drama the sexual element occurs in. Our psychological and sexual nature, like our physical, never stand still in development unless a pain or problem freezes them at a particular level of maturity. Therefore, our sexual dreams, even if our sex life is satisfactory, show us what growth, what new challenge, is being met.

Example: "My lover was standing behind me, and John, my husband, was standing in front of me. I was asking John to have sex with me and at the same time thinking, 'Oh, hell, if he does he will think we have something going between us.' I felt no flow toward John but felt somehow I was trying to tell my lover that I was desirable." (Sally A.) Sally's dream needs no interpretation. Such clear dreams show that Sally is ready to be directly aware of what she is doing in her relationships. If the sex in the dream is deeply symbolized, it suggests the dreamer is less willing to be aware of their motivations or connected painful feelings. Even though Sally's dream was clear, it was still dealing with an area of her sexuality she was not clearly conscious of. If she had been aware, it is doubtful whether she would have dreamt it.

Example: "I was in a farmyard. A small boy climbed all over the bull. It became terribly angry. It had been chained without attention too long. Now it tore away and sought the cows. The gates were closed, but the bull smashed through the enclosing fence. I rushed to the fence and sat astride it, but on seeing that, the bull smashed it like match wood. I looked around for some safe place. The bull charged the first cow to mount it, but so terrible was its energy and emotion that it could not express as sex. It smashed the cow aside as it had done the fence. Then it rushed the next and tossed it over its head, charging and smashing the next. I climbed into somebody's garden, trying to get out of the district." (Arthur J.) Although this dream depicts Arthur's "chained" sexual drive as the bull, it is still fairly obvious. If we consider the setting and plot of the dream, as suggested above, we see that Arthur is desperately trying to avoid responsibility for, or trying to escape, his own sexual drive—figuratively "sitting on the fence."

sex and dreams

general information about sex in your dreams   Whenever a healthy man dreams, he experiences an erection, no matter what the subject of the dream. Women also experience such stimulus while dreaming.

While dreaming you can safely allow any form of sexual pleasure you desire. Don't let the useful morals of waking life intrude into your dreams. If your sexual dreams are frustrating, or do not lead to deep pleasure, drop the fears and limiting attitudes that are blocking the full flow of your excitement.

Your longing for sexual partners that isn't openly expressed will attempt to become real in your dreams. It doesn't mean that you are dissatisfied with your present partner if you have sex with other people in your dreams. All of us have such secret longings, and it is healthy for them to be allowed as we sleep.

Sometimes sexual pleasure is depicted in dreams as a tidal wave, or a snake, or something you may be resisting. This is because full sexual bliss floods the whole body, releasing tensions, bringing peace and a healing action physically and psychologically. To achieve this, learn to let go of rigid self-control and be ready to be emotional.

Enjoying sexual pleasure with an animal, such as being kissed or licked by a cat, is the way dreams describe your sexual urges at their most uncomplicated and basic level. It doesn't mean you are weird. In such dreams you are dropping the complicated social rules that usually direct how you express yourself.

The energy behind the sexual drive is enormously important. It can flow in many different ways. It not only expresses as genital sex, but also in caring for others. If it is blocked, illness can result. Your dreams show in detail just how you are dealing with this most important area of your life, and what is standing in the way of satisfaction and health. Do not accept the ready-made formulas of popular sexual norms. Your dreams will show your intimate and unique needs. Remember your dreams and be enriched by them. See **animals; adolescent; affair; devil; Christ;** *the shadow* under **archetypes.**

sex and identity   Many dreams show how we gain much of our identity out of our sexual relationship or lack of it. Men and women often feel they are inadequate or lacking in personal worth if they are not in a relationship where their partner is fascinated by them sexually. As suggested in the entry on **individuation,** our sense of personal value and positive existence may be constructed from many things, but can ultimately become less dependent upon particulars such as physical attractiveness or sexual partnership. While the identity is still dependent upon sexual partnership, lack of sexual intercourse can produce powerful feelings of loneliness, loss of self-esteem, and a strange feeling of isolation and distance from other people—especially one's sexual partner. This brings about an urge to establish sexual contact again, and illustrates the dependence one has upon sex for a sense of well-being. See **gender.**

shadow, shade   The unaccepted or repressed aspects of one's own personality; feeling "put in the shade"; feelings still overshadowing one from past experiences or relationships; feeling inferior; protection; occasionally a sense of the dead or fear of the unknown; negative emotions; the subtle presence or "soul" of the person whose shadow it is. A shadow can also be a sign of coming events, the shadows cast from the future. This is because we often see someone's shadow before we see them. Idioms: afraid of one's shadow; shades of; shadow of one's former self; worn to a shadow. See *the Shadow* under **archetypes; shadowy figure.**

shadowy figure   Your rejected emotions or potentials. It is the aspect of yourself you reject, the secondary side of your personality, its nondominant traits. In the example below, Gloria is meeting her own feeling of fear. This is obvious because the shadowy thing felt the fear also. In, fact it, *is* the feeling of fear. See *the Shadow* under **archetypes.**

Example: "A shadow thing came very quickly up the stairs, along our corridor, and into the bedroom, over to the bed to bend over me. I felt fear as I never felt it before and I started to make a noise. It was also the shadow making the noise and it was frightened, and moved toward the window. I felt sorry it was frightened too, but then it was too late, as it had gone. I woke up making a howling noise. My husband said he felt the fear in the room strongly too." (Gloria F.)

shampoo   Attempt to clear away thoughts or attitudes that are not useful, or interfere in clear thinking. See *hair* under **body.**

shapes, symbols   These are visual presentations of our internal or psychological structure. Because the mind and emotions in some ways appear so abstract, it is difficult to have a clear image of our differences compared with other people, or to see changes that occur through maturing. Shapes, symbols, and patterns give us a clear image of our inner world.

center, middle   Emphasizes the importance of the thing, person, or animal in that position; conflict, where the middle is between opposites; obstruction when something might be in the middle of the road, corridor, etc.; feelings of being involved, when in the middle of a crowd, for instance. When something is in the middle of a circle or square, can represent the self or spirit. Idioms: middle of the road; piggy in the middle; center of attention.

circle, round   Yourself; personal identity; wholeness; it suggests a good harmony between all the aspects of your being—thus a feeling of pleasure, centeredness, and openness, physical, mental, and transcendent; may be used to depict the self; eternity; female sexuality; "the same dull round" of routine suggested by Blake, in which one might be trapped if there is no alternative; if the circle is irregular, suggests imbalance or lack of harmony. <u>Idioms:</u> go round in circles; come full circle; vicious circle; circle of influence/friends. See **ring.**

crescent   Femininity; the vagina; the process of feminine creativity. <u>Crescent moon:</u> the beginning or ending of something to do with one's feelings or inner life.

cross   Difficulties or tribulations we carry, perhaps unnecessarily; human life and its whole spectrum of experience, physical, sexual, mental emotional, cosmic—painful and delightful; wrongness, as with tick being correct, cross being wrong or forbidden; completion, as when crossed off list; the body, upon which consciousness is nailed or fixed during life. If <u>cross upright, as +:</u> being upright; correct; self-assertion; balanced. If <u>cross as X:</u> the four extremities; reaching out; crossing out. Like the square, it can also represent wholeness, solidity, especially if the arms are equal length.

diamond   Choices or direction, like the compass needle.

line   Distance; movement; movement in space or time; a dividing force, or a division, such as a boundary. This is expressed in the phrases "at this point I draw the line," "this is the bottom line." If there is a suggestion of this in the dream, someone drawing a line for instance, then it suggests their decisiveness, or their boundary. <u>Tangled line:</u> changes and decisions in life; indecision or confusion. <u>Zigzag line:</u> movement; change; the basic pleasure or achievement of leaving one's mark.

mandala   This is any circle or square within which shapes, objects, or other symbols appear. The mandala can be a square garden with round pond in it, square with circle in it, etc. It depicts what we have done with our life, what qualities or balance we have achieved through our effort or self-responsibility. It shows whether we have dared meet the darkness and light in our nature and bring balance; whether we have found the courage to have our boundaries of thought and viewpoint split asunder by a greater vision or despair, and what we have done with the pieces of wonder and pain we have found. The mandala often appears as a form of compensation also. In this sense it is a spontaneous attempt to bring order and integration at times when our mental and emotional life may be very shattered and disconnected. See **compensation theory;** *spiral* below.

oblong   An area of our experience—might be sex, mind, etc.; boundaries of our awareness or what we dare let ourselves experience; physical reality; oneself contained within the boundaries of our experience and social and personal constraints.

patterns   Concepts or realizations, made up of interblending pieces of information and experience; the order or chaos of our inner world of thoughts and feelings; the patterns we live by, such as habits, and beliefs; insight into the cycles or patterns underlying human and animal life; the actual patterns of one's pulse and breathing—these may be represented by patterns of dots for the pulse, or wavy or short lines may represent breathing.

round   See *circle, round* above.

sphere, ball   Wholeness; an "all round" view or a rounded character. Ball: interaction between two people, sexual and otherwise—the "ball" is in your court—in that throwing the ball may show someone trying to get one's attention and response. Ball games, being thrown a ball: challenges, prowess, competition in the game of life; having and letting go; sex play; masturbation; a man's "balls"; wholeness. Id-

<u>ioms:</u> have a ball; ball at one's feet; one's eye on the ball; start the ball rolling; new ball game; play ball with someone; he has/hasn't the balls. See *the self* under **archetypes; games.**

spiral   Things we repeat over and over like habits; movement toward greater awareness or insight.

Example: "We walk around, go upstairs, and I notice a staircase leading to a room or rooms. The stairs are painted in green too, and they go up square, about eight steps in a flight, but round and round—spiral. I am scared by them, don't want to go up, but am curious. We move in and nobody but myself has really taken any notice of the stairs. Nobody has been up. Halfway up I can see there is a glass roof, the wooden frames painted green. I am terrified but have to go on. Then I wake. Next dream I got up there. It smelt very musty. Lots of draw sheets covering things. I bent to lift a sheet. It was raining. I could hear it thrashing on the glass. Then I woke." (Nadine T.) In this example we have the spiral and the square combined in the stairs. In this way the dream manages to combine many different ideas, such as climbing to the unknown, spiraling or circling something, and the squareness or down-to-earth nature of what is being discovered. There are things we have learned, yet not realized consciously. Like a jigsaw puzzle, we have all the pieces, and we sense the connection, but we have never formed it into a conscious thought or verbal idea. It therefore remains as a feeling sense or hunch, but not a rational idea. Nadine is spiraling toward, or circling around, such a realization. She is frightened because it may be difficult—one may realize that all the years of marriage point to having been used as a doormat.

square   Down-to-earth; reality; the physical experience; stability; the materializing of an idea, feeling, or plan. Leonardo da Vinci's diagram of the man in the circle within the square represents a complete balance of the various aspects of human nature—as he may have achieved himself. See *mandala* above.

star Aspiration; the transcendent aspect of self. *Six-pointed:* personal harmony between physical, mental, and transcendent. <u>Five-pointed:</u> one's body, oneself, and one's sensed kinship with all life.

triangle Oneself being capable of "standing"; the three major aspects of human nature—body, personal experience, and impersonal consciousness; similar to the number three—See **numbers.** The <u>triangle with point upward:</u> depicts the physical aspects of human nature moving toward the personal or conscious. <u>Triangle with point downward:</u> the areas of consciousness moving toward physical expression. <u>Triangles linked in Star of David:</u> complete balance in human nature; Judaism. Sometimes the points of the triangle are used to represent the three stages of human development. The first is the undifferentiated or preconscious stage; the second is the sense of individuality, feeling "otherness" in regard to the world; and the third is the relationship of the self to the "other" in people and the world.

shark See *shark* under **fish, sea creatures.**

shave Making oneself socially acceptable, and therefore might infer feelings of anxiety about how others see you; refreshing one's sense of self; fear of hurting/cutting oneself; sometimes depicts the saying "a close shave." See *hair* under **body.**

sheep See *sheep* under **animals.**

shell The defense we use to avoid being hurt emotionally, or to defend the integrity of our identity. See *shellfish* under **fish, sea creatures.** <u>Shell as in armament:</u> a possibly explosive situation; stored anger or violence that can be launched into an attack.

shine Containing a lot of our personal energy. See **aura; light.**

ship   See **boat, ship.**

shirt   See *shirt* under **clothes.**

shit   See **excrement; toilet.**

shiver   Fear or conflict; excitement such as held-back sexual passion; getting near to release of unconscious material. <u>Idioms:</u> give one the shivers; send shivers up one's spine.

shoes   See *shoes* under **clothes.**

shop, shopping   Desires; something we are looking for or want—love, fame, sex; place of work, or business. <u>Idioms:</u> shop around; set up shop; shut up shop; talk shop; closed shop. See **purchasing;** *shopkeeper* under **roles.**

shot, shooting   <u>Being shot:</u> a traumatic injury to feelings, often out of parental or other close relationship. It need not be something dramatic, like being assaulted, but can be a quiet injury, like not bonding emotionally with parents; feeling as if you have been a target for other people's ridicule or attack; occasionally a bullet wound suggests some sort of illness in the part of the body indicated. <u>Someone/something else shot:</u> still usually refers to dreamer. <u>Dreamer shooting someone/something:</u> anger; fear or defense against meeting feelings or insights; aggressive sexuality; exploring feelings about death. <u>Idioms:</u> get shot of; shot across the bows; shot in the arm; all shot to pieces; shot in the dark.

shoulder   See *shoulder* under **body.**

shovel, spade   Introspection; the work of digging into your memories; the techniques you are using to uncover your past experience or what is unconscious and therefore buried.

shrink

shrink   If <u>dreamer or people shrink:</u> return to a child-hood feeling state or point of view; losing face or feeling "small." If <u>other things shrink:</u> they are becoming less threatening or interesting or play less important part in one's life; are seen as connected with the unconscious, aspects of which are often seen as of "little" significance, yet are full of the sort of power that motivates or undermines our resolves.

sick   <u>Idioms:</u> fall sick; make one sick; sick and tired of; sick as a dog; sick to death of.

vomiting   Bad feeling you are discharging; feeling sick of a relationship or situation; being pregnant. If <u>feeling sick, in the sense of illness:</u> See **illness; vomit.**

side   See *side* under **positions.**

sidewalk   A safe place to be in the activities—traffic—of life. Your public activities, open to the influence of other people, or social influences. Your present direction, and so an indication of what you are meeting in your life at present.

sight   See **seeing, saw, sight.**

signature   Agreement; what you will; your mark in the world; yourself.

silence   Uneasiness; unspoken feelings; expectancy; being unable to voice one's feelings; condoning; absence of life—death; the silence—nonexistence or void—out of which personal life emerges.

silver   Old, precious, or sad memories or intuitions.

sing   Expressing inner feelings, one's real self, and thus expressing more of one's creative potential. Because of this there may be a feeling of great satisfaction because you are being more yourself; touching the flowing feelings of our life; other people's self-expression and daring.

sinking   Despairing; losing ground; loss of confidence. <u>Idioms:</u> be sunk; sinking feeling; sink or swim; sink to someone's level.

sister   See *sister* under **family, family relationships.**

size   How important we see something, or what feeling impact it has on us, or how we feel in relationship to the person or object.

big, large   Importance; relationship—as when we feel small beside somebody with a "big" reputation. <u>Idioms:</u> big of somebody; big brother; big fish/noise/wheel/ shot; big guns; big head; go down big; big time; too big for shoes; big-time.

little, small   Of little importance; feeling "small"; relating to childhood. See also **shrink.**

six   See *six* under **numbers.**

skating   Sense of balance and proportion in life. Skill in keeping balanced in a difficult circumstance. See **ice, iceberg.**

skeleton   Feelings about death; part of your ability or basic strength, feelings or talent you have "killed off" or allowed to die at some time.

skin   See *skin* under **body.**

skirt   See *skirt* under **clothes.**

sky   The mind; your potential. Dream scenes—such as the sky opening and people or objects appearing, or threatening

sky

things falling from the sky—are graphic descriptions of how suddenly a new thought or viewpoint or event appears from nowhere; or for no apparent reason anxious or depressing thoughts occur "out of the blue." Floating or flying in sky: avoiding anxiety; escape into daydreaming or the mind; having a wider awareness of a situation; exploring potential. Color or mood of sky: your view of or feeling about life at the moment. Idioms: sky's the limit; sky high; pie in the sky; out of the blue. See **flying; space.**

sleeping   Not being aware; avoidance of feeling or looking at something; surrender of waking self; withdrawal from involvement with others. Idioms: lose sleep over; sleep around; put it to sleep; sleep in; sleeping partner; sleep like a log; let sleeping dogs lie; sleep off; sleep on something; sleep together; sleep with; sleep rough.

smell   See **perfume, scent, smell.**

smoke   Intuition of danger, or anxiety about danger; smoldering passions or emotions. Idioms: go up in smoke; put up a smoke screen; no smoke without fire. See **fire.**

smoking   Attempt to control anxiety; something controlling our decisions—habits; sometimes connects with hidden sexual desires; comfort or a change in mood, such as might occur when we meet a friend.

snack bar   Something you are hungry for or looking for; relationship with a person or group—the atmosphere in the dream would indicate what the quality of the relationship is. See **food.**

snail   Vulnerability—its shell depicting our defense against being hurt; feelings of repulsion for some people. Probably repulsion regarding "squirmy" feelings regarding their body or sexuality.

snake   See *snake* under **reptiles, lizards, snakes.**

snow   Depending on feeling reaction to the snow—emotional coldness or frigidity; pureness; beauty. Skiing or winter sports: Freedom, relaxation.

soap   Cleansing or melting of emotions, resulting in a feeling of release or well-being; feeling one needs to "clean up one's act" in some way, or "come clean"; sense of grubbiness; guilt or conscience.

sock   See *socks* under **clothes.**

soft toy   See **toys; teddy bear.**

solar plexus   See *abdomen* under **body.**

solder   Friendship; unity; strong bonds.

soldier   See *soldier* under **roles.**

solicitor   See *lawyer* under **roles.**

son   See *son* under **family, family relationships.**

sounds   Sounds in dreams are similar in impact as sounds we hear in waking. They carry information to you very directly. So you feel fear or pleasure depending on the sound. Therefore, the important thing is to define what feeling reaction you have to the sound, and what information you gather from it. Take this as the thing to consider in understanding your dream. Ask yourself, is the sound a warning? Does it carry information? Is it producing pleasure? Sounds are sometimes a power in dreams. They reach out and cause something to happen at a distance. This suggests a use of positive will, a confident expression of yourself in a way that you expect a result to follow.

soup

soup   See *soup* under **food.**

south   The genital area of self; warmth; lightness; feelings. <u>In the southern hemisphere:</u> coldness; darkness; death.

space   <u>Space in a building:</u> one's potential or what has not been used up in activity yet; opportunity; sense of independence and freedom. <u>Cosmic space:</u> beyond thinking or limited concepts and ego boundaries; beyond what is established already; being out of touch with reality. <u>Awareness of space:</u> awareness of experience going beyond the present view of the world one has created. The realization one's personal experience is not all there is. <u>Person or yourself in space:</u> depending on dream, it may suggest feeling out of touch with other people; introverted because of feeling ill-at-ease with oneself; awareness of transcendent life beyond the boundaries of the physical senses; expanded awareness.

spaceship   Your means of exploring reaches of inner experience beyond the limited awareness given by the senses. Therefore might mean exploring inner resources through intuition, or opening new aspects of mental function or experience, such as happens in altered states of consciousness, or unusual mental functioning. See **altered states of consciousness; UFO.**

spade   See **shovel, spade.**

speaking   This depicts some form of communication, often between your unconscious view of life and your waking self, or between an aspect of yourself that does not dominate your behavior and your mainstream self. <u>Difficulty in speaking:</u> this can mean that you have something you want to express, but it is still largely unconscious, or is held back through uncertainty. You therefore need to imagine yourself speaking it clearly, allowing it to come out, perhaps first in private; feeling a lack of power or authority when confronted by others; fear of saying something stupid, or being thought a fool for your opinions; indecision, conflicting ideas, perhaps arising from criticism or punishment during your early years. See **paralysis—while asleep or trying to wake.**

spear This has many meanings, depending upon how it is used in the dream. It can depict male sexuality, but usually in the form of confidence or self-affirmation. Such power can of course wound oneself or others, but it can also penetrate what is guarded or hidden. The spear therefore can represent a penetrating intellect or inquisitiveness. In some cultures the spear represented manhood in the sense of the skill to be independent and provide for others.

spectacles See **glasses—spectacles.**

speed Progress, or lack of it. A state of tension; patience; desire to get somewhere. Also the intensity, or lack of it, of your feelings or the experience. Perhaps, if the speed is terrible, it shows difficulty in meeting demands.

spell See **bewitched.**

sperm This indicates not only the power of cooperation in pregnancy, but also all the immense influence and background that lies behind a human birth. Thousands of generations of experience lie latent in the sperm and ovum. It is also eternal, in that although the body carrying it dies, the sperm, if it passes on in reproduction, carries on living. It therefore has an unbroken existence back to the beginning of life. It can therefore represent your whole long history, all your forebears in the male line, all your potential for the future.

spice Sex; pleasure; variety or change.

spider See *spider* under **insects; web.**

spinster   <u>Man's dream:</u> possible hope for sexual partner; husband prior to marriage; unmarried male friend; or if the man is married in real life, hopes that he were single. <u>Woman's dream:</u> oneself if unmarried; desire for freedom; comparison with present if married.

spirit body   See **out-of-body experience.**

spirits   Feelings or intuitions about the dead or death; fears concerning one's own unconscious memories or feelings—i.e., being haunted by the past, perhaps because it has never been fully felt. This full experience of it is a sort of exorcism, banishing the ghost; intuitions arising from one's own mind and awareness, as it exists beyond the preconceptions and boundaries of prejudice or fear. <u>Idioms:</u> be with someone in spirit; high/low spirits; public spirit; spirit away; spirit is willing. See **ghost;** *devil* under **archetypes; masturbation.**

splinter   Minor irritation; hurtful words or ideas; harbored ideas that bring negative feelings or pain.

spots   See skin under **body.**

spring   New growth; what was latent emerging; what was dead coming to life again; the seeds of what had already been sown springing into life or manifestation; a new start in business or relationship; childhood or youth. <u>Spring of water:</u> free-flowing feelings; rejuvenating energy; can sometimes refer to one's source of life and consciousness in a transcendent sense, especially if the spring is in a cave or underground. It then suggests one's personality is becoming more aware of the collective unconscious and its contents. <u>Metal spring:</u> ability to recover or take shocks. See **water.**

spy   Suspicion; underhandedness; secrecy; something you could be in trouble about if you were found out. See **burglar, intruder.**

stab Feeling "wounded" by someone else's remarks, actions, or attitude; aggressive sexuality. If we are stabbing someone, especially if it is a parent or someone we have linked with emotionally or sexually, there may sometimes exist behind the action the need to sever or kill any dependence upon or bonding with that person. Any anger being felt, in this case, is about the depth of our need or dependence, and the pain at having to sever the connection. Such severance and angry killing of our feelings for someone else usually gives rise to guilt. See **weapons.**

stadium See **arena, amphitheater.**

stage See **theater.**

stairs See *stairs* under **house, buildings.**

stars Intuitions about the cosmos; the perhaps almost unnoticeable promptings or motivations that occur through life, leading us in a particular direction—destiny; hopes, or wishes. See *star* under **shapes, symbols.**

starvation Something in oneself not given due attention; the impoverished and ignored aspect of self; attempts to deny the body because there is anxiety about its needs and urges.

station See **railroad, railway, train.**

statue, idol An unfeeling or "dead" part of self; feelings that someone is unresponsive or cold; social memory. <u>Idol:</u> values you have created, false or otherwise.

stealing Taking love, money, or opportunity under false pretenses; not giving as good as you get; feeling you are undeserving or unloved, and what you get is stealing because it is given unwillingly. <u>Being stolen from:</u> feeling cheated or not respected; may refer to sexuality or love—do you give

stealing

it, or does it feel as if it is taken from you?; can also refer to death—that life is being "stolen" from one. <u>Idioms:</u> steal one's heart; steal someone's thunder; steal the show.

steam Emotions under pressure; expressed emotions; something transitory. <u>Idioms:</u> getting steamed up; full-steam ahead; get up steam.

steeple A landmark in one's life; may also refer to the body, as "bats in the belfry" does, suggesting the head. The top of the steeple is the mind and wider awareness; male sexuality.

sterilize Fear of illness; reference to infection in the body; cleaning out sources of negative feelings or hurts.

stick Often used to suggest anger, courage, defensiveness, or the need for them. Someone brandishing a stick therefore suggests a threat from someone else, or threatening someone else. <u>Stick used for walking:</u> an aid in supporting oneself, such as certain beliefs or friends might be; something or someone you can lean on. See **walking stick.**

stiffness Sensing that you are either holding yourself back in relationships or endeavors, or you are too formal; anxiety or tension.

sting Hurt by what has been said or done by someone. To be stung to action, means pain has stimulated you to do something about it.

stomach See *abdomen* under **body.**

stone Hardness, loss of feeling, or unfeeling; mystery of life. <u>Idioms:</u> cast the first stone; leave no stone unturned; stone-dead; stone-deaf; blood out of a stone; stone broke; heart of stone; stoned. See **rock.**

store See **shop, shopping.**

stork See *stork* under **birds.**

storm Anger; emotional outburst; feeling battered by events or emotions; an argument with someone; difficulties. <u>If storm is approaching:</u> a sense of difficult times ahead; anger or passion building up; passions or anger you feel about someone but have not yet expressed. <u>Idioms:</u> bend before the storm; storm in a teacup; take by storm; weather the storm.

stove See **oven; fire.**

strangle Holding back feelings; trying to kill emotions or sexuality. Most of our feelings create sounds, such as laughter or crying, a sigh, words of anger or love, cries of pain. The attack on the neck is therefore often an attempt to stifle these. See **danger.**

string Attempts to make something secure; mending a situation or relationship; trying to hold something together—a business, a marriage; connection with others. <u>Idioms:</u> have someone on a piece of string; hold the purse strings; string along; string someone along; strung up; no strings attached; pull strings; apron strings.

submarine Ability to meet the depths of feelings in the unconscious, as well as functioning okay in the everyday world. Any sort of boat has the possible suggestion of relationship also, especially if there is some expression of this in the dream. Therefore, the feelings expressed in the dream may refer to unconscious feeling in a relationship. <u>If the submarine is threatening:</u> fears of internal emotions or urges. If the submarine is surfacing, the emotions may be breaking through into your everyday life. See **ship.**

subway   Your journeys into what is usually unconscious in you—such as realization of childhood traits still active in you as an adult, meeting repressed sexuality, discovery of unexpressed potential or insight; something alternative you are considering or involved in—as in "underground" newspaper; your unconscious connections with other people or things. See **tunnel; underground.**

sucking   Emotional hunger; experiencing childhood longings, dependence, or feelings. <u>Being sucked at:</u> if other than child-parent relationship, feeling one's energy drained; having a sense of another person, or an aspect of oneself, being parasitic—not giving as well as receiving, or having baby needs; sexual feelings. <u>Idioms:</u> suck up to someone; bloodsucker.

suffocating   Usually to do with a sense that the external environment, or one's inner attitudes or fears, are threatening to kill one's pleasure in living; feeling imprisoned by another person's will or emotional pressure and demands; there may be a connection with some sleep problems.

sugar   Pleasure; substitute for relationship or love; may refer to body health. <u>Idioms:</u> all sweetness and light; sweet on someone; a sweet tooth; the sweets (rewards) of.

suicide   Remembering that most people in dreams depict an aspect of oneself, this may be illustrating that we lack pleasure in life or have little to live for in the way of satisfaction; suicide may also be a sign of interiorized anger, where instead of admitting our anger, we destroy parts of our feelings; may depict business or relationship suicide. If it is <u>someone we know:</u> often shows us hoping person will get out of our life; intuition.

suitcase   The womb; what one carries inside oneself, such as longings, attitudes, fears; how we see ourselves socially—the luggage might be a sign of status, how we rate ourself; also a symbol of independence or going somewhere; what we are hiding from others, or what others cannot see; a secret and perhaps dangerous thing, but certainly often unknown. See **bag.**

summer   Mid-life; success; fruitfulness; pleasure; warmth; a peak of life or effectiveness.

sun   Warmth; vitality; conscious awareness; the self, or source of one's life energy; the radiant life-energy of the father as an inner power. <u>Sunlight:</u> being aware; warmth; positive feelings in body and mind; relaxation; health. <u>Sunbathing:</u> allowing the flow of inner energies to give pleasure. <u>Sunrise:</u> realization; a new start; childhood; hope and energy to grow. <u>Midday:</u> maturity; middle life; time to be working at one's life. <u>Sunset:</u> old age; death; return to latent period prior to a new birth. See **time;** *rebirth, resurrection* under **archetypes.**

superhero   See *hero/ine* under **archetypes; individuation.**

surfing   Facing challenges and keeping one's emotional and social balance. Riding waves of pleasure, excitement, influence, sexuality, or difficulties. Learning to relate to life in a skillful way that lets you get pleasure from it. See **sea.**

surgery   <u>A surgery:</u> one's health, emotional or physical. <u>Having surgery:</u> feeling "got at" by someone; having someone "get under one's skin"; difficult but healing changes in self; feelings about surgery if imminent.

swallowing   Holding back emotions; swallowing words or anger; taking in something. <u>Idioms:</u> swallow one's pride; he/she swallowed it.

swamp Feelings that undermine confidence and well-being; might depict feelings about a relationship, perhaps with mother. See **sink.**

sweeping Clearing away outmoded attitudes, anxieties, or emotions; getting feelings about someone out of one's life. <u>Idioms:</u> make a clean sweep; sweep someone off their feet; sweep something under the carpet; sweep the board; sweep the floor with.

sweets Childhood pleasures or rewards. So sweets may relate to something you want desperately or hunger for in a childlike way. See **sugar.**

swimming Confidence in dealing with the impacts, anxieties, or emotions that cause some people to "go under," either in relationships or something like running a family or business; being able to meet the many influences, urges, and thoughts in which we exist; expressive motivation; trusting oneself, life, and our sexuality. There is an element of personal survival in swimming. A parent dreaming about its child swimming might very well be considering whether they will "sink or swim" in their dealings with life. Many women dream of swimming or being in the water during menstruation. <u>Hanging about, not getting in:</u> hesitation about a change or something new in life. <u>Learning to swim:</u> learning to survive in a new environment, such as happens when we emerge from childhood into adult sexual drives, or the school or work environment. <u>Swimming against the current/tide:</u> meeting opposition, either from within or from others; moving against general opinions; feeling difficulties. <u>Swimming underwater:</u> taking awareness into what was unconscious; looking within; seeing what goes on under the surface in relationships, the body, etc. If easy, it suggests ease meeting the varied aspects of one's being. <u>Swimming with other people:</u> sharing common feelings, goals, etc.; connections with others. <u>Diving in:</u> taking the plunge in a new activity, relationship, or way of life. <u>Idioms:</u>

in the swim; swim against the tide; sink or swim. See **diving; pool; sea; swimming pool; water.**

swimming pool   The way we share experience with other people or are involved with other people. It therefore often refers to relationships with others, especially the aspect of relationship where feelings or influence permeates us from others. For instance, we might be part of a social group that starts using drugs, and be influenced to join in drug usage. The swimming pool may also represent the magical inner world of our mind, fantasy, and imagination, especially in relationship with other people. Being underwater in the pool: something that is "submerged," such as feelings about a past relationship that still exist, but are not "on the surface" of one's mind. Or perhaps an aspect of one's personality that has not yet been recognized consciously; it suggests seeing what is going on unconsciously or under the surface in a group. See **pool; swimming; water.** Idioms: in the swim, out of your depth.

swing   Like rocking, may refer to way we relax ourselves facing stress; self-gratification, sex or masturbation; feelings of pleasure; daily ups-and-downs. Idioms: get into the swing of things; go with a swing; in full swing.

sword   See *sword* under **weapons.**

symbols and dreaming   Words are themselves symbols of objects, ideas, or feelings. Whether we look at mathematical equations, a film, a novel, or a business logo, each involves the use of symbols. When we look at a thermometer we lose sight of it as a real object, and see it as temperature. Throughout our everyday life we use things symbolically without noticing. A name on the label of goods may depict quality to us. A face can represent love or brutality. In the struggle toward human awareness, and its increasingly subtle use of symbols such as language to think and express with, there must have been stages of development. This is a side of "history" seldom given attention, yet is very important. Perhaps our dream "thinking" is using an earlier form of symbols, one that might have been more an everyday event prior to language.

Even though we exist as an individual integrated with today's world, our earlier levels of thinking still exist. Unconsciously we still see the thermometer as temperature; the car as status, independence, or ease in getting to work; we perceive the inside of our house as an expression of ourselves—if we didn't we would not take pains to make it nice for guests. Through these unconscious feeling connections or symbolic views we have of things, dreams create their store of images and scenes. Processing a dream is an attempt to discover what values we ourselves unconsciously place upon the people, animals, objects, and situations around us. The way we unconsciously use symbols relates to more than simply our dream life and feeling connections with such things as a car. Because symbol "thinking" is now largely unconscious and links with more basic emotional responses, we often unconsciously use symbols in our body. A physical disability or illness can sometimes symbolize a powerful emotion or hurt that we cannot meet consciously. Often, people take on a profession that symbolizes important fears or attitudes they have. See **unconscious.**

syringe Intercourse; a sense of what influence other people's opinions or criticism is having on us; for some, drug dependence. See **injection.**

T

table   See *table* under **furniture, furnishings.**

tablet   See **pill.**

tail   As the tail can be raised and lowered, can refer to sexual excitement; the penis; what you are carrying with you from the past; instinctive urges or responses.

tailor   See *tailor* under **roles.**

talking   An attempt at contact or a sense of being in contact with whatever/whoever you are talking to; expressing what you feel and think; standing up for what you believe or feel strongly about; attempt at justification or correcting an opinion. <u>Difficulty in speaking or not speaking:</u> restrained anger or difficult feelings; anxiety or lack of confidence; absence of real contact or communication. <u>Speaking and not being understood:</u> feeling of not being listened to; frustration. <u>Idioms:</u> on speaking terms; know someone to speak to; nothing to speak of; speak as one finds; speak for someone; speak out; speaks for itself; speaks volumes; speak with forked tongue; speak one's mind. See *mouth* under **body;** *paralysis, paralyzed* under **body; silence.**

tank   Aggressiveness; defensiveness through the use of anger or aggression. <u>Water tank:</u> the womb, especially if

tank

fairly small and containing fishes or tadpoles; one's inner feelings and processes; stored emotions, perhaps restrained emotions. It might also at times represent your bladder or that you are retaining too much water in your body.

tap   See **faucet**.

tapestry   Reflection of your inner condition or history; the tapestry or many strands of life experience, its richness and symmetry. See *patterns* under **shapes, symbols**.

taste   Likes, dislikes, desires, and standards. The words used to describe taste often refer equally as well to feelings—bitter, sweet, sour. <u>Idioms:</u> bad taste; taste blood; have a taste for; leaves a nasty taste; acquired taste.

tattoo   Indelible memory of an experience or relationship—might relate to pain also; tribal or group identity.

tax   Feeling "taxed"; what we owe to life and society for our existence; how much of self we want to give.

taxi   Desire for help; other people's influence in your life; help you have to pay for. See **car**.

tea   Sociability; uplifting or energizing influence; allowing oneself time to "drink in" one's surroundings or experiences. See **drink**.

teacher   See *teacher* under **roles**.

teddy bear   Desire for comfort; wanting sympathy and love that cannot hurt us or respond negatively; childhood state of relationship. As a child, the people we depend utterly on for our sense of security may be out of our control. For instance, our mother may go to work, and though we may beg for her to stay, she still goes. So in this sense, as a child one has no control over one's feelings. The teddy bear, because it is always there for us, may be a sole source of security. See **toys.**

teenager See **adolescent.**

teeth See *teeth* under **body.**

telepathy See **ESP in dreams.**

telephone Desire or attempt to communicate; attempt to make contact with an aspect of oneself or someone else. Cellular phone: similar to telephone but may have associations with need to be available; status; emergency communication links; fear of being out of the circle of friends. Dreamer not answering phone: avoiding contact or communication; someone is trying to "get through" to you. No reply to dreamer's call: feeling someone is out of contact with you, not aware of your feelings; having a feeling of being alone in the world, or nobody being there for you. Emergency call: probably a crisis in your relationship or life; reaching out for help; moral dilemma. Telephone number: if it is of someone known, most likely an attempt to communicate with that person. See **fax machine, fax; numbers.**

telescope Taking a "closer look" at whatever is being viewed; making something bigger than it is.

television TV set: the function of seeing what is going on, or what is the news from within oneself. Watching TV: watching one's internal activity, values, politics; relaxation. Television personality: see **famous people.**

temperature See **hot; cold; ice, iceberg.**

temple See **church.**

ten See *ten* under **numbers.**

tennis

tennis   See **games, gambling.**

tent   One's relationship with natural forces in self; feeling of being on the move, not putting down roots; getting away from everyday responsibilities.

terror   Inability to face or cope with those emotions, fears, ideas, or urges represented in the dream. It is important to find where you felt that sort of terror in the past. This releases its hold on you. This is not easy, because many memories have never been verbalized, or occurred either prior to learning speech, or when you were under anesthetic. But they can be realized through steady dreamwork.

tests   Measuring oneself against others or the opinion of others; self-assessment; feelings of being compared or criticized, or self-criticism; stress caused by competitive work situation, or need for qualifications. <u>Medical tests:</u> concern about health.

testicles   See *testicles* under **body.**

thaw   Change in emotional responses; forgiveness; melting of frigidity, or emotional distancing through withdrawal of feelings.

theater   Observing the "play" of one's own thoughts and feelings, hopes, fears, and fantasies; acting something out and not being real. <u>Onstage:</u> feeling in the public eye, or wanting to be noticed; going through a "stage" of one's life. If particular emotions are being expressed onstage, it suggests these feelings are something you are dealing with in your public relations. <u>The stage:</u> a situation you are meeting or in the midst of, perhaps demanding you play a particular role. <u>Looking at stage:</u> what is claiming attention at present; looking within oneself; experimenting with or exploring an idea or situation such as a relationship; role or situation. <u>Idioms:</u> set the stage for; stage fright; stage-manage; act a part; act of God; act on; catch somebody in the act; get in on the act; get one's act together; act one's age; play the fool. See **famous people;** *actor/actress, acting* under **roles.**

thermometer   Concern about health if medical thermometer; one's emotional warmth or lack of it.

thief   The loss of things valued; the perhaps quiet or surreptitious taking of valuable time, energy, love, either by your carelessness or through relationship with others. Or perhaps you are taking these from someone else. It may also refer to feelings of resentment or anger. See **burglar, intruder.**

thirst   To have an inner need for something; to long for satisfaction, probably in regard to one's emotional or transcendent needs, but can be sexual too. See **drink.**

threaten, threatened   See **anger.**

three   See *three* under **numbers.**

throat   Self-expression; vulnerability; the link between thoughts and feelings. <u>Idioms:</u> at each other's throats; cutthroat competition; cut one's own throat; lump in the throat; jump down someone's throat; ram something down someone's throat; stick in one's throat. See *neck* under **body.**

thunder   Repressed emotions being released; warning of emotional outburst; external difficulties. See **storm.**

ticket   The price we pay to achieve something or get somewhere; sense of right to something, therefore confidence; proof or validity; sometimes ability or correct view of something; symbol of money. <u>Idioms:</u> that's the ticket; just the ticket; meal ticket; work one's ticket.

tidal wave

tidal wave   See Tidal wave under **sea.**

tide   See Tide under **sea.**

tie, tied   See **knot.**

time of day   The passage of time in life; our age; sense of ease or pressure.

the daylight hours   Conscious waking life; our area of choice, and ability to make decisions. Most dreams deal only with one day. Where several days pass in the same dream, or even longer periods: the dream is expressing periods of change; different stages of growth in one's life; or very different conditions through which one has lived or might live. Being late: feeling we have left something too late or we have missed out on something; realizing we have not acted quickly enough to avert a situation; avoidance of responsibility.

afternoon, evening   The end of life; middle or old age; the more subtle feeling areas of experience or relationship, period of relaxation.

hours of the day   May refer to age; period of life, 12 noon being mid-life; something that happens at that time of the day; 11 may be eleventh hour. See **numbers.**

midday   Mid-life; fully awake, as opposed to the unconscious; activity, or work projects.

morning   Youth or the first part of life; energy; enthusiasm.

night   Example: "Three of us were on our way to a lively night out and I suggested a short cut through Richmond Park" (Eloise K.). In Eloise's dream the night depicts her feelings of relaxation, pleasure and sexual encounter. This aspect of night also suggests feeling the absence of the workaday world; time for reflection and being by oneself; intimacy with others; introspection.

Example: "It was a very dark night with thunder and lightning, heavy rain and high winds. I am in a waiting room at Heathrow Airport" (Mrs P. H.). Night in this dream shows a period of difficult change in the dreamer's life. It represents a period of darkness or depression; loneliness; difficulties; sometimes negative feelings about old age and death.

Example: "I was creeping through a field at night. In darkness I and others were trying to accomplish some secret act, rather as spies or underground agents might. I also remember another where I was near a house at night. There was some special reason for getting to the house. Again an 'agent' sort of feeling." (Sam K). Sam is experiencing areas of his unconscious or unknown self, thus the secrecy, as he probably has hidden something from himself. This aspect of night suggests turning our attention inwards to an extent where we discover insights, memories or mysteries that were previously unknown to us. These can be painful areas of our experience, or very positive and life enhancing realizations. It depicts the times in life when feelings arise from within when we are alone, or in a receptive mood—or go in search of who we are. Idioms: it's about time; all in good time; at one time; do time; for the time-being; half the time; gain time; have no time for someone; lean times; time after time; time flies; behind the times; big time. See **dark; light; sun.**

tire   See *tire* under **car.**

toad   See *toad* under **reptiles, lizards, snakes.**

toilet   The actual room: privacy; your need for time where you are not always considering what others need or want of you. If it is a bathroom and toilet: possibly includes the need for cleaning up one's sexual attitudes or

toilet

general attitude to others and self. <u>Toilet bowl:</u> the part of you that can deal with the body wastes, and the emotions you need to discharge; female sexual organ; "sexpot." <u>Going to the toilet:</u> expressing natural needs; releasing feelings, often creative; letting go of tightly held attitudes, the past, or sexuality; acceptance of one's own natural drives and needs. <u>What we put down the toilet:</u> what we consider to be the least important or most unpleasant aspects of ourselves or our experience; what we want to get out of life—my small son, who had depended for long years on a pacifier, one day decided he no longer wanted to have that dependency, or be seen as needing it. He took the pacifier out of his mouth, put it down the toilet, and flushed it away.

tomato   Passion; sexuality; if dream shows body reactions, may show personal reaction to tomato as food. See **eating;** *fruits* under **food.**

tomb   Feelings or insights about death; fears we face when beginning the meeting with contents of our unconscious; unconscious family influences; the denial or killing of needs and feelings, leaving us feeling dead or only half living life; burial of our past, past love, past hopes and dreams, or feelings of guilt. If <u>bodies in tomb:</u> our potential; aspects of self that "died" in the past, or were buried, perhaps by the immediate needs of bringing up children, or some other aspect of outer life. If <u>trapped in tomb:</u> illustrates a withdrawn or autistic aspect of self—a part trapped by fears or pain; how we bury our living potential by withdrawing from difficulty, pain, or life. See **grave; cemetery.**

tools   Practical abilities we have; suggestion of things we might need to do in life—hammer out a situation with someone, cut away old attitudes, drill through resistances to discover real feelings, etc.; male sexuality in different aspects.

drill   Working through the emotions and fears that resist insight; sex when there is little feeling contact or there are fears preventing intimacy.

hammer   Aggression; desire to hammer home one's point; energy to break through resistances or break old patterns of behavior.

saw   Energy to reshape old attitudes; wordplay on "see"; sex as the relationship meets hesitations; masturbation; criticism, cynicism, a questioning state of mind; inquiry; cutting remarks or experiences.

torch   Confidence in meeting the dark or unknown aspects of self; insight. See **searchlight.**

tornado   Emotions and urges against which we feel powerless, and which may become obsessive. See **storm; wind; whirlwind.**

torpedo   Unconscious or unadmitted sexual drive that could be destructive; unconscious aggression.

tortoise   See *tortoise* under **reptiles, lizards, snakes.**

totem   A sense of your connection with your forebears and nature. The intuition the unconscious has of your links with the past.

touching   Being aware of; becoming conscious; meeting and becoming intimate; contacting. Touching also sometimes shows a linking up with something, as when a person touches a power line and gets shocked. This suggests we have "touched" feelings or drives that are a shock to us. Often directly or indirectly sexual. The absence of touching in otherwise intimate scene: can suggest lack of ability to reach out or express one's need for contact; a passive attitude in which you want the other person, or a more

touching

automatic aspect of oneself, to take responsibility and risks. <u>Active avoidance of touching</u>: shows feelings of anger. The anger may be passive, but such avoidance of contact is as vicious as hitting. The dreamer moves toward a healthier state by expressing her anger. Touching is also a means of communicating emotions or intentions. This can be love, anger, sympathy, or a statement that attempts to break down insularity. <u>Idioms:</u> get in touch; keep in touch; lose touch; lose one's touch; out of touch; touch-and-go; touch someone; touched up; touch something off; touch upon; common touch; Midas touch; touch bottom; soft touch; touch wood.

tower   Something built or created in life. As such, it can be an outer achievement or erection of inner attitudes, such as defensiveness, isolation, insularity, or an attempt to reach the heights of awareness or recognition; male sexuality and drive that may not be expressed satisfactorily, and thus be the source of aggression toward females and society. This also has the elements of insularity and defense.

town   See **city, town; capital.**

toy   Childhood attitude to life or people; not taking something or someone seriously, but just "playing" at life or love; can also show an attitude of play that is positive and creative—not killing one's creativity by being too serious; the toy dream may be a way of "playing" with emotions and sexuality that allow the dreamer to explore and mature these areas in a safe way. <u>Toy animal, cuddly toy:</u> a childhood attitude to one's natural drives; one's desire for a nonthreatening emotional or sexual relationship. As such, the toy—a teddy bear, for instance—may be one's sole certainty for emotional comfort, the only emotional contact one has any control over in one's childhood. See **doll; games, gambling; teddy bear.**

track   A little used, unconventional, or more natural way of going about something. <u>Idioms:</u> off the beaten track; in one's tracks; lose track of something; make tracks for; hard on someone's track; on the right/wrong track; track record; on the track of; blaze a trail. See **road;** or **railroad, railway, train** for railway track.

train See **railroad, railway, train.**

tramp, dropout The ignored or little expressed side of oneself; a threatening aspect of oneself; the "yes but" syndrome—I would make an effort in life but I'm broke, people put me down, others are against me, I come from a broken home—the I've had a hard time in life, life owes me a living feeling. <u>In a woman's dream:</u> may refer to the negative feelings and thoughts connected with your urge toward personal identity and success—feelings and attitudes such as "a woman can't make it in the world," "it's a man's world," "my husband puts me down."

transparent Available to insight and awareness; something we can "see through"—therefore suggesting gaining discernment; may also show us feeling vulnerable, because others can see parts of our nature usually hidden, or that we are revealing more of self.

trapped Not being able to break free of old fears, attitudes, or relationships; being held by beliefs or religious views not conducive to personal growth. See **imprisoned; cage, cell;** *wolf* under **animal; escape; holding.**

trash See **garbage.**

trash can See **garbage can.**

travel What you are doing with your life—thus, your destiny or direction in life; the direction or function of your personal growth at time of dream; the movement of life through the aging process. <u>Traveling without goal:</u> having no aim in life; confused about direction; taking life

413

travel

as it comes. <u>Going on holiday:</u> moving toward giving yourself more free time; growth toward allowing yourself to fulfill your needs instead of always considering other people. <u>Traveling to an island:</u> becoming more independent; isolating oneself. <u>Traveling alone:</u> independence; loneliness. <u>Traveling to far, mysterious country:</u> trying to find one's way through the strange mists of the mind and memory, to realize parts of childhood experience that are important, but now seem far off. <u>Traveling with others:</u> involvement with others; relationship; social relationships; how you compare yourself with others; what feelings and attitudes influence you. See **railroad, railway, train; boat; road; airplane.**

treasure The riches of your wholeness—the wonder, wisdom, or value of life; something we have had to face difficulties to gain, such as personal achievement, mature love, self-realization, wholeness; something that is enormously valuable in bringing wholeness and health to oneself—such as a balancing of dry intellectual achievement with deeply felt love, or an introverted personality with outward activity.

trees The tree depicts the living structure of your inner self. Its roots show your connection with your physical body and the earth, your family background and influences, and cultural roots; its trunk, the way you direct the energies of your being—growth, sex, thought, emotion. The branches are the abilities, directions, and many facets you develop in life—varied and yet all connected in the common life-process of your being. The tree can also symbolize new growth, stages of life, and aging, with its spring leaves and blossoms, then the falling leaves. The top of the tree, or the end of the branches, are your aspirations, the growing vulnerable tip of your personal growth and transcendent realization. From this point of view, the leaves may represent your personal life, this particular life with its many activities and desires that may fall off the tree—

414

die—but what gave it life continues to exist. The tree may also at times represent a place of safety or refuge, as when we climb it to escape. The tree is our whole life, the urge that pushes us into being and growth. It depicts the force or process that is behind all other life forms—but seen as it expresses in personal existence.

The phrase "family tree" describes a way the unconscious uses the image of a tree to represent something that is an internal reality. Within the unconscious there is an awareness that our present personality is built upon the lives and character of our forebears. So our face may be presented on the top or surface of the tree, but behind our face, or on lower branches, or in the trunk, lie the lives of our ancestors stretching back throughout the ages.

In some old manuscripts, pictures show a man lying on the ground and his penis growing into a tree, with fruits, birds, and perhaps people in its protective shade. This illustrates how one's personal life energy can branch out from its source in the basic drives, and become creativity, fruitfulness, something given to others. The tree can also represent the spine, and the different levels of human experience—physical, sensual, sexual, hungers, emotions, relatedness, communication, thought, self-awareness.

A <u>wood, collection of trees:</u> the natural forces in your being, therefore one's connection with or awareness of the unconscious; other people's personal growth and connection with self. <u>Branches:</u> members of your family; directions or possibilities in your life. <u>Christmas tree, other evergreen:</u> the eternal or unchanging aspect of your transitory experience. <u>Climbing a tree:</u> exploring or becoming aware of the directions and facets of your personal growth; using your skills or strength to get away from anxiety or danger, such as you do when climbing to get away from a dangerous animal. <u>Dead branch:</u> a direction that no longer has life or motivation in it; a member of your family dying or leaving you. <u>Dead tree:</u> past way of life; something that was full of life for you in the past, but is now dead; dead relative. <u>Falling tree:</u> sense of threat to one's

trees

identity; loss of relative. <u>Flowering tree:</u> fertility; femininity. <u>Oak:</u> strength, perseverance, mightiness, sheltering, protection, hardiness, fruitfulness. Continuance in the face of difficulties, or facing of hardship. This has probably arisen from some of the harsh climates oaks grow in, like on rocky sea cliffs. Many people translate or understand the cross of Jesus to be a tree. Artists have often depicted Jesus nailed to a tree. Often, this is the oak, which symbolizes the power of physical life, the power behind material creation. <u>Leaves:</u> the living, growing part of you. The part that is still vulnerable because of its newness, or outworn (depending on color of leaf) part of your thinking or feeling. You can also be blown like a leaf, suggesting separation from your roots and main growth; or you can take a leaf from someone's notebook, thus following their example or idea. The leaves as a whole, if falling, can represent the end of your life, the passing ego that dies, but leaves the trunk, the process that gave life. <u>Roots:</u> your connection with the past, with your family heritage or influences; the things you are tied to by necessity or love; your fundamental physical characteristics as they express in your personality. <u>Tree trunk:</u> your family background and connections. <u>Idioms:</u> top of the tree; family tree; barking up the wrong tree; tree of knowledge; dead wood; can't see the trees for the wood. See *death* and *rebirth, resurrection* and *the self* under **archetypes; individuation.**

trespassing   Feeling that you are not respecting someone else's boundaries or wishes—or vice versa.

truck   Similar to car—drives, such as ambition, what motivates one—but usually connected with work or our more commercial relationship with people. For instance, one's personal motivations or activities meeting the influence of big unified groups, such as the police or large businesses. But also one's efforts to get something done, to get things moving. See **car.**

trunk Similar to **chest,** except it may be wordplay on one's physical chest. In either case, it often refers to what we have stored away and perhaps forgotten. Therefore might point to emotions or memories that we still hold within us, perhaps even locked in the chest or trunk as muscular tensions. For car trunk see Car boot, trunk under **car.**

tsunami See Tidal wave under **sea.**

tunnel Pathways you have created into your unconscious; ways you have evolved to deal with innermost feelings and memories; exploring inner ideas or tendencies; vagina or being in the womb. An attempt to get out of a tunnel, especially if small and difficult, can refer to memories of birth; strategies developed to reach inner resources and bring them to the surface. See *death* and *rebirth, resurrection* under **archetypes; corridor; enclosed, enclosure; end; swimming.**

turquoise See Turquoise under **jewels.**

turtle See *turtle* under **reptiles, lizards, snakes.**

twelve See *twelve* under **numbers.**

two See *two* under **numbers.**

U

UFO Suggests some change in yourself, or personal growth; becoming aware of something new, or some new aspect of yourself. For instance, a change might be occurring in the way you relate to people or events. Our mind has the ability to view experience as a whole, rather than in parts. What we sense unconsciously in this way is presented to the conscious mind as images, such as UFOs or circles of light. Another way of explaining this is to realize that our conscious self is only a tiny part of the whole process of life active in us. There are amazing potentials in each of us that might only be glimpsed in stress situations. Occasionally this more powerful or bigger side of ourselves breaks through and is experienced as an alien, or great being. Because of the hallucinatory aspect of the dream process, and the fact that in dreaming we see exterior imagery as real, when this breaks through while we are awake, it is difficult to accept the source of it as our unconscious. See **altered states of consciousness; space; spaceship.**

The <u>ball of light or fire:</u> this is a common waking experience as well as dream image. It occurs when the person touches their sense of wholeness as described above. We see this mentioned in the description of Pentecost—the flame on top of the head—and may account for cases of people seeing flying saucers. Example: "A flying saucer dropped a man on our lawn. He was seven feet tall and stood in a ring of light. The sky was vivid pink and a peculiar airplane flew over. It was the shape of a cross." (Natalie

D.) The circle, the light, the shape of the cross and the big man, are all symbols of the self. See *the self* under **archetypes; hallucinations, hallucinogens; satellite; unconscious.**

ulcer   See **abscess.**

umbilical   Dependence upon others for one's needs; emotional tie to mother; prenatal life.

umbrella   The coping skills we use to ward of difficult feelings and changes in circumstance.

uncle   See *uncle* under **family, family relationships.**

unconscious   As dreams apparently emerge from what has been named the unconscious, it is helpful to understand ideas regarding it and something of its nature.

Taking into account not only Freudian and Jungian approaches to the unconscious, but something of more recent research, the term "unconscious" must be taken to represent many functions and aspects of self, rather than something we can neatly define. Therefore, we might think of the term as being like the word "body," which means a whole spectrum of organs, functions, chemical processes, neurological events, systems, cell activities, as well as one's experience of these.

In general, a helpful way of thinking about the unconscious is to realize its function in memory and skills. For instance, a mass of your experience is presently not in your conscious awareness. It is therefore unconscious. But if I pose the question "What is your present home address?" what was unconscious a moment ago becomes known and communicable. Millions of bits of other information lie unconscious in you at any one moment, along with skills not being accessed, and other functions not used. So in this sense your conscious self is a tiny part of your total potential.

There is also an action of the unconscious level of mind

unconscious

that scans life experience and attempts a healing or balancing process in your personality. It urges you through dreams or intuitions and feelings toward actions or experiences that are more expressive of your total self rather than the one-sidedness of conscious viewpoints. Dreams not only reflect this drive arising from wholeness, but also present potentials you have that you might otherwise ignore because they lie outside daily experience.

There are many other aspects of the unconscious, such as memories of childhood trauma, the dream process, the image formation process and sensory apparatus, as well as most body functions and processes. It is enough to begin with if we recognize that a lot of oneself and one's potential remains unknown to us because it remains unconscious, or a part of unconscious processes.

under/underneath   The person we are beneath our social mask; the feelings and urges we have but may not admit to others or even ourselves; the less expressed or capable side of our nature; something we hide. If <u>dreamer is under something or someone:</u> feeling suppressed; feeling weighed down or worried about something; feeling the underdog. If <u>dreamer sees something under them:</u> feeling the top dog; seeing your less capable functions or self; looking down on others; having a wider view. <u>Idioms:</u> come under; down under; under one's wing; under the weather; under the thumb; under one's hat; under a cloud; under one's nose; under the counter; under the influence. See **above.**

underground   <u>Under the ground:</u> the hidden side of yourself; what is going on underneath the everyday—street level—of your life; your unconscious depths of experience—ancient strata of psychological and physiological processes in you; parts of yourself you have ignored or buried. See **subway.**

undress   Revealing one's real feelings; revealing one's sexual feelings; being intimate. See **clothes; nude.**

unearth Bring to consciousness; reveal to oneself, or realize; become aware that you have buried—feelings about a past love, old hurts, etc.

uniform Identification with a role, such as soldier or nurse; identification with, or conformity with, collective likes and dislikes—being "in" with the group; social pressure to conform; feeling a sense of being accepted or rejected by a group or work situation; social correctness; loss of your uniqueness.

union, unity, united This can suggest conformity due to outer pressure rather than inner direction, or the power of united emotions, energies, ideas. <u>United or merged with someone or something:</u> this is like love, in which you absorb qualities from the other person. In some dreams you might even become them as you make big life changes and allow new aspects of yourself to emerge.

university Individual potential and learning ability; something important you are learning; something important you have to offer. Or it can link with your experiences of university life. In which case, it is worth defining what your overall impression of university was—loneliness, pleasure, intense friendships? See **school.**

up, upper Looking through dreams in which the words "up," "upwards," "upper," or "upstairs" are used, again and again one sees the same feeling as expressed in the example below—getting away from being "pulled down" by difficult feelings, by depression, by everyday duties, by difficulties in relationships, and so on. It expresses the technique we use when worried, such as reading a book, being entertained, having a drink—anything to take attention away from the difficult feelings. This does not remove the anxieties. It would be longer-lasting if we faced them and transformed them; moving upwards, of course, also depicts positive change; shifting toward mental activity; gaining a wider view of things; promotion. <u>Idioms:</u> one up on; on the up and up; up a gum tree; up and down; ups and downs; up the pole; up the wall; up the spout; up to the hilt. See **ascending.**

Example: "When I was very small, probably even pre-school, I often dreamt of flying. I was mostly dressed only in my short vest and usually floating upwards to escape adults who were clawing at my legs to pull me down." (Kathleen A.)

urine, urinate   Release of tension; letting go of re-strained feelings; release of sexual feelings; other people's sexual attitudes, or their negative sexual attitudes; the flow of life through us. Dreams in which we try to go to the toilet but it is mysteriously locked or closed may be due to the need to pee during the night.

uterus   See *vagina, uterus* under **body.**

V

vacation See **holiday**.

vaccination See **injection**.

vagina See *vagina, uterus* under **body**.

valley Being down-to-earth; outward activity; fertility; depression or gloominess; female sex organs—*"cwm"* in Welsh means "the valley between the hills;" occasionally associated with death—valley of the shadow of death.

vampire The fear associated with emotional or sexual relationships; feeling that someone is too demanding; the sense of not being able to be independent of one's parent/lover, and feeling your personal independence or will is sucked away by them. We create this creature out of doubts or fears. The energy-sapping fears and dependences are depicted as the vampire; the energy-sapping experience of sex.

vanish Thoughts and feelings constantly appear and then disappear, sometimes never to be seen or captured again. This is the magical world of mind and emotion, where things emerge out of the vast world of the unconscious, and vanish again. Therefore, vanishing suggests one is losing awareness of something. In this case it suggests something that is manipulated or emerges from the unconscious. <u>Person/animal who vanishes:</u> love for

423

vanish

someone that has gone; something we realized or learned that we have lost sight of; an autonomous part of self that we cannot yet direct. See **autonomous complex.**

vase   Womb; receptivity; ability to contain something. With flowers: sense of beauty and growth emerging out of receptivity; could be brothers and sisters. See **cup.**

vault   The womb; your store of resources; sexual potency; memories; unrealized wisdom, influences from the past. If the vault is used for burial, then it links with feelings you have about death, dying, or the dead.

VD   Sense of uncleanness in sexual life or an unhealthy sexual attitude; feeling infected by another person's sexual attitudes; awareness of the fears and hurts that infect one's sexual life.

vegetables   See *vegetables* under **food.**

vermin   See **insects;** *mouse* and *rat* under **animals.**

victim   Feeling victimized; having a passive relationship with others, or one's own internal aggression; the aspect of self that one has injured or murdered by repression or moral condemnation. See *victim* under **roles; murder; aggression.**

vine   Your connections with family and ancestors; growth or fruitfulness of parts of self; the transcendent in your life. Idioms: clinging vine. See **trees.**

violet   See *indigo, violet* under **colors.**

violin   See **fiddle; music; musical instrument.**

virgin   Free of preconceptions; receptivity; girlhood or innocence. In a woman's dream: oneself if still a virgin; a daughter. That one has had sex doesn't mean that one's girlhood feelings actually were met and mated with. These might very well reappear in a new relationship or in a phase of one's marriage. In a man's dream: one's feeling self that is receptive; one's soul or psyche; the aspect of oneself that can connect with expanded awareness because it can rid itself of preconceptions.

virus   See **bacteria, germs, virus.**

visions   See **hallucinations, hallucinogens; religion and dreams; unconscious; ESP in dreams.**

vitamin   Intuition about health needs; anxiety about health—hypochondria; thoughts or feelings that are healthy—for instance, the confidence that you gain by taking vitamins might be healthier for you than the vitamins.

voice   Expression of yourself, not simply ideas, but subtle feelings or realizations. Spontaneous speech, a voice that speaks through or to one: your personality or mind is not a totally unified whole. We do not identify with some aspects of ourselves. Because we disown them, or fail to connect with them, they become split from our main expression. Contacting them may be like meeting a stranger—thus, in dreams they are shown as exterior to self, or a separate voice, perhaps disembodied; some aspects of self express spontaneously—see **autonomous complex.** The voice may therefore be one's intuition; expression of unconscious but not integrated parts of self; fears; the self being met in the dream. See **talking.**

void   In living a full life, at some time we may meet an experience of facing emptiness, of something so primal that it has no form, no future, no past, nothing. This may be a very frightening experience because this void, this basis to existence, feels as if it will take everything away. If we are in love, meeting the void seems to say that nothing matters,

void

nothing is important because in the end all is void, all is empty. The strange thing is that if we dare to meet the experience of the void, it holds in it a wonderfully transforming influence. Because it is nothing it has the possibility of everything. It helps break through boundaries that previously held us captive. It frees us from limiting ideas and beliefs. It is a power for change and liberation. When meeting the void, it isn't that the truth about things we experience is taken away, what happens is that everything is seen as true. Every opposite becomes true for a while, and this is incredibly unnerving. In dreams this void may be represented by standing on the edge of a cliff, or by a mysterious emptiness or perhaps by an enormous pit. See **abyss.**

Example: "I was standing in front of a mysterious emptiness. It wasn't like a mist, as it was transparent, yet I couldn't see through it. I felt slightly anxious about it but wanted to explore it. So I slowly extended my hand and arm into it. As my hand entered, it disappeared. But as my hand went deeper, a hand slowly emerged from the translucent emptiness, and I realized that whatever I put into this mysterious void came back to me." (Dan)

volcano Long-held emotions or hurts. If <u>erupting</u>: emotional release—possibly hurts from many years past will surface, and if allowed, express in a healing way.

vomit Discharge of feelings and ideas that one's system finds irritating or poisonous to well-being.

voyage A new undertaking, relationship, or way of life. Sometimes the voyage of discovery into one's inner life. See **travel; boat.**

vulture See *vulture* under **birds.**

W

wage   See **pay; money.**

waiter/waitress   See *waiter/waitress* under **roles.**

waiting   Looking to others or circumstances for your cue. Idioms: waiting in the wings; lady in waiting; wait on someone hand-and-foot; a waiting game; lie in wait. See *waiter/waitress* under **roles.**

wake up   To realize something; to "wake up" to one's situation; to come out of a period of withdrawal. Idioms: rude awakening; wake up to something; wide awake.

walking   See *walking* under **postures, movement, body language.**

wall   Such as garden wall: defensive attitudes; boundaries that give us feelings of security; working boundaries directing an activity; social barriers; boundaries created by anxiety or view of life—a nationalistic attitude might act as a barrier to seeing other viewpoints on history. Dependence upon our physical senses gives a boundary to awareness, and a wall may also express such a frontier of awareness. For house wall, see wall under **house, buildings.** Wall of prison, trap: fear; pain; ignorance; prejudice; anger; sense of being an outsider; family attitudes or responsibilities one feels restrained or trapped by. Idioms:

wall

drive somebody up the wall; go to the wall; writing on the wall; back to the wall; head against a brick wall; fly on the wall. See **fence;** *wall* under **house, buildings.**

wallet   Similar to money, but may have more of a leaning toward power, or being in power; social effectiveness or ability to survive socially; one's sense of self-worth and value, thus related to one's identity, or how one sees oneself. See **money.**

wallpaper   Surface appearance of things; the surface layers of your feelings and awareness; cover-up. It can also represent the world we create from sensory impressions, and personal attitudes. This is a world that can be dropped away by such things as sudden illness or war. Then it is as if another world is revealed underneath the wallpaper.

want, wanting   Wanting is a primal drive that through socialization we may crush and thereby lose contact with what we want from feelings and needs. In doing so we may also lose much of our decisiveness and creativity. When it is a "don't want" in the dream, it is helpful to change it to a positive. "I didn't want to go with my mother" could become "I wanted to do my own thing." Because what we want is complex and often in conflict, our dream characters may want something that we oppose.

war   Internal conflicts—there might be a bloody battle between one's moral code and sexual needs, for instance; or between what we allow ourselves to feel and the self-healing process that attempts to release childhood pain; or between intellect and body needs or emotions. Conflict can also occur between your personal drives and the social, political, or economic regime you live in. The war might also represent a battle going on between your gender identity and the opposite gender; between yourself and another person; or your conscious attitudes and your unconscious biological processes and intelligence. Jung reports an interesting fact that men involved in actual war scenes, or people involved in threatening ongoing everyday life, seldom dream about it. During the first World War, if men began to dream repeatedly of the war scenes they were involved in, it was considered that their psychic immunity was breaking down and it was time to take them away from the active front. <u>Idioms:</u> in the wars; on the warpath; war of nerves; declare war. See **attack; fight;** *soldier* under **roles; bomb; air raid.**

wardrobe   See *closet cupboard, wardrobe* under **furniture, furnishings.**

warehouse   See *warehouse* under **house, buildings.**

warmth   Often appears alongside sunlight and comfort in dreams; physical comfort and well-being; supportive family feelings; love, cheerfulness, or hopefulness; feeling of emotional situation "warming up."

warning   <u>Warning bell, voice, signal:</u> intuition that something needs attention in your life, internally or externally. <u>Being warned by someone else or voice:</u> sense of not living up to your standards; something you have noticed unconsciously but need to become consciously aware of.

washing   Getting rid of negative feelings, such as despair or self-doubt; fears about health—neurotic phobias about one's own wholeness. <u>Washing hair:</u> changing one's attitude; altering the way one thinks about something or one's viewpoint. <u>Washing vagina or penis:</u> clearing negative sexual feelings; dealing with the results of pent-up sexuality or reproductive drive. <u>Hanging up washing:</u> allowing change to come into your life; letting other people see one's new attitudes. <u>In a mother's dream:</u> may refer to caring for the family emotionally. <u>Washing hands:</u> getting rid of feelings about something you have done or been involved in. <u>Idioms:</u> all come out in the wash; lost in

washing

the wash; it won't wash; wash dirty linen in public; wash one's hands off. See **soap; bath, bathing.**

wasp See *wasp* under **insects.**

watch (wrist) If a present, probably relates to giver or circumstances of giving. See **time; presents; clock.**

watching Being aware of; observing something—perhaps something you have noticed from everyday events but not made conscious, or something about self; watching out for what other people are doing to you—suspicion; learning something or trying to understand. Idioms: be on the watch for; watch out; watch one's step; watch over; watch someone like a hawk. See **seeing, saw, sight.**

water Emotions, moods and flow of feeling energy. Because of the nature of water, it lends itself to depicting how we relate to our feelings. For instance, one can "drown" in or feel swept away by some emotions. At other times we can feel cleansed and refreshed. It also represents our potential to experience many emotions, because water can take any shape or move in so many ways. How we relate to the water shows how we are meeting emotions and moods. In a collective sense, as a lake or the sea, it can represent the mysterious source of life, the womb, and the processes that bring us about; women frequently dream during menstruation of being in water or swimming. The dream content will show something about what is happening in the body at such times, or even if there is excessive water retention. Entering water: entering into strong feelings, such as might arise in a relationship or new job; sexual relationship; emotions that might stand in one's way—as a deep lake might, or turgid water. Deep water: the deeps of one's inner life. Hot water: strong emotions; facing difficult situations, such as social criticism. Electricity and water: emotions that can generate a very powerful reaction to a situation—such as jealousy or anger. Idioms: make water;

muddy the waters; tread water; water something down; turn on the waterworks; water under the bridge; hold water; in hot water; head above water; pour cold water onto something. See **pool; river; rain; sea; spring.**

water creatures   See **fish, sea creatures.**

wave   See Waves under **sea.**

weapons   Guns, rockets, knives, spears, etc. depict desire to hurt someone, or if we are <u>being shot or hurt</u> in the dream, how we have internalized aggression or past hurts or fear of being hurt; also, defense against fears or being hurt. If we <u>shoot or stab someone or something,</u> we need to consider what part of ourselves we are turning aggression upon. If we <u>kill or injure a recognizable person,</u> we may be harboring the desire to hurt or kill that person, even if only in reputation. All weapons can represent male sexual drive or aggressive sexuality. The <u>situation in which the action takes place:</u> defines what the weapon expresses. <u>Ineffective weapons:</u> feelings of inadequacy. A <u>work tool used as a weapon:</u> skill or authority turned against ourselves or someone else—as might happen if a doctor got sexual favors through his position. See **rocket; shot, shooting; stab.**

arrow   Something that has really got into us, like hurtful words or actions; or being pierced by a powerful emotion, such as love; turning attention inward in a wounding way; sometimes a message, perhaps of love or endeavor.

bullets, ammunition   If it is <u>something someone else has:</u> things that you feel others can use against you, such as lies, criticism, anger, etc. If it is <u>something you have:</u> attitudes or thoughts you use to bolster your confidence; things you feel or think that could be used to wound other people or even yourself; ways we defend against other people's attack. <u>Lacking ammunition:</u> feeling without hope

431

for some difficulty you are involved in, perhaps an emerging conflict with a partner or at work.

gun   Penis; male sexuality; anger; confidence in defending oneself against criticism, etc.; fears or anxieties; attitudes we use as a defense against emotions or realizations—a man might feel depressed about growing old, and defend himself against this with positive thoughts; also, the bulldozer emotions we sometimes use against others, like a pistol held to their head. When <u>shot by gun:</u> feeling hurt, wounded; being the target of criticism or hurtful remarks; fear of sex. <u>Idioms:</u> shot in the arm; shot across the bow; shot to pieces; shot in the dark; long shot.

knife   Penis, cutting intellectual insight, aggression, depending on how used in the dream; an attempt to wound someone; ability to cut through things that trap or bind you. <u>Idioms:</u> get one's knife into someone; on a knife edge; under the knife (surgery); cut it out; cut the air with a knife.

sword   Because it often has a cross as a handle, has mixed meanings. Erection; conflict or a fight; doing battle with someone; anger; social power; justice; transcendent strength. <u>Heirloom:</u> a heritage of attitudes from one's family; willpower or discrimination; strength to defend oneself and one's rights. Consider background of dream for meaning. <u>Sword coming point-first out of mouth:</u> angry words; argument or vicious verbal attack. <u>Sword hanging by a thread:</u> threats hanging over one. <u>When sheathed:</u> power or anger under control, perhaps even forgiveness; strength held in reserve; the soul or self in the body. <u>Idioms:</u> cross swords with someone; double-edged sword; sword of Damocles. See *cross* under **shapes, symbols; fight; attack; shot, shooting; war.**

weather   Changing external situations, or internal response to situations; moods and emotions. The following idioms give indications of the meaning. <u>Idioms:</u> sunny disposition; things don't look so bright; things will brighten up; it never rains but it pours; like living under a cloud; things are a bit rough/stormy/overcast. See **blizzard; rain; flood; cloud; snow; lightning; thunder.**

web   A sticky situation you feel yourself in; feeling caught up in something that might trap you; being trapped by the power of someone else's emotions or expectations; a web of lies; the symmetry of the self; the delicate or sometimes imperceptible but real connections linking you with other people, events, and the world. This link may be supportive or threatening; the circle of life, as with a mandala, the center suggesting a merging back into the primal energy of life. Through this link one may sense what is going on in the world and in relationships. At its most fundamental level, this sensing tells us whether what is happening or approaching can be eaten, or whether it will eat us. At its subtler levels, we sense our connection with all of life and can find a personal place in the scheme of things. This aspect connects with the symbol of the labyrinth as the difficult journey to self-discovery. See **maze.** Sometimes the web made by a spider is a cocoon, and so is protective. Often this relates to very delicate processes of change going on in us, perhaps ones that need us to be a little withdrawn or protected from the world in order for the process to work out and mature.

wedding   See **marriage, wedding.**

weeds   Things you have developed in your life that are not contributing much, or might even be stopping more positive personal growth; misplaced endeavor or energy. See **plants.**

weight   Seriousness; sense of a burden or responsibility; importance. Weight of someone on dreamer: feeling they are being too dependent or a burden in one's life. Idioms: carry weight; pull one's weight; throw one's weight around; worth one's weight in gold. See **fat person.**

well

well   Access to your deepest resources of life—therefore personal transcendent wisdom or information from the unconscious; the source of "well-being"; the vagina; a view into one's depths. See **water.**

werewolf   See **vampire; animals.**

west   Where the sun sets—death or the end of something; physical life; down-to-earth self.

whale   See *whale* under **fish, sea creatures.**

wheat   Wisdom of experience; the harvest of life experience; fruitfulness.

wheel   The ability to meet changes, to be mobile. <u>Large waterwheel or funfair wheel:</u> the ups and downs of life; the wheel of life—birth and death; karma. <u>Idioms:</u> behind the wheel; set the wheels in motion; take the wheel; wheeling and dealing; wheels within wheels; oil the wheels; spoke in one's wheel. See **shapes, symbols.**

whip   Hurtful remarks; angry feelings; sexuality that has as its base a desire to hurt; desire to control through threats or pain. <u>Idioms:</u> whip hand; whipping boy.

whirlwind, vortex   Conflict—energies storming in one; emotional turmoil; meeting the impact of a past trauma. See **tornado.**

whiskey   See **alcohol.**

white person   Depends on skin color of dreamer. <u>If black:</u> feelings about whites; or if known, what you feel about them. <u>If white:</u> same as any person dream.

widow   Fears or feelings about breakup of relationship, or desire to break relationship; feelings connected with someone you know who is a widow; loss in a relationship; feelings of loneliness. <u>Married woman dreaming of being a widow:</u> fears of losing husband; desire to be free of husband. <u>Unmarried woman dreaming of being or meeting a widow:</u> might refer to uncertainties or fears about a relationship you are in, or whether you will be happily married.

wife   See *wife* under **family, family relationships.**

wig   False ideas; unnatural attitude. If <u>dreamer wears wig:</u> feelings about being bald. See *hair* under **body.**

wind   The movement of consciousness or mind; the hidden influences in your life; ideas and conceptions that move you. <u>Flying with the wind:</u> uplift of sexual energies into the mind to become a wider view or an integration of experience; upliftment. <u>Strong wind:</u> powerful urges; being moved by ideas and beliefs that have a strong influence on you. See **tornado.**

window   See *window* under **house, buildings.**

windsurfing   See **surfing.**

wine   See **alcohol.**

winter   Emotional coldness; a quiescence awaiting an appropriate period for growth; the end of a cycle of action and fruitfulness; absence of relationship; an unfruitful period of life; old age; death.

wireless   What we listen to or hear going on around us or inside us; company; other people's "noise." <u>Inside wireless:</u> our mind; inside oneself.

wise man   Father; the self; what we have learned from our active experience, but might not be expressing or

435

wise man

actualizing. See *the self* under **archetypes;** *wise old woman/ wise old man* under **archetypes.**

wise woman   Mother; wisdom about feelings and relationships and the mysteries of birth and death. See *the self* under **archetypes,** *wise old woman, wise old man* under **archetypes.**

witch   The fears or difficult feelings and relationship habits we have developed in relationship with our mother. Because these feelings are now part of ourselves, if female, we can of course become the witch in relationship to someone else. Also vindictiveness, jealousy, etc.

Example: "I talked about my mother, she was standing before me in full anger and blaming me for bringing out the witch in her. She said, 'Look at my eyes.' They were horrid to see, all red and angry, and she was dark." (Margaret T.)

withdrawal   Whether the dream shows the withdrawal movement or form—such as pulling back one's hand, or in the form of deep introversion—it depicts some aspect of pulling back the subtle extensions of oneself made in work, relationships, and life involvement. Consider the clues given in the dream to define what you are withdrawing.

wizard   See *magician* under **roles.**

wolf   See *wolf* under **animals.**

woman   A <u>woman in a woman's dream:</u> an embodiment of what you deeply need, fear, hope for, or avoid. What the woman is doing in the dream gives a clue to what the need, feeling, or fear is. The example below helps make this plain.

Example: "I gave birth to a baby girl I named Charlotte. I had mixed emotions about this, uncertainty, excitement.

I wanted to share the news with my friends. I phoned one, a woman in Australia. I told her with enthusiasm, but she listened quietly and remained silent. I felt uneasy, then she said, 'We lost Luke'—her son—'the week before.' I then woke with muddled feelings." (Roseanne) Roseanne explored her feelings about the dream characters. It all fell into place when she asked herself what she had "lost" recently. She had left a lover of some years standing. This gave her a lot more freedom and new opportunity, depicted by the baby, but also muddled feelings of loss. Her Australian friend represents her feelings of grieving for the "death" of her relationship. Her muddled feelings arise because she both loves the new life that opens up, but grieves the death of her romance.

Goddess, holy/oriental woman: the dreamer's highest potential; what she is capable of but may not yet have lived; her intuition and wisdom transcending her own personality. Older woman: could be the dreamer's mother; her feelings about aging; her sense of inherited wisdom. One woman, one man: behavior patterns arising from parental relationship. Two women and the dreamer: conflicting or different feelings or drives. Woman's sister, female children: particularly used to represent herself. The character of the dream woman—loving, angry, businesslike, lazy, sexual—gives a clue to what part of the dreamer it is referring to. If the dream woman is a person known well, the above can still be the case, but the woman may represent what the dreamer feels about that person. Woman younger than the dreamer: oneself at that age.

Woman in a man's dream: this is fundamentally about your felt relationship with a particular woman, or women in general. What is happening in the dream will depict the aspect of relationship being illustrated. The dreamer's present relationship with his own feelings and intuitive self; his sensitivity and contact with his unconscious through receptivity; or how he is relating to his female partner. The latter is especially so if the woman in the dream is his partner. Old woman: usually the dreamer's mother. The woman, because she is his feelings, is obviously also his sexual desires and how he meets them. <u>Oriental woman in occidental dream:</u> the aspect of mind and emotions that links the conscious personality with its unconscious transcendental wisdom and intuition, and perhaps the capacity to love. <u>Two women and the (male) dreamer:</u> an "eternal triangle" situation; conflicting feelings. <u>Younger woman:</u> can depict his desires for a woman of that age, or his more vulnerable emotions. The conditions or situations of the woman, see under appropriate entries, such as **illness, murder, swimming,** etc.

womb Fundamental state of awareness; the state or condition prior to your development of personality—this can be personal, but it also relates to all human creatures, so is historical or evolutionary. It is a condition without ego, with a sense of being life itself; fears connected with birth and or sex. <u>Going back to the womb or to the condition of withdrawal:</u> regression to the "womb" state of awareness—therefore, perhaps a time of not being able to meet the stress of having a personality with self-awareness—a time of gaining respite and perhaps touching one's roots of being in order to gain new strength.

So much of our foundations of experience are connected with our experience of prenatal life and birth that we may need to touch these experiences to heal or free parts of our nature for further growth. See **individuation; nest; breath;** *blue* under **colors.**

wood <u>Wooden things:</u> the past, or structures of thought or behavior we have built, which originally had life but are now habitual; being "wooden"—lacking life or feeling. <u>Wooden room/house:</u> a part of our nature that has been carefully cultivated or created out of past experience. For woods see **trees.**

wood with trees Allowing oneself to be natural, and for the mind and emotions to move in their own way.

wordplay, puns According to Freud, one of the major processes of the unconscious is condensation. This means that within one element in a dream, such as the strange room we dream we are in or the unusual name a person has in the dream, are condensed many associated emotions, memories, or ideas. Talking about a pea pod that appeared as part of her imagery, Constance Newland shows how it represented her father's penis. The pea associated with pee or urine, and the pod with a seed carrier, the testicles. Freud gives the example of a patient who dreamt he was kissed by his uncle in an "auto." The patient immediately gave his own association as autoeroticism. A psychologist whose patient dreamt she was going on a trip on a boat called *Newland,* correctly inferred that the patient was getting better, because the name suggested new territory traversed. One woman dreamt about a busy intersection, and realized it was referring to inter-sex-on.

So we need to consider how we might be unconsciously playing with words, then check if this helps us gain insight. Also, phrases are used in the same way. We might see such words as "I felt a prick," "keeping it up was difficult," "dead end," and so on, in writing down our dream.

work <u>At work:</u> concerns or issues connected with one's work or lack of it. <u>Working:</u> actively trying to change a situation in one's life—one might be working at one's marriage or learning something, depending on dream surroundings. <u>Idioms:</u> have one's work cut out; set to work; worked up; work like a horse; work off; work out; dirty work; donkey work; spanner in the works.

world The sphere of one's experience; one's own world of awareness and activity; the way one experiences the world/life; the personal interaction one has with the "world." <u>End of the world:</u> end of the way you have been experiencing or relating to life; fears or feelings about death; anxieties about external events; big change in one's personal growth. See **end-of-world dreams and**

world

fantasies. Other worlds/dimensions: new ways of experiencing oneself and life; new paradigm; breakthrough to new realizations; a part of yourself separated by circumstances, pain, or suppression. Idioms: a world of; on top of the world; out of this world; think the world of; best of both worlds; small world.

worm Feeling insignificant or ineffective; something you treat as insignificant; the penis. Worms: ill health; health worries. Idioms: even a worm will turn. See **maggots.**

wound Hurt feeling; trauma from the past. If wounding someone: desire to hurt someone, or to destroy some aspect of oneself. If pierced: apart from hurt feelings, may also show one being opened by new experiences, even love.

writing Thinking about something; sorting out one's ideas and decisions; communication; leaving one's mark in life; expressing inner feelings and ideas; one's personal history. What someone you know has written: what you feel about them; their influence in your life and mind.

X

x Sometimes represents an error; X marks the spot; ten; the cross; an unknown quantity.

x rays Something influencing your life unconsciously; seeing into a situation or oneself; fear of illness.

Y

yacht   See **boat.**

yard   See **garden.**

yawn   Boredom; tiredness; unconscious trying to say something—yawning is a movement arising from the self-regulatory process. See **movements during sleep.**

yeast   Ideas or intangible influences that can yet change one's life or situation.

yellow   See *yellow* under **colors.**

yes   Wherever we say yes to a person or situation in a dream, we are opening to the influence of that aspect of ourselves. It is important to define what leads us to agreement in the dream. Is it that one says yes because of feelings that one should, or it was expected? Was the yes out of anxiety? Was it said because that was what you agreed with, or because it was the most useful response?

yoga and dreams   The aim of yoga in relationship to dreams is to move through the apparent reality of our dreams by remaining lucid in sleep. Perhaps another way of describing it is to see if the dream can be resolved into its constituent components. The reason being that the practitioner of traditional yoga was, or is, in search of the real—something that does not break down under analysis or awareness. One of the examples of this is told in yoga when the teacher asks the student to say what a house is. Gradually the student is led to see that it is a sum of parts, the bricks, the mortar, the wood, the nails, the windows, and so on. In breaking it down to its parts it disappears as a house. Similarly when human personality is looked at in the same way, it is not a stable reality, but a sum of parts. So the yogi is looking to see what lies behind the parts, until there is something indivisible. In fact yoga philosophy claims a self existent reality is discoverable as the noise of our thoughts and emotions are quietened.

yogi   The self; withdrawal from outward activity.

youth   Oneself at that age; the attitudes and responses developed at that age. If <u>dreamer younger than youth:</u> one's potential of growth and change; the part of self growing toward that age. See **boy; girl.**

Z

zero See *zero* under **numbers.**

zip Connections with others; ability to be "open" or "closed" with others.

zoo Natural urges and instincts, such as sexuality, parental caring, social grouping. What is happening to the animals shows how you are relating to the natural side of yourself—and how it is responding to your conscious attitudes and activities. Life processes in us are not inert, they constantly respond to what we do and what we are. See **animals.**

Bibliography

✳

Aaronson and Osmond, *Psychedelics,* Doubleday, 1970.

Adler, Gerhard, *Studies in Analytical Psychology,* International Universities Press, 1967.

Ackroyd, Eric, *A Dictionary of Dream Symbols,* Blandford Press, 1993.

Alex, William, *Dreams, the Unconscious and Analytical Therapy,* C. D. Jung Institute of San Francisco, 1992.

Anch A. and others, *Sleep: A Scientific Perspective,* Prentice Hall, 1988.

Anon., *The Universal Interpreter of Dreams and Visions,* Baltimore, Md., 1795.

Antrobus, John, *The Mind in Sleep,* Hillsdale, 1978.

Arthos, John, *Shakespeare's Use of Dream and Vision,* Bowes and Bowes, 1977.

Barclay, David and Therese Marie. *UFOs: The Final Answer?* Blandford Press, 1993. Has a great deal about dreams, the mind, and environmental influence on the mind and hallucinations.

Becker, Raymond De, *The Understanding of Dreams—and Their Influence on the History of Man,* Hawthorn, 1968.

Bonime, Walter, *The Clinical Use of Dreams,* Da Capo Press, 1983.

Bro, Harmon, *Edgar Cayce on Dreams,* Warner Books, 1970.

Bibliography

Bro, Harmon, *Seer out of Season: The Life of Edgar Cayce,* Aquarian, 1990. Biography of Edgar Cayce.

Bro, Harmon, *Dreams in the Life of Prayer,* Harper and Row, New York, 1970.

Brook, Stephen, *The Oxford Book of Dreams,* Oxford University Press, 1983. A dream anthology, from pre-Christian to present times.

Bunker, Dusty, *Dream Cycles,* Para Research, 1981.

Burroughs, William S., *My Education: A Book of Dreams,* Viking Press, 1995.

Caldwell, W. V., *LSD Psychotherapy,* Grove Press, 1969.

Campbell, Joseph, *Myths to Live By,* Paladin, 1988. Wonderful reading, although not directly about dreams.

Campbell, Joseph, *The Portable Jung,* Viking Press, 1974.

Cannegeiter, Dr. C. A., *Around the Dreamworld,* Vantage Press, 1985.

Capacchione, Lucia, *The Creative Journal,* Newcastle Publishing, Co., 1993.

Caprio, Betsy and Hedberg, Thomas M., *At a Dream Workshop,* Paulist Press, 1988.

Carskadon, Mary A., *Encyclopedia of Sleep and Dreaming,* Macmillan, 1992.

Cartwright, Rosalind, *A Primer on Sleep and Dreaming,* Addison Wesley, 1978.

Cartwright, Rosalind, *Crisis Dreaming,* Aquarian Press, 1993.

Chetwynd, Tom, *Dictionary for Dreamers,* Paladin, 1974. Good dictionary.

Circlot, J. E., *A Dictionary of Symbols,* Routledge & Kegan Paul, 1962.

Clift, J. D. and W., *Symbols of Transformation in Dreams,* Crossroad, 1986.

Bibliography

Cooper, J. C., *The Illustrated Encyclopaedia of Traditional Symbols,* Thames and Hudson, 1993.

Corriere, Karle, *Dreaming and Waking,* Peace Press, 1980. Exploring the idea of whether, if we meet the feeling content of dreams, they gradually cease to be symbolic. A landmark in dream theory.

Cotterell, Arthur, *A Dictionary of World Mythology,* Oxford University Press, 1986.

Coxhead, David and Susan Hiller, *Dreams—Visions of the Night,* Thames & Hudson, 1981.

Crisp, Tony, *Do You Dream?,* Spearman, 1971.

Crisp, Tony, *The Instant Dream Book,* C. W. Daniel Co., Ltd., 1984.

Crisp, Tony, *Mind and Movement,* C. W. Daniel Co., Ltd., 1987.

Crisp, Tony, *The New Dream Dictionary,* Little, Brown, 1994.

Crisp, Tony, *Liberating the Body,* Aquarian, 1992. Using the dream process to access resources of the unconscious for health and intuition.

Crisp, Tony, *Dreams and Dreaming,* London House, 1999.

Cunningham, Scott, *Sacred Sleep: Dreams and the Divine,* Crossing Press, 1992.

Dee, Nerys, *Your Dreams and What They Mean,* Aquarian, 1984.

Delaney, Gayle, *New Directions in Dream Interpretation,* State University Press, 1983.

Delaney, Gayle, *Living Your Dreams,* Harper & Row, 1988.

Delaney, Gayle, *Breakthrough Dreaming,* Bantam, 1991.

Delaney, Gayle, *Sexual Dreams,* Piatkus, 1994.

deVries, Ad, *Dictionary of Symbols and Imagery,* North Holland Publishing Co., 1974.

Bibliography

Diamond, Edwin, *The Science of Dreams,* Eyre & Spottiswoode, 1962. A fascinating collection of researched information on dreams.

Edinger, Edward, *Ego and Archetype,* Shambhala, 1991.

Eliade, Mircea, *Yoga Immortality and Freedom,* Princeton University Press, 1970.

Empson, Jacob, *Sleeping and Dreaming,* Faber and Faber, 1989.

English, Jane, *Different Doorway: Adventures of a Caesarean Born,* Earth Heart, 1985. Description of dreams and work leading up to Jane's memory of her caesarean birth and its influence on her life.

Evans, Christopher, *Landscapes of the Night,* Victor Gollancz, 1983. The computer theory of dreaming, with excellent survey of other theories.

Fagan and Shepherd, *Gestalt Therapy Now,* Harper Colophon, 1970. Contains an explanation of Fritz Perls' approach to achieving insight into one's dreams.

Faraday, Ann, *Dream Power,* Hodder and Stoughton, 1972. Good basic textbook, written for laypeople, but intelligently.

Fraday, Ann, *The Dream Game,* Harper & Row, 1974.

Fay, Maria, *The Dream Guide,* Centre for the Healing Arts, 1978.

Fordham, Freida, *Introduction to Jung's Psychology,* Penguin Books, 1972.

Freud, Sigmund, *The Interpretation of Dreams,* Allen & Unwin, 1955. The first of all modern dream books.

Fromm, Erich, *The Forgotten Language,* Allen & Unwin, 1952. This is subtitled *An Introduction to Dreams, Fairy tales and Myths.*

Garfield, Patricia, *Creative Dreaming,* Ballantine, 1974. Clear description of taking dreams to satisfaction.

Garfield, Patricia, *Pathway to Ecstasy.* Holt, Rinehart and Winston, 1979.

Bibliography

Garfield, Patricia, *Your Child's Dreams,* Ballantine, 1984.

Gaskell, G. A. *Dictionary of All Scriptures and Myths,* Crown, 1960.

Gendlin, Eugene, *Let Your Body Interpret Your Dreams,* Chiron, 1986.

Gnuse, Robert Karl. *The Dream Theophany of Samuel: Its Structure in Relation to Ancient Near Eastern Dreams and Its Theological Significance,* University Press of America, 1984.

Green, Celia, *Lucid Dreams,* IPR, 1968. The foundation research on lucidity in dreams.

Hadfield, J. A., *Dreams and Nightmares,* Penguin, 1954. Hadfield proposes a biological theory of dreams that stands between Freud, Jung, and more modern theories. It is also an interesting book.

Hall, Calvin S., *The Meaning of Dreams,* Harper & Row, 1953. Hall worked a lot with series of dreams, and with content analysis. This is the result of his research, written in easily readable form.

Hall, James P., *Jungian Dream Interpretation: A Handbook of Theory and Practice,* Inner City Books, 1985.

Hamilton, Edith, *Mythology,* New American Library, 1991.

Hannah, Barbara, *Encounters with the Soul: Active Imagination,* Sigo Press, 1981.

Harary, Keith, *Lucid Dreams in 30 Days,* Aquarian, 1990.

Harding, M. Ester, *The I and the Not I,* Princeton University Press, 1965.

Harris, Thomas, *I'm OK—You're OK,* Pan Books, 1975.

Hartmann, Ernest, *The Nightmare,* Basic Books, 1984.

Hearne, Dr. Keith, *Visions of the Future,* Aquarian, 1989. An investigation of premonitions.

Heyer, G. R., *Organism of the Mind,* Kegan Paul, 1933.

Hillman, James, *Re-Visioning Psychology,* Harper, 1975.

Bibliography

Hobson, J. Allan, *The Dreaming Brain,* Penguin, 1990. Latest information on research into dreams and the brain. A good section on understanding dreams—not as things with hidden meanings, but as straightforward expressions of our unique self.

Hodgson and Miller, *Self Watching,* Century Publishing Co., 1982.

Holbech, Soozi, *The Power of Your Dreams,* Piatkus, 1991.

Hubbard, Ron. *Dianetics,* Bridge, 1985.

Hunt, Harry, *The Multiplicity of Dreams,* Yale University Press, 1991.

Jobes, Gertrude, *Dictionary of Mythology, Folklore and Symbols,* Scarecrow, 1962.

Johnson, Robert A., *Inner Work: Using Dreams and Active Imagination for Personal Growth,* Harper & Row, 1986.

Jung, Carl, *Dreams,* Ark Paperbacks, 1986. Very technical consideration of the subject.

Jung, Carl, *Mandala Symbolism,* Princeton University Press, 1972.

Jung, Carl, *Man and His Symbols,* Aldus, 1964. The breadth and depth of dreams. It is in paperback, excellent reading.

Jung, Carl, *Memories, Dreams, Reflections,* Routledge & Kegan Paul, 1963.

Jung, Carl, *Modern Man in Search of a Soul,* Kegan Paul, 1933.

Jung, Carl, *On the Nature of Dreams,* Princeton University Press, 1974.

Jung, Carl, *The Portable Jung,* edited with an interpretive introduction, chronology, notes, and bibliography by Joseph Campbell, Viking Press, 1971.

Jung, Carl and Wilhelm, Richard, *Secret of the Golden Flower,* Kegan Paul, 1942. Jung's commentary on this ancient Chinese book on meditation is wonderful reading for those seriously interested in their own inner life.

Keller, Helen, *The World I Live In,* Random House, 1947.

Kelsey, Morton, *Dreams—A Way to Listen to God,* Paulist Press, 1978.

Kent, Caron, *The Puzzled Body,* Vision Press, 1969.

Kleitman, Nathaniel, *Sleep and Wakefulness,* University of Chicago Press, 1963.

Kluger, Yechezkel, *Dreams and Other Manifestations of the Unconscious.*

Krippner, Stanley, *Dreamtime and Dreamwork,* Jeremy Tarcher, 1990.

Krippner, Stanley, *Dreamworking,* Bearly, 1988.

LaBerge, Stephen, *Lucid Dreaming,* Ballantine Books, 1985.

LaBerge, Stephen and Rheingold, Howard, *Exploring the World of Lucid Dreaming,* Ballantine Books, 1990.

Langs, Robert, *Decoding Your Dreams,* Unwin Hyman, 1989.

Layard, John, *The Lady of the Hare,* Faber and Faber, 1944.

Leach, Maria, and Friens, Jerome, eds., Funk and Wagnall's *Standard Dictionary of Folklore, Mythology and Legend,* Harper, 1984.

Lee, S.G.M. and Mayes, A. R., eds., *Dreams and Dreaming,* Penguin, 1973.

Lincoln, J. S., *The Dream in Primitive Cultures,* Cresset Press, 1935.

Ling and Buckman, *Lysergic Acid and Ritalin in the Cure of Neurosis,* Lambarde Press, 1964.

Linn, Denise, *A Pocketful of Dreams,* Piatkus, 1993.

Mackenzie, Norman, *Dreams and Dreaming,* Bloomsbury Books, 1989.

Mahoney, Maria, *The Meaning in Dreams and Dreaming,* Citadel Press, 1987.

Martin, P. W., *Experiment in Depth,* Routledge & Kegan Paul, 1964.

Mathews, Boris, *The Herder Symbol Dictionary,* Chiron Publications, 1993.

451

Bibliography

Mattoon, Mary Ann, *Understanding Dreams,* Spring Publications,1978.

Maybruck, Patricia, *Romantic Dreams,* Pocket Books, 1991.

Meddis, Dr. Ray, *The Sleep Instinct,* Routledge & Kegan Paul, 1977.

Mindell, Arnold, *Dreambody: The Body's Role in Revealing the Self,* Sigo Press, 1982.

Mindell, Arnold, *Work with a Dreaming Body,* Viking Penguin, 1989.

Moffitt, Alan, *The Function of Dreaming,* State University Press, 1993.

Monroe, Robert, *Journeys out of the Body,* Anchor Press, 1975.

Moody, Raymond A., *Life After Life,* Mockingbird Books, 1975.

Moon, Sheila, *Dreams of a Woman,* Sigo Press, 1991.

Moorcroft, William, *Sleep, Dreaming and Sleep Disorders,* University Press of America, 1994.

Murray, Alexander, *Who's Who in Mythology,* Studio, 1992.

Natterson, Joseph, *The Dream in Clinical Practice,* Jason Aronson, 1994.

Neihardt, John G., *Black Elk Speaks,* University of Nebraska Press, 1979. The story of an American Indian Holy Man.

Newland, Constance, *Myself and I,* Frederick Muller Ltd., 1963. The connection with dreaming is the enormously rich and potent fantasies she met and dealt with during her LSD analysis. The book is therefore a powerful description of the world one meets in dreams, and the personal fears and forces that underlie the strange imagery of the unconcious. She also spontaneously understood some of her dreams.

Noone, Robert and Holman, D., *In Search of the Dream People,* William Morrow, 1972.

O'Connor, Peter, *Dreams and the Search for Meaning,* Paulist Press, 1987.

Oswald, Ian, *Sleep,* Penguin, 1966. The great landmark in researched basis of sleep and dreams.

Bibliography

Parker, Julia, *The Secret World of Your Dreams,* Piatkus, 1990.

Partridge, Eric, *Origins,* Routledge & Kegan Paul, 1966.

Perls, Fritz, *The Gestalt Approach,* Science and Behaviour, 1989.

Priestly, J. B., *Man and Time,* Aldus Books, 1964.

Rainer, Tristine, *The New Diary,* Angus and Robertson, 1980.

Rawson, Wyatt, *The Way Within,* Vincent Stuart, 1965. Interesting results of a dream group working together over some years. Arising from the work of P. W. Martin.

Reed, Henry, *Getting Help from Your Dreams,* InnerVision, 1985.

Reich, Wilhelm, *The Function of the Orgasm,* Noonday Press, 1961.

Rennick, Teresa, *Inner Journeys,* Turnstone Press, 1984. Handbook on the use of visualization and fantasy in problem solving and personal growth. It is useful to work with dream images in this way, especially in taking the dream forward toward satisfaction.

Rossi, Ernest, *Dreams and the Growth of the Personality,* Pergamon Press, 1972.

Russon, Richard, *Dreams Are Wiser Than Men,* North Atlantic Books, 1987.

Rycroft, Charles, *The Innocence of Dreams,* Hogarth Press, 1991.

Rycroft, Charles, *Anxiety and Neurosis,* Penguin Books. 1968.

Sanford, John A., *Dreams and Healing,* Paulist Press, 1978.

Sanford, John A., *Dreams—God's Forgotten Language,* Lippincott, 1968.

Seafield, Frank (Alexander Grant), *The Literature and Curiosities of Dreams,* 1865.

Sechrist, Elsie, *Dreams—Your Magic Mirror,* Cowles, 1968. Expressive of the Edgar Cayce view of dreams.

Shohet, Robin, *Dream Sharing,* Thorson, 1985. Working as a dream group.

Bibliography

Sparrow, Gregory Scott, *Lucid Dreaming—Dawning of the Clear Light*, A.R.E. Press, 1976.

Stafford and Golightly, *LSD—the Problem Solving Drug*, Award and Tandem Books.

Stevens, William Oliver, *The Mystery of Dreams*, Allen & Unwin, 1950. Examples of different types of dreams.

Sugrue, Thomas, *There Is a River*, ARE Press, 1984. The first biography of Edgar Cayce. The chapter on the philosophy arising from the Cayce readings is well worth studying.

Talbot, Michael, *The Holographic Universe*, Grafton Press, 1991. Not directly about dreams, but fascinating reading for those trying to understand the dimension out of which dreams occur, and occasionally reach beyond the normal.

Tart, Charles, *Altered States of Consciousness*, Doubleday Anchor, 1969. Has a whole section on dreaming and self-induced dreams.

Taylor, Jeremy, *Dreamwork*, Paulist Press, 1983.

Ullman, Montague, *Working with Dreams*, Delacorte, 1979.

Ullman, Montague and Krippner, Stanley, *Dream Studies and Telepathy*, Turnstone, 1973. Researched results of telepathy during dreaming.

Ullman, Montague and Limmer, Claire, *Variety of Dream Experiences*, Continuum, 1987.

Ullman, Montague and Zimmerman, *Working with Dreams*, Crucible, 1989.

Van de Castle, Robert L., *Our Dreaming Mind*, Aquarian, 1994.

Von Franz, Marie-Louise, *On Dreams and Death*, Shambhala, 1987.

Von Franz, Marie-Louise, *The Way of the Dream*, Windrose, 1988. Recorded conversations with von Franz taken by Frazer Boa—a transcript of the film *The Way of the Dream*.

Walker, Barbara G., *The Woman's Encyclopaedia of Myths and Secrets*, Harper & Row, 1983.

Bibliography

Weaver, Rix, *The Old Wise Woman*, Vincent Stuart Ltd., 1964.

Weatherhead, Leslie, *Psychology in Service of the Soul*, Epworth Press, 1929.

Webb, W. B, *Sleep, The Gentle Tyrant*, Prentice Hall, 1975.

West, Katherine L., *Crystallising Children's Dreams*.

Whitmont and Perera, *Dreams: A Portal to the Source*, Routledge, 1991.

Williams, Strephon K., *Jungian-Senoi Dreamwork Manual*, Aquarian Press, 1991.

Wiseman, Ann Sayre, *Nightmare Help*, Ansayre Press, 1986.

Zeller, Max, *The Dream, the Vision of the Night*, Sigo Press, 1990.

Zimbardo, Philip, *Psychology and Life*, Scott, Foresman and Co., 1992.

Zweig, Stefan, *Mental Healers*, Cassell, 1933. (Contains a chapter on Anton Mesmer.)

About the Author

✳

TONY CRISP has had a long working relationship with dreams. In 1972 he wrote one of the earliest self-help books on dreams. In those years he also started one of the first human growth centers in the U.K., teaching people how to use dreams and the dream process for healing and personal growth. Since then three more of his books on dreams have been published, along with others on working with the dream process while awake, using spontaneous movement.

A previous version of *Dream Dictionary* has been translated into seven languages worldwide. Tony Crisp's insight into the dream process was so valued that he was London Broadcasting Company's dream therapist for seven years.